VISUAL QUICKSTART GUIDE

# LIVESTAGE PROFESSIONAL 3

## FOR MACINTOSH AND WINDOWS

**Martin Sitter**

 Peachpit Press

Visual QuickStart Guide
## LiveStage Professional 3 for Macintosh and Windows
Martin Sitter

**Peachpit Press**
1249 Eighth Street
Berkeley, CA 94710
510/524-2178
800/283-9444
510/524-2221 (fax)

Find us on the World Wide Web at: http://www.peachpit.com
To report errors, please send a note to errata@peachpit.com

Peachpit Press is a division of Pearson Education

Copyright © 2002 by Martin Sitter

Project Editor: Jill Marts Lodwig
Editor: Nikki Echler McDonald
Production Coordinator: Connie Jeung-Mills
Copyeditor: Kathy Simpson
Tech readers: Steve Israelson, Selwyn Wan
Compositor: Owen Wolfson
Indexer: Joy Dean Lee
Cover design: The Visual Group

### Notice of Rights
All rights reserved. No part of this book may be reproduced or transmitted in any form by any means, electronic, mechanical, photocopying, recording, or otherwise, without the prior written permission of the publisher. For information on getting permissions for reprints or excerpts, contact permissions@peachpit.com.

### Notice of Liability
The information in this book is distributed on an "As Is" basis, without warranty. While every precaution has been taken in the preparation of the book, neither the author nor Peachpit Press shall have any liability to any person or entity with respect to any loss or damage caused or alleged to be caused directly or indirectly by the instructions contained in this book or by the computer software and hardware products described in it.

### Trademarks
Visual QuickStart Guide is a registered trademark of Peachpit Press, a division of Pearson Education. Apple, Mac, Macintosh, and QuickTime are trademarks of Apple Computer, Inc., registered in the U.S. and other countries. Macromedia is a registered trademark and Macromedia Flash and Flash are trademarks of Macromedia. LiveStage and LiveStage Professional are trademarks of Totally Hip Software.

Throughout this book, trademarks are used. Rather than put a trademark symbol in every occurrence of a trademarked name, we state that we are using the names in an editorial fashion only and to the benefit of the trademark owner with no intention of infringement of the trademark.

ISBN 0-201-77142-X

9 8 7 6 5 4 3 2 1

Printed and bound in the United States of America

To the loving memory of
Monica Lehune.

# Acknowledgments

Thanks above all else go to my family, who, though at times perplexed, have always had faith. Without all of you, I wouldn't have the courage to quest for my dreams.

Thank you, Marjorie Baer, for giving me Dream Number 1.

Thank you, Nikki Echler McDonald, for your unyielding patience, commitment, and sentinel eyes.

I'd also like to thank everyone at Totally Hip Software for producing a killer product. Special thanks to Eric Bin and Guillaume Iacino for all their invaluable feedback and creative direction as I wrote this book, and to Steve Israelson and Selwyn Wan, my technical yodas.

Thanks to all of my friends and co-conspirators, who have understood the conspicuous absences but kept the invitations coming nonetheless.

Last, I'd like to thank The Vancouver Film School's New Media faculty, and especially Francesco Schiavon for unwittingly pushing me down the path, if not straight off the cliff....

# TABLE OF CONTENTS

**Introduction**     **ix**
Who Needs This Book? ......................... x
How to Use This Book ......................... x
Getting Started .............................. xii

**PART 1:**    **BUILDING A PROJECT**     **1**

**Chapter 1:**    **The Tracks Tab**     **3**
About the Tracks Tab.......................... 4
About Tracks.................................. 6
About Samples................................ 10
About the Timeline........................... 13

**Chapter 2:**    **The Stage and Library**     **17**
About Stage Basics ........................... 18
About Using the Stage........................ 20
About Grids.................................. 23
About Align Tools ............................ 26
About Draw Settings ......................... 28
About the Library ............................ 30

**Chapter 3:**    **Setting Track Properties**     **35**
About the Track Tab.......................... 36
About the Spatial Tab ........................ 39
About the Composition Tab ................... 42
About the Advanced Tab ..................... 51

**Chapter 4:**    **The Script Editor**     **53**
About the Script Editor....................... 54
About Events ................................ 57
About the Script Edit Field ................... 62
About QScript Syntax ........................ 68
About Action Statements ..................... 72
About QScript Properties..................... 75
About the QScript Reference Window .......... 78

## Table of Contents

**Chapter 5: Setting Movie Properties** — 81
- About the Play Section .......................... 82
- About the Movie Section ........................ 87
- About Looping Movies .......................... 91
- About QuickTime Properties .................... 92
- About Intermovie Communication .............. 95
- About Exporting ................................ 97

**PART 2: EXPLORING TRACKS** — 101

**Chapter 6: Basic Visual Tracks** — 103
- About Color Tracks ............................ 104
- About Picture Tracks ........................... 109
- About Skin Tracks ............................. 113
- About External Tracks ......................... 117

**Chapter 7: Movie Tracks** — 119
- About Movie Tracks ............................ 120
- About Child Movies ............................ 122
- About Slaving Child Movies .................... 130
- About MIAM Playback Parameters ............. 133
- About the Layout Pop-Up Menu ................ 135
- About Loading Child Movies ................... 137

**Chapter 8: Text Tracks** — 141
- About Text Attributes .......................... 144
- About Text Margins ............................ 150
- About Text Appearance ........................ 154
- About Text Effects ............................. 156
- About Animated Text .......................... 159
- About Hotspots ................................ 162
- About Formatting Hotspots .................... 165
- About Advanced Hotspot Editing .............. 170
- About Chapter Tracks .......................... 173

**Chapter 9: Streaming, Flash, and VR Tracks** — 177
- About Streaming Tracks ........................ 179
- About Flash Tracks ............................ 184
- About Scripting Flash Tracks .................. 190
- About Flash Buttons ........................... 194
- About VR Tracks .............................. 199
- About VR Tracks and QScript ................. 201
- About VR Hotspots ............................ 204
- About Multi-Node VRs ........................ 206

## Table of Contents

**Chapter 10: Sprite Tracks** — **209**
- About Sprite Images .......................... 211
- About Sprites ................................ 214
- About Sprite Layout Properties............... 217
- About Sprite Backgrounds .................... 223
- About Behaviors ............................. 226
- About Sprite Buttons......................... 230
- About Scripting Sprites ..................... 232
- About Image Override......................... 235

**Chapter 11: Animations and Manipulations** — **237**
- About Source Pop-Up Menus................... 238
- About Tween Tracks .......................... 239
- About Cel-Based Animations.................. 246
- About Effect Tracks ......................... 253
- About Transitions............................ 255
- About Filter Effects ........................ 258
- About Special Effects........................ 260

**Chapter 12: Working with Audio** — **263**
- About Sound Tracks .......................... 264
- About Track Volume .......................... 266
- About MIDI................................... 268
- About Instrument Tracks ..................... 271
- About Playing Instruments.................... 276

**Chapter 13: Advanced QScript** — **281**
- About Constants.............................. 282
- About Variables.............................. 285
- About Debugging Projects..................... 289
- About Conditional Statements ................ 291
- About Custom Events.......................... 292

**Appendix A: Keyboard Shortcuts** — **295**

**Appendix B: Online Resources** — **297**

**Appendix C: Useful QScripts** — **299**
- Switching Fonts Based on Platform............ 300
- Checking Connection Speed.................... 301
- Making a JavaScript Pop-Up Window............ 302
- Monitoring a Movie's Download Progress ....... 303

**Index** — **305**

# INTRODUCTION

A decade ago, when Web sites were measured in the thousands rather than billions, the World Wide Web was used for little more than displaying crude home pages of text. As modems got faster and compression algorithms grew more sophisticated, pictures began to change the way we see and work with the Web. Now skyrocketing connection speeds are paving the way for video to create the next revolution in Web design. Working quietly in the background to make that happen is QuickTime.

QuickTime displays hypertext, all popular picture formats, and Macromedia Flash files on any computer platform. QuickTime is an enabling technology that provides other applications access to advanced multimedia tools. If you have QuickTime Pro, you can turn those tools to your advantage, using sprite, text, VR, and Flash tracks to make interactive, low-bandwidth QuickTime movies.

Like QuickTime Pro, LiveStage Professional 3 (herein referred to as LiveStage) taps into QuickTime's multimedia architecture. But LiveStage goes further by providing a graphical user interface that makes creating QuickTime movies easy and intuitive.

If Web-based video (or even CD-ROM video) is your medium, you need QuickTime, and to create interactive QuickTime movies, there is no better tool than LiveStage.

# Introduction

## Who Needs This Book?

This book is designed for beginning to intermediate LiveStage users. Although you don't need to be an experienced multimedia author to use the program, some knowledge of graphics software applications is required. LiveStage is not a content-creation program; it's a content-assembly program. To create the content for your projects, you'll need Adobe Photoshop, Adobe After Effects, Macromedia Flash, or similar applications. If you've already created graphics and sound files and now want to assemble them into an interactive QuickTime movie, this book is for you.

**LiveStage 3 users.** This book is written with you in mind, and I do mean *all* of you. With the release of version 3.0, Totally Hip Software introduced a new community into the LiveStage family: Windows users! This book includes screen shots, shortcuts, and tips for both Mac and Windows platforms.

**LiveStage 3 demo users.** Not quite sure you want to invest in the latest version of LiveStage? Try before you buy, and download the demo version from Totally Hip Software's Web site (www.totallyhip.com). The demo offers all the features of the full release but doesn't let you save your projects. It will, however, export your projects into compiled, interactive QuickTime movies. Use this book as a reference guide the same way you'd use it with the full-price version of LiveStage.

**LiveStage 2 users.** Although LiveStage 3's interface has been redesigned to reflect an expanded feature set, LiveStage 2 works similarly to LiveStage 3. LiveStage 3 boasts several additions that version 2 lacks—notably, skin tracks, the enhanced QScript library, and expanded text-editing features. LiveStage 2 users can simply skip those sections in this book.

## How to Use This Book

*LiveStage Professional 3 for Macintosh and Windows: Visual QuickStart Guide* is divided into two parts. Part 1 (chapters 1 through 5) covers LiveStage basics that apply to every project you'll make in LiveStage. You'll get to know the LiveStage authoring environment while learning key concepts such as how to resize and rearrange your project's media and use the script editor to add interactivity. New LiveStage users should read Part 1 from start to finish. After you've read these chapters, you should feel comfortable making simple movies with basic QScripting to provide interactivity.

Part 2 gets into the nitty-gritty of LiveStage's many tracks. As your projects become more sophisticated, you will have pointed questions about the inner workings of each track type. You may need to raise or lower the volume of a sound track, wire a Flash button with your own QScript, or create hyperlink-like hotspots in a text track. As you develop questions, Part 2 delivers answers.

Following in the tradition of all *Visual QuickStart Guides*, this book uses clear screen shots and step-by-step instructions to break the LiveStage authoring process into easy-to-digest chunks. Whether you pick up this book with a question in mind or read it from front to back, you will find this *Visual QuickStart Guide* to be a valuable learning and reference tool.

## Cross-platform issues

Although the Mac-vs.-Windows debate continues to rage, in multimedia circles, there is just one choice: use the platform that works best for your purpose. No matter which platform you use, LiveStage comes to you.

Totally Hip Software has designed LiveStage to work exactly the same way on both platforms. All menus, dialogs, windows, and editors are organized similarly for Macintosh and Windows computers. As you read this book, you will see many screen shots for both Windows and Mac platforms. With the exception of a few cosmetic differences, both authoring environments work the same way; you should have little difficulty translating between this book's screen shots and what you see on your monitor.

If you're a Macintosh user, you'll notice that all Macintosh screen shots are taken in Mac OS X. For Mac OS 9.x users, LiveStage looks similar to LiveStage for Windows and you shouldn't have any trouble making sense of the screen shots included in this book. All the features are the same; they just look a bit different.

If you're using an operating system older than Mac OS 9.1, you need to update your CarbonLib to version 1.2.5. To do so, use the CarbonLib 1.2.5 installer on the LiveStage program CD-ROM.

## Keyboard shortcuts

Many of LiveStage's menu commands have keyboard shortcuts that help speed the authoring process. When this book first introduces a command, it also lists the keyboard shortcut (where applicable). For a complete list of keyboard shortcuts, see Appendix A, "Keyboard Shortcuts," at the back of this book.

## Putting movies on the Web

LiveStage makes wired (fully interactive) QuickTime movies, and this book shows you how to use LiveStage. It does not, however, show you how to put those movies on the Internet. Appendix B, "Online Resources," lists several links that will help you embed your movies in a Web page properly. Still, there's no substitute for a good book, and to that end, I suggest reading *QuickTime Pro for Macintosh and Windows: A Visual QuickStart Guide*, by Judith Stern and Robert Lettieri. That book contains detailed instructions for distributing your movies on the Internet and is an excellent companion to the book you are reading.

## Getting help

Several online forums are dedicated to using LiveStage, and some very clever people lurk in those dark places. Totally Hip Software provides two forums where you can get the help you need. Blue Abuse (www.blueabuse.com), caters to novice LiveStage users. More advanced authors, however, may prefer the LiveStage Talk mailing list. Either way, if you have a question about LiveStage that this book doesn't answer, the solution is often just a forum post away.

To learn more about the LiveStage forums or to find other useful links, see Appendix B.

# Getting Started

If you're one of those people who shake your Christmas presents the night before the big morning, you've probably already installed LiveStage, opened it, and taken a look. For the others, the remainder of this introduction holds important information about installing LiveStage, setting startup preferences, and creating and saving projects.

### To install LiveStage on a Macintosh:

1. On the LiveStage CD-ROM, locate the LiveStage Professional folder (**Figure i.1**).

2. Drag the entire folder to your hard disk.
   There is no installer for the Macintosh version of this program; dragging it to your hard disk is all you need to do. Be sure to note the serial number on the back of your CD-ROM package, as you will need it the first time you launch LiveStage.

### To install LiveStage on a Windows PC:

1. On the LiveStage CD-ROM, locate the LiveStage Professional installer icon.

2. Double-click the installer icon to begin the installation process.
   The installation program walks you through the steps needed to install LiveStage on your computer. Be sure to note the serial number on the back of your CD-ROM package, as you will need it the first time you launch LiveStage.

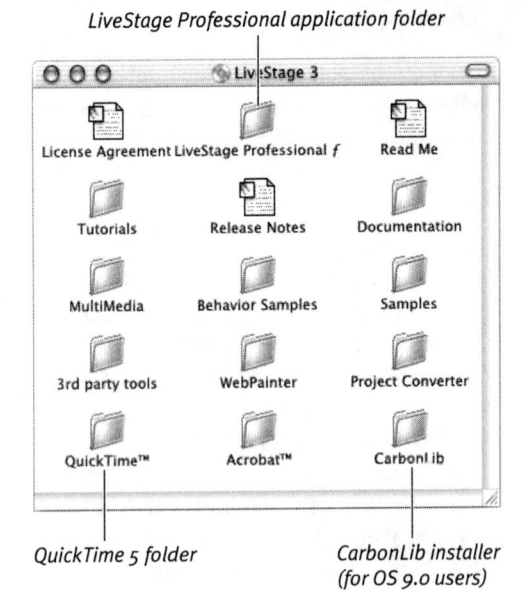

**Figure i.1** The LiveStage Professional application folder in the Macintosh program CD-ROM.

Introduction

**Figure i.2** The LiveStage Professional splash screen.

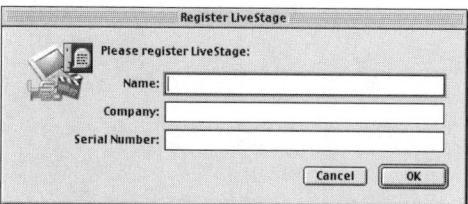

**Figure i.3** The first time you launch LiveStage, you will need to enter your name, your company, and the program's serial number.

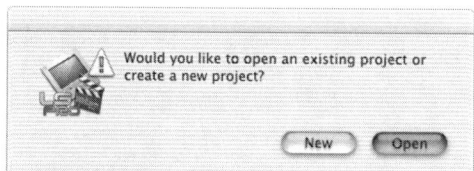

**Figure i.4** This dialog appears by default when you launch LiveStage.

## To launch LiveStage:

1. In the Finder (Mac) or on the desktop (Windows), double-click the LiveStage application icon.

    LiveStage opens, and a splash screen appears (**Figure i.2**). If you're using the program for the first time, however, a dialog appears, asking for your name, your company, and serial number (**Figure i.3**). Enter the appropriate information to get back to the splash screen.

2. In the splash screen, click OK.

    A dialog prompts you to create a new project or open an existing one (**Figure i.4**).

3. Click the New button to create a new project or the Open button to open an existing project.

**GETTING STARTED**

xiii

Introduction

## Setting startup preferences

You can define a startup preference, telling LiveStage to open in a specific way every time you launch the program. If you always begin your LiveStage sessions with a new project, for example, set the startup preference to create a new project automatically upon launch.

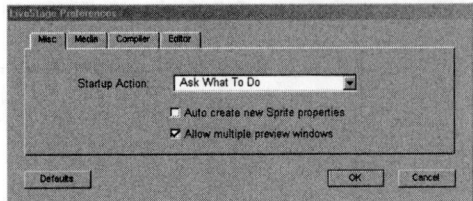

**Figure i.5** The LiveStage Preferences dialog, displaying the Misc tab.

### To define startup preferences:

1. Choose Edit > Preferences or, in Mac OS X, choose LiveStage Pro > Preferences.

    The LiveStage Preferences dialog opens (**Figure i.5**).

2. Select the Misc tab.

3. From the Startup Action pop-up menu, choose a startup action (**Figure i.6**).

    Your choices are:

    **Ask What to Do.** This default action prompts you to open an existing file or create a new one.

    **Create New Document.** LiveStage creates a new project file each time that you open the program.

    **Open Existing Document.** Upon startup, you're prompted to open an existing LiveStage project from the Open dialog.

    **Reopen Last Document.** LiveStage opens the last project that you worked on.

    **Do Nothing.** LiveStage launches but doesn't open or create a project.

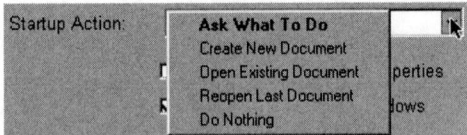

**Figure i.6** Possible startup actions. The choice you make defines the action LiveStage will perform each time it is launched.

### ✔ Tip

- By clicking the Defaults button in the LiveStage Preferences dialog, you restore all preferences to their default values, including those set in other tabs of the dialog.

# Introduction

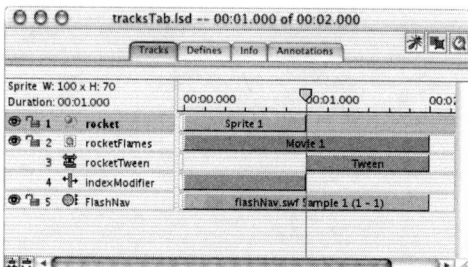

**Figure i.7** The Tracks tab is covered in detail in Chapter 1.

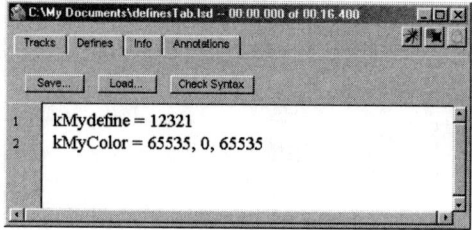

**Figure i.8** The Defines tab. To learn more about defines, flip to Chapter 13.

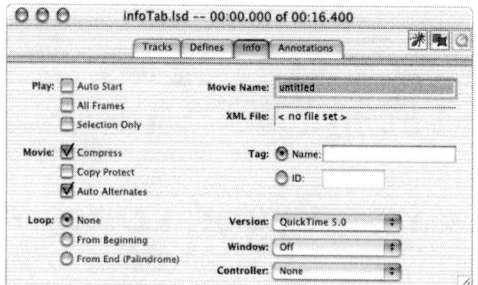

**Figure i.9** You'll learn everything there is to know about the Info tab in Chapter 5.

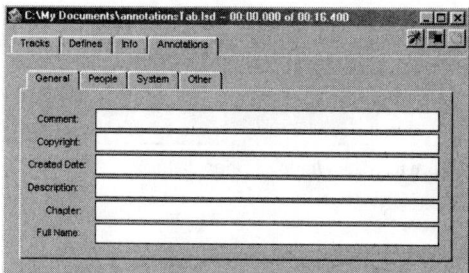

**Figure i.10** The Annotations tab, as its name implies, lets you annotate your movie with information about its author and copyright.

## Using the Project window

The first thing you see when you start a new project is an empty Project window, which serves as the base for each LiveStage project. All work you do in LiveStage stems from one of the four tabs at the top of the Project window:

**Tracks,** where you assemble and sequence your project's content by using tracks and samples on the Timeline (**Figure i.7**)

**Defines,** where you define constants for your *QScripts*, LiveStage's proprietary scripting language (**Figure i.8**)

**Info,** where you set playback characteristics that control how QuickTime displays your movie (**Figure i.9**)

**Annotations,** where you enter information about the movie itself, such as its author, copyright, and creation date (**Figure i.10**)

Introduction

## To create a new project:

- Choose File > New Project (Command/Ctrl-N).

    A new, untitled Project window appears (**Figure i.11**).

## To open an existing project:

1. Choose File > Open (Command/Ctrl-O).

    The Open dialog appears (**Figures i.12** and **i.13**).

2. Navigate to the project file that you want to open.

3. Click Open.

    LiveStage opens the file as a project.

## ✔ Tips

- To open a file quickly, double-click its icon or drag it from the Finder (Mac) or desktop (Windows) and drop it on the LiveStage application icon.

- To open a recently modified movie, choose File > Open Recent and then choose a file from the submenu.

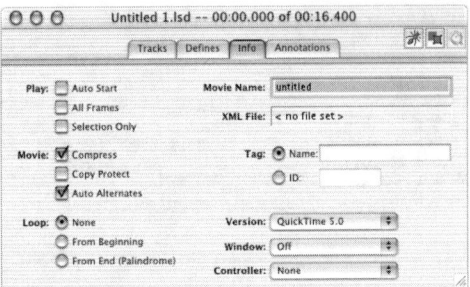

**Figure i.11** The Project window in Mac OS X, with the Info tab displayed.

**Figure i.12** The Mac OS X Open dialog.

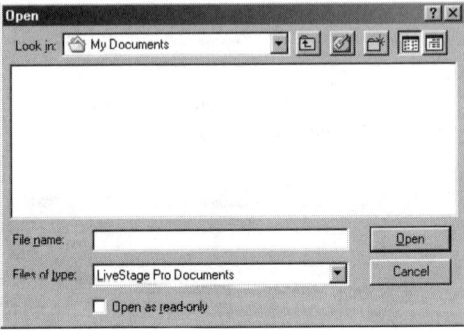

**Figure i.13** The Windows Open dialog.

Introduction

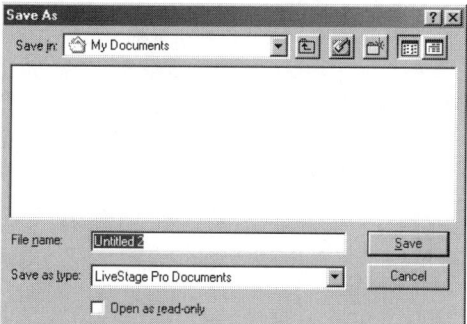

**Figure i.14** The Save dialog lets you save your project to your hard disk.

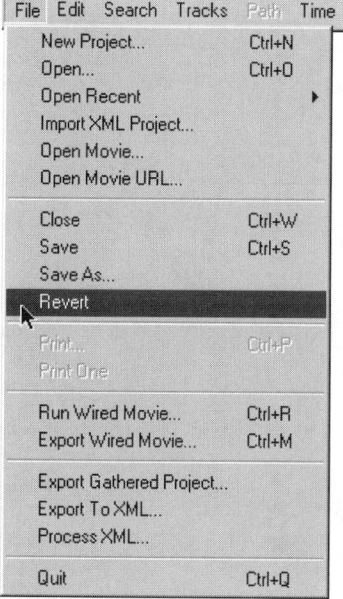

**Figure i.15** The Revert command opens the last saved version of your project.

## To save a project:

1. Choose File > Save (Command/Ctrl-S). The Save dialog appears (**Figure i.14**).

2. In the File Name text box, type a name for your project file.

3. Click Save.

## To revert to the last saved version:

◆ Choose File > Revert (**Figure i.15**). LiveStage discards all changes that you've made since the last time you saved.

## ✔ Tip

■ At this time, LiveStage offers only one level of undo. If you've made several changes in your project but then decide you don't like them, use the Revert command to return to the beginning.

## To close a project:

◆ Choose File > Close (Command/Ctrl-W) or click the close box at the top of the Project window.

  LiveStage closes the active Project window but does not quit.

GETTING STARTED

xvii

# PART 1

# BUILDING A PROJECT

| Chapter 1: | The Tracks Tab | 3 |
| Chapter 2: | The Stage and Library | 17 |
| Chapter 3: | Setting Track Properties | 35 |
| Chapter 4: | The Script Editor | 53 |
| Chapter 5: | Setting Movie Properties | 81 |

# THE TRACKS TAB

When most people think of movies, they picture a moving visual track accompanied by some sort of audio. Indeed, most QuickTime movies you see on the Internet are made up of only one audio and video track. But QuickTime is much more versatile than this. In fact, a QuickTime movie can have an unlimited amount of tracks, and these tracks can hold videos, sounds, pictures, MIDI, or any of the other special track types that are part of QuickTime.

When you make a QuickTime movie with LiveStage you have access to any of the track types QuickTime understands. Furthermore, LiveStage provides an editor that makes it easy to arrange these tracks into a coherent movie. That editor is the Tracks tab.

The Tracks tab forms the base for any project you create with LiveStage Professional. You'll spend most of your time using this tab to add and edit all the different forms of media (pictures, videos, and sounds) that combine to make a project. This chapter covers the Tracks tab, exploring the relationship between tracks and samples and how they are arranged in the Tracks tab's Timeline.

Chapter 1

# About the Tracks Tab

To appreciate the Tracks tab's role, imagine that a project is like a house you have built out of many smaller bricks of media, such as pictures, text, and sounds. A strong house must stand on a solid foundation, and that foundation is built in your project's construction yard: the Tracks tab (**Figure 1.1**).

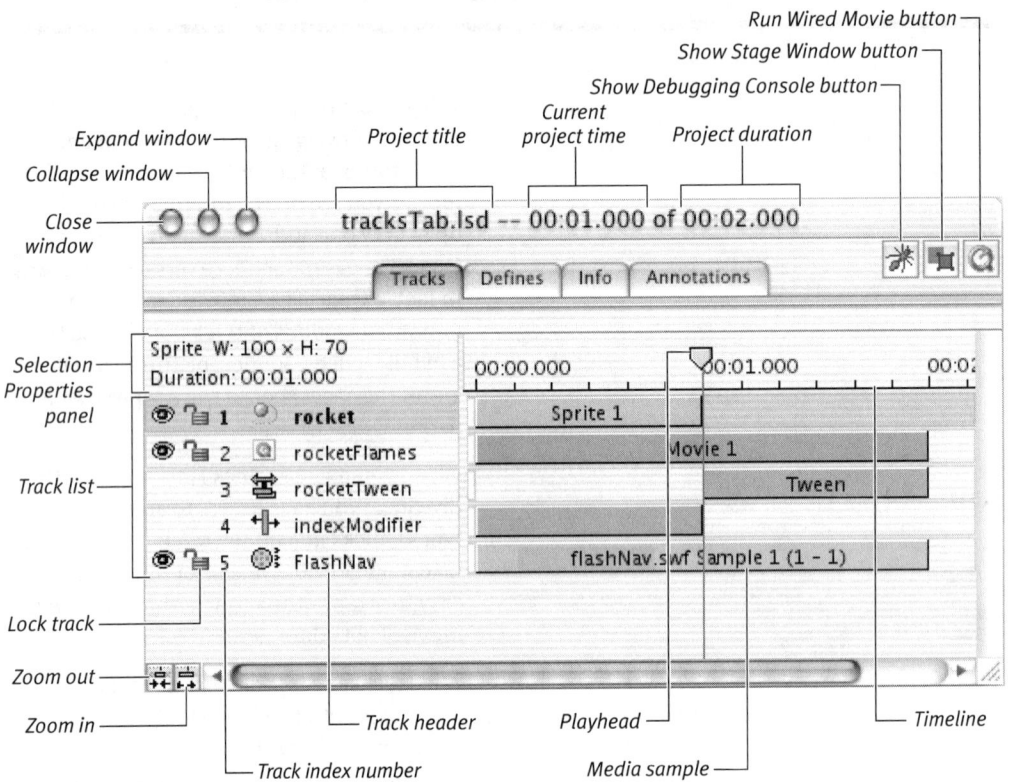

Figure 1.1 The Project window's Tracks tab.

# The Tracks Tab

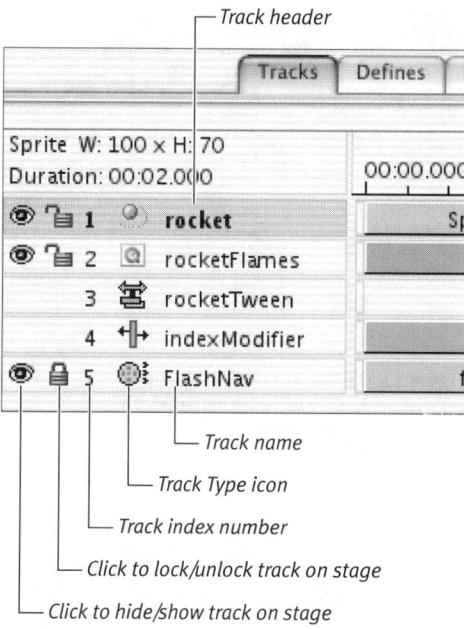

**Figure 1.2** The Track list.

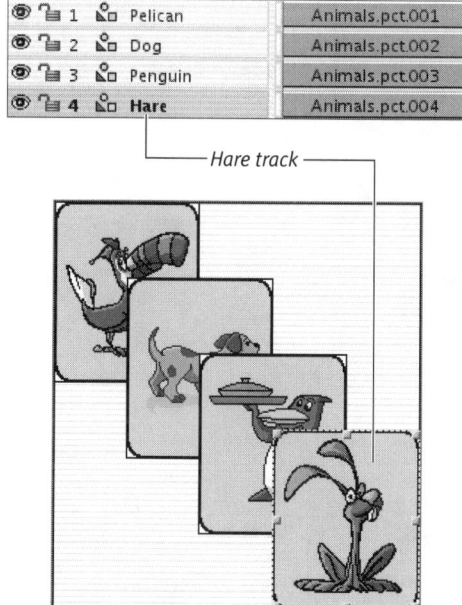

**Figure 1.3** The hare track is at the bottom of the Track list, which means that it appears on top of all other tracks on the stage.

As its name implies, the Tracks tab contains tracks, which stretch horizontally across the window like rows of bricks in a wall. The left side of the Tracks tab displays your project's Track list (**Figure 1.2**). As you add new tracks, each one is placed at the bottom of the list and is given an identifying index number, starting at 1 for the track at the top of the list, 2 for the next track, and so on. Tracks at the bottom of the list are placed in front of tracks toward the top, so the newer tracks appear to be on top of the older tracks above them (**Figure 1.3**).

The right side of the Tracks tab houses your project's Timeline, which in turn houses your project's media samples. A *media sample* can contain pictures, sounds, QScript, or data, depending on its track. The sample's position in the Timeline defines *when* its content will appear in your movie. Like a stonemason, you can resize, reorder, remove, and add samples in the Timeline. Double-click one of the colored blocks, and you'll call up a sample editor that you can use to edit that sample's content.

## About Tracks

A solid project is built from the ground up. Track after track, row after row, you add and arrange your movie's content—the movie's size and scope remaining entirely up to you. Though you can complete most projects with 10 or fewer tracks, you can add as many tracks as you need; there's no limit to your project's size.

Fortunately, you don't have to worry about adding tracks in their order of appearance. LiveStage offers you a flexible construction environment, allowing you to reorder track position easily. You can duplicate tracks, delete them, or even offset their start time to a point much later in the project.

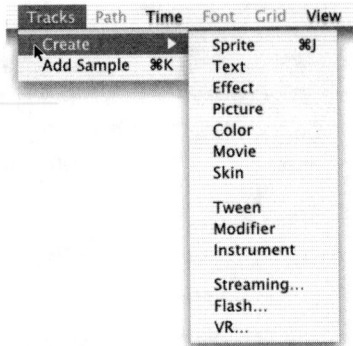

**Figure 1.4** The Tracks menu is available only while you are working in the Tracks tab of the Project window.

### To create a new track:

1. From the Tracks menu, choose Create (**Figure 1.4**).

   A submenu of available track types pops out to the right of the Tracks menu.

2. Choose a track type from the submenu.

   LiveStage creates a new track and places a default sample in the Timeline (**Figure 1.5**).

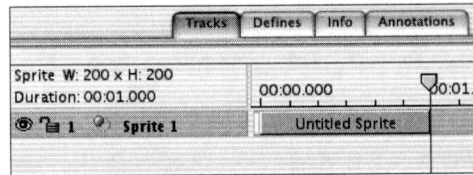

**Figure 1.5** The Tracks tab, showing a newly created track and sample.

### ✔ Tips

- Macromedia Flash tracks, streaming tracks, and VR tracks cannot hold empty samples. Creating one of these tracks causes the Open dialog to appear. Use this dialog to navigate to the file you want to add to your project.

- To create tracks in LiveStage quickly, drag your pictures, movies, or audio files into the Project window directly from the Finder (Mac) or desktop (Windows). This action creates a new track and fills the track with a sample containing your media. As an added time-saving feature, the new track is sized to the exact dimensions of the source media file!

# The Tracks Tab

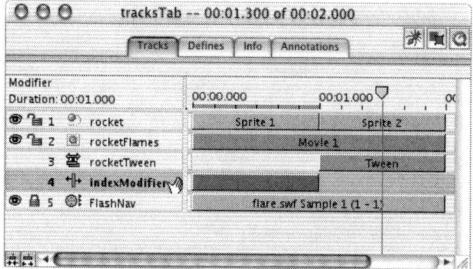

**Figure 1.6** To alter a track's position, drag it up or down in the Track list.

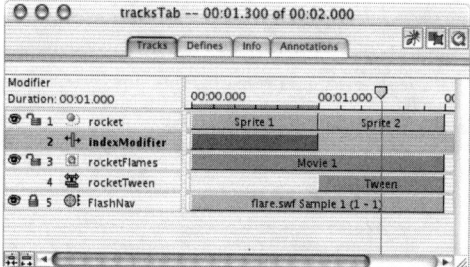

**Figure 1.7** The track named "indexModifier" in its new position. Notice that the index number has changed to reflect its current place in the Track list.

## Working with tracks

Like layers in Flash or Adobe Photoshop, each track has a position in the project's stacking order. As mentioned earlier in this chapter, visual tracks that are lower in the Track list appear to be on top of the tracks above them. If you grab a track from the bottom of the Track list and drag it to the top, that track will move behind the other tracks. To identify the track's position in the list quickly, look at its index number. The topmost track always has an index value of 1, the next track down is 2, and so on. When you reposition a track in the Track list, all index values update to reflect the new order.

### To rearrange track order:

1. In the Track list, select a track (**Figure 1.6**).

   The track header is highlighted, indicating that you may move it.

2. Drag the track to a new position.

   The track jumps to its new position in the Track list, and LiveStage updates each track's index value to reflect the move (**Figure 1.7**).

### ✔ Tips

- Your track's drawing-layer number also affects its position in the project's stacking order. To learn more about drawing layers, see Chapter 3, "Setting Track Properties."
- If you have more than one project open, you can drag tracks between the Tracks tabs of the different Project windows.

**ABOUT TRACKS**

7

Chapter 1

## To duplicate a track:

1. In the Track list, select the track that you want to duplicate.

   The track is highlighted.

2. Choose Edit > Duplicate (Command/Ctrl-D) (**Figure 1.8**).

   A new track is added at the bottom of the Track list.

## To delete a track:

1. In the Track list, select the header of the track that you want to delete.

   The track is highlighted.

2. Choose Edit > Clear, or press the Delete key.

   The track is deleted from the Track list.

## To select multiple tracks:

1. In the Track list, select a track.

   The track is highlighted.

2. Hold down the Shift key while selecting a second track (**Figure 1.9**).

   The second track is selected and highlighted.

## To resize the Track list:

1. Select the bar immediately to the left of the Timeline's time scale (**Figure 1.10**).

   The pointer changes to the resize pointer.

2. Drag to resize the Track list.

**Figure 1.8** The Edit menu lets you duplicate, copy, paste, and delete tracks.

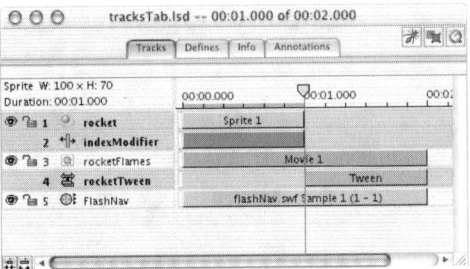

**Figure 1.9** To move or delete multiple tracks at the same time, hold down the Shift key as you select tracks from the Track list. Selected tracks are highlighted.

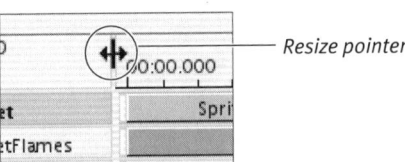

**Figure 1.10** Moving the resize pointer to the left makes the Timeline bigger; moving the pointer to the right shrinks the Timeline.

# The Tracks Tab

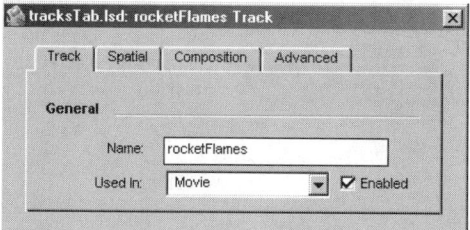

**Figure 1.11** The Track Properties window.

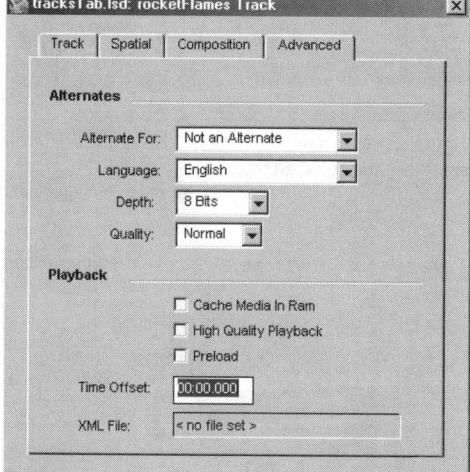

**Figure 1.12** The Track Properties window's Advanced tab. The Time Offset text box is at the bottom of this window.

*The offset track's start point*

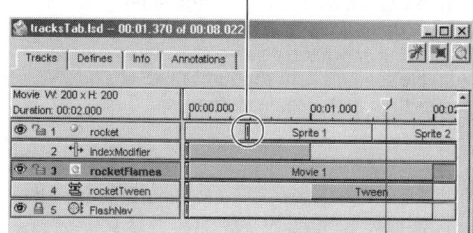

**Figure 1.13** The bar at the beginning of a track indicates that it is offset. To quickly alter a track's offset time, grab the bar and drag it along the Timeline.

## Offsetting a track

You can compare offsetting a track to moving an entire row of bricks sideways. The track's start time changes, but the relative timing of its samples does not. Picture a row of bricks sliding to the right. Each brick changes position relative to bricks in other rows but not relative to bricks in its own row. This trick comes in handy if you've spent a lot of time lining up multiple picture, sprite, or movie samples, but then find that you have to delay their start time to a point later in the project.

### To offset a track:

1. In the Track list, double-click the header of the track that you want to offset.

   The Track Properties window opens (**Figure 1.11**). The Track Properties window has several tabs that you will explore in Chapter 3, "Setting Track Properties." For now, however, you will look at only one section of the Advanced tab.

2. Select the Advanced tab (**Figure 1.12**).

3. In the Time Offset text box, enter a new start time for the track.

4. Click the close box at the top of the window.

   In the Timeline, the beginning of the track jumps to the offset time you specified (**Figure 1.13**).

### ✔ Tip

- To offset a track directly from the Timeline, grab the bar at the track's left edge and drag it to a new start position. As you drag the bar, hold down the Option key (Mac) or Ctrl-Alt keys (Windows) to force the track to snap to the beginning or end of other tracks and samples.

# Chapter 1

## About Samples

In LiveStage, each track may only contain one distinct type of sample. Think of samples as being colored bricks, with each color representing a separate type of media. Tween samples are mauve, for example; text samples are dusky violet, and audio samples are green. In LiveStage, each track must contain bricks of exactly the same color. Thus, tween tracks can hold only tween samples, text tracks can hold only text samples, and instrument tracks can hold only instrument samples.

### To add a new sample:

1. In the Track list, select the header of the track to which you want to add a sample. The track is highlighted.

2. Choose Tracks > Add Sample (Command/Ctrl-K) (**Figure 1.14**).
   An empty sample is added after the last sample in the selected track (**Figure 1.15**).

### ✔ Tip

- Flash tracks, modifier tracks, streaming tracks, and VR tracks do not allow you to add new samples. Instead, you have to create a new track and then offset it to begin after the last track has ended.

### To alter a sample's start time:

1. Double-click a sample.
   The sample editor opens (**Figure 1.16**).

2. In the Start Time text box at the top of the sample editor, type a new start time (**Figure 1.17**).
   In the Timeline, the sample jumps to the specified point.

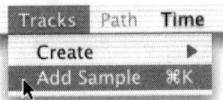

**Figure 1.14** The Tracks menu lets you add new samples to selected tracks.

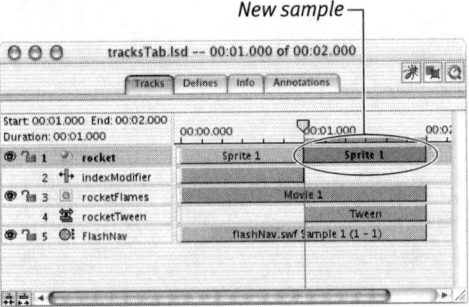

**Figure 1.15** New samples are added after the last sample in the selected track.

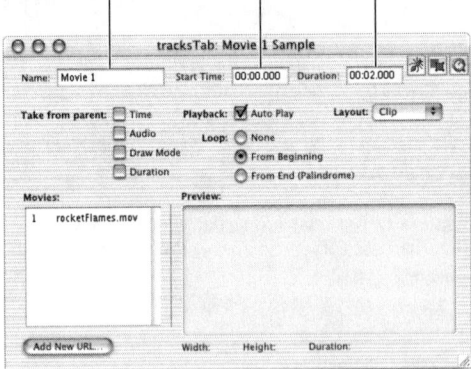

**Figure 1.16** A movie sample editor. Although each sample editor looks and functions differently, depending on what type of track it belongs to, all editable samples have the same three text boxes across the top: Name, Start Time, and Duration.

**Figure 1.17** You use the Start Time text box to change a sample's start position in the Timeline.

# The Tracks Tab

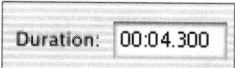

**Figure 1.18** The Duration text box specifies the length of time that a sample covers in the Timeline.

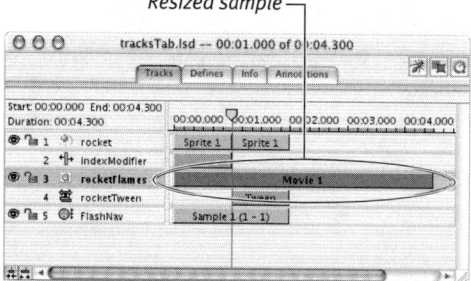

**Figure 1.19** If you change a sample's duration, it will appear to reduce or expand in the Timeline.

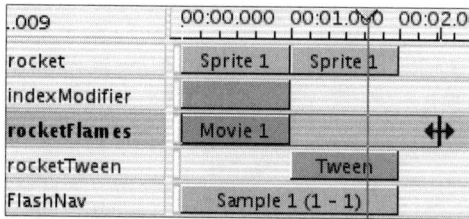

**Figure 1.20** Drag the handle at the end of a sample to resize the sample in the Timeline.

## ✔ Tip

- Flash tracks, modifier tracks, streaming tracks, and VR tracks do not allow you to alter their start times through a sample editor. Instead, offset the tracks to adjust when they start relative to the other tracks in your Project window.

## To alter a sample's duration:

1. Double-click a sample.
   The sample editor opens.

2. In the Duration text box at the top of the sample editor, type a new duration (**Figure 1.18**).
   In the Timeline, the sample updates to reflect its new length (**Figure 1.19**).

## ✔ Tips

- The sample editor for Flash, streaming, and VR samples does not have a Duration text box. To learn more about resizing these samples, see Chapter 6, "Basic Visual Tracks," and Chapter 9, "Streaming, Flash, and VR Tracks."

- You can also resize a sample directly in the Timeline by dragging its resize handle—a double-headed pointer that appears at either end of a sample when you mouse over it. You can align the end of a sample by dragging the handle to a new time position. As you drag the handle, hold down the Option key (Mac) or Ctrl-Alt keys (Windows) to force the sample to snap to the beginning or end of other samples in the Timeline (**Figure 1.20**).

Chapter 1

### To reposition a sample:

1. In the Timeline, select the sample you want to reposition.
   The sample is highlighted.

2. Drag the sample to a new position (**Figure 1.21**).
   As you move the sample, a ghost outline shows its new position.

### ✔ Tip

- You cannot move a sample to a space smaller than the sample itself. In such a case, try resizing the sample before moving it.

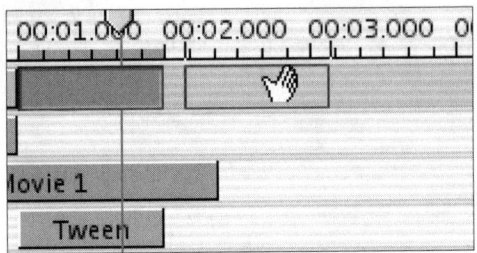

**Figure 1.21** You can move a sample in the Timeline by dragging it to a new position.

### To duplicate a sample:

1. In the Timeline, select a sample.
   The sample is highlighted.

2. Choose Edit > Duplicate.
   A duplicate sample is placed after the last sample in the track.

### To delete a sample:

1. In the Timeline, select the sample to be deleted.
   The sample is highlighted.

2. Choose Edit > Clear; or press the Delete key.
   The sample is deleted from the Timeline.

# The Tracks Tab

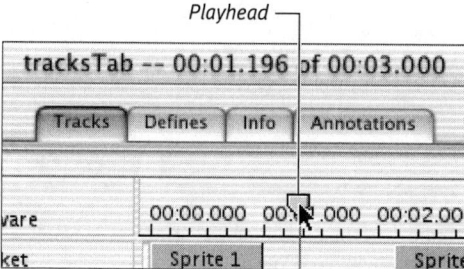

**Figure 1.22** The Project window's title bar displays the current time in your movie, as reflected by the playhead's position in the Timeline.

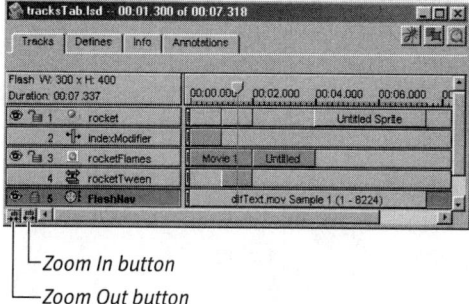

**Figure 1.23** Zoom out on the Timeline to fit more of your project in the Project window.

## About the Timeline

Just as people are slaves to time, projects are ruled by the minutes, seconds, and fractions of seconds that make up the Timeline. The Timeline shows your movie's linear progression from its beginning (the left edge of the Timeline) to its end (the right edge of the last sample in the Timeline). To navigate around the Timeline, you use the playhead.

The *playhead* is a pointer with a red indicator line emanating from its tip. It sits at the top of the Timeline and indicates exactly "when" you are in your project by means of a time value displayed in the Project window's title bar. This time value, which always reflects the playhead's position in the Timeline, is called the movie's *current time* (**Figure 1.22**).

The playhead works in conjunction with the Stage window to show the visual content of your movie at its current time. (To learn more about the Stage window, see Chapter 2, "The Stage and Library.") If you need to arrange the graphic content of your movie at a particular time, first you must move the playhead to that time value in the Timeline. The stage will update automatically to display your project's visual content at that time, allowing you to change its layout.

### ✔ Tip

- If you want to zoom out on the Timeline for a broader view of how your samples are lining up, click the Zoom Out button at the bottom of the Tracks tab (**Figure 1.23**). To view the Timeline in more detail, click the Zoom In button.

# Chapter 1

## To jump to a specific point in the Timeline:

1. Choose Time > Go to Time.
   The Go to Time dialog opens (**Figure 1.24**).
2. Type a time value in the text box.
3. Click OK.
   The playhead jumps to the specified point in time.

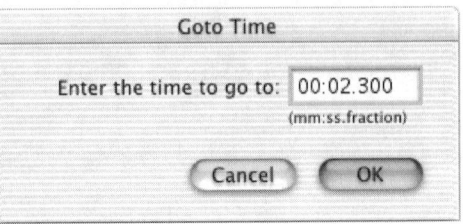

**Figure 1.24** The Go to Time dialog, accessible from the Time menu, lets you jump to an exact point in the Timeline.

**Table 1.1**

### Time-Scale Conversions

| LiveStage Ticks | Time Value |
| --- | --- |
| 1 | 1/600 second |
| 10 | 1/60 second |
| 60 | 1/10 second |
| 300 | 1/2 second |
| 600 | 1 second |
| 18000 | 30 seconds |
| 36000 | 1 minute |

## The LiveStage Time Scale

Most video-editing programs use a time scale measured in frames per second. But LiveStage is much more than just a video-editing program; it can mix movies of different time scales in one project. Why is that capability important? Well, if you want to use two movies in your project—one with a time scale of 12 frames per second, for example, and the other with a time scale of 29.97 frames per second—you need a time scale that can accommodate these different frame rates. As a result, LiveStage divides its time scale into fractions of a second.

The default time scale for LiveStage is 600 time units per second (**Table 1.1**). This fine resolution allows you to incorporate any movie, regardless of frame rate, into your project. LiveStage breaks this time scale into more-manageable chunks by allowing you to use minutes and seconds in time-entry dialogs.

Time-entry dialogs look similar to the display on a digital clock, using a colon to separate minutes from seconds and a period to separate seconds from fractions of a second. To enter a time value of 1 minute, 30 and one-half seconds in a time-entry dialog, you would type `01:30.300`.

# The Tracks Tab

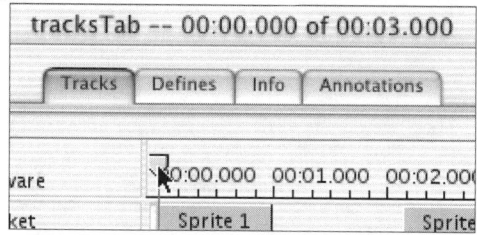

**Figure 1.25** Dragging the playhead along the Timeline is a quick way to jump from place to place within your project.

## To move the playhead along the Timeline:

- In the Timeline, click the playhead and drag it to a new position (**Figure 1.25**).

    The movie's current time, as reflected by the playhead, is updated and displayed in the Project window's title bar.

## ✔ Tip

- To snap the playhead to the beginning or end of a sample, hold down the Option key (Mac) or Ctrl-Alt keys (Windows) as you move the playhead along the Timeline.

- To jump backward through samples quickly, press the left-arrow key or choose Time > Go to Previous Frame. To jump forward through frames, press the right-arrow key or choose Time > Go to Next Frame.

# The Stage and Library

In Chapter 1, you saw how to use the Tracks tab to create, reposition, and modify tracks and samples so that you can set them to appear *when* you want them in your movie. To see how all the visual pieces look together, however, you'll need to head to the stage.

When you're working in the Timeline, your media look like nondescript, multicolored bricks of different sizes (durations). In the Stage window, however, the visual content stored in those simple bricks takes on its true form, allowing you to see how your content works together. In the Stage window, you can tweak and align all your visual content, including picture, Flash, VR, video, and sprite tracks.

The first part of this chapter tells you how to use the stage, including arranging and aligning visual media, zooming in and out, and mastering grids. The second part is designed to get you organized. When you're neck deep in pictures, movies, and animations, you'll be lost unless you learn to keep them all organized with LiveStage's library. The end of this chapter introduces the library and shows you how to use it to streamline your workflow.

Chapter 2

# About Stage Basics

When you first open LiveStage or create a new project, the Stage window is not visible. Before you can use the stage, you must open it.

### To open the Stage window:

◆ Choose Window > Show Stage Window.
   or
   Click the Show Stage Window button in the top-right corner of the Project window (**Figure 2.1**).

   If the Stage window was open before but hidden behind other windows on your screen, clicking the Show Stage Window button brings the stage to the top (**Figure 2.2**).

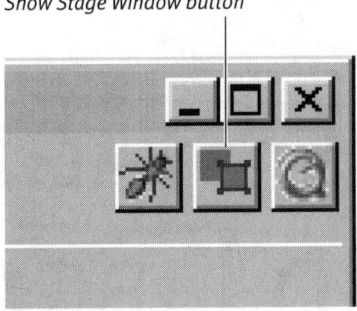

**Figure 2.1** The Project window's Show Stage Window button is a great shortcut for opening the Stage window.

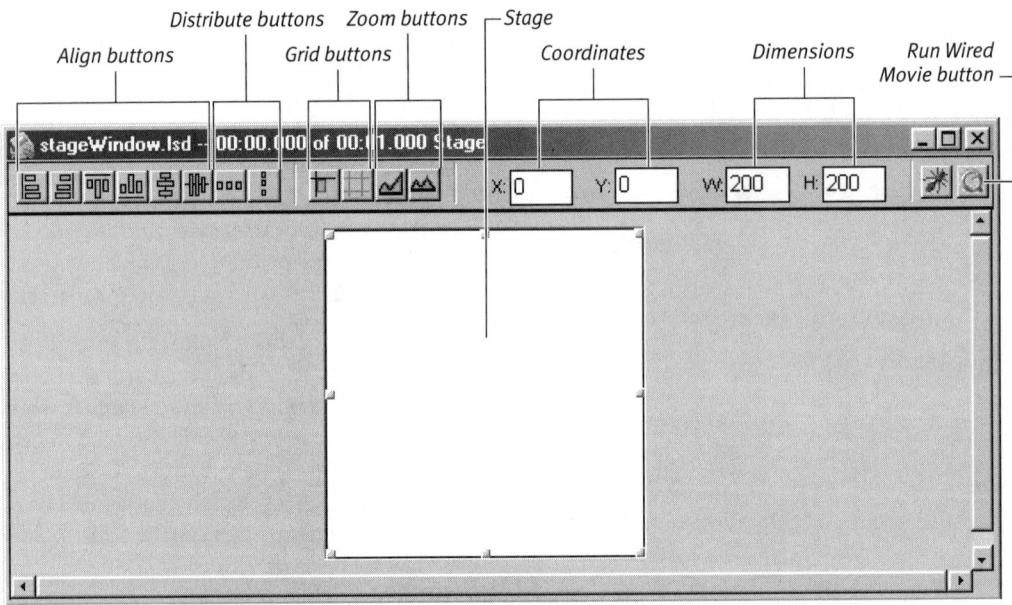

**Figure 2.2** The Stage window.

# The Stage and Library

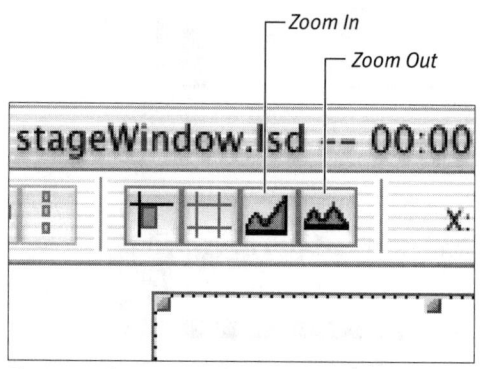

**Figure 2.3** The zoom buttons make the stage appear bigger or smaller.

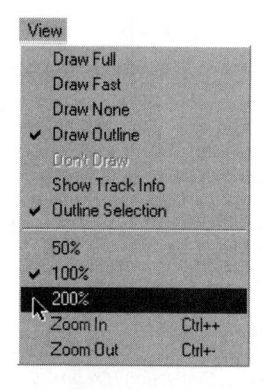

**Figure 2.4** The View menu contains many options, including zoom values, that control the stage's appearance.

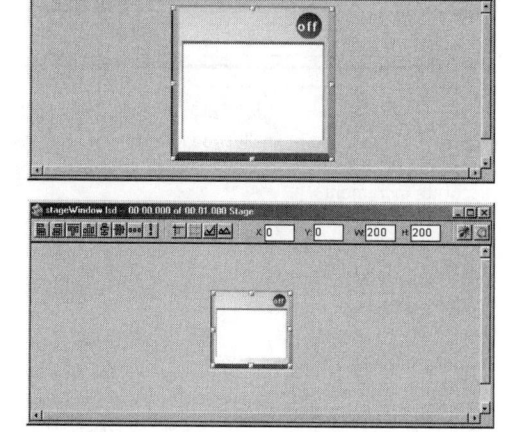

**Figure 2.5** The result of zooming in and out on the stage.

In theory, you can make your project as tall and wide as you like. In practice, you'll probably stay within 1600 x 1200 pixels—the highest screen resolution of most monitors on the market today. If you're working on a very large project, you'll need to zoom out on the stage to fit the whole project in the Stage window. Conversely, if your project is very small, you'll need to zoom in to see enough detail to place tracks and sprites accurately.

### To zoom in or out on the stage:

◆ To zoom in, press Command/Ctrl—]; to zoom out, press Command/Ctrl—[.

◆ In the Stage window, click the Zoom In or Zoom Out button (**Figure 2.3**).

◆ From the View menu, choose a zoom value (**Figure 2.4**).

Depending on the zoom value you select, the stage reduces or enlarges (**Figure 2.5**).

## Stage Properties

If you're used to working in multimedia programs such as Macromedia Flash or Director, setting the stage's size and background color is one of the first things you do upon starting a project. In LiveStage, however, you cannot set a predefined stage size and background color. Instead, the stage expands and contracts to encompass all your project's visual tracks. To work around this behavior, use a color track as a backdrop for your project. (To learn more about color tracks, see Chapter 6, "Basic Visual Tracks.")

ABOUT STAGE BASICS

19

## About Using the Stage

You can reposition or resize visual tracks directly on the stage in a couple of ways. If accuracy isn't an issue, simply select a track and drag it to a new position. If you need to be more precise, the text boxes at the top of the Stage window let you reposition and resize tracks in pixel-accurate increments.

### To reposition a track:

1. In the Stage window, select the track you want to reposition.

   The track is highlighted with a blue outline.

2. Drag the track to a new position on the stage (**Figure 2.6**).

   or

   Enter a new X and/or Y value in the coordinate text boxes at the top of the Stage window (**Figure 2.7**).

   The track moves to its new position on the stage.

### ✔ Tips

- To move several tracks at the same time, press the Shift key, select the tracks to be moved, and drag them to a new position on the stage.

- Use the arrow keys to move selected tracks 1 pixel at a time. If you hold down the Shift key, selected tracks will jump 10 pixels each time you press an arrow key.

- If a sprite is the same size as the sprite track that contains it, you may experience problems while trying to select and move the entire track. Press Command-Option (Mac) or Shift-Ctrl (Windows) to move troublesome sprite tracks easily.

**Figure 2.6** To reposition a track, select and drag it across the stage.

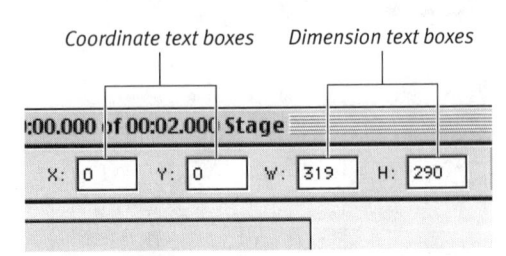

**Figure 2.7** These text boxes let you alter the coordinates and dimensions of tracks in pixel-accurate increments.

## The Stage and Library

**Figure 2.8** The result of resizing a track on the stage. Resize handles appear only around tracks. If you need to change a sprite's dimensions, use the Dimension text boxes at the top of the Stage window.

### To resize a track:

1. In the Stage window, select the track you want to resize.

   The track is highlighted, and eight resize handles surround it.

2. Enter new width and/or height values in the appropriate text boxes at the top of the Stage window.

   *or*

   Drag a resize handle until the track is the correct size (**Figure 2.8**).

### ✔ Tips

- To maintain the track's aspect ratio (proportions), press Option (Mac) or Ctrl-Alt (Windows) *before* you select and drag a resize handle.

- Resize handles work only with tracks. If you have selected a sprite on the stage, the eight resize handles do not appear. You can still resize the selected sprite, however, by entering new width and/or height values in the text boxes at the top of the Stage window. To learn more about sprites, see Chapter 10, "Sprite Tracks."

## Locking tracks

If you have several tracks in close proximity on the stage, you may have a problem selecting the track you want to move. Locking the surrounding tracks alleviates this problem, as locked tracks cannot be selected or moved from their positions. Hiding the surrounding tracks serves a similar purpose and has the added advantage of allowing you to focus on just the objects you need to arrange. Although hidden tracks are not visible on the stage, they remain part of your project and *will* be visible in the final movie.

## Chapter 2

### To lock a track's position:

♦ In the Tracks tab of the Project window, click the Lock icon in the track's header (**Figure 2.9**).

The lock snaps shut, indicating that the track is locked and cannot be moved or selected on the stage.

### To hide a track:

♦ In the Tracks tab of the Project window, click the Eye icon in the track's header.

The Eye icon closes, indicating that the track is no longer visible on the stage.

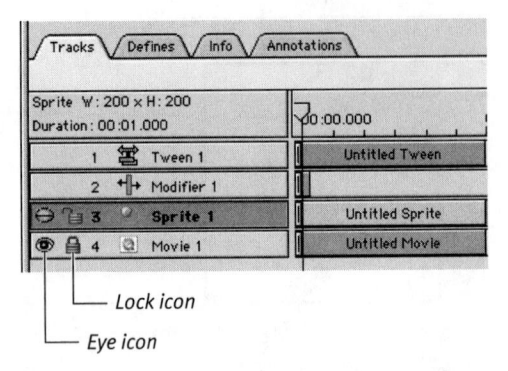

**Figure 2.9** Only visual tracks have headers containing Eye and Lock icons. Nonvisual tracks, such as tween, modifier, and sound tracks, are not visible on the stage and thus do not need to be hidden or locked.

## Opening editors from the stage

While you're in the thick of arranging objects on the stage, you occasionally need to open a sample editor to change image content or update QScripts. Ordinarily, you would open a sample from the Tracks tab, but jumping back to the Timeline is time-consuming and inconvenient. Luckily, you can open sample editors directly from the stage.

### To access a sample editor from the stage:

♦ On the stage, double-click a track.

A sample editor opens. If you clicked a track that does not have a sample editor, such as a video or sound track, a media preview window opens and displays the track's content.

### ✔ Tip

■ You can also open a sprite editor from the stage. Double-click any sprite, and its sprite editor will appear.

## About Grids

A grid is a crosshatch of lines dividing the stage into square cells, similar to the boxes on a piece of graph paper (**Figure 2.10**). The grid's intersecting lines let you assess the alignment of visual tracks accurately and then shift any tracks that are not placed properly.

LiveStage also has a handy function that causes objects to snap to grid intersections as you drag them around the stage.

### To enable or disable grid display:

◆ Choose Grid > Show Grid, or click the Show Grid button at the top of the Stage window (**Figure 2.11**).

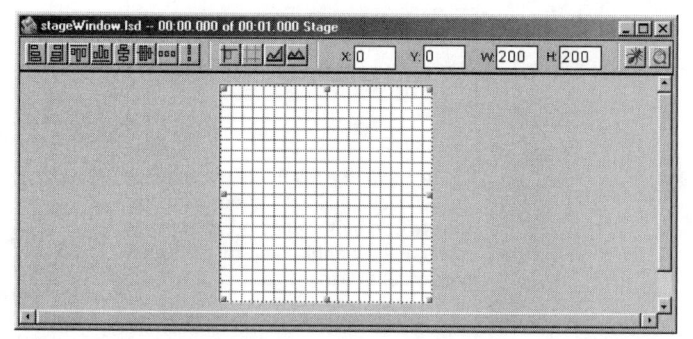

**Figure 2.10** The grid provides a reference field of evenly spaced horizontal and vertical lines that make it easy for you to align objects on the stage.

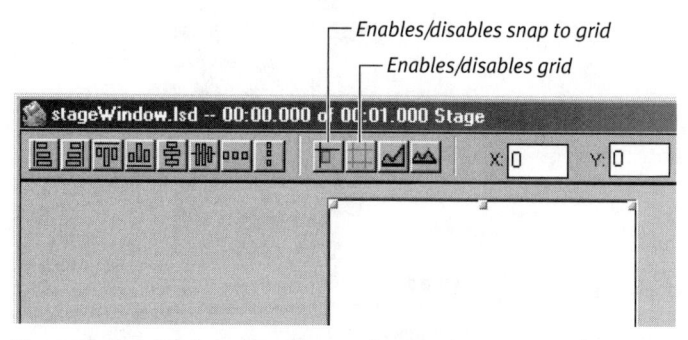

*Enables/disables snap to grid*
*Enables/disables grid*

**Figure 2.11** The stage's toolbar offers two buttons that control the grid. The button on the right turns the grid on and off; the button on the left enables and disables the snap to grid function.

Chapter 2

## To enable the snap to grid function:

◆ Choose Grid > Snap to Grid, or click the Snap to Grid button at the top of the Stage window (**Figure 2.12**).

Sometimes, you need to align objects to a point on the stage that does not correspond to a grid intersection. Should this situation occur, you need to alter the grid's size.

## To set a new grid size:

1. Choose Grid > Set Grid Size (**Figure 2.13**). The Grid Settings dialog appears (**Figure 2.14**).
2. Enter a pixel value in the Grid Size text box.
3. Click OK.
   The grid expands or contracts to match the setting you entered.

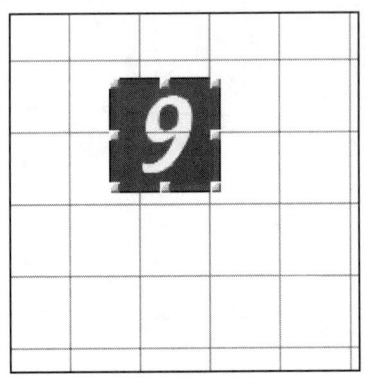

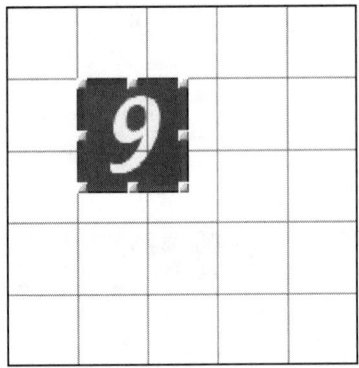

**Figure 2.12** In the top figure the graphic sits between grid intersections. With the Snap to Grid button enabled, the top left corner of the graphic jumps to meet grid intersections on the stage.

**Figure 2.13** The Grid menu mirrors the functions of the toolbars at the top of the Stage window.

ABOUT GRIDS

24

# The Stage and Library

**Figure 2.14** The Grid Settings dialog defines how your grid looks on the stage. Use this dialog to change the grid's size and color.

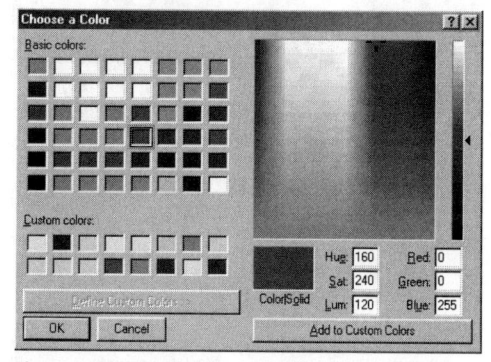

**Figure 2.15** Click the Grid Color box in the Grid Settings dialog to open the Color Picker, which you can use to set the grid's color.

By default, the grid is drawn in blue. If your project has a blue background or if the grid lines don't contrast with your project's colors, you can make the grid more visible by setting a new color.

### To set a new grid color:

1. Choose Grid > Set Grid Size.

    The Grid Settings dialog appears.

2. Click the Grid Color box.

    The Color Picker opens (**Figure 2.15**).

3. Select a new color for your grid.

4. Click OK to close the Color Picker.

5. Click OK to close the Grid Settings dialog.

    The stage updates to reflect its new color setting.

**ABOUT GRIDS**

25

# About Align Tools

The alignment toolbar in the top-left corner of the Stage window offers alignment options that line up several tracks or sprites. You can align objects by their top, bottom, left, or right edges or by their horizontal or vertical centers (**Figure 2.16**).

The alignment toolbar also contains two spread options that distribute and space tracks evenly by their horizontal or vertical center lines (refer to Figure 2.16).

*Arrow buttons unaligned*

*Arrow buttons aligned by their top edges*

*Round buttons spread improperly*

*Round buttons spread horizontally by their centers*

**Figure 2.16** Without the stage's alignment features, organizing the buttons in this project would be very difficult. When you use a combination of alignment and spread options, each button moves to an appropriate position automatically.

# The Stage and Library

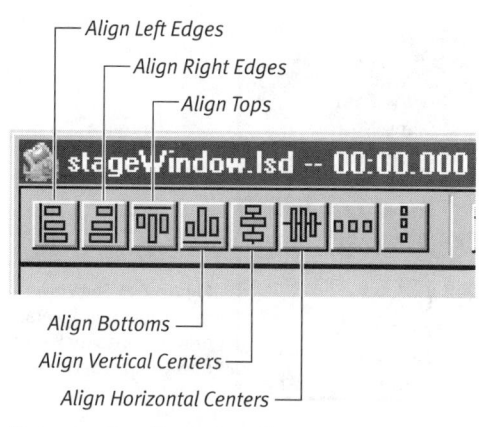

*Figure 2.17* The alignment toolbar.

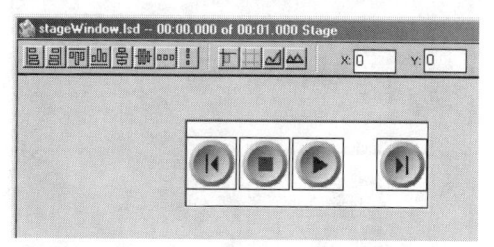

Labels: Align Left Edges, Align Right Edges, Align Tops, Align Bottoms, Align Vertical Centers, Align Horizontal Centers.

*Figure 2.18* The result of using the Align Horizontal Centers button.

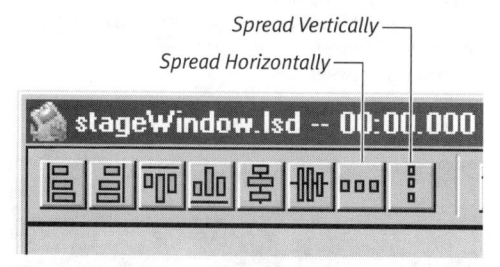

*Figure 2.19* The spread toolbar.

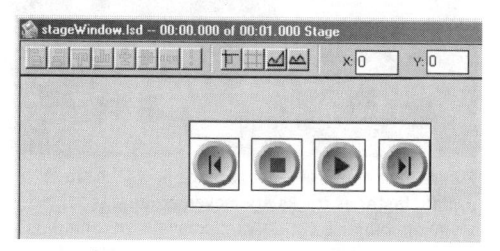

Labels: Spread Vertically, Spread Horizontally.

*Figure 2.20* The result of using the Spread Horizontally button.

## To align tracks:

1. In the Stage window, hold down the Shift key and select the tracks or sprites you want to align.

   Each selected track is highlighted, and the alignment buttons along the top of the Stage window are enabled (**Figure 2.17**).

2. From the Grid menu, choose an alignment option.

   *or*

   Click a button in the alignment toolbar at the top of the Stage window.

   The selected visual elements are aligned (**Figure 2.18**).

## To distribute tracks:

1. In the Stage window, hold down the Shift key and select the tracks you want to distribute.

   Each selected track is highlighted, and the alignment buttons along the top of the Stage window are enabled (**Figure 2.19**).

2. From the Grid menu, choose a spread option.

   *or*

   Click a spread button in the alignment toolbar at the top of the Stage window.

   The selected tracks are spread evenly, and the distance between their center points is equalized (**Figure 2.20**).

**ABOUT ALIGN TOOLS**

27

# Chapter 2

## About Draw Settings

A complicated project with a lot of tracks can take its toll on the stage, causing it to update more slowly when you move objects around. To speed things, choose one or more appropriate draw settings from the View menu (**Figure 2.21**):

- **Draw Full:** draws visual elements accurately, including graphics modes, transparency settings, and text antialiasing. (To learn more about graphics modes and transparency settings, see Chapter 3, "Setting Track Properties.") This setting is more processor-intensive but provides the truest representation of your final movie (**Figure 2.22**).

- **Draw Fast:** draws visual elements quickly but does not display graphics modes, transparency settings, or text antialiasing. Graphics may also appear slightly pixilated, though they look normal in the final movie (**Figure 2.23**).

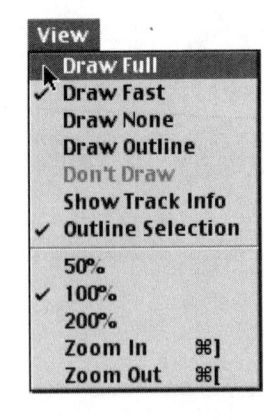

**Figure 2.21** The View menu contains several draw settings that affect how your media appear on the stage.

**Figure 2.22** Use the Draw Full setting to make tracks appearing on the stage look as they will in the final movie. Note how these pictures have smooth transitions between colors.

**Figure 2.23** The Draw Fast setting allows the stage to update faster as tracks are moved around, but the stage no longer accurately reflects how your final movie will display. The colors in this example are noticeably pixilated.

**Figure 2.24** Draw None is useful only if you are suffering extreme stage redraw delays, such as those that occur when working on very slow computers.

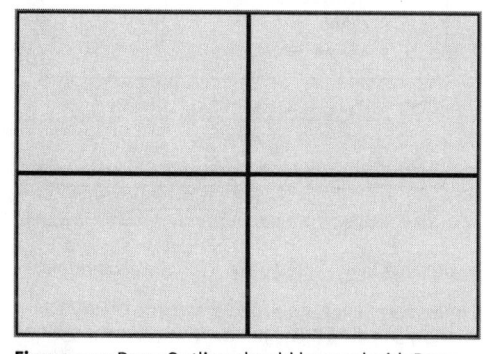

**Figure 2.25** Draw Outline should be used with Draw None so that you can see where tracks are placed on the stage.

**Figure 2.26** Show Track Info displays individual track names in their top-left corners.

- **Draw None:** visual tracks are not displayed on the stage, though you can still select and move them. If choosing the Draw None option, you should also choose Draw Outline; otherwise, you will not be able to see the boundaries of tracks on the stage and you will not know what you are selecting (**Figure 2.24**).

- **Draw Outline:** draws a 1-pixel-wide black outline around each object on the stage. (**Figure 2.25**).

- **Don't Draw:** affects only tween editors. To learn more about this option, see Chapter 11, "Animations and Manipulations."

- **Show Track Info:** displays the name of the track or sprite in its top-left corner. This mode can be used in conjunction with any of the other draw settings (**Figure 2.26**).

- **Outline Selection:** draws a 1-pixel-wide blue outline around any object selected on the stage. This mode can be used with any of the other draw settings.

### ✔ Tip

- It's a good idea to keep the Stage window closed when you're not using it. As you work in other Project windows and tabs, the stage monitors your actions and redraws constantly to reflect any changes you make. This redrawing slows your system, especially if you have a lot of tracks in the project.

# Chapter 2

## About the Library

Rather than scatter your media files haphazardly around your hard disk, you can use the LiveStage library to sort and organize videos, pictures, sounds, QScripts, and any other content you use in your projects. The Library window can be accessed from the Window menu and opens to show three tabs across the top (**Figure 2.27**):

- **Media.** This tab works on a global scale, holding files that are available to all your projects. If you have a set of button graphics that you want to use in multiple projects, store them here, and they'll be available every time you open LiveStage.

- **Local.** The Local tab is used to store files that are only available to the project you are currently working on. If you have more than one project open at the same time, as you switch between projects the Local tab's content will change to show media from the presently active project.

- **Scripts.** The Scripts tab collects AppleScripts, Behaviors, and QScripts for use in any of your projects.

### ✔ Tip

- The first time you save a project, LiveStage creates a local Library folder in the same directory as the project file (**Figure 2.28**).

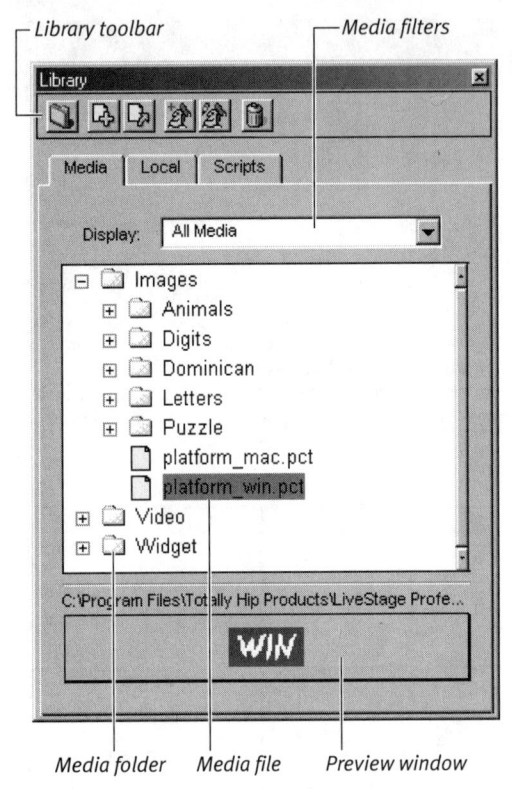

**Figure 2.27** Simply drag media from the Library window and drop them into the Tracks tab for use in your projects.

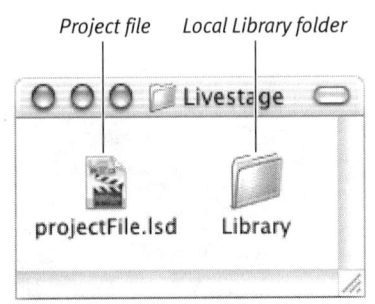

**Figure 2.28** The first time you save a project, a local Library folder is created in the same directory as your project file. This folder is an ideal place to collect media files used in that project.

## The Stage and Library

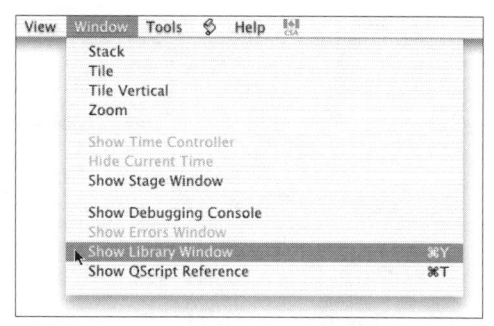

**Figure 2.29** The Window menu can be used to show or hide the Library window.

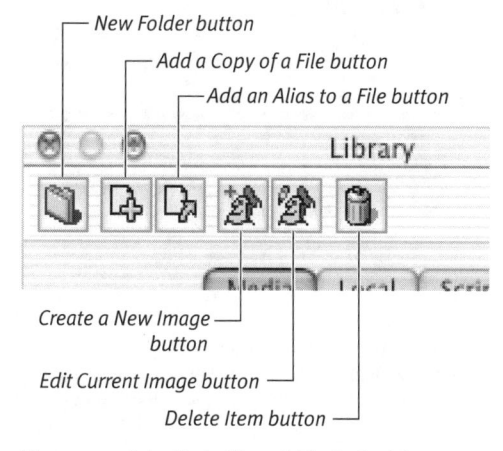

**Figure 2.30** Selecting a file or folder in the Library window enables the buttons in the Library toolbar.

- New Folder button
- Add a Copy of a File button
- Add an Alias to a File button
- Create a New Image button
- Edit Current Image button
- Delete Item button

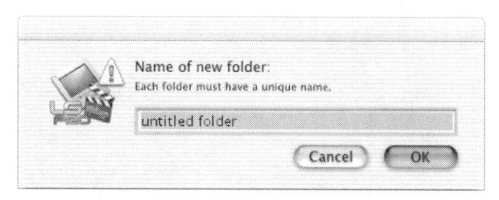

**Figure 2.31** Give your new folder a unique name.

### To open the Library window:

◆ Choose Window > Show Library Window (Command/Ctrl-Y) (**Figure 2.29**).

To add files to the library, create a new folder in one of the tabs and then add your media to that folder.

### To create a new folder:

1. Select a file or folder in the Library window.

    This action enables the New Folder button in the Library toolbar (**Figure 2.30**).

2. Click the New Folder button.

    A dialog opens asking you to name the new folder (**Figure 2.31**).

3. In the text box, type a name for the new folder.

4. Click OK.

    A new folder is created in the library (**Figure 2.32**).

New folder

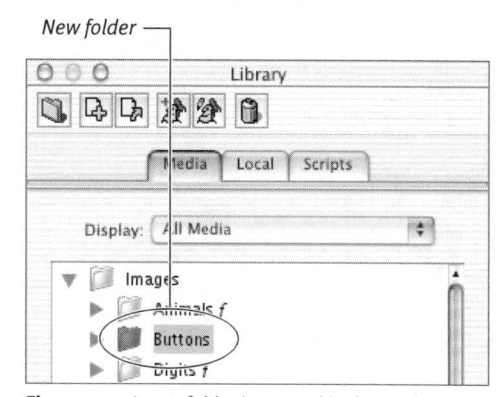

**Figure 2.32** A new folder is created in the media list.

**ABOUT THE LIBRARY**

31

## Adding files to the library

When you add a file to the library, the original file is left on your hard disk, and a copy of it is placed in the selected Library folder. This arrangement makes it easy for you to keep all your files organized in one place on your computer. Sometimes, however, you need to change workstations or move to another computer. If you save your work files in the library's Local tab, they're placed in a Library folder that's saved with your project, making it easy for you to transfer the project between computers without losing important data.

### To add a file to a folder:

1. Select the folder to which you'd like to add the file.

   The folder is highlighted.

2. In the Library toolbar, click the Add a Copy of a File button.

   The Open dialog appears.

3. Navigate to the file that you want to add to the Library folder.

4. Click OK.

   A copy of the file is added to the selected folder (**Figure 2.33**).

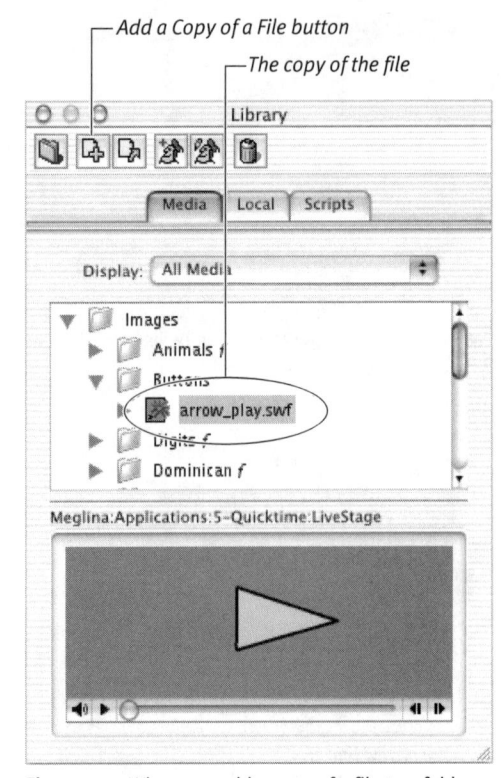

**Figure 2.33** When you add a copy of a file to a folder, the original file is left untouched on your hard disk and a copy is placed in the selected Library folder.

The Stage and Library

— Add an Alias to a File button
— The alias of the file

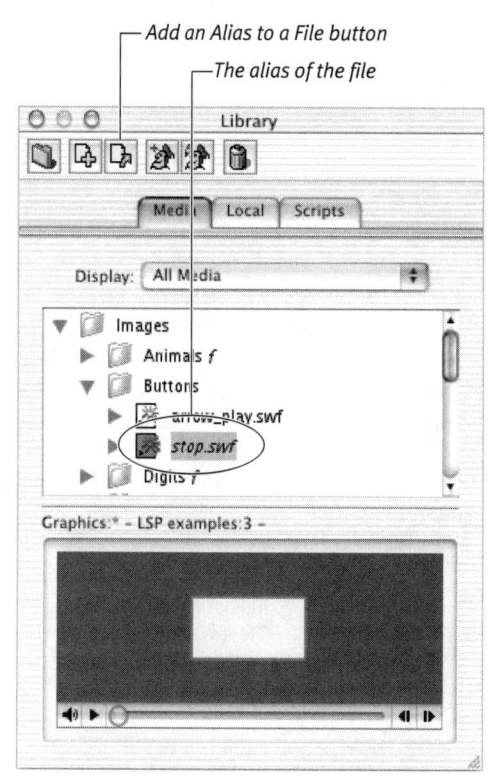

**Figure 2.34** Alias file names are printed in italics, clearly distinguishing them from other Library files.

## Adding aliases

An *alias file* is a pointer to a media file that exists elsewhere on your hard disk or on a local artwork server. Alias files are handy if you work with a production team, because your graphic designers can continue refining media content while you create the project. When you use aliases, every time you compile the project, it updates automatically to include the updated media files.

### To add an alias file to a folder:

1. Select the folder to which you'd like to add the file.

   The folder is highlighted.

2. In the Library toolbar, click the Add an Alias to a File button.

   The Open dialog appears.

3. Navigate to the file that you want to add to the Library folder.

4. Click OK.

   An alias file is added to the selected folder (**Figure 2.34**).

---

### Populating the Local Library

To activate the command buttons across the top of the Library window, you must select one of its files or folders first. When you create a new project, the Local tab is empty. Because there aren't any files or folders to select, you're unable to use the buttons to create *new* files or folders, resulting in a sort of vicious circle.

Fortunately, a workaround is available. The first time you save a project, LiveStage creates a local Library folder next to the project file on your hard disk. Find this folder, and put a media file in it. When you go back to LiveStage, the media file will appear in the Local tab. Select the file to activate the Local tab, making it available to store and organize files. Note that this will be fixed in a future update of LiveStage 3.0.

ABOUT THE LIBRARY

## To delete files or folders:

1. Select a file or folder to be deleted.
   The file or folder is highlighted.

2. In the Library toolbar, click the Delete Item button.
   Deleting a file or folder moves it to your computer's wastebasket. You cannot undo this action. Be sure that you really want to delete the file before you click that trash can icon!

Filters let you find a particular media type quickly among the many files in your library. If you're looking for a certain video, for example, use a media filter to make the library show only video files.

## To use a media filter:

1. Select the Media tab of the Library window.

2. From the Display pop-up menu, choose a media type (**Figure 2.35**).
   Only the selected media type will be displayed in the library (**Figure 2.36**).

## To move files between library folders:

◆ Select the file that you want to move, and drag it to the appropriate folder.

## ✔ Tip

■ You can change the size of the Library window's preview window by dragging the bar that separates it from the library's list of objects (**Figure 2.37**).

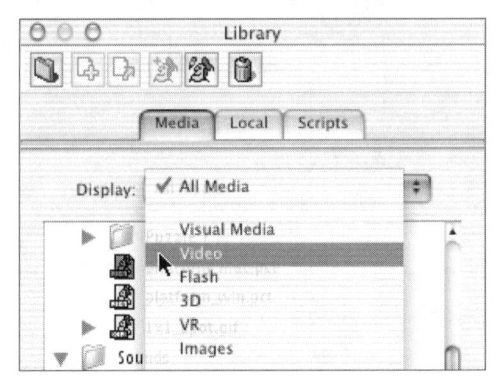

**Figure 2.35** Media filters let you locate a particular file type quickly.

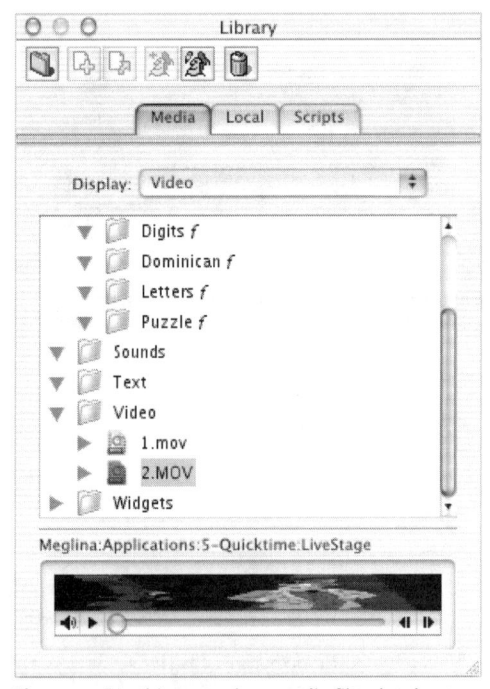

**Figure 2.36** In this example, a media filter has been used to hide everything but video files.

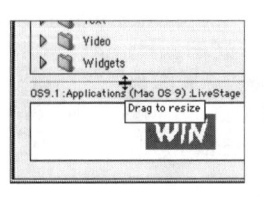

**Figure 2.37** Drag the bar below the Library's media list to resize the preview window.

# SETTING TRACK PROPERTIES

**Figure 3.1** The Track Properties window controls the display of individual tracks. If the track has more than one sample, the choices you make here will apply to every sample.

So far, you've tackled the basics of creating and editing tracks with both the Timeline and the stage. If all you ever want to do with LiveStage is create simple slide shows of still images, this may be all you need to know. Chances are good, however, that you'll want to tweak your tracks to create more advanced effects for your movies. In this case, you'll need to acquaint yourself with the Track Properties window (**Figure 3.1**).

Every track has a Track Properties window, which holds properties that apply to the entire track and every sample within it. When you open the Track Properties window, you always see Track and Advanced tabs, as these tabs hold properties common to every track. All visual tracks also have Spatial and Composition tabs. This chapter covers these common track properties and provides important tips about their use in LiveStage.

## To open the Track Properties window:

◆ In the Tracks tab, double-click the track's name in the Track list.

The Track Properties window opens, defaulted to the Track tab.

# About the Track Tab

The first thing you see when you open the Track Properties window is the Track tab, which sets general track properties. Although each track has a General section, a few tracks—such as sprite, text, and Flash tracks—have additional sections that set properties unique to those tracks. You'll learn about these additional sections in the chapters that deal explicitly with those tracks. For now, you'll explore the General section.

## Setting general track properties

The Track tab's General section serves two valuable functions: it lets you name the track, and it lets you determine whether it will be enabled in the final movie.

When you're new to LiveStage, you might forget to name your tracks, and that's fine. When your projects involve only a couple of tracks and samples, it's easy to remember what's what. As your projects grow, however, naming your tracks becomes an important tool for project navigation, as unique names make your tracks easily recognizable in the Track list. As you delve deeper into LiveStage, you will also use the track's name to target it through QScript. For more on using QScript to target tracks, see Chapter 4, "The Script Editor."

### To name a track:

1. In the Track Properties window, select the Track tab.

2. Type a new name in the Name text box (**Figure 3.2**).

   The default name is replaced by the new name you've entered. In the Track list, the track's header updates to reflect the change (**Figure 3.3**).

**Figure 3.2** Naming tracks lets you identify them efficiently as you work on your project.

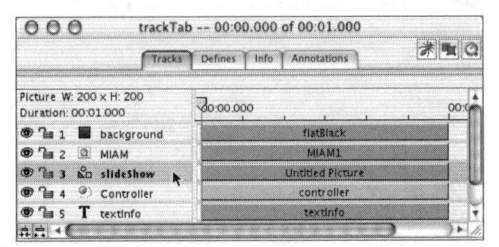

**Figure 3.3** The name you give your track appears in its header in the Track list.

# Setting Track Properties

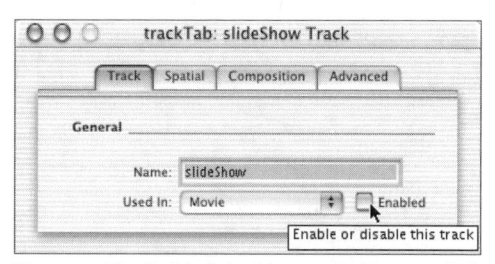

**Figure 3.4** The Enabled checkbox works like an on/off switch for your track. When you disable a track, it remains part of your movie, but won't be visible until it is enabled again.

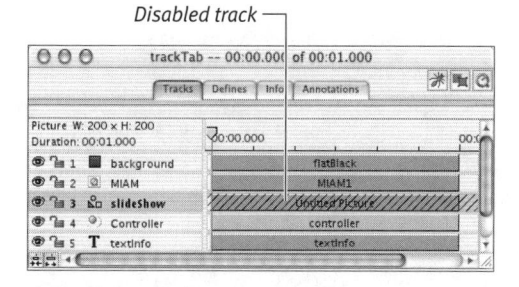

**Figure 3.5** Disabled tracks are grayed out in the Timeline.

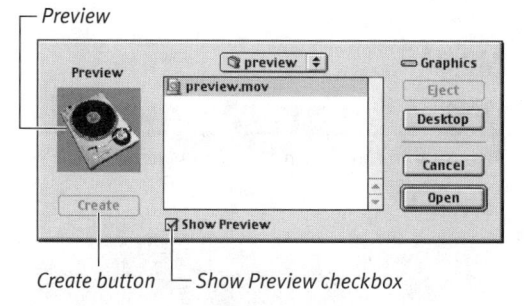

**Figure 3.6** An Open dialog showing a movie preview. For the preview to be displayed, you must check the Show Preview checkbox. If the preview is still not visible, click the Create button at the bottom of the Preview section.

The Enabled checkbox acts like an on/off switch, allowing you to hide tracks and prevent them from appearing while your movie plays. A common trick is to turn off a track by disabling it and then use QScript to turn it back on at run time. You can use QScript to turn a sound track on and off, for example, creating background music for your movie. (To learn more about turning tracks on and off with QScript, see Chapter 4, "The Script Editor.") Although disabled tracks are invisible during playback, they're still in the movie's file, taking up valuable space. If you don't plan to use QScript to turn the track back on at run time, don't just disable it—delete it!

### To enable or disable a track:

1. In the Track Properties window, select the Track tab.

2. Check or uncheck the Enabled checkbox (**Figure 3.4**).

   If you disable a track, its samples appear grayed out in the Timeline (**Figure 3.5**). Though the track remains part of your movie, it will not be displayed when the movie plays.

## Creating posters and previews

If you've ever searched for one particular file in the morass of movies on your hard disk, you'll appreciate previews. A *preview* is an image or short movie that plays in the Open dialog of QuickTime-compatible applications (**Figure 3.6**), helping you identify the file's content without opening it. You can create previews for sound, picture, Flash, video, and VR tracks.

*continues on next page*

When a user saves your movie as a favorite, QuickTime Player displays a poster image of the movie in its Favorites tab (**Figure 3.7**). If you do not create a poster image for your movie, QuickTime generally uses the first frame as the poster frame. Only tracks with visual content can be used as poster images.

### To create a preview and/or poster:

1. In the Track Properties window, select the Track tab.

2. From the Used In pop-up menu, choose a preview or poster type (**Figure 3.8**). Choices include:

   **Movie.** The track is only used in the movie, not as a preview or a poster. This option is the default setting.

   **Preview.** The track is used only as a preview. It will *not* be visible in the final movie.

   **Poster.** The track is used only as a poster. It will *not* be visible in the final movie.

   **Movie and Poster.** The track is used as a poster image and is also visible in the final movie.

   **Movie and Preview.** The track is used as a preview and is also visible in the final movie.

   **Poster and Preview.** The track is used as both a preview and a poster image. It will *not* be visible in the final movie.

   **All.** The track is used as a poster, as a preview, and also in the movie.

### ✔ Tips

- LiveStage creates previews that run about 3 seconds. If you're on a Macintosh, you can make a longer preview by using the preview AppleScript, which you access from the AppleScript menu (**Figure 3.9**).

- Try making a preview from a panoramic VR track. The preview retains its VR functionality.

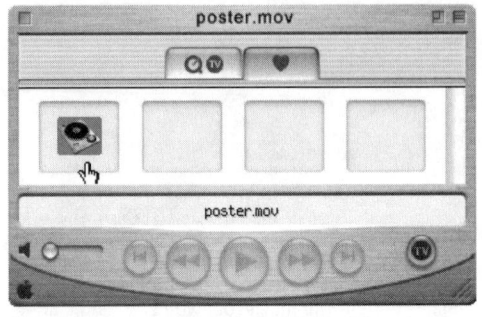

**Figure 3.7** A poster image in QuickTime Player's Favorites tab.

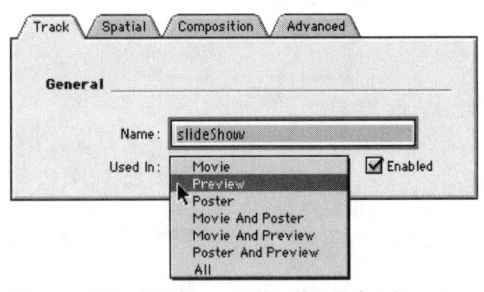

**Figure 3.8** The Used In pop-up menu makes it easy to create a poster or preview from any visual or audio track.

*AppleScript menu icon*

**Figure 3.9** The Macintosh AppleScript menu.

Setting Track Properties

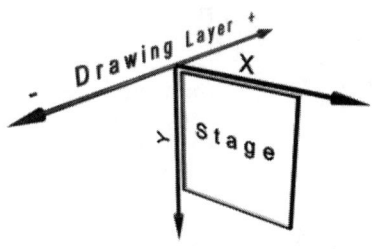

**Figure 3.10** Though the stage may appear to be two-dimensional on your screen, it actually functions in three dimensions, using the track's drawing layer as a pseudo Z axis.

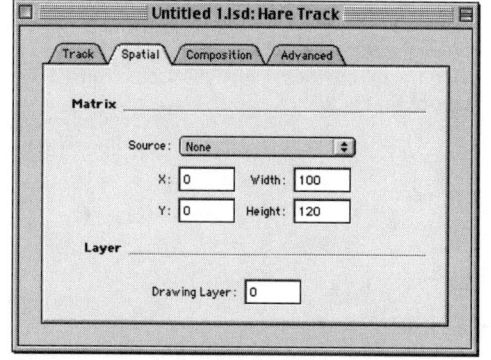

**Figure 3.11** The Spatial tab contains a Matrix editor, which you use to set a track's width, height, and X,Y coordinates, rather than opening the stage.

**Figure 3.12** When you adjust a track's dimensions in the Track Properties window, its size on the stage changes.

## About the Spatial Tab

As in the real world, LiveStage projects exist in three dimensions. The Spatial tab lets you place tracks anywhere in this three-dimensional space. Using this tab, you can move tracks to the left and to the right, as well as up and down. You can also place them behind or in front of other tracks. Picture your project's work space as a graph with an X, a Y, and a Z axis. The top-left corner of each track represents its (X, Y) value, and its Z value is defined by its drawing layer (**Figure 3.10**). Drawing layers are discussed later in this chapter. First, however, take a moment to look at the Matrix editor.

## Using the Matrix editor

The Matrix editor, which mirrors the settings in the Coordinate and Dimension text boxes of the Stage window, allows you to set a track's size and position without having to open the stage.

You'll find this feature handy when you're working with visual tracks. LiveStage creates each new visual track at a default size of 200 pixels by 200 pixels. If your media differs from that size, as it probably will, you'll need to adjust the track's dimensions to fit it.

### To set track dimensions:

1. In the Track Properties window, select the Spatial tab.

2. In the Matrix editor section of the tab, enter new width and/or height values (in pixels) in the appropriate text boxes (**Figure 3.11**).

   The track reduces or expands to the new dimensions (**Figure 3.12**).

# Chapter 3

## To set track coordinates:

1. In the Track Properties window, select the Spatial tab.

2. In the Matrix editor, enter new X and/or Y values in the appropriate text boxes (**Figure 3.13**).

   The track jumps to its new position on the stage (**Figure 3.14**).

### ✔ Tips

- Using QScript to change the X,Y coordinates of a track can yield interesting results when your movie is played in QuickTime Player. Wire a track with QScript to move beyond the stage at run time, for example, and QuickTime Player's display area expands to encompass the track's new position, making the movie appear to grow.

- The Matrix editor also contains a Source pop-up menu from which you can choose a tween or modifier track as an animation source. To learn more about tween and modifier tracks, see Chapter 11, "Animations and Manipulations."

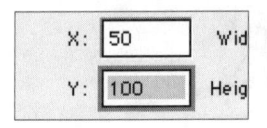

**Figure 3.13** The Matrix editor's X and Y text boxes specify the coordinates of your track's top-left corner on the stage.

**Figure 3.14** When you adjust a track's coordinates in the Track Properties window, its position on the stage changes.

---

### Track Registration Points

The top-left corner of each track is its *registration point*. QuickTime Player uses this registration point to position the track properly in your movie. This point cannot be moved relative to the track itself. Thus, when you set a track's X,Y coordinate, you are actually setting its registration point.

Setting Track Properties

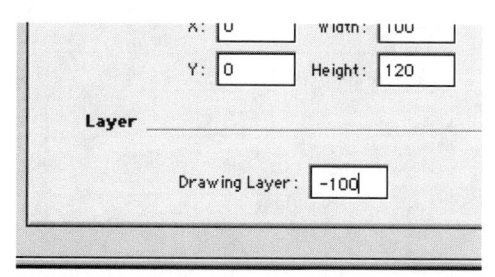

**Figure 3.15** The Layer editor sits at the bottom of the Spatial tab and is used to move a track above or below other tracks in your project. Negative drawing layer values cause a track to appear "on top" of tracks with higher drawing layer values.

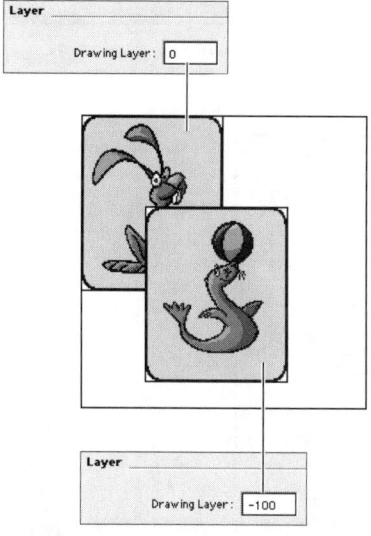

**Figure 3.16** The Rabbit picture track has a drawing layer set to the default value of 0. The Seal track has a drawing layer set to −100, and consequently appears in front of the Rabbit track on the stage.

## Understanding drawing layers

In Chapter 1, you saw how a track's position in the Track list defines its place in the project's stacking order. Tracks lower in the list appear above tracks that are higher in the list. Similarly, you can use drawing layers to place one track above another.

Drawing layers work a bit differently than you might expect. Tracks with lower drawing layer values are placed in front of tracks with higher drawing layer values, and negative values are accepted. A track with a layer value of −100, for example, is placed on top of a track with a layer value of 100. As LiveStage lets you select any drawing layer between −32,768 and 32,768, you will never run out of layers for your tracks.

### To change a drawing-layer value:

1. In the Track Properties window, select the Spatial tab.

2. In the Layer editor section of the tab, enter a new value in the Drawing Layer text box (**Figure 3.15**).

   If you enter a positive value, the track is moved behind any track with a lower drawing-layer value. If you enter a negative value, the track is moved in front of any track with a higher value (**Figure 3.16**).

### ✔ Tip

- A track's drawing layer value takes precedence over its position in the Track list. If Track A has a drawing layer set to −1, and Track B has a drawing layer set to 0, Track A will *always* be drawn in front of Track B, even if Track B is lower in the Track list.

ABOUT THE SPATIAL TAB

41

# About the Composition Tab

The Composition tab groups properties that define how a visual track interacts and blends with other visual tracks in your movie (**Figure 3.17**). Using this tab, you can combine (composite) visual media to create fantastic effects that are often impossible in real life, such as Superman flying through the sky or astronauts roaming the surface of Mars.

Although you can use the Composition tab to color-correct or blend tracks artistically, the tab's most important feature is its capability to create transparent effects with graphics modes.

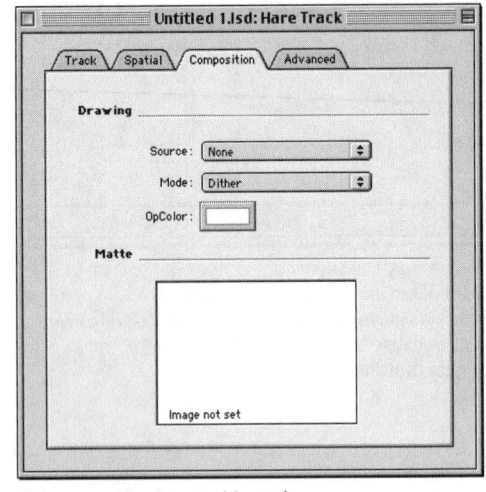

**Figure 3.17** The Composition tab.

## Using graphics modes

Graphics modes blend overlapping tracks by specifying how pixels from one track interact with pixels from underlying tracks. Although you can use graphics modes to create all sorts of special effects, you'll most often use them to create transparencies. (For a full description of the other graphics modes, see "Appendix 2: Graphics Mode Reference" in the LiveStage Professional manual.)

Graphics modes are *composited* (blended) by the user's computer while the movie plays. This situation allows you to create dynamic effects by setting tracks to blend on the fly. Imagine a Halloween display with ghosts flying across the screen. When you first bring the ghost image into LiveStage, you will not be able to see through it. A solid ghost is not very effective. But by applying a graphics mode, you can make that ghost semitransparent. As the ghost flies around the screen, the graphics mode continues to let the background image show through, achieving your haunting effect.

But be warned: unrestrained use of graphics modes can put a huge strain on slower computers, which will result in dropped frames and unsteady playback.

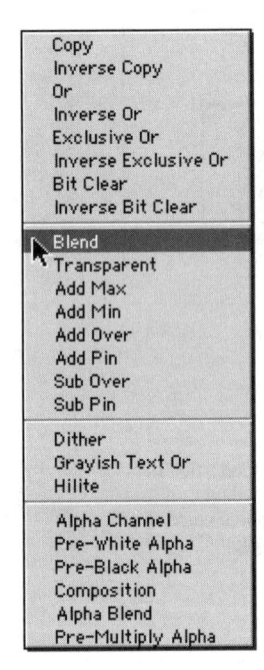

**Figure 3.18** The Mode pop-up menu lists QuickTime graphics modes.

Setting Track Properties

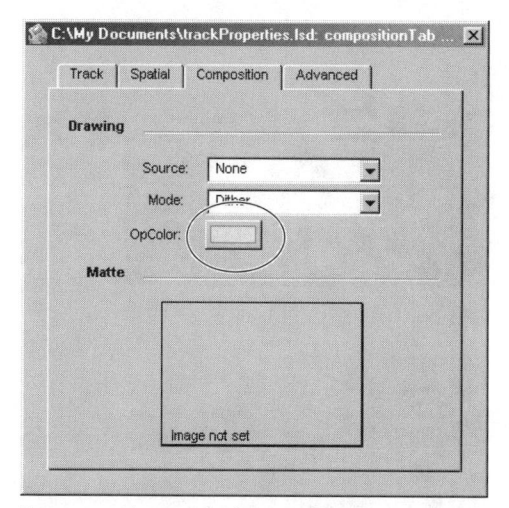

**Figure 3.19** The OpColor box specifies the control color to be used with your graphics mode.

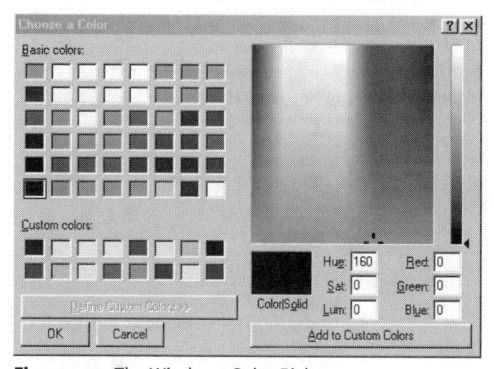

**Figure 3.20** The Windows Color Picker.

## To set a track's graphics mode:

1. In the Track Properties window, select the Composition tab.

2. From the Mode pop-up menu, choose a graphics mode (**Figure 3.18**).

   Some graphics modes, such as Transparent and Blend, work in conjunction with a control color, called the *OpColor*. The OpColor controls the amount and/or tint of pixel blending.

## To specify an OpColor:

1. In the Composition tab, click the OpColor box (**Figure 3.19**).
   The Color Picker opens.

2. Select a new control color (**Figure 3.20**).

3. Click OK.
   Depending on the mode you've chosen, you may have to run a preview movie to see the results of your choice, as not every graphics mode displays on the stage.

4. In the Project window, click the Run Wired Movie button.
   LiveStage compiles the movie, and the result of your OpColor selection is shown in the preview window.

### ✔ Tip

- If your selected graphics mode is not visible on the stage, make sure that Draw Full is selected in the View menu. If Draw Full is selected, but you still can't see the effects of the graphics mode, you will have to run a preview movie.

Chapter 3

## Using alpha channels

The best way to create transparent effects is to create your images in a graphics program such as Adobe Photoshop or After Effects. These programs let you create *alpha channels*, which act like mattes, allowing background tracks to show through the transparent areas of the tracks on top of them (**Figure 3.21**). When you bring the image into LiveStage, you can unlock the alpha channel with a graphics mode to make the masked areas transparent. In fact, if your media has an alpha channel, you *must* specify an appropriate graphics mode. Otherwise, LiveStage will render the alpha channel as white instead of transparent, and you will not be able to see through it to the visual tracks below.

**Figure 3.21** The top movie does not utilize the plane image's alpha channel, while the bottom movie does. As a result, in the top movie a white rectangle obstructs the view of the tracks below, while in the bottom movie you can see through the transparent areas of the plane image to the visual objects below.

### About Alpha Channels

Alpha channels let you create transparency for your visual tracks. To really understand how an alpha channel works, you need to know a bit about color channels in pixels.

When you create an image in a graphics program such as Adobe Photoshop, you start by specifying its dimensions. If you create an image that is 200 pixels by 200 pixels, you end up with a square made of 40,000 individual pixels. Furthermore, each of these pixels is assigned a distinct color. When you look at the completed image, you see an array of tiny, uniquely colored pixels that your eye blends into a coherent graphic.

Most images that you use in LiveStage are created with an RGB (red, green, blue) color model. In the RGB color model, each pixel's color is defined by the value of three color channels: red, green, and blue. Furthermore, each of these color channels is assigned a separate 8-bit value that determines how much of that color will be present in the pixel.

An alpha channel is a fourth 8-bit channel that defines how transparent each pixel will be. If you were to remove an alpha channel from the image, you would see something that looked like an 8-bit grayscale image. This grayscale image acts like a matte for the RGB image to which it is applied. Where the alpha channel is black, the image is transparent. Where the alpha channel is white, the image is opaque (you can't see through it). Where the alpha channel is gray, the image is translucent, and you can just see through it to the background.

## Setting Track Properties

### To use an alpha channel:

♦ In the Composition tab, open the Mode pop-up menu, and choose an alpha-channel type that matches the alpha channel in your medium (**Figure 3.22**).

The alpha channel will *not* be updated on the stage but will be rendered transparent in your final movie.

## Using Transparent mode

Transparent mode takes a color value that you assign and makes it invisible. If your visual medium is set against a solid-color background, you can use Transparent mode to drop out the background color. This trick is handy if you have a file (such as a Flash button) that does not have an alpha channel but needs a transparent background.

Flash creates vector files with sharp, clearly defined lines and large blocks of solid, uniform color. This is exactly what you need when working with Transparent mode. Files that mildly blur your image's colors (such as JPEGs) do not work well, as there are minute color differences in the background pixels. Even though these color differences are barely perceptible, your computer sees them clearly and will not make these pixels transparent. Consequently, Transparent mode is best suited for images with large blocks of uniform color, such as GIFs, PNGs, SWFs, and media compressed with the animation codec.

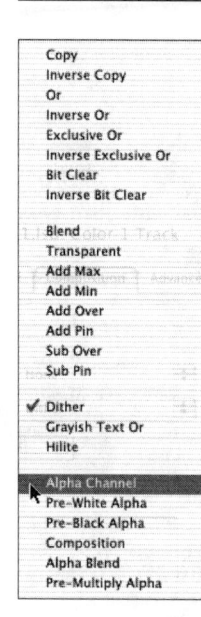

**Figure 3.22** The bottom of the Mode pop-up menu lists alpha channels supported by LiveStage.

Chapter 3

**To set a transparent color:**

1. In the Composition tab, choose Transparent from the Mode pop-up menu.

2. Click the OpColor box.
   The Color Picker opens.

3. Select a transparency color that matches the one you want to drop out of your image.

4. Click OK.
   The transparent color is applied to your source medium (**Figure 3.23**). The results of this action will not be visible on the stage. To test your transparent color, you must run a preview movie.

✔ **Tip**

- Macintosh users can use the eyedropper tool to sample any color on the screen, including the file's background color. To enable the eyedropper, open the Color Picker and hold down the Option key.

**Figure 3.23** Transparent mode has been used to drop out the solid color between the seal and the frame surrounding it.

Setting Track Properties

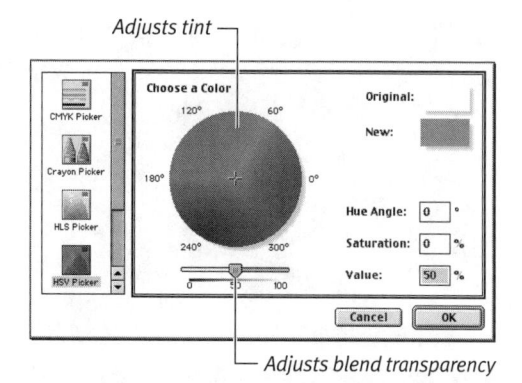

Adjusts tint

Adjusts blend transparency

**Figure 3.24** The Hue/Saturation/Value Color Picker. The value slider at the bottom of the picker controls the amount of blending; the crosshair in the circle above defines the track's tint color.

**Figure 3.25** The result of Blend mode with a value of 50. The seal is rendered 50 percent transparent.

## Using Blend mode

When you blend a track, you adjust the transparency setting of each of its pixels in a uniform way. If you give a track a blend value of 50 percent, for example, the track becomes 50 percent translucent, allowing you to see it and the tracks below it. You can use Blend mode to blend tracks or tint them by selecting an appropriate OpColor.

### To blend a track:

1. In the Composition tab, choose Blend from the Mode pop-up menu.

2. Click the OpColor box.
   The Color Picker opens.

3. Change the source track's transparency by moving the slider to adjust its grayscale value (**Figure 3.24**).

   A value of 0 (black) makes your source track completely transparent. A value of 100 (white) makes your source track completely opaque. Values between 0 and 100 create varying degrees of transparency (**Figure 3.25**).
   
   or
   
   Change the track's tint by adjusting the hue and saturation values.

4. Click OK.
   The blend is applied to your track, and the Stage window updates to show this change.

### ✔ Tip

- If you need to blend a file with an alpha channel, use Alpha Blend mode. This mode is a combination of the Alpha Channel and Blend modes. Use the OpColor box to change image opacity and/or tint.

Chapter 3

## Using Dither mode

Dither mode is one of the few graphics modes that affects only one layer. When you dither an image, each pixel is blended with the pixels surrounding it, resulting in smooth color transitions across the entire image. If you have a monitor set to a color depth of millions or even thousands of colors, you probably won't notice the difference. Users with monitors set to only 256 colors, however, will see a dramatic improvement in movie quality (**Figure 3.26**).

Dither is the default graphics mode and generally is the one you will use most often, as it provides the best display of the track's visual content across the widest range of monitors.

**Figure 3.26** The same image displayed with three different dither settings on a monitor with a color depth of 256 colors. The top image is not dithered. Note the extreme amount of banding that occurs. The middle image is rendered with Dither mode. The bottom image uses a combination of Dither mode and the High Quality Playback option, selected in the Advanced tab of the Track Properties window.

# Setting Track Properties

## To dither a visual track:

◆ In the Composition tab, choose Dither from the Mode pop-up menu.

The track now dithers on monitors with a color resolution set lower than the track's resolution.

## ✔ Tip

■ High-quality error-diffusion dithering makes your tracks look even better than normal dithering on monitors with a lower bit depth than your visual tracks. To enable high-quality error-diffusion dithering, check the High Quality Playback checkbox in the Track Properties window's Advanced tab. But be warned: High Quality Playback is best used only on still images, as it takes a lot of processor power and will result in dropped frames.

## Using track mattes

Although it's easier to create transparencies by using graphics modes, you can also make tracks transparent by using track mattes if your media does not have an alpha channel. A *matte* is a grayscale image that acts like a stamp. Just as a stamp places a black ink pattern on white paper, a matte uses a black pattern to create a patch of visibility for your track (**Figure 3.27**). All other parts of the track are made transparent.

*continues on next page*

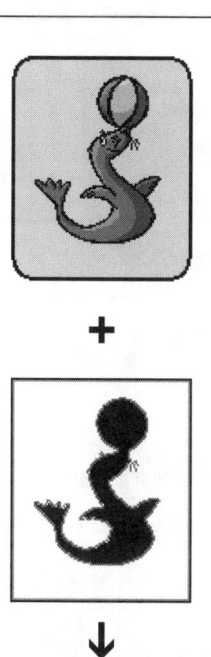

**Figure 3.27** Track mattes use a grayscale image to create transparency over an entire track. The black part of the matte stamps a visible pattern on the track it is attached to, and the white part becomes transparent.

---

### About Matte Images

Alpha channels are like 8-bit grayscale images that create transparency in a visual file. If you were to extract an alpha channel from an RGB image, you would have the inverse of a matte image. A *matte image* is just an alpha channel that you created on your own. After you've made a matte image, you can apply it to any visual track in your project.

# Chapter 3

To achieve varying degrees of transparency, use an 8-bit grayscale image as a matte. Although black pixels are fully opaque and white pixels are transparent, gray pixels result in varying degrees of translucence (**Figure 3.28**). A matte image can be used with several different tracks, allowing you to build layers of transparency in your movie.

### To create a track matte:

1. In the Track Properties window, select the Composition tab.

2. From the Library window, Finder (Mac), or desktop (Windows), drag a grayscale image into the Matte image box (**Figure 3.29**).

   The matte image's black areas will be visible in your movie, and the white areas will be transparent, letting visual tracks below shine through (refer to Figure 3.27).

### ✔ Tip

- After you've set a matte, you can see where the matte-image file is on your hard disk by resting your pointer on the matte image for a moment.

### To delete a track matte:

1. In the Track Properties window, select the Composition tab.

2. Select the matte image.

   A thin blue line surrounds the image box.

3. Press the Delete key.

   The image is deleted.

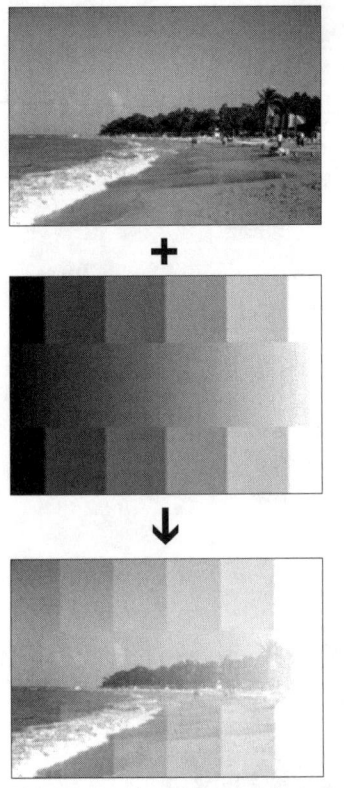

**Figure 3.28** Using 8-bit grayscale matte images creates varying degrees of transparency. In this example, the matte image is fully black on the left side. Consequently, the left side of the beach graphic is completely opaque. The right side of the matte image is fully white. As a result, you cannot see this side of the beach image, because it is fully transparent. The gray parts in between vary in transparency, depending on the darkness of the matte image.

**Figure 3.29** To set a matte image, drag an 8-bit grayscale image into the Matte section of the Composition tab.

# Setting Track Properties

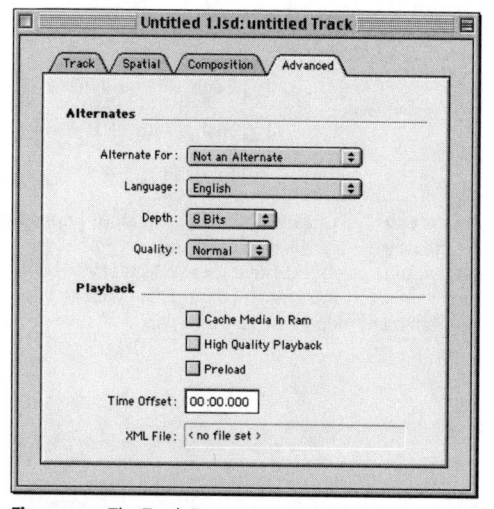

**Figure 3.30** The Track Properties window's Advanced tab.

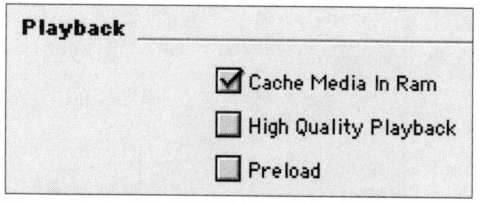

**Figure 3.31** Caching a track's media in the host computer's RAM makes that track available for playback instantly and can improve your movie's performance.

## About the Advanced Tab

The Advanced tab is divided into two sections: Alternates and Playback. The Alternates section works in conjunction with the Project window's Info tab, and as a result, I'll discuss this section in Chapter 5, "Setting Movie Properties." For now, I'll concentrate on the Playback section.

The Playback section groups track properties that QuickTime uses to optimize movie playback for the viewer's computer. If you check the Cache Media in Ram checkbox, while QuickTime plays the movie, it will store the track's media content in the displaying computer's RAM. If the user needs to recall the track later, his or her computer can access it from RAM, which speeds movie playback.

### To cache a track in RAM:

1. In the Track Properties window, select the Advanced tab (**Figure 3.30**).

2. Check the Cache Media in Ram checkbox (**Figure 3.31**).

   The track is stored in the RAM of the viewer's computer. If your movie needs to recall that track later, the track will be played from RAM.

Preloading a track works similarly to caching a track in RAM, with one important difference. When you select the Preload option, rather than interleaving the track with all the others in the project, LiveStage stores that track at the beginning of the movie, so it is among the first of the tracks to be downloaded and stored in RAM. Although doing so is not necessary, you can improve your movie's performance by preloading any tracks you want to appear first in your movie, such as background images, sound tracks, or any tracks that contain important scripting.

*continues on next page*

### To preload a track:

1. In the Track Properties window, select the Advanced tab.
2. Check the Preload checkbox.

   This track is moved to the front of the QuickTime file, and its media will download before the media from other tracks.

   When you check the High Quality Playback checkbox, you're telling QuickTime to display the track at the highest possible quality allowed by the viewer's system. This option is particularly effective when used in conjunction with Dither mode. Unfortunately, choosing this option may slow your movie, as QuickTime assigns more resources to the display than to your movie's playback performance.

   Because this option can place a strain on the viewer's system, use it only when necessary. If you're using QuickTime to display a family portrait on your grandma's old 256-color monitor, for example, you might want to use High Quality Playback to make sure that she can see her grandchild's smile in the best possible detail. But, because of the consequences it can have on movie playback, you usually will want to keep High Quality Playback turned off.

### To display a track at the highest possible quality:

1. In the Track Properties window, select the Advanced tab.
2. Check the High Quality Playback checkbox (**Figure 3.32**).

   The movie now places more emphasis on the display of your track and less on its real-time playback performance.

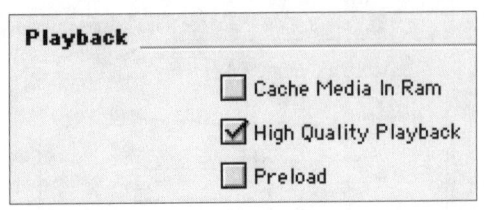

**Figure 3.32** High Quality Playback places more emphasis on the way the track is displayed and less emphasis on real-time playback. The track looks great even on monitors set to 256-color bit depths, but your movie may lurch and skip frames as it plays.

# The Script Editor

By definition, LiveStage is a QuickTime authoring environment for the creation of *wired,* or scripted, interactive movies. You can create interesting projects without ever getting into QScript, but to do so would be to harness only a fraction of LiveStage's power. Fortunately, QScript is a simple and functional scripting language that anyone can learn with ease.

Only four types of tracks in LiveStage are scriptable: sprite, text, Flash, and VR. Scriptable tracks can be programmed to monitor events in your movie, such as a mouse click, the press of a key, the loading of a scripted sample, or even the passing of time. When an event occurs, a scriptable track responds to that event by executing a handler, or *QScript*, that tells your movie to do something.

Of course, before a scriptable track can respond to an event, you, as the programmer, must tell the track what event to look for and what action to take when the event occurs. To do this, you use the track's script editor.

This chapter shows you how to use the script editor to create your very own wired actions. Along the way you'll learn the basics of QScript syntax, including how to properly construct action statements that tell your movie what to do. You'll finish the chapter by learning about QScript properties, which harvest information about your movie's sprites, tracks, and other objects.

# About the Script Editor

The script editor is divided vertically into two parts (**Figure 4.1**). The section on the left is the Event Handler list, and the section on the right is the script edit field. These two sections work in tandem. To write a QScript, you first select an event in the Event Handler list. Your movie will watch for that event and, when the event occurs, will execute the QScript that you write in the script edit field. Along the top of the script edit field are three buttons, which you use to save, load, and check QScript syntax.

Each of the four scriptable tracks has uniquely tailored script editors that look different but work exactly the same way. The remainder of this chapter covers the script editor in detail. Before you learn to use the script editor, however, take a moment to open one and familiarize yourself with its parts.

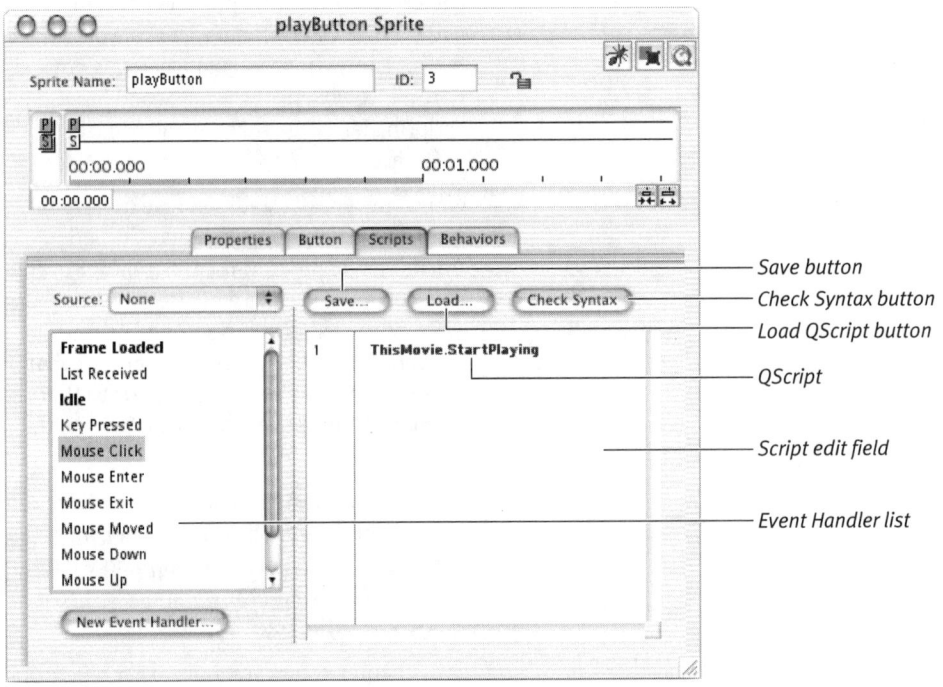

**Figure 4.1** The script editor is where you enter, arrange, and manage QScripts, which add interactivity to your movies.

# The Script Editor

**Flash script editor**

*Event Handler list* — *Script edit field*

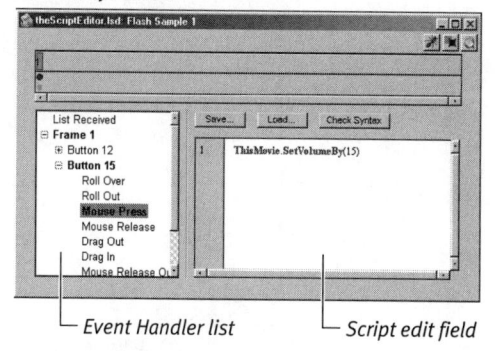

**Text script editor**

*Event Handler list* — *Script edit field*

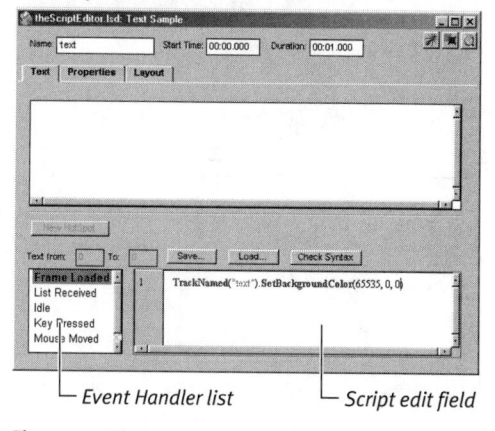

**Figure 4.2** When you open a Flash or text sample, the script editor is the first thing you see.

## To open a script editor:

**1.** In the Timeline or on the stage, double-click a scriptable track sample.

If you've opened a text, Flash, or VR sample, the script editor is the first thing you see (**Figure 4.2**). If you've opened a sprite sample, you must take a few more steps to open the script editor. (To learn more about sprites, see the sidebar "What Are Sprites?" below.)

*continues on next page*

---

## What Are Sprites?

As anyone who has ever studied Shakespeare knows, a *sprite* is a small or elusive supernatural being. In many ways, the sprites in LiveStage live up to this reputation, as they are very complex and can be tough to understand at the start.

When you create a sprite track in LiveStage, you are actually creating a container that holds sprites. You can think of sprites as being actors on the stage provided by the footprint of the sprite track. Like any stage, the sprite track has *wings* where the actors (sprites) can sit offstage, unnoticed by the audience (the viewer), waiting for their chance to run out and interact with other characters on the stage. Each sprite is made up of an image, and like any actor, it has lines to speak in your movie. Of course, sprites don't speak English. Instead, their lines consist of the QScripts you write for their event handlers. To learn more about sprite tracks, see Chapter 10, "Sprite Tracks."

ABOUT THE SCRIPT EDITOR

55

## Chapter 4

2. In the Sprite list on the left side of the sprite sample editor, select the sprite that you want to edit (**Figure 4.3**).

3. If the Scripts tab is not already open, select it in the group of tabs in the middle of the sprite sample editor.

   The sprite's script editor is revealed (refer to Figure 4.3).

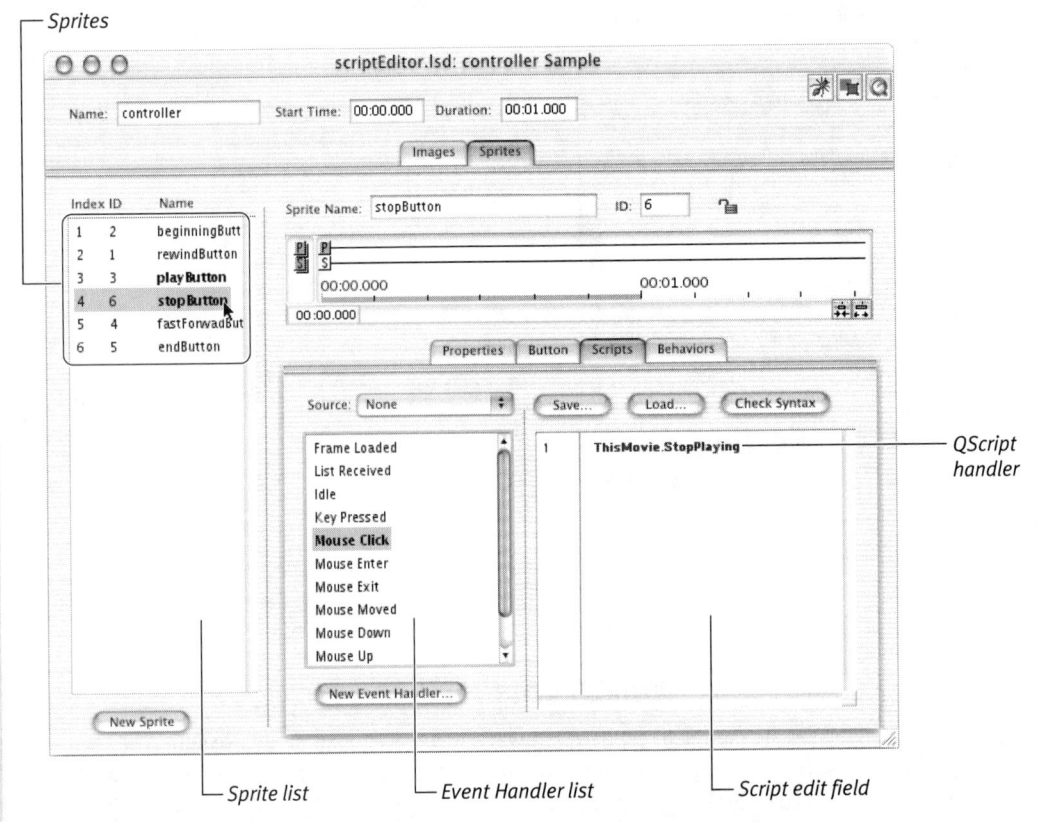

**Figure 4.3** Sprite samples are by far the most complex samples used in LiveStage. A sprite sample can contain many sprites, which are listed in the Sprite list on the left side of the sample editor. Additionally, each sprite has its own script editor, which you open by clicking the Scripts tab. This hierarchy is daunting initially, but as you become more adept at scripting with LiveStage, you will appreciate the flexibility it offers.

# The Script Editor

*Events that can trigger a QScript*

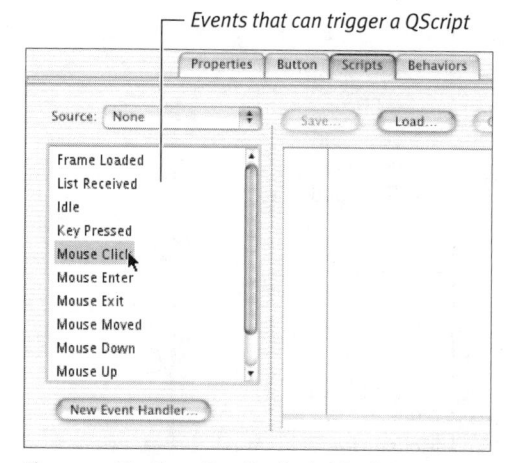

**Figure 4.4** The Event Handler list holds all the events that you can use to trigger a QScript.

## About Events

LiveStage is event-driven, meaning that something must happen to trigger a QScript. As the movie's author, you decide which event triggers an action by choosing, or specifying, an event in the Event Handler list.

The Event Handler list occupies the left side of a script editor and comes stocked with two types of common events: object events and track events. These predefined events make it easy for you to decide what should trigger an action, as all you have to do is look down the list and pick one. Possible events include `Mouse Enter`, `Mouse Exit`, `Mouse Click`, `Frame Loaded`, and `Idle`.

### To specify an event:

◆ With the script editor open, select an event handler in the Event Handler list (**Figure 4.4**).

The event handler is highlighted, and you can enter a QScript in the script edit field on the right side of the script editor.

### What's an Event Handler?

An event handler is a two-headed beast. When you make a selection in the Event Handler list, you are specifying the event that will trigger the handler, or QScript, that appears in the script edit field on the right side of the script editor. Together, the trigger event and the QScript handler make up an event handler.

57

# Chapter 4

## Understanding object events

*Object events* are triggered by direct interaction between the viewer and an object in a scriptable track, such as a sprite, a Flash button, a QTVR hotspot, or a text hotspot. If you've written a `Mouse Enter` event handler for a sprite, for example, the handler will execute when the user's pointer passes over the sprite. The sprite is the object, and the pointer passing over it triggers the object event (**Figure 4.5**).

Object events include:

**Mouse Click.** Event is triggered when the viewer clicks and releases the pointer button while the pointer is directly over an object in a scriptable track.

**Mouse Enter.** Event is triggered when the user's pointer moves over an object in a scriptable track.

**Mouse Exit.** Event is triggered when the user's pointer leaves the area occupied by an object in a scriptable track.

**Mouse Down.** Event is triggered when the user clicks and holds the pointer button over an object in a scriptable track.

**Mouse Up.** Event is triggered when the user releases the pointer button after clicking on an object in a scriptable track.

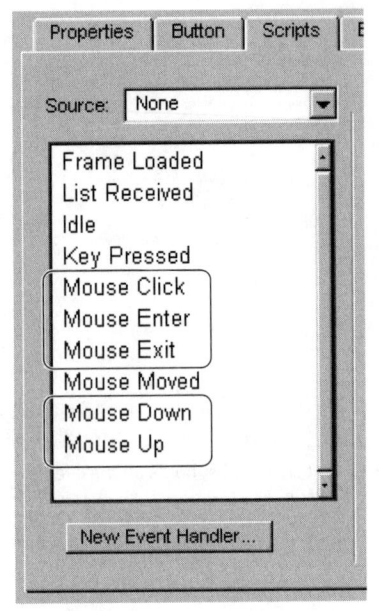

**Figure 4.5** LiveStage Object events.

## The Script Editor

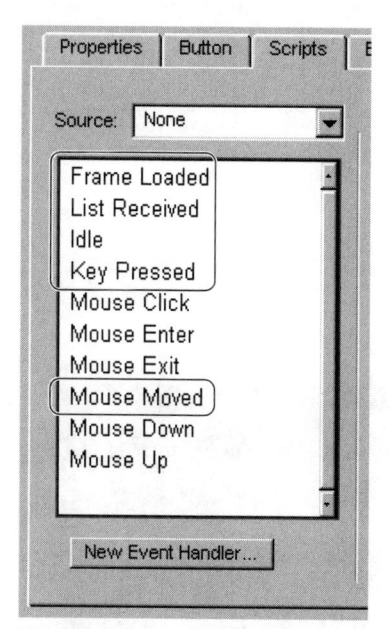

**Figure 4.6** LiveStage Track events.

## Understanding track events

*Track events* work on a larger level than object events, responding to actions that affect the entire track rather than individual objects within the track. In fact, for track events, the track itself is the object of the event.

Track events often do not need any user interaction to trigger them. A Frame Loaded event, for example, will fire automatically as soon as the sample containing it is loaded (**Figure 4.6**). Other track events, such as Mouse Moved, monitor user interaction with the track.

Track events include:

Frame Loaded. Event is triggered when a sample containing an event handler is loaded.

Idle. Event is triggered by the scriptable track's idle frequency, which acts like an internal clock for text, sprite, and VR tracks.

Key Pressed. Event is triggered when the user presses a key.

Mouse Moved. Event is triggered when the user moves the pointer while it is inside the boundary of a sprite or text track.

# Chapter 4

## Using the Idle event

Of all the predefined events that you can use to trigger a QScript, the `Idle` event is the most complex. This event executes as time passes in the movie, whether or not the movie is playing, and is independent of user interaction. Because the `Idle` event executes continuously, you can use it to create a sprite animation by sequencing through a series of sprite images, or you can use it to rotate a VR panorama continuously (**Figure 4.7**).

The `Idle` event's timing is controlled by its idle frequency. Simply put, *idle frequency* is the clock that tells the `Idle` event when to fire. This frequency is measured in ticks per second; 1 tick is equal to 1/60 second.

Each tick of the idle-frequency clock causes one `Idle` event to execute. To specify how many times per second your `Idle` event executes, you need to adjust its track's idle frequency.

Only three of the scriptable tracks (sprite, text, and VR tracks) contain `Idle` events. If you have more than one of these tracks in your project, you can set an individual idle frequency for each track. You could set a sprite track to rotate through a series of 12 sprite images once every second (one image every 1/12 second), for example, and set a VR track in the same project to rotate 5 degrees every 1/4 second.

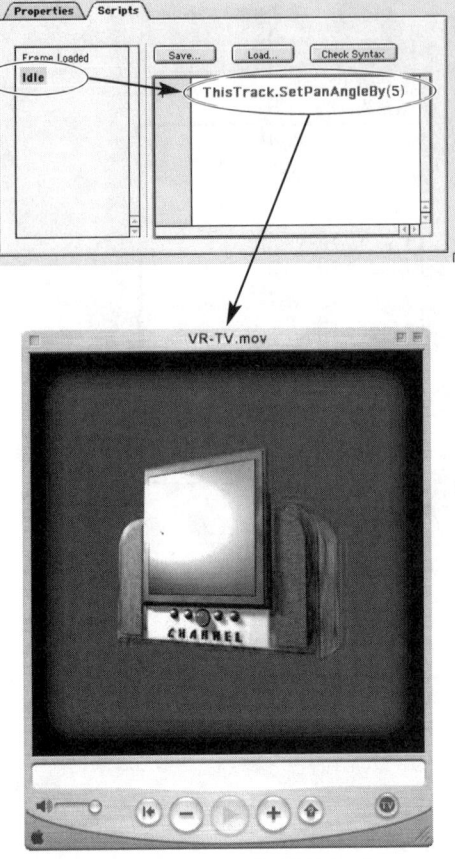

**Figure 4.7** `Idle` events are perfect for simple animations, such as this VR animation. When placed in the VR sample's `Idle` event, this QScript action spins the VR five degrees each time the VR track's idle frequency ticks.

## The Script Editor

*Sprite track properties section*
*Idle Frequency text box*

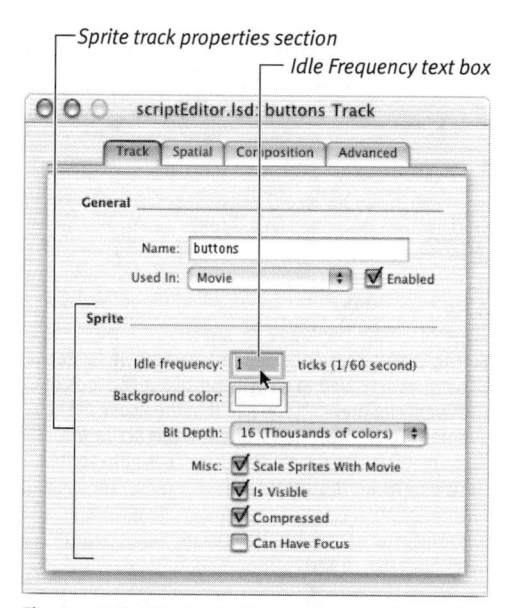

**Figure 4.8** The Track tab of the sprite Track Properties window includes a Sprite section, which holds properties unique to sprite tracks. One of these properties is the sprite track's idle frequency.

### To set idle frequency:

1. In the Tracks tab of the Project window, double-click the track header of a sprite, text, or VR track.

   The Track Properties window opens, displaying the Track tab (**Figure 4.8**).

2. Enter a new value in the Idle Frequency text box.

   The `Idle` event executes at the rate you've specified.

---

### The Idle Frequency Time Scale

Idle frequency is measured in ticks per second, with 1 second being equal to 60 ticks. (Do not confuse this system with the movie time scale, in which 1 second is equal to 600 time units.)

By default, sprite tracks have an idle frequency of 1, whereas text and VR tracks have an idle frequency of −1. At an idle frequency of 1, the `Idle` event handler executes 60 times per second. At −1 (or any other negative value), the idle frequency is turned off, and the `Idle` event handler is not executed.

Every time an `Idle` event occurs, the host computer has to dedicate some of its resources to executing the handler. If you have several `Idle` event handlers in your movie, and each one is set to a frequency of 1, each `Idle` event handler competes for computer resources every 1/60 second. This situation forces the computer to think very hard, which can slow movie playback.

As a result, you should use an idle frequency that's just fast enough to allow the smooth execution of scripts attached to the `Idle` event. For most practical purposes, you can get away with setting your idle frequency to 5 or higher, meaning that the `Idle` event handler executes 12 or fewer times per second.

**ABOUT EVENTS**

# About the Script Edit Field

After you've decided what type of event should trigger your QScript, the next step is writing the script. You do all your QScript composing in the script edit field, which functions in many ways like a full-featured text editor. You can type your QScript in this field, or you can cut, copy, and paste it a line at a time. You can even save QScripts and reload them later, much the same way that you might save or open a text file in a text editor.

Before you get into writing QScripts, however, you should familiarize yourself with the basics of using the script edit field.

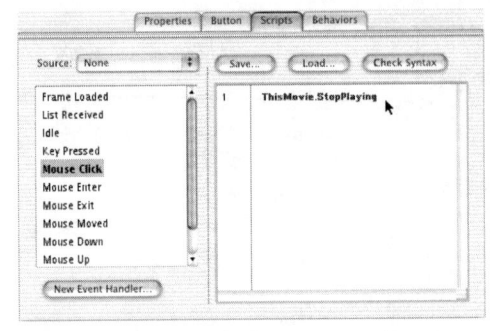

**Figure 4.9** This script, which causes a movie to stop playing, is attached to a sprite button. If you look at the Event Handler list, you see that the Mouse Click event is highlighted. Consequently, this script will stop the movie as soon as the user clicks the sprite button to which it is attached.

### To enter a QScript:

1. Select an event from the Event Handler list. The event is highlighted.

2. Type a QScript in the script edit field (**Figure 4.9**).

### ✔ Tip

- In the script edit field, some words vary in size and color. LiveStage color-codes QScript language elements, which makes them easier to read. If you would prefer something other than the default colors, you can change them; choose Edit > Preferences, and click the Editor tab of the Preferences dialog. (If you're using Mac OS X, choose LiveStage Pro > Preferences > Editor Tab.)

# The Script Editor

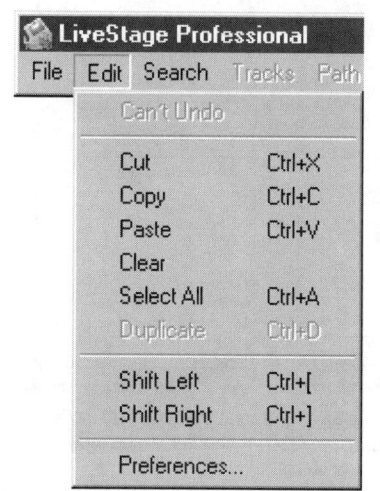

**Figure 4.10** While you're working in the script edit field, you can choose commands from the Edit menu to copy, paste, and select QScripts.

## To delete a QScript:

◆ Select the QScript text that you want to delete and then choose Edit > Clear (**Figure 4.10**).

## To copy a QScript:

◆ Select the QScript text that you want to copy and then choose Edit > Copy (Command/Ctrl-C).

The highlighted QScript is copied to your computer's Clipboard. You can paste this QScript into any script editor or text application.

## To paste a QScript:

◆ Click the script edit field to place the insertion point where you want to paste the script, and then choose Edit > Paste (Command/Ctrl-V).

The contents of your computer's Clipboard are pasted into the script edit field.

## ✔ Tip

■ So many keyboard shortcuts are available that it would be impractical to list them all here. For a full list, see Appendix A, "Keyboard Shortcuts."

# Managing scripts

If you've written a script that you know will be useful at some point in the future, you can save the script and load it into a different project later.

There is no way to save just a small portion of a QScript, so when you save a QScript, you actually are saving an entire handler. You can recall that handler at any time by loading it into any event. Thus, a handler you've written for a Mouse Click event, once saved, can be loaded and attached to a Mouse Down event or even a Frame Loaded event.

### To save a QScript:

1. In the Event Handler list, select the event handler that you want to save.

    If the script edit field currently contains a QScript, the Save button at the top of the script editor becomes active. If no QScript appears in the script edit field, the Save button is unavailable.

2. Click the Save button (**Figure 4.11**).

    The Save dialog opens.

3. Navigate to the directory where you want to save the QScript, and type a file name.

4. Click the Save button.

    The QScript is saved in the directory you specified and is ready to be reloaded whenever you need it (**Figure 4.12**).

### ✔ Tip

- If you know that you will be using your saved QScript in a different project, save it in the library's Scripts folder. The script will be available in the Library window when you create or open a new project.

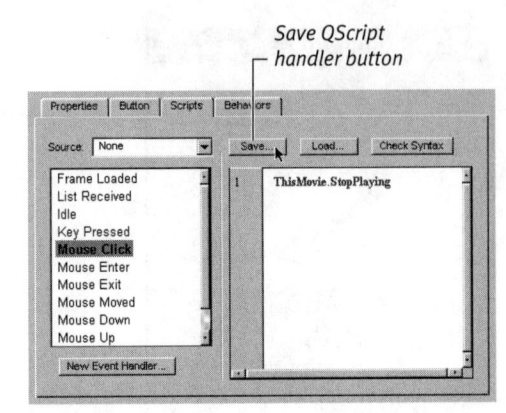

**Figure 4.11** The Save button at the top of the script editor lets you save QScript handlers to be recycled in other tracks or projects.

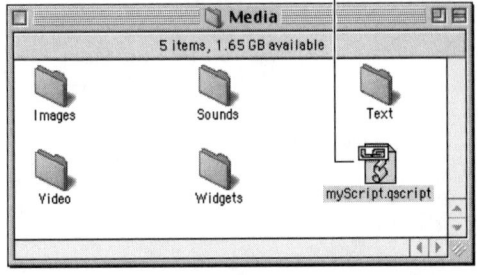

**Figure 4.12** A saved script looks like any other file on your computer. To edit the script from outside LiveStage, open the QScript in any text editor.

## The Script Editor

*Load QScript handler button*

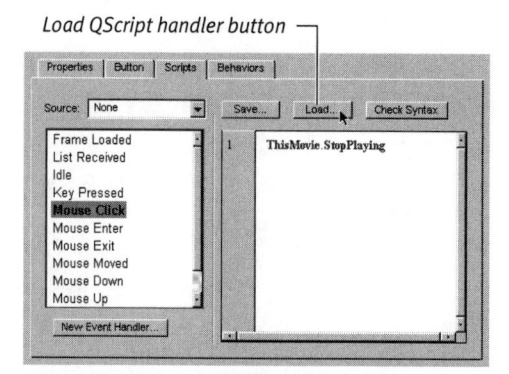

**Figure 4.13** The Load button at the top of the script editor lets you load QScript handlers that you've previously saved to your hard disk.

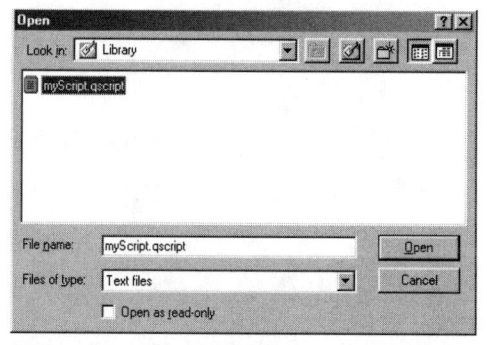

**Figure 4.14** Use the Open dialog to navigate to a QScript file saved on your hard disk.

### To load a QScript:

1. In the Event Handler list, select the event into which you want to load a QScript.

2. Click the Load button (**Figure 4.13**). The Open dialog appears.

3. Select the QScript file that you want to load, and click the Open button (**Figure 4.14**).

   The selected QScript file opens in the script edit field, replacing whatever was there previously.

### ✔ Tip

- If you've created a QScript in an outside text editor, save it as a plain-text file with the .txt extension. Then you can open this text file by clicking the Load button.

Chapter 4

## Checking QScript syntax

For a QScript to function properly, it must be written according to certain rules of syntax. If you follow the guidelines outlined in the "About QScript Syntax" section later in this chapter, you will have no problems making your QScripts syntactically valid. Still, mistakes happen. You can check the validity of your QScript by clicking the Check Syntax button.

### To check QScript syntax:

◆ In the script editor, write a QScript in the script edit field, and click the Check Syntax button (**Figure 4.15**).

If your QScript syntax is valid, LiveStage issues a three-toned, bell-like upward arpeggio indicating this fact. If the QScript is not valid, a groan sound plays, and the Errors window opens (**Figure 4.16**).

### ✔ Tip

■ In the Errors window, if you double-click an error, LiveStage automatically opens the appropriate script editor and, in most cases, also highlights the line of script that contains the error.

Check QScript syntax button

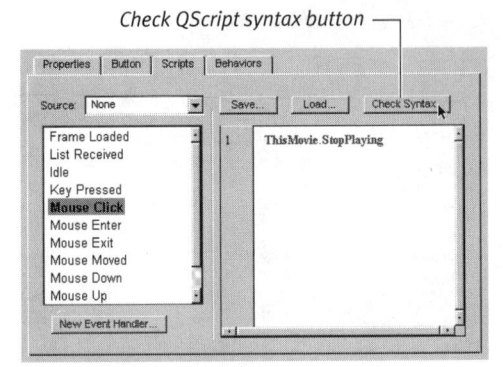

**Figure 4.15** The Check Syntax button validates any QScript displayed in the script edit field. Use this button to locate scripting errors quickly.

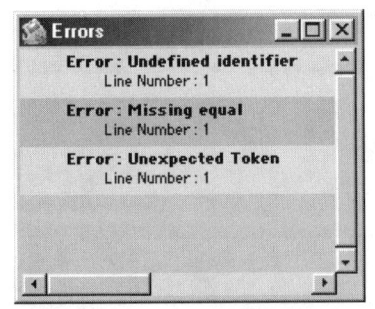

**Figure 4.16** If your QScript contains syntax errors, the error window alerts you to the type and location of the error.

ABOUT THE SCRIPT EDIT FIELD

66

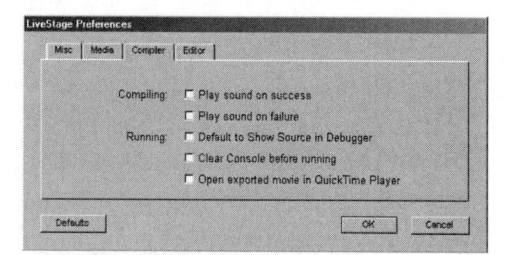

**Figure 4.17** The Compiler tab of the Preferences dialog lets you turn off compiler sounds, including the sounds that occur when you check QScript syntax.

## Disabling compile sounds

Compile sounds occur every time you check QScript syntax, run a wired movie, or export your movie to a finished QuickTime file. When you compile a movie, LiveStage assembles all the QScript you've written into a form that QuickTime understands. If some of your QScript is not correctly written, LiveStage is unable to compile the movie, and a groan-like alert sound occurs. Otherwise, you are greeted with a happy dinging, indicating that everything is fine. In some situations you will want to turn these compile sounds off.

### To turn off compile sounds:

1. Choose Edit > Preferences (in Mac OS X, choose LiveStage Pro > Preferences).

    The Preferences dialog opens.

2. Select the Compiler tab (**Figure 4.17**).

    The top of the Compiler tab holds two checkboxes: Play Sound on Success and Play Sound on Failure.

3. Deselect one or both of the checkboxes.

    No sound occurs when you check your scripts' syntax.

# About QScript Syntax

QScript is a simple object-oriented scripting language that is similar to other scripting languages, such as JavaScript, C++, and Lingo for Macromedia Director. If you have any experience with these scripting languages, you'll feel at home with QScript. If not, don't worry; QScript is easy to learn.

At its most basic level, a QScript is made of language elements, including keywords, that you snap together to make a sentence that LiveStage understands. Keywords are like real words in English. They even look like English, which makes them very easy to work with, especially for beginners.

A QScript sentence usually has two parts. The first part is the *target specifier*, which tells your QScript which movie object it will target (**Table 4.1**). The second part of the sentence is an action, which tells the object to do something, or a property, which harvests information about the target object. In either case, the target object indicated by the target specifier is the focus of the QScript statement.

> ### Omitting Target Specifiers
>
> Target specifiers that start with the word "this" can be omitted from your QScript actions. The following QScript actions do exactly the same thing:
>
> `ThisTrack.SetEnabled(False)`
>
> `SetEnabled(False)`
>
> Both action statements turn off the track to which they belong.

**Table 4.1**

### Common Target Specifier Keywords

| Target Specifiers | Description |
| --- | --- |
| ThisMovie | Specifies the current movie |
| ThisTrack | Specifies the current track |
| ThisSprite | Specifies the current sprite |
| MovieNamed("MovieName") | Specifies a movie by its tag name |
| MovieOfID(MovieID) | Specifies a movie by its tag ID number |
| TrackNamed("name") | Specifies a track by its name |
| TrackOfIndex(TrackIndex) | Specifies a track by its index number |
| SampleNamed("SampleName") | Specifies a sample by its name |
| SpriteNamed("SpriteName") | Specifies a sprite by its name |
| SpriteOfIndex(SpriteIndex) | Specifies a sprite by its index number |
| SpriteOfID(SpriteID) | Specifies a sprite by its ID number |
| ChildMovieNamed("ChildName") | Specifies a child movie by its name |
| ChildMovieOfID(ChildID) | Specifies a child movie by its ID number |

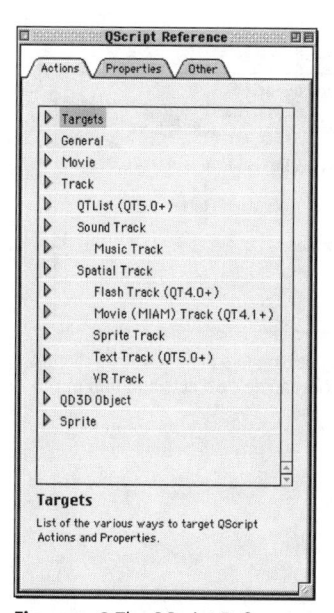

**Figure 4.18** The QScript Reference window holds every QScript keyword available to LiveStage.

# Using QScript language elements

Like any language, QScript is created from a combination of language elements that combine to form a statement. Each language element has a different purpose. Just as English sentences have nouns, verbs, and adjectives, QScript sentences have target specifiers, actions, and properties.

But that's just the tip of the iceberg. If you used only nouns, adjectives, and verbs to compose your English sentences, you would be able to communicate, but you would sound like a caveman. To wax eloquent, you need to understand the language's other elements. The same is true of QScript. As you delve deeper into scripting, you will use many of the following language elements:

**Keywords.** Predefined words that have special meaning in LiveStage (**Figure 4.18**).

**Data.** Information stored as constants and variables.

**Variables.** Objects that store information that can be set and altered as the movie runs. In the following examples, X and Y are variables. The information on the right side of the equal sign is the value (data) assigned to those variables.

```
X = 23
Y = ThisMovie.MaxLoadedTimeInMovie
```

**Constants.** Predefined data that cannot change as the movie runs. Examples:

```
1234
http://www.djinn.ca
```

**Boolean Constants.** Predefined constants that can be used in logical expressions or control statements. Examples:

```
True
False
```

*continues on next page*

Chapter 4

**Properties.** Data that returns values associated with attributes of LiveStage objects (**Figure 4.19**). Examples:

MovieVolume

TrackHeight

**Commands.** QScripts that tell your movie to do something, typically referred to as QScript actions. Examples:

ThisMovie.SetVolumeTo(200)

TrackNamed("MyTrack").MoveMatrixTo(50)

**Operators.** Sybols that work on numbers to compare, combine, or otherwise operate on data from your movie. Examples:

+ - < > * /

**Expressions.** Groups of numbers and operators that combine to generate values. Expressions often appear on the right side of an assignment statement. Examples:

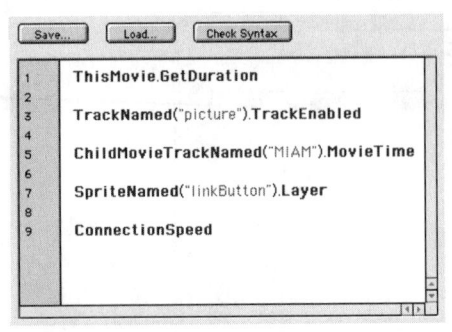

9 * 7

(4 + 8)/2

```
ThisMovie.GetDuration
TrackNamed("picture").TrackEnabled
ChildMovieTrackNamed("MIAM").MovieTime
SpriteNamed("linkButton").Layer
ConnectionSpeed
```

**Figure 4.19** Properties are like little windows that let you peek inside your movie's objects and find out information about them.

## About Object-Oriented Scripting Languages

The first thing you may wonder is, "What does object-oriented mean?" Although I could get very technical, the answer is really quite simple. Every script you write must be directed toward one particular object. In LiveStage, an object can be a sprite, a sample, a track, the movie itself, a child movie, or even a different movie open on the same Web page.

At the most basic level, you can work with an object in only two ways: instruct an object to do something or ask it to tell you something about itself. When you instruct an object to do something, you are telling it to perform an action, such as rotate or move to a different position. If you ask an object to tell you something about itself, you are requesting a property, such as its current position in the movie, its width, or its height.

In either case, the script you write is *oriented* toward an object, meaning that one object is the focus of that script.

ABOUT QSCRIPT SYNTAX

# The Script Editor

**Figure 4.20** Action statements tell your movie what to do.

## Understanding statements

*Statements* are instructions that tell your movie how to handle data elements. Think of statements as being bits of QScript that *do* something. Statements may contain keywords, operators, and expressions.

Statements fall into the following four categories:

**Assignment statements.** A combination of a variable and the data or properties it is assigned. Assignment statements always have three parts: the variable being assigned the value, an equal sign (=) that separates the halves of the statement, and an expression. To learn more about assignment statements, see Chapter 13, "Advanced QScript." Examples:

X = 5
Y = X
Count = Count + 1

**Control statements.** Statements that allow your QScripts to make logical decisions as your movie runs. To learn more about control statements, see Chapter 13, "Advanced QScript." Example:

```
IF (MaxLoadedTimeInMovie =600)
    ThisMovie.StartPlaying
ENDIF
```

**Action statements.** Statements used to issue commands that tell a movie object to do something, such as start playing or move to a different position (**Figure 4.20**).

**Comments.** Text that helps you document parts of your QScripts. LiveStage ignores comments. Examples:

```
// this is a comment
/*this is a
    multi-line comment
*/
```

# About Action Statements

An action statement generally has two parts. The first part is the *target*, or the object of the action. The second part is the *command*, or the part of the script that tells the target what to do. In other words, a target acts like a noun in a sentence, whereas a command takes on the role of the verb; it is the action that the object undertakes.

Think of an action statement as though it were plain English. "He moves," "she rotates," and "the boy named Xavier disappears" are all plain-English action statements. In each case, the object of the sentence does something. QScript works exactly the same way, but it uses target objects from your movie (**Figure 4.21**). The preceding sentences, when translated into QScript, would say, "This track moves," "That sprite rotates," and "The track named Xavier disappears."

A QScript statement, however, cannot have spaces between keywords. Instead, QScript links words with a *dot,* or a period. This syntax is called dot syntax, and it allows QScript to understand which keywords combine to make an action statement. In the following example, the action statement disables a text track as soon as it is loaded by the movie.

### To use an action statement:

1. In the Project window, select the Tracks tab.

2. Choose Tracks > Create > Text.

   A new text track is created, with the default dimensions of 200 square pixels, and an empty sample is placed in the Timeline.

3. Double-click the text track's header.
   The Track Properties window opens.

4. In the Name text box, change the text track's name to textTrack (**Figure 4.22**).

The boy named Xavier disappears

↓

The track named Xavier disappears

↓

TrackNamed("Xavier").SetEnabled(False)

**Figure 4.21** To write a QScript, you use syntax similar to everyday English. Just as *The boy named Xavier* is the target object of the first sentence, TrackNamed("Xavier") is the target object of the last sentence. Similarly, *disappears* is the equivalent of SetEnabled(False).

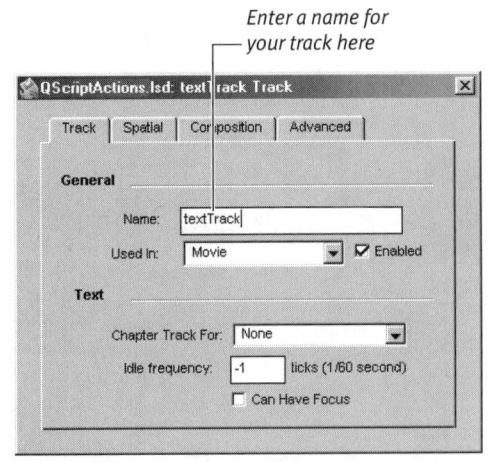

**Figure 4.22** In LiveStage, the most common way to target a track for use with QScripts is by name or index number. Index numbers change as you move tracks in the Track list, so it's better to target your tracks by name.

## The Script Editor

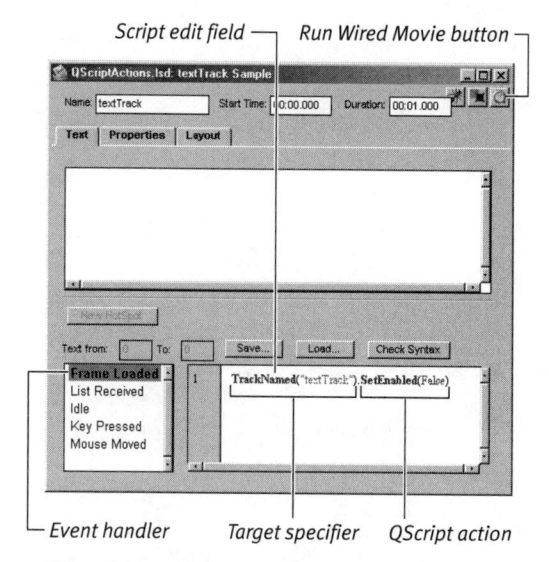

**Figure 4.23** A text sample's script editor appears automatically when you open the text sample. Make sure that you enter your QScripts in the script edit field and not the text box above it.

*(Labels on figure: Script edit field, Run Wired Movie button, Event handler, Target specifier, QScript action)*

**Figure 4.24** The text track in this movie was scripted to turn off upon loading, resulting in the empty preview window that you see here. Your movie is running, but there's nothing to see.

5. Click the close box at the top of the Track Properties window or press Command/Ctrl-W.

   The Track Properties window closes. In the Track list, the text track's header updates to reflect the name change.

6. Double-click the text sample.

   The sample's script editor opens.

7. In the script editor's Event Handler list, select the Frame Loaded event handler.

   If you want the text track to turn off as soon as the movie opens, you must use the Frame Loaded event to trigger the QScript handler.

8. In the script edit field, enter the following QScript (**Figure 4.23**):

   TrackNamed("textTrack").SetEnabled
   → (False)

9. Click the Run Wired Movie button at the top of the Project window.

   Even though the text track has a dimension of 200 square pixels, the preview window displays only a thin bar (**Figure 4.24**). Your action statement made the text track disappear when the movie launched.

**ABOUT ACTION STATEMENTS**

73

## Using data in action statements

Almost every action uses some form of data to tell it what to do. In the `SetEnabled(False)` action used in the preceding section, the word `False` is a form of data called a *Boolean constant*. Another common action is the sprite action, such as `MoveTo(x,y)`. In this case, if you replace x and y with numbers, those numbers are also data, but data in the form of a numeric constant.

In QScript, data represents information that your scripts can read and use. Data can be stored as either a constant or a variable. A *constant* is a form of data that never changes. Constants include:

**Numbers** (`54321`, `-54321`)
**Text strings** (`"Hello World!"`)
**Boolean constants** (`True`, `False`)

*Variables*, on the other hand, can change as the movie plays. For more information on variables, see Chapter 13, "Advanced QScript." For now, you'll focus on using constants and QScript properties.

---

### About Dot Syntax

Dot syntax links commands to targets. In QScript, as in most scripting languages, target objects are separated from commands by a period, or a dot. That small period puts the *dot* in *dot syntax* and is the key to making an action statement work. Thus, a QScript action statement generally looks like this:

`Target_Specifier.Command`

Dot syntax uses a hierarchical structure that in many ways resembles a path name in an HTML hypertext reference. Just as you use a slash (/) in HTML to bore through progressively nested directories in search of a file, you can use dot syntax to delve deeply into a movie and target the correct object. The following QScript, for example, is a perfectly legitimate and syntactically correct use of dot syntax:

`MovieNamed("myMovie").ChildMovieTrackNamed("myChild").TrackNamed("myTrack").`
`→ SetLayerTo(-100)`

## About QScript Properties

Properties provide a way for your scripts to obtain information from LiveStage objects. Properties let your scripts determine an object's name, its enabled status, or even its coordinate position in the movie. Properties are a bit harder to understand than QScript actions. Think of properties as being things that return values about an object. These values are data and can be used in any way that data can be used. Thus, a property can be used as the expression on the right side of an assignment statement or can even be fed into a QScript action (See "Using Properties in QScript Actions" at left.)

Like action statements, properties rely on dot syntax to harvest a value associated with a specific target object. To determine a property of an object, you would use the following syntax:

`Target_Specifier.QScript_Property`

The most important thing to remember about properties is that they return values. Properties are read-only. The `TrackEnabled` property, for example, looks at the target object it is attached to and determines whether that track is enabled. If so, the `TrackEnabled` property returns a value of `True`. If the track is not enabled, this property returns a value of `False`. You can use this data as a component of a QScript action statement.

As is true of action statements, the best way to understand properties is to use one. The example on the next page builds on the project you created in "About Action Statements" earlier in this chapter. In this example, you'll harvest the enabled property of the track named textTrack and use it to set the enabled status of a different track.

### Using Properties in QScript Actions

Most (but not all) action statements have three parts: a target specifier, a QScript action, and a bit of data that controls what the QScript action does. When you use the `SetLayerTo(Layer)` action, for example, the `SetLayerTo` keyword is the action, and the numeric value that you enter as the `Layer` is a bit of data that controls what the action does.

Similarly, the `SetEnabled(False)` action disables a targeted track. In this action, `False` is actually a Boolean constant. But the Boolean constant `False` is also a value that can be returned by the track property `TrackEnabled`.

Now the fun begins. If properties return data values, and if data is used to control actions, why not nest a track property inside an action? Using this technique, you can do very complex things, such as set one track's enabled status based on the enabled status of a second track. Here's the QScript you would use to do so:

```
TrackNamed("Track_B").SetEnabled
 (TrackNamed("Track_A").TrackEnabled)
```

If Track A is enabled when this action is executed, Track B is also enabled. If Track A is disabled, so is Track B.

Chapter 4

## To use a property:

1. Choose Window > Show Library Window > Media tab.

2. Drag an image from the Images folder to the Tracks tab of the Project window.

   A new picture track is created at the bottom of the Track list (**Figure 4.25**).

3. Double-click the picture track's header.

   The Track Properties window opens.

4. Change the picture track's name to pictureTrack.

5. Click the close box at the top of the Track Properties window or press Command/Ctrl-W.

   The Track Properties window closes. In the Track list, the picture track's header updates to reflect the name change (**Figure 4.26**).

   Picture tracks are not scriptable, so you have to use the text track's script editor to change the picture track's enabled status.

6. Double-click the text sample.

   The sample editor opens.

7. Select the Frame Loaded event handler (**Figure 4.27**).

   The Frame Loaded event is highlighted, and the script that you wrote in the preceding exercise is visible in the script edit field.

8. Click the script edit field just behind the last text character of the existing QScript action statement.

   An insertion point is placed behind the existing action statement.

9. Press Enter or Return.

   The insertion point jumps down to the next line.

*Image from library*

*New picture track*

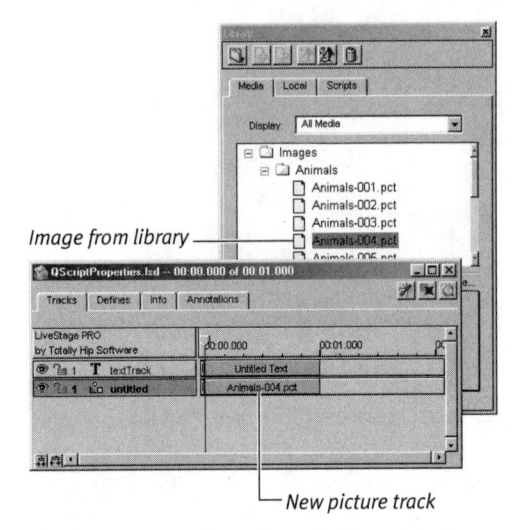

**Figure 4.25** Drag an image from the library into the Tracks tab.

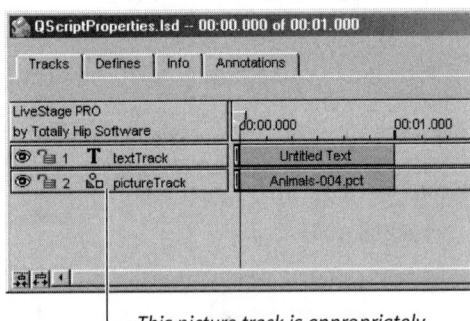

*This picture track is appropriately named and can be targeted by QScript*

**Figure 4.26** The picture track's header reflects the name you've assigned it using the Track Properties window.

ABOUT QSCRIPT PROPERTIES

The Script Editor

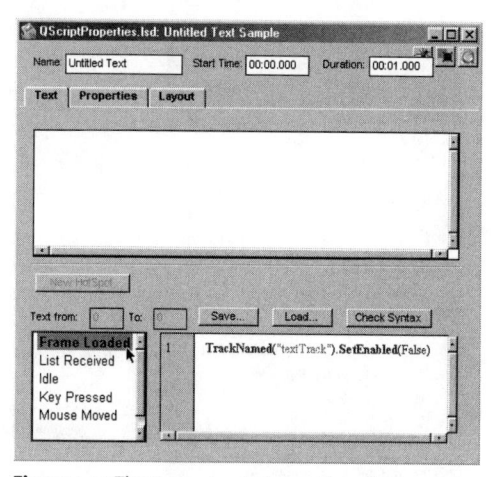

**Figure 4.27** The Frame Loaded event handler.

**10.** Enter the following QScript (**Figure 4.28**):
TrackNamed("pictureTrack").
→ SetEnabled(TrackNamed
→ ("textTrack").TrackEnabled)

**11.** Click the Run Wired Movie button at the top of the Project window.

The preview window displays only a thin bar, and neither track is visible. You used the text track's enabled property to disable the picture track (**Figure 4.29**).

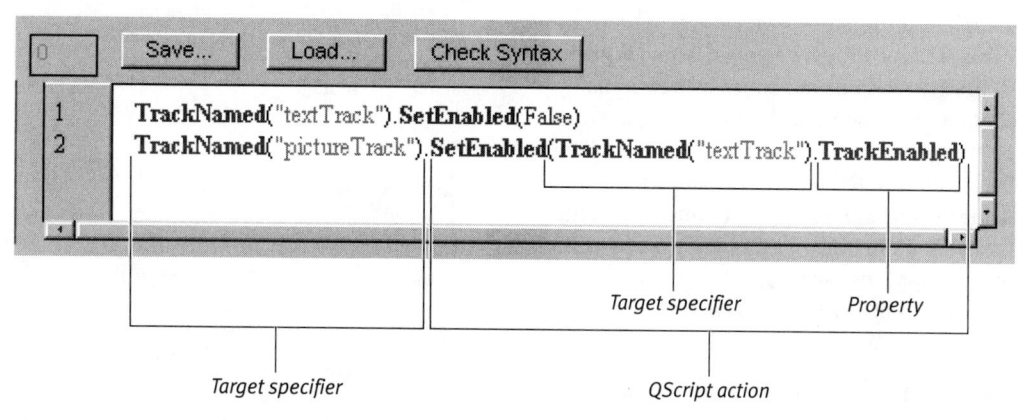

**Figure 4.28** The text track now holds two action statements. The first statement sets the enabled status of the track named textTrack to False. The second sets the enabled status of the track named pictureTrack to equal the enabled status of the track named textTrack, which is False.

**Figure 4.29** As soon as the track named textTrack loads, both tracks are turned off, and the preview window shows up empty.

# About the QScript Reference Window

By now, you know that QScript is composed of many language elements called keywords. Each target specifier is a keyword, as are each individual action and property. To make a script, you snap together one or more QScript keywords in the script edit field, following the basic rules of syntax outlined earlier in this chapter. Remembering all the keywords, however, is difficult even for seasoned LiveStage users. Fortunately, the QScript Reference window provides a categorized list of every QScript keyword available to LiveStage.

The QScript Reference window has three tabs: Actions, Properties, and Other (**Figure 4.30**). The Actions tab contains keywords that tell your movie to do something, such as start playing or go to a specified URL. The Properties tab lists keywords that return values, such as the movie's volume or current time. The Other tab contains all the remaining QScript language elements, including logical operators (<, +, =, >) and control statements (IF...ELSE...ENDIF).

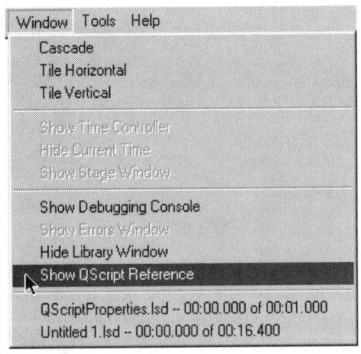

### To open the QScript Reference window:

◆ Choose Window > Show QScript Reference (Command/Ctrl-T) as shown in **Figure 4.31**.

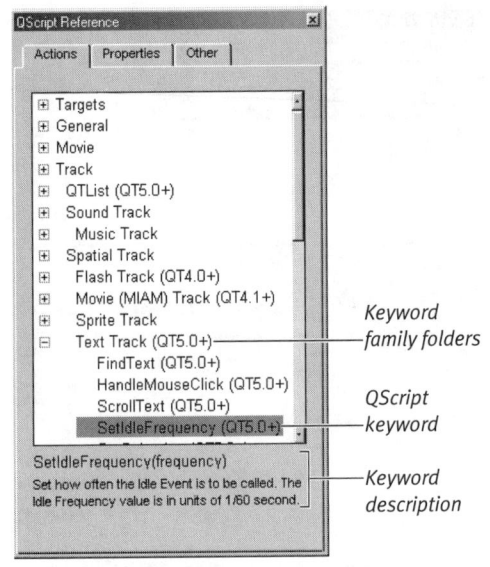

**Figure 4.30** The QScript Reference window contains every QScript keyword and language element available to LiveStage.

**Figure 4.31** To open the QScript Reference Window, choose Window > Show QScript Reference.

The Script Editor

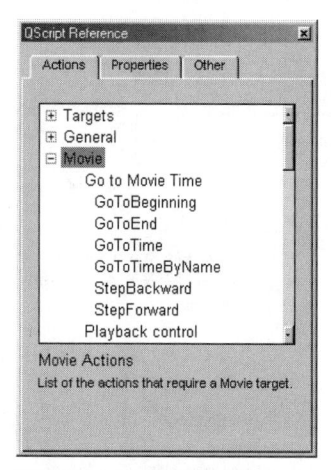

**Figure 4.32** To expand a QScript folder, click the plus sign (Windows) or the arrow (Mac).

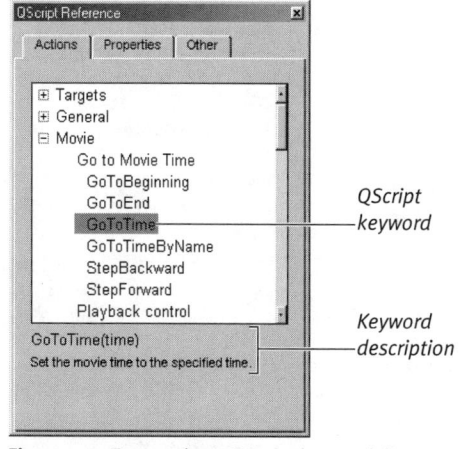

**Figure 4.33** To see what a QScript keyword does, select it and then read the description at the bottom of the QScript Reference window.

## Selecting a QScript keyword

Each tab is further divided into categorized folders containing families of QScript keywords that operate on the same type of object. All actions that operate on text tracks, for example, are grouped in the Actions tab inside a folder named Text Track. When you follow these simple hierarchies, it is very easy to find any keyword you might be after.

### To select a QScript keyword:

1. In the QScript Reference window, select the Actions, Properties, or Other tab.

2. Locate the folder containing the appropriate keyword family.

3. Click the arrow (Mac) or plus sign (Windows) to the left of the folder (**Figure 4.32**).

   The folder opens to reveal all QScript keywords in that family.

4. Select a keyword by clicking it (**Figure 4.33**).

   To see what the keyword does, look at its description at the bottom of the QScript Reference window.

### ✔ Tip

- A common QScript syntax error involves selecting a keyword from the wrong family for the target you are specifying. This error is very easy to avoid, as actions and properties are grouped in families named for the target objects with which they work. If you have a track and want it to do something (perform an action, for example), open the QScript reference window, click the Actions tab, and look in the Track folder to see what track actions are available.

ABOUT THE QSCRIPT REFERENCE WINDOW

79

## Using QScript keywords

After you've found the right QScript keywords, writing a QScript is as simple as dragging the keywords into a script editor's script edit field. That's it! A quick look at the QScript Reference window is sure to turn up the keyword you need, so you don't need to memorize keywords. Save that brainpower for more important things, such as creating quality movies.

### To use a QScript keyword:

1. In the script editor, click the script edit field.

2. Drag a keyword from the QScript Reference window into the script edit field (**Figure 4.34**).

### ✔ Tip

- If the insertion point is flashing in an active script edit field, you can double-click a keyword in the QScript Reference window, and the keyword will jump straight into the script edit field.

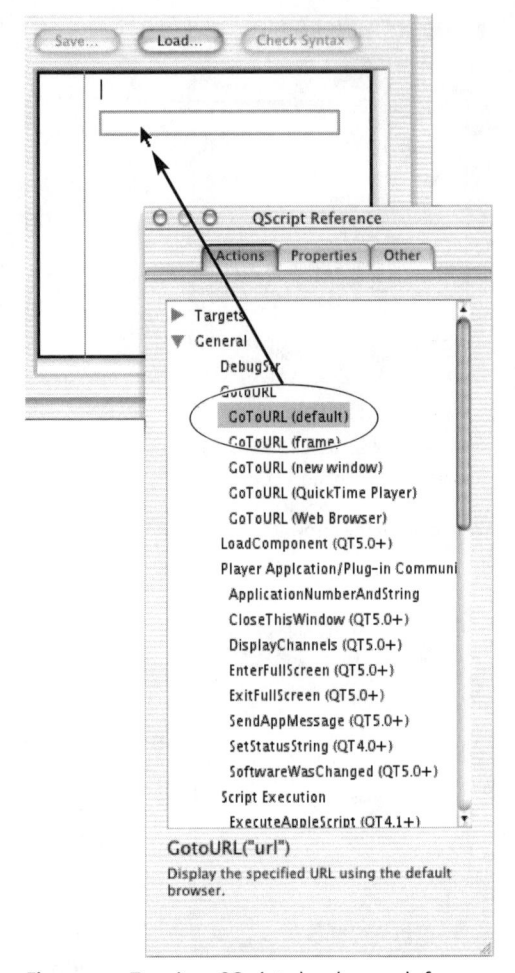

**Figure 4.34** To write a QScript, drag keywords from the QScript Reference window straight into any script edit field.

# Setting Movie Properties

## 5

In Chapter 1, "The Tracks Tab," you learned how to snap together and arrange pictures, video, and sound files to create a project. Chapter 3, "Setting Track Properties," went a step further, exploring the properties that affect how each track is displayed in the final movie. This chapter wraps up the process by discussing properties that determine how QuickTime displays that finished movie.

Movie properties include Auto Start, which tells QuickTime to play the movie automatically, and Loop settings, which cause a movie to play indefinitely. LiveStage conveniently groups all movie properties in the Info tab, which you'll get to know intimately in this chapter. You'll also learn how to turn your finished project into a QuickTime movie file that others can view outside the confines of the LiveStage interface.

Many of the Info tab's functions work in tandem with other aspects of your movie and may require QScript. If you're still uncomfortable using QScript, don't worry. Chapter 4, "The Script Editor," provides you with enough information to tackle any of the scripting in this chapter confidently.

## About the Play Section

The Info tab divides movie properties into three sections: Play, Movie, and Loop (**Figure 5.1**). The Play section (rather obviously) holds properties that affect the way QuickTime plays your movie, including Auto Start, All Frames playback, and Selection Only playback.

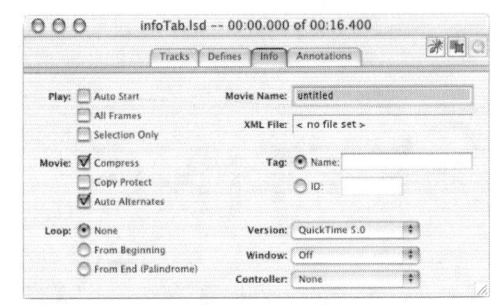

**Figure 5.1** You use the Info tab to set properties that affect the way QuickTime displays your movie.

### Understanding Auto Start

In a Web browser, several things happen when you set a movie to Auto Start. First, QuickTime determines how quickly the file is downloading to your computer. Next, it calculates the length of time it will take to download the entire file. When the time left in the download is less than the total length of the movie, QuickTime starts playback. But be warned: Auto Starting a movie can lead to stuttering, which occurs when QuickTime starts playing but then quickly stops because not enough of the movie has downloaded to allow smooth playback.

The first section of all QuickTime movie files contains the movie resource. This section of the file is pure data, which is small and downloads quickly. As a result, QuickTime is sometimes tricked into thinking the movie is downloading faster than it really is and may begin playing the movie before enough of it has downloaded. QuickTime will play for a second, quickly catch up to the end of what has already downloaded and then stop (stutter). It then recalculates the time needed to download the file and resumes playback only when enough of the file has downloaded to allow unimpeded playback.

Stuttering is most noticeable with audio tracks; the user hears the sound start and then suddenly stop. You can prevent stuttering by enabling the Preload track property for audio tracks (see Chapter 3, "Setting Track Properties"). This property tells QuickTime to download the track into RAM before playing it.

## Setting Movie Properties

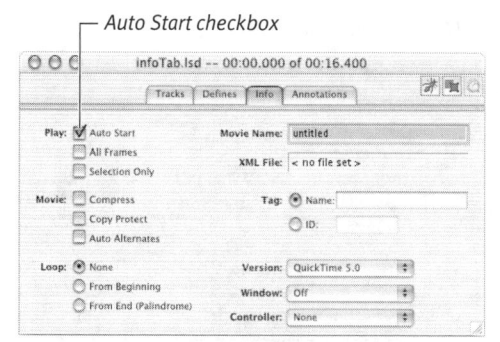

**Figure 5.2** When a movie is first opened in QuickTime Player, it normally just sits there, waiting for the viewer to click Play. If you select the Auto Start movie property, your movie plays as soon as enough of it has loaded to facilitate unimpeded playback by the QuickTime browser plug-in.

## Using Auto Start

When you check the Auto Start checkbox, QuickTime begins playing your movie just as soon as enough of it has downloaded to allow uninterrupted playback of the entire file.

### To Auto Start a movie:

◆ With the Info tab open, check the Auto Start checkbox (**Figure 5.2**).

## Using All Frames playback

As QuickTime plays back your movie, it attempts to maintain a steady playback rate that keeps the visual portion of your movie synchronized with the audio portion. On slower computers, QuickTime must drop frames to accomplish this task.

But dropping frames can lead to a very serious problem. If you've used a small sprite sample in your movie, QuickTime might leap right over it as it drops frames. If the sprite sample holds only images, this situation may not matter. But if the sample holds a sprite with an important script attached—such as one that tells the movie to stop or to jump to a different point in the Timeline—the script will not be executed, and your movie will not play as expected.

This can be a big problem for projects that incorporate a scripted Flash track. A typical scripted Flash movie contains frame actions that control internal looping and navigation. Most authors output their scripted Flash files at the default frame rate of 12 frames per second. At that rate, one frame lasts only 1/12 of a second. Should QuickTime happen to skip a frame with an important action attached to it, the navigation structure of your Flash track will fall apart.

*continues on next page*

## To prevent frame skipping:

◆ Make the scripted sample at least a half second long.

At this length, it is unlikely that QuickTime will skip the frame.

*or*

In the Info tab, check the All Frames checkbox (**Figure 5.3**).

QuickTime is forced to play every frame of your movie so that no important scripts are missed.

## ✔ Tip

■ When you force every frame of your movie to play, QuickTime cannot synchronize the audio to the movie's visual content. As a result, QuickTime disables your audio tracks, which means that your movie will have no sound.

## Using playback selections

Setting a playback selection is rather like telling QuickTime to hike only a small section of a large trail. If you set a playback selection, QuickTime will play only the specified section of the movie when the file is opened.

Selections are often used with loop playback to make sure that QuickTime loops your movie at exactly the right point. But that isn't the only thing you can do with selections. If you haven't aligned the ends of your tracks exactly, for example, parts of your movie may go blank when QuickTime reaches the end of the file. You can prevent this situation by setting a playback selection that forces QuickTime to stop playing just before the blank bits appear.

*All Frames checkbox*

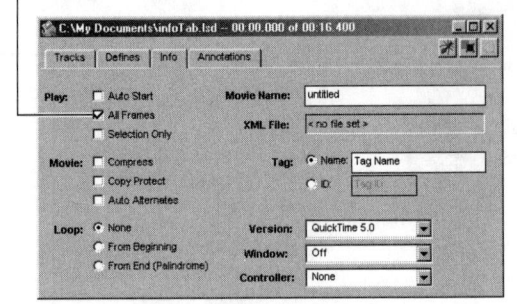

**Figure 5.3** Selecting All Frames playback causes QuickTime to play every frame of your movie but disables your movie's audio tracks.

## Setting Movie Properties

*Selection Only checkbox*

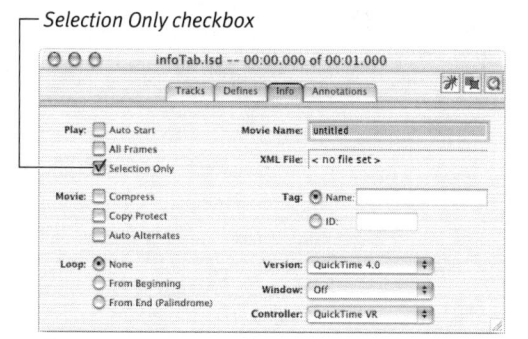

**Figure 5.4** Checking the Selection Only checkbox tells QuickTime to play only a specified section of your movie.

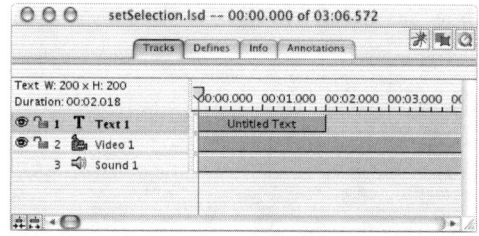

**Figure 5.5** This text track has been moved to the top of the Track list, effectively hiding it behind the movie's other tracks.

*Script edit field*
*Event Handler list*
*Run Wired Movie button*

**Figure 5.6** An open text sample.

### To set a playback selection:

1. With the Info tab open, check the Selection Only checkbox (**Figure 5.4**).

   QuickTime is told to play only the specified selection. But this step is only the first in setting a playback selection. The next several steps specify the selection that QuickTime will play.

2. Create a text track by choosing Tracks > Create > Text.

   A new text track is created, and an empty sample is placed in the Timeline.

3. In the Tracks tab, select the text track's header, and move it to the top of the Track list (**Figure 5.5**).

   The text track is hidden behind all the other tracks in your movie. If you left the text track at the bottom of the Track list, it would appear in your movie as a 200-square-pixel patch of white sitting on top of your other tracks.

4. Double-click the text sample to reveal the script editor (**Figure 5.6**).

5. In the Event Handler list on the left side of the script editor, select the Frame Loaded event handler.

   It is important to select the correct event handler. For this example, you need QuickTime to jump to the specified playback selection as soon as the movie is opened or loaded. To achieve this result you must use the Frame Loaded event handler.

   The Frame Loaded event handler is executed as soon as the sample containing the SetSelection QScript is loaded, which allows QuickTime to jump to the set selection before the movie begins playing.

   *continues on next page*

**ABOUT THE PLAY SECTION**

85

Chapter 5

6. Type the following QScript in the script edit field (**Figure 5.7**):

   ThisMovie.SetSelection(start_time,
   → end_time).

   The start_time value is the point in time in your movie when you want the selection to start. The end_time value is the moment when you want the selection to end.

   Make sure that you use the proper time scale for the start and end times. If you want the selection to start at 2 seconds and end at 4-1/4 seconds, for example, use a start time of 00:02.000 and an end time of 00:04.150.

7. Click the Run Wired Movie button in the top-right corner of the text sample.

   When the movie file opens, only the specified selection plays (**Figure 5.8**).

✔ **Tips**

- If you already have a scriptable track sample at the beginning of your project, you do not need to create a new text track to hold your QScript. Instead, place the SetSelection QScript in the Frame Loaded event handler of the existing scriptable track sample.

- If you've created a looping audio movie, you may notice a pause at the movie's loop point. Setting a playback selection significantly reduces this pause. In particular, audio files created with MP3 compression may have a fraction of a second of silence tacked onto the end, leading to a looping stutter. Setting a playback selection allows you to trim off this excess silence accurately without altering the source audio file.

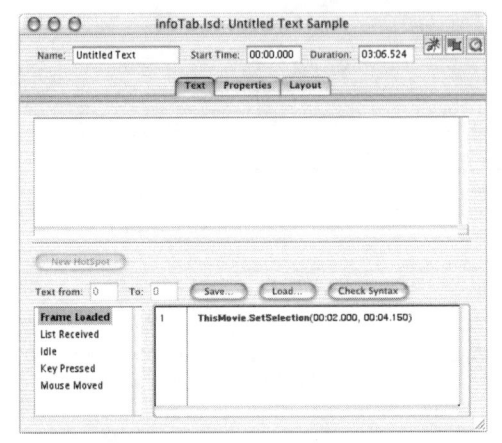

**Figure 5.7** Because it is in the Frame Loaded event handler, this SetSelection QScript executes as soon as the movie opens.

*Playback selection*

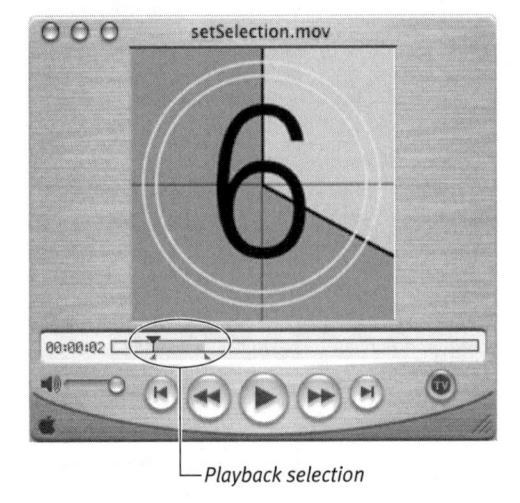

**Figure 5.8** If you open the movie in QuickTime Player, the playback selection is highlighted.

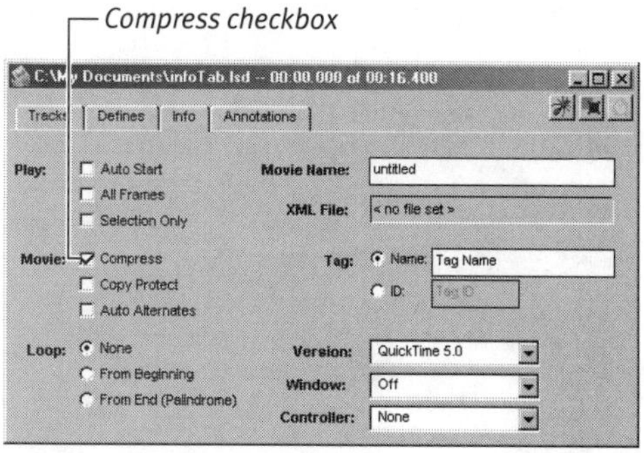

## Setting Movie Properties

*Compress checkbox*

**Figure 5.9** Compressing your movie's resource makes it smaller and, thus, better suited for Internet delivery.

## About the Movie Section

The Movie section groups three loosely related movie properties: Compress, Copy Protect, and Auto Alternates.

### Compressing the movie resource

A QuickTime movie file has two parts. The first part, called the *movie resource,* contains all the information about the movie's tracks and samples, including their dimensions, graphics modes, and spatial/temporal position in the movie. The second part of the file holds the movie's video, image, and sound files.

The movie resource can be compressed to make your files smaller and better suited for the Internet. You may not notice a difference in file size if your movie is very large, as the movie resource is tiny in comparison with the entire file. If your movie is small (less than 40 KB), however, any decrease in file size is beneficial. Typically, you'll want to leave the Compress checkbox checked.

### To compress the movie resource:

◆ In the Info tab, check the Compress checkbox (**Figure 5.9**).

## Copy-protecting movies

The Info tab's Copy Protect feature prevents viewers from modifying your movie or saving it from their Web browsers. But don't let this feature lull you into a false sense of security. A viewer's Web browser may store a copy of your movie in its cache, from which it's easily retrieved. There is no 100 percent effective way to copy-protect your movie. You might as well resign yourself to the fact that if someone wants to steal your movie, he or she will find a way.

**To copy-protect your movie:**

◆ In the Info tab, check the Copy Protect checkbox (**Figure 5.10**).

## Using alternate tracks

Alternate tracks let you create foreign-language subtitles by substituting one track for another based on the language setting of the viewer's operating system.

Each alternate track remains a part of your movie and consequently increases its file size. You need to keep this fact in mind if you intend to distribute your movie over the Internet.

**To enable alternate tracks:**

◆ In the Info tab, check the Auto Alternates checkbox (**Figure 5.11**).

**To create an alternate language track:**

1. From the Tracks tab, double-click the track header of the track you want to make an alternate language track.

    The Track Properties window opens (**Figure 5.12**).

2. In the Track Properties window, select the Advanced tab.

*Copy Protect checkbox*

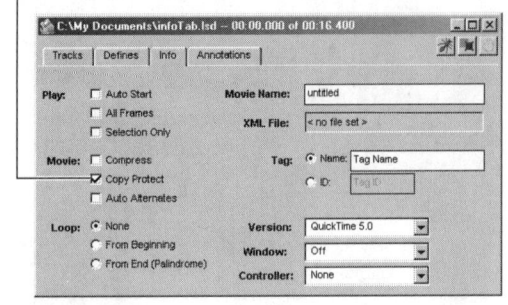

**Figure 5.10** Copy-protect your movie if you want to make it difficult for viewers to download your work to their hard disks.

*Auto Alternates checkbox*

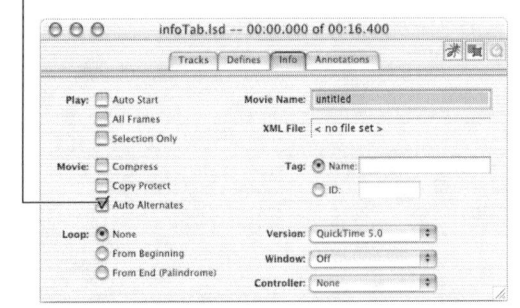

**Figure 5.11** The Auto Alternates checkbox tells QuickTime to display a track that corresponds to the language of the user's operating system.

*Advanced tab*

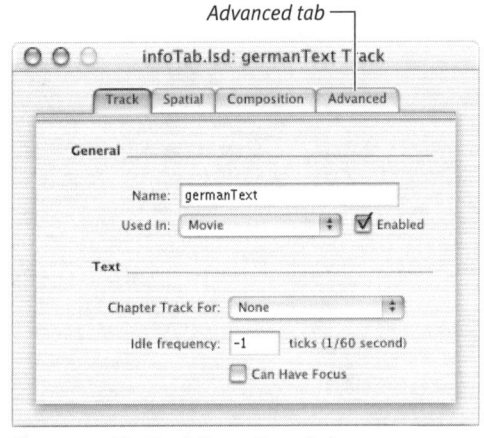

**Figure 5.12** The Track Properties window.

## Setting Movie Properties

**Figure 5.13** The Alternate For pop-up menu lets you choose which track will be disabled if the proper alternate track conditions are met.

**Figure 5.14** If the movie opens on a computer that has an operating-system language matching the language you specify, this track will be played instead of its alternate.

3. From the Alternate For pop-up menu, choose the track for which this track is an alternate (**Figure 5.13**).

   You cannot make a track an alternate for itself; the alternate track's own name is unavailable in the Alternate For pop-up menu.

4. From the Language pop-up menu, select a language for this alternate track (**Figure 5.14**).

   If the user's computer is set to the language you selected, this track plays instead of its alternate (**Figure 5.15**).

### ✔ Tip

- If you're using different sound tracks to deliver a narrative in several languages, you can conserve file size by making the sound tracks separate child movies that load from a URL when a language is needed (see Chapter 7, "Movie Tracks").

**Figure 5.15** The default English sound track is disabled, replaced by this German alternate text track.

89

## Testing alternate language tracks

Testing alternate language tracks can be a bit difficult. QuickTime currently uses the language setting of the viewer's operating system to decide which alternate track to display. Changing the language setting in QuickTime's Preferences dialog does *not* affect which alternate language track you experience. This situation may change in future versions of QuickTime, but for now, you must use QuickTime Player's Choose Language option to test your alternate language tracks.

### To test alternate language tracks:

1. Open your movie in QuickTime Player.

2. In QuickTime Player, choose Movie > Choose Language (**Figure 5.16**).

   If your movie contains no alternate language tracks, the Choose Language command is unavailable. If your movie does have alternate language tracks, the Choose Movie Language dialog opens (**Figure 5.17**).

3. Select the language of the track that you're testing.

   The alternate language track is displayed.

**Figure 5.16** To test an alternate language track, open it in QuickTime Player and then choose Movie > Choose Language.

**Figure 5.17** The Choose Movie Language dialog displays all the alternate language tracks in your movie. Choose one for QuickTime Player to display.

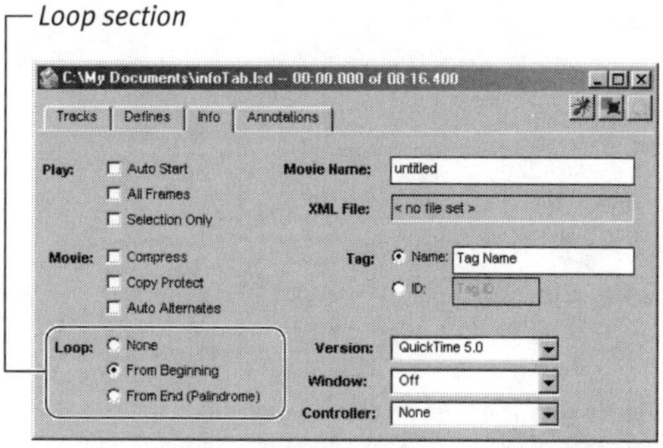

**Figure 5.18** Selecting a Loop value other than None causes your movie to play back continuously until the viewer clicks Stop or Pause.

*Loop section*

## About Looping Movies

Movies normally play through to the end and then stop. If you set a Loop value, however, the movie continues playing indefinitely or until the viewer pauses it.

You can set the Info tab's Loop property to one of three values:

**None.** The movie plays to the end and stops. No looping occurs.

**From Beginning.** The movie plays to the end and then immediately starts replaying from the beginning. The movie loops continuously until playback is halted.

**From End (Palindrome).** The movie plays to the end and then plays in reverse until it reaches the beginning, where it reverses direction once more. Palindrome looping is sometimes called *ping-pong looping*, as the movie appears to bounce between end points like a Ping-Pong ball bouncing back and forth over a net. The movie loops continuously until playback is halted.

### To loop a movie:

- In the Loop section of the Info tab, click the appropriate radio button (**Figure 5.18**).

### ✔ Tip

- Looping a movie sometimes causes audio tracks to stutter during the transition from the end of the movie to the beginning. This situation is a problem if you're using a short audio clip to provide background music for your movie. Prevent this problem by caching the audio track in RAM (see Chapter 3, "Setting Track Properties") and/or setting a playback selection.

# About QuickTime Properties

The three pop-up menus in the bottom right corner of the Info tab are used to set QuickTime properties. You can use these menus to assign a standard QuickTime controller to your movie, or to tell QuickTime Player to enter present movie mode (in present movie mode, QuickTime displays your movie across the viewer's entire screen). If you need your movie to be compatible with older versions of QuickTime, you can use the Version pop-up menu to select a QuickTime version.

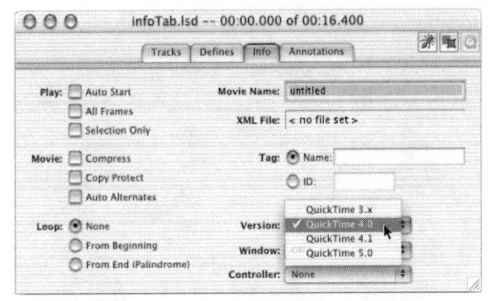

**Figure 5.19** The Version pop-up menu lists older versions of QuickTime. As LiveStage compiles your movie into a finished QuickTime file, it checks to make sure all of your QScripts are compatible with the QuickTime version you have selected.

## Setting QuickTime version compatibility

The Version pop-up menu is important if you know that your movie will be played on a version of QuickTime that's older than 5.0 or if you want to make your movie available to the widest possible audience. When LiveStage exports your project to a finished QuickTime movie file, it normally produces a movie that is compatible with QuickTime 5.0 and later. Users who do not have QuickTime 5.0 installed will not be able to view your movie without first upgrading their copies of QuickTime. If you want to ensure that your movie will work on computers using older versions of QuickTime, choose a QuickTime version from the Version pop-up menu.

**Figure 5.20** The Errors window.

### To set QuickTime version compatibility:

◆ In the Info tab, choose a QuickTime version from the Version pop-up menu (**Figure 5.19**).

After compiling the movie, LiveStage checks your QScripts for compatibility with the QuickTime version you selected. If your movie contains incompatible QScripts, the Errors window appears (**Figure 5.20**).

## Using present movie mode

Present movie mode only works if your movie is opened in QuickTime Player. In present movie mode, your movie is displayed in the center of the viewer's monitor, and any space between your movie's boundaries and the edge of the screen is displayed in black (**Figure 5.21**). Even the menu bar across the top of the screen disappears.

### To set a present movie mode:

◆ In the Info tab, choose a display size from the Window pop-up menu (**Figure 5.22**).

To make QuickTime present your movie as soon as it's launched, choose an auto screen size.

To enable present movie mode through QScript while the movie is playing, choose a manual screen size.

### ✔ Tip

- Using QScript, you can create a wired event to enter or exit present movie mode at run time. To do so, choose Full Screen (Manual) from the Window pop-menu, create a sprite button (see Chapter 10, "Sprite Tracks"), and attach the `EnterFullScreen` QScript to its `Mouse Clicked` event handler. When the sprite button is clicked, QuickTime Player will enter present movie mode. `ExitFullScreen` causes the movie to revert to the original. This QScript works only with QuickTime Player 5 and later.

**Figure 5.21** Present movie modes are particularly effective for presentations, as your movie is the only thing that appears on the screen.

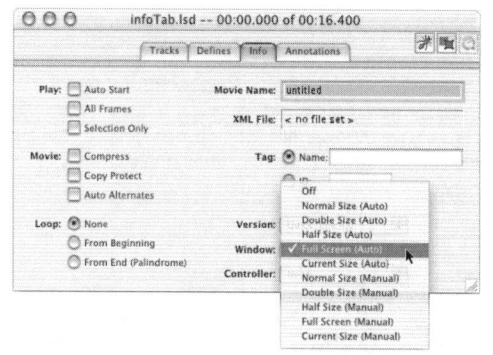

**Figure 5.22** The Window pop-up menu contains all available present movie modes.

# Chapter 5

## Using QuickTime controllers

QuickTime uses two types of standard controllers to give viewers power over the playback of your movie. The first, called a *linear controller*, allows the viewer to play, pause, and change the volume of movies or videos that progress in a forward direction (**Figure 5.23**). The second, called a *VR controller*, lets the viewer zoom, pan, and change the volume of QuickTime Virtual Reality movies (**Figure 5.24**).

By default, LiveStage outputs your movie without a controller. This situation is great if you've used QScript and a few sprite buttons to provide your own custom navigation structure. If you haven't, you should use one of QuickTime's standard controllers so that viewers can control your movie's playback.

### To select a movie controller:

◆ In the Info tab, choose a controller type from the Controller pop-up menu (**Figure 5.25**).

When your movie is opened, it contains the type of controller you specified (**Figure 5.26**). If you are creating a normal movie, use the standard controller. VR movies need a VR controller to operate properly.

### ✔ Tip

■ To learn how to design your own custom controllers, see Chapter 10, "Sprite Tracks."

**Figure 5.23** The Macintosh (top) and Windows (bottom) QuickTime linear controllers.

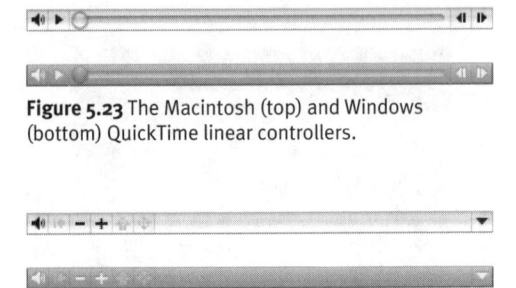

**Figure 5.24** The Macintosh (top) and Windows (bottom) QuickTime VR controllers.

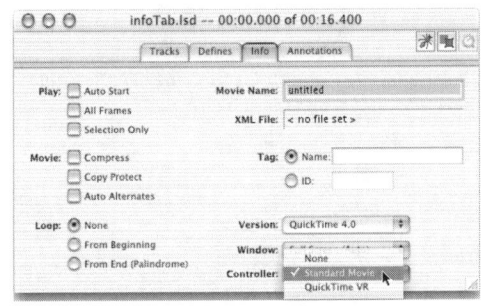

**Figure 5.25** The Controller pop-up menu lets you assign a standard, VR, or even no controller to your movie.

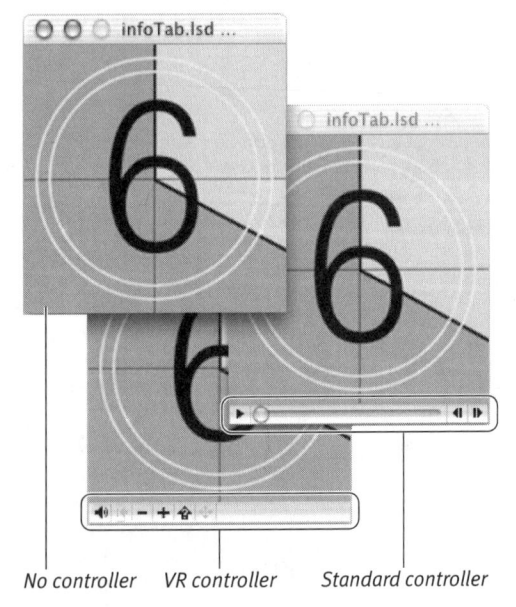

**Figure 5.26** An example of the three controller options.

# Setting Movie Properties

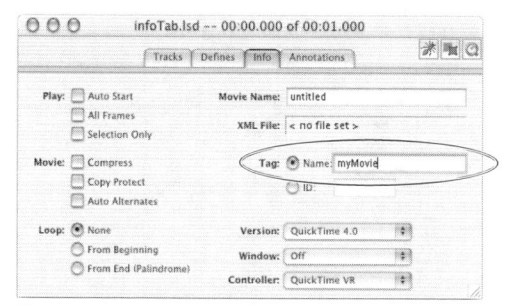

**Figure 5.27** To target a movie by its tag name, first select the Name radio button and then enter a tag name for the movie in the text box.

**Figure 5.28** An example of intermovie communication. The video in the top browser frame is controlled by the controller movie in the bottom browser frame.

## About Intermovie Communication

If your finished movie is like a cleverly constructed house, intermovie communication is like a phone line between your house and other houses on its block. Intermovie communication allows two or more movies embedded in the same Web page (or open at the same time in QuickTime Player) to "talk" to each other—even if they are in different frames. Intermovie communication lets you design one movie to control the playback of another, pass variables between two open QuickTime files, or even design a compass in one Web page frame that spins to reflect the focal position of VR movies loaded into another frame.

To use intermovie communication, you must specify a unique tag name or tag ID number for your movies. This unique tag name or tag ID lets QuickTime identify each movie. You then target the movie by using the `MovieNamed` or `MovieOfID` QScript.

### To assign a tag name:

1. In the Tag section of the Info tab, click the Name radio button (**Figure 5.27**).

2. Enter a name in the text box.

   QuickTime uses this name to target the movie for intermovie communication (**Figure 5.28**).

95

Because tag IDs are numbers, they generally are not as intuitive to use as names. If you are looking at a list of movies identified by the numbers 1, 2, 3, 4, and 5, it's pretty hard to remember what movie contains what. Nonetheless, LiveStage lets you do so.

### To assign a tag ID:

1. In the Tag section of the Info tab, click the ID radio button (**Figure 5.29**).

2. Enter a number in the text box.

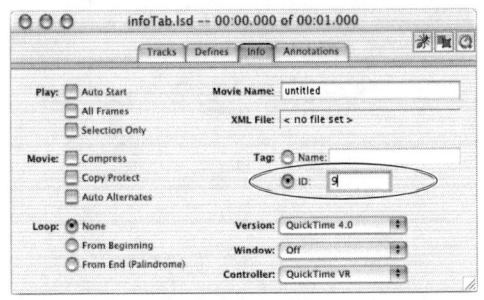

**Figure 5.29** To target a movie by its tag ID, first select the ID radio button and then enter a number in the text box.

### ✔ Tips

- For some purposes, tag IDs provide a bit more versatility than tag names. It's easy to write a QScript that generates numbers, for example, but hard to write one that generates names. By using tag IDs, you can write a QScript that generates target-movie IDs dynamically at run time.

- To target a movie by ID, use the `MovieOfID("ID")` target specifier.

Setting Movie Properties

**Figure 5.30** To export your movie to a QuickTime file, choose File > Export Wired Movie.

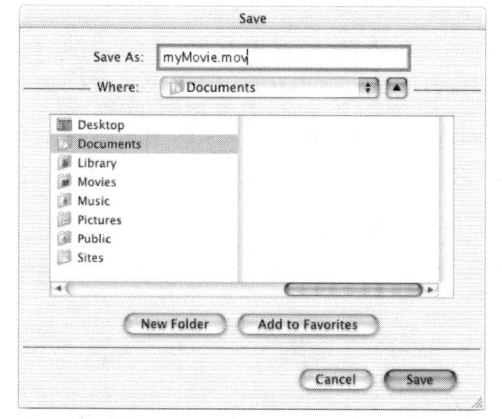

**Figure 5.31** Use the Save dialog to save your project as a QuickTime movie on your hard disk.

**Figure 5.32** The finished QuickTime file.

## About Exporting

When you export a project, LiveStage assembles all of its tracks, sprites, and QScripts into a format that QuickTime can understand. Exporting a project creates a QuickTime movie file that you can open in QuickTime Player or distribute on a CD-ROM or over the Internet.

### To export your movie to a QuickTime file:

1. Choose File > Export Wired Movie (Command/Ctrl-M) (**Figure 5.30**). The Save dialog opens.

2. Enter a name in the Save As text box (**Figure 5.31**).

3. Navigate to the place on your hard disk where you want to save your movie, and click Save.

   If your QScript is valid syntactically, LiveStage compiles your movie into a QuickTime movie file (**Figure 5.32**). If your QScript contains syntax errors, the Errors window opens.

### ✔ Tip

- Do not name your exported movie the exact same thing as your LiveStage project file or you may replace your project file with the exported movie.

97

## Setting an export file name

Although the Movie Name property is often overlooked, it can be a great time-saver. Use the Info tab's Movie Name text box to specify a file name for your movie. When you export your movie, this name automatically appears in the Save dialog's Save As text box. This feature saves you the hassle of retyping the file name every time you export your project.

### To set a movie file name:

◆ In the Info tab, enter a name in the Movie Name text box (**Figure 5.33**). Don't forget to include the .mov extension to ensure full cross-platform compatibility.

Your movie name appears in the Save dialog's Save As text box.

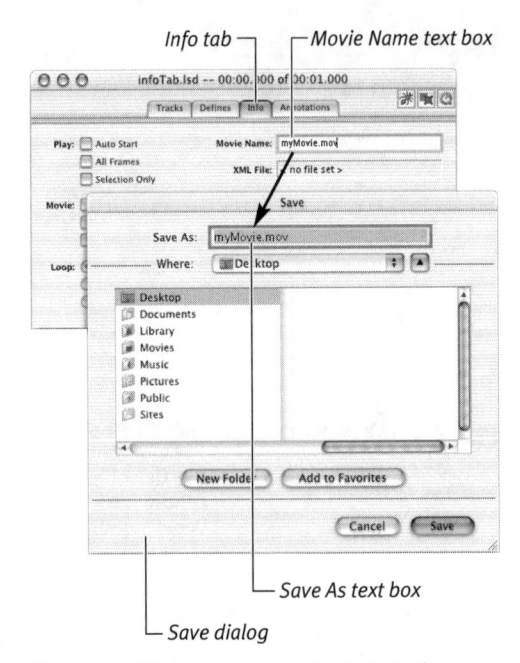

**Figure 5.33** When you export a wired movie, the name you enter in the Info tab's Movie Name text box is entered automatically in the Save dialog's Save As text box.

## Collecting a project

If you added media to your project by dragging it into the Tracks tab from the Finder (Mac) or desktop (Windows), your media files probably are distributed over many directories on your hard disk. Fortunately, LiveStage contains a command that will gather all of your project's media in one common Library folder. When you finish creating a project and are ready to back it up by saving it to a CD-ROM or some other storage medium, use LiveStage's Export Gathered Project command to make sure that you haven't left important media files behind.

**Figure 5.34** Use the Export Gathered Project command to gather all your project's media in one common Library folder.

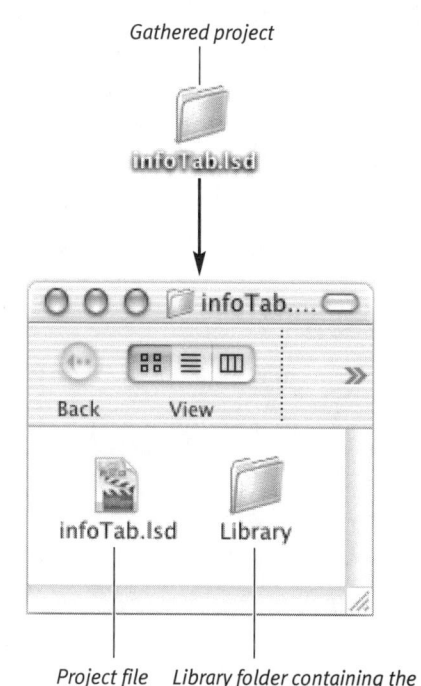

### To collect a project's media files:

1. Choose File > Export Gathered Project (**Figure 5.34**).

   The Save dialog opens.

2. Type a name in the Name text box.

3. Navigate to the place on your hard disk where you want to save the gathered copy of your project, and click Save.

   In the directory you have selected, LiveStage creates a new folder with the same name as your project (**Figure 5.35**). In this new project folder, LiveStage places a copy of your project file and a Library folder containing copies of the media files.

### ✔ Tip

- If two media files have exactly the same name, only one of them will be saved with the gathered project. Make sure you check the names of all of your media files so that none get left behind.

**Figure 5.35** The Export Gathered Project command creates a new folder and places a copy of the project file in it, along with a Library folder filled with the project's media.

*Setting Movie Properties*

**ABOUT EXPORTING**

99

# PART 2

# EXPLORING TRACKS

| Chapter 6: | Basic Visual Tracks | 103 |
| Chapter 7: | Movie Tracks | 119 |
| Chapter 8: | Text Tracks | 141 |
| Chapter 9: | Streaming, Flash, and VR Tracks | 177 |
| Chapter 10: | Sprite Tracks | 209 |
| Chapter 11: | Animations and Manipulations | 237 |
| Chapter 12: | Working with Audio | 263 |
| Chapter 13: | Advanced QScript | 281 |
| Appendix A: | Keyboard Shortcuts | 295 |
| Appendix B: | Online Resources | 297 |
| Appendix C: | Useful QScripts | 299 |

# Basic Visual Tracks

By now, you should be familiar with the LiveStage authoring environment and ready to tackle the program's various track types in more detail. Beginning with this chapter, you'll explore track types, learning how they work and mastering authoring techniques that will speed your work flow and enable you to create complex projects easily.

This chapter covers visual tracks, including color, picture, skin, and external tracks. These tracks are more or less passive containers for visual media. You can modify their properties (position in the movie, graphics modes, and track mattes), but you cannot alter the media that they contain. Furthermore, these basic visual tracks are not scriptable, and the viewer cannot interact with them (although you can target them from a scriptable track and use QScript to alter their position, enabled status, or graphics mode).

# About Color Tracks

Color tracks are a quick way to create large swaths of color for fills or movie backdrops (**Figure 6.1**). Because color tracks are rendered with QuickTime's vector codec, they add very little to your movie's file size.

### To create a color track:

◆ Choose Tracks > Create > Color (**Figure 6.2**).

A new color track is created at the bottom of the Track list.

### ✓ Tip

■ If you intend to use a color track as a background for your project, you will have to move it to the top of the Track list or increase its drawing-layer value. (For more information on drawing layers, see Chapter 3, "Setting Track Properties.")

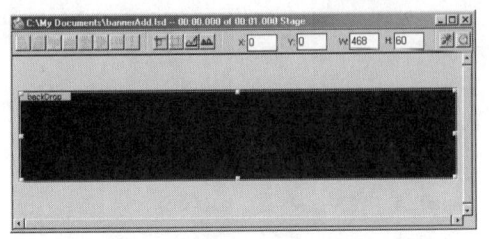

**Figure 6.1** If you're working on a project that must meet certain dimensions, such as a banner ad, use a color track to define your stage's size and background color. You know that your final movie will be the right size as long as you stay within the color track's boundaries.

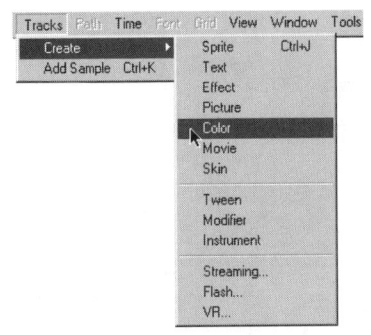

**Figure 6.2** To create a color track, choose Tracks > Create > Color.

---

## Making a Backdrop

The stage is organic; like an amoeba, it expands and contracts to encompass all your project's visual tracks. When it comes to laying out your movie, this behavior can create problems. First, any area of the stage not covered by a track will appear gray (QuickTime Player) or white (QuickTime Plug-in) in your final movie, which may not be the effect you are after. Additionally, if you are designing your project as a component of a larger Web page, the project must have certain dimensions to integrate seamlessly with the other parts of the page. If you can't set a stage size, it's difficult to make sure that all your visual tracks fall within the dimensions you've decided upon for the movie.

Fortunately, color tracks offer a quick solution to this problem. If you need to specify a stage size and color, simply use a properly sized color track as a backdrop.

Basic Visual Tracks

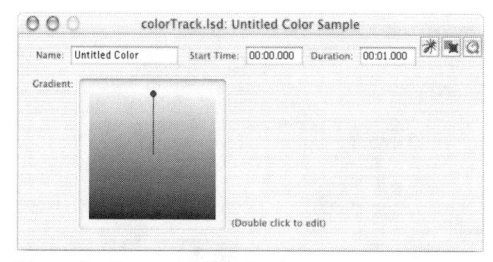

**Figure 6.3** An open color sample.

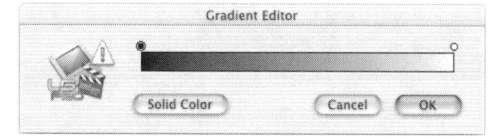

**Figure 6.4** The Gradient Editor dialog.

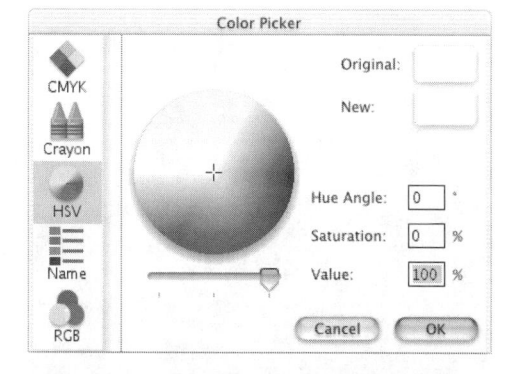

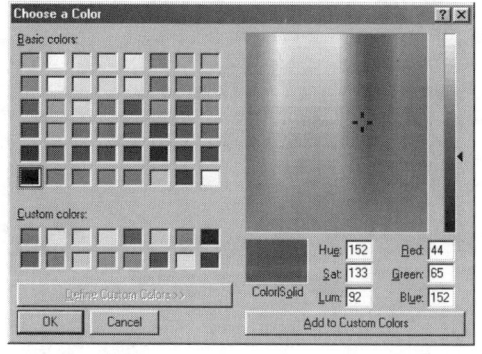

**Figure 6.5** The Macintosh Color Picker (top) and the Windows Color Picker (bottom).

## To define a solid color:

1. Double-click a sample in the color track that you want to change.

   The color sample opens to reveal a Gradient box (**Figure 6.3**).

2. Double-click the gradient box.

   The Gradient Editor dialog opens (**Figure 6.4**). By default, the dialog shows a simple black-to-white fade.

3. Click the circular color chip at the left end of the gradient bar.

   The Color Picker opens (**Figure 6.5**).

4. Choose a color, and click OK.

   The Color Picker closes, and you return to the Gradient Editor dialog, where the gradient bar updates to reflect your newly selected color.

5. Click the Solid Color button (**Figure 6.6**).

   *continues on next page*

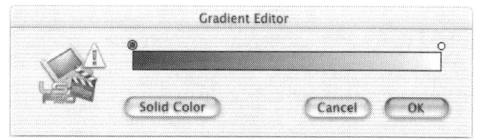

**Figure 6.6** If you click the Solid Color button at the bottom of the Gradient Editor dialog, the color in the left color chip uniformly fills the color track.

ABOUT COLOR TRACKS

105

# Chapter 6

6. Click OK to close the Gradient Editor dialog.

   The color sample's Gradient box turns a solid color, as does your color track on the stage (**Figure 6.7**).

7. Close the color sample.

## Creating multiband gradients

Color tracks can produce much more than simple solid colors. In fact, you can turn a color track into a multiband gradient containing all the colors of the rainbow (**Figure 6.8**).

### To create a multiband gradient:

1. Double-click the color track's sample.

   The color sample opens.

2. Double-click the Gradient box.

   The Gradient Editor dialog opens.

3. Drag one of the circular color chips toward the middle of the gradient bar (**Figure 6.9**).

   The circular color chip turns into a square, and the Color Picker opens.

4. Select a new color, and click OK.

   The Color Picker closes, and you return to the Gradient Editor dialog.

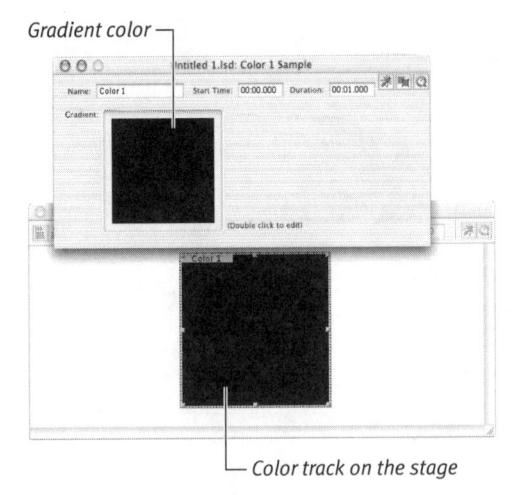

**Figure 6.7** The color of the Gradient box fills the color track on the stage.

**Figure 6.8** The sky in this picture is actually a color track. By designing your gradients carefully, you can achieve some startlingly realistic effects.

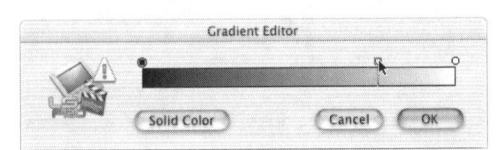

**Figure 6.9** To create a new gradient band, drag one of the circular color chips toward the middle of the gradient bar.

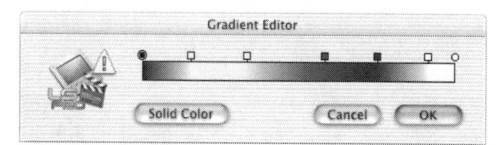

**Figure 6.10** You can make complex multiband gradients by dragging many color chips into the center of the gradient bar.

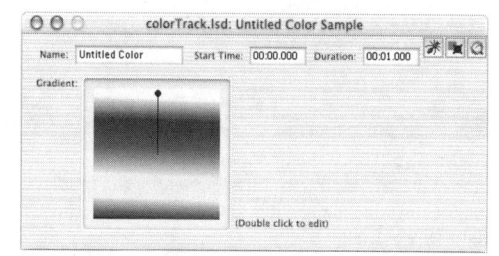

**Figure 6.11** A multiband gradient.

5. Continue dragging color chips into the center of the Gradient Editor and picking colors from the Color Picker until you have selected as many colors as you need (**Figure 6.10**).

6. Click OK to close the Gradient Editor dialog.

   The color sample updates to reflect your color selections (**Figure 6.11**).

7. Close the color sample.

### To delete a gradient color:

1. In the Gradient Editor dialog, select a square color chip.

2. Press the Delete key.

   The square color chip is deleted, and that color is removed from the gradient.

## Altering gradient alignment

You are not stuck with horizontal gradients. The Gradient box contains an angle control lever that you can use to spin your gradient in any direction (**Figure 6.12**).

### To change gradient alignment:

1. In the Gradient box, select the red circle at the top of the angle-control lever (**Figure 6.13**).
2. Drag the angle-control lever until the gradient is aligned properly (**Figure 6.14**).

### ✔ Tip

- The angle-control lever snaps to 30-degree increments. To disable snapping, press Option (Mac) or Ctrl-Alt (Windows) before you select and drag the angle-control lever.

**Figure 6.12** The sky behind these mountains was made with a color track. The alignment of the gradient makes the sun look like it is shining down from the right side of the picture.

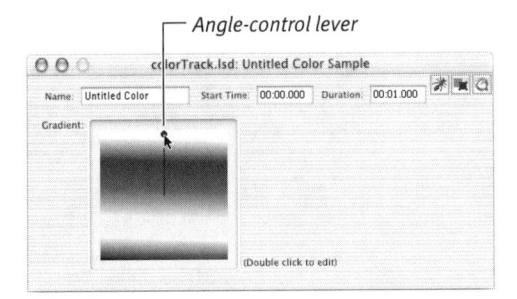

**Figure 6.13** The angle-control lever lets you change the alignment of a color track's gradient.

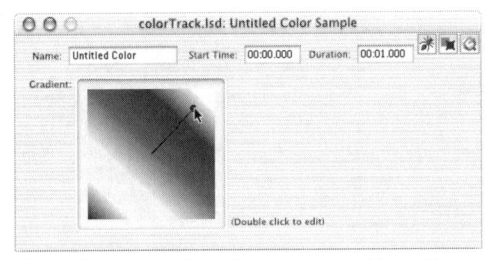

**Figure 6.14** As you drag the angle-control lever, the gradient's alignment changes.

# Basic Visual Tracks

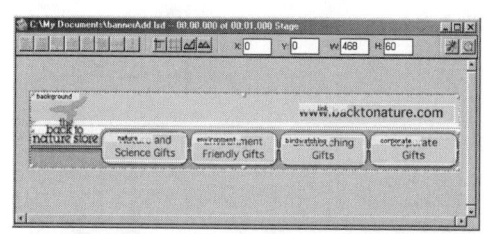

**Figure 6.15** The background of this QuickTime banner ad is a picture track, but all the hot spots on top are text tracks.

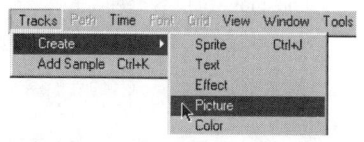

**Figure 6.16** To create a picture track, choose Tracks > Create > Picture.

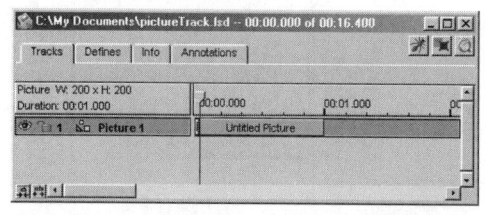

**Figure 6.17** A newly created picture track and sample.

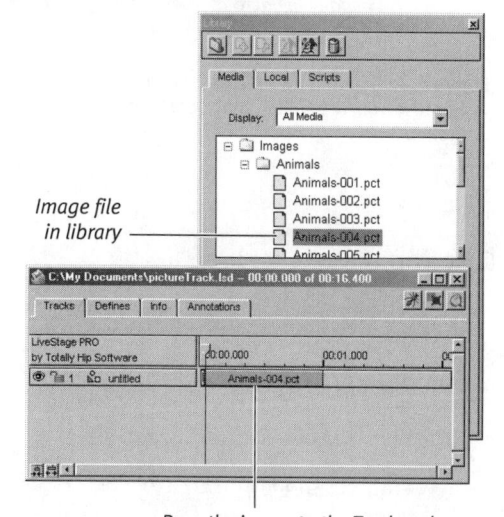

*Image file in library*

*Drag the image to the Tracks tab*

**Figure 6.18** To create a picture track quickly, drag an image to the Tracks tab from the library, Finder (Mac), or desktop (Windows).

## About Picture Tracks

Although a creative mind could find unlimited uses for picture tracks, these tracks typically are used for slide shows and background images (**Figure 6.15**). Picture tracks are slightly restricted in that each picture sample can hold only one image. If you need to display more than one still image at a time, you will have to create multiple picture tracks or use a sprite track (see Chapter 10, "Sprite Tracks").

### To create a picture track:

◆ Choose Tracks > Create > Picture (**Figure 6.16**).

A new picture track is created at the bottom of the Track list, and an empty picture sample is placed in the Timeline (**Figure 6.17**). The new picture sample is created at the default track dimensions of 200 square pixels.

*or*

Drag an image from the Finder (Mac), desktop (Windows), or library to the Tracks tab of the Project window (**Figure 6.18**).

A new picture track is created at the bottom of the Track list, and a sample containing the image is placed in the Timeline. When you drag an image to the Tracks tab, the new picture track is assigned the same dimensions as the source-image file.

Chapter 6

### To set or switch a picture-sample image:

1. In the Tracks tab, double-click a picture sample.

   The picture sample opens (**Figure 6.19**).

2. Drag an image file from the Finder (Mac), desktop (Windows), or library to the open picture sample (**Figure 6.20**).

   If the picture sample was empty, it is now populated with this new image. If the picture sample already contained an image, the old image is replaced with the new one.

### ✔ Tip

- To see a full-sized preview of the image in a picture track, double-click the image inside the picture sample.

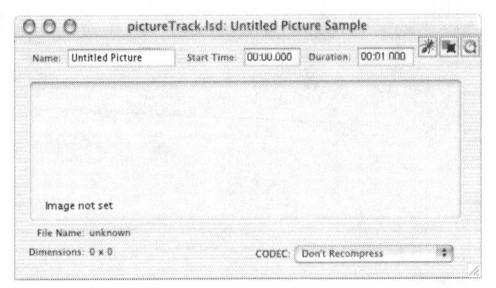

**Figure 6.19** When you create a picture track, its sample is empty, and a prompt in the bottom-left corner tells you that no image file has been set.

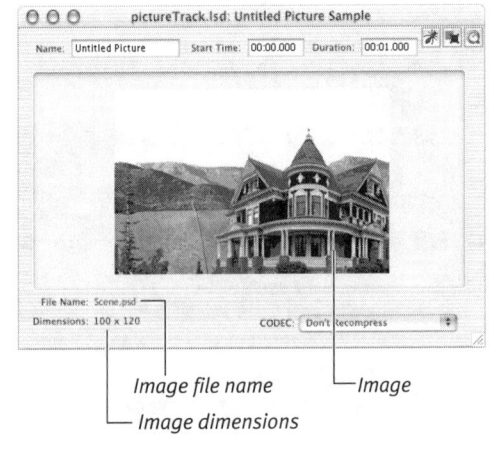

**Figure 6.20** To populate a picture sample, drag an image to it from the Finder (Mac), desktop (Windows), or library.

---

## Common Track Actions

With the exception of skin tracks, the following QScript actions can be used with any visual track in LiveStage, including color, picture, and external tracks:

`SetEnabled(True/False)`. Turns the track on or off.

`ToggleEnabled`. Switches the track's enabled status to the opposite of its current state.

`SetGraphicsModeTo(mode, red, green, blue)`. Sets a new graphics mode and control color.

`SetLayerTo(layer)`. Moves the track back and forth in the project's stacking order.

`MoveMatrixTo(x, y)`. Moves the track's top-left corner to the new (x, y) position.

Basic Visual Tracks

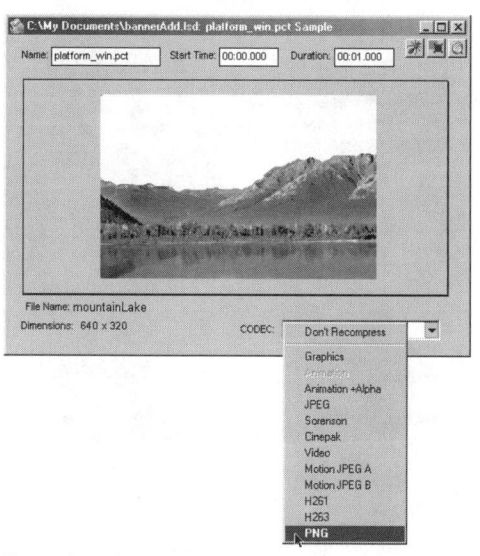

**Figure 6.21** The CODEC menu gives you access to several of QuickTime's compression codecs. For image compression choose either JPEG or PNG.

LiveStage supports many image formats, including uncompressed Photoshop images, which offer excellent quality but produce very large files. If you plan to distribute your movie over the Internet, you will need to compress all uncompressed images. Fortunately, the picture sample gives you access to many of QuickTime's compression codecs, which you can use to decrease image file size significantly.

### To compress a picture sample:

◆ In the picture sample, choose the appropriate compression codec from the CODEC pop-up menu in the bottom-right corner (**Figure 6.21**).

 You can choose any codec, but only two of them are well-suited for compressing still images: JPEG and PNG.

*continues on next page*

### Common Track Properties

With the exception of skin tracks, the following properties can be used with any visual track in LiveStage, including color, picture, and external tracks:

GetDuration. Returns the track's duration.

TrackEnabled. Returns the track's enabled status.

TrackHeight. Returns the track's height, in pixels.

TrackWidth. Returns the track's width, in pixels.

TrackLayer. Returns the track's drawing-layer value.

MouseHorizontal. Returns the pointer's current x coordinate.

MouseVertical. Returns the pointer's current y coordinate.

## ✔ Tips

- If your image has already been compressed in GIF, JPEG, or PNG format, do not recompress it. Whenever you compress an image file, compression artifacts occur that degrade the visual quality of your file. If you recompress a compressed image, these compression artifacts become more noticeable. Even worse, recompressing an image sometimes increases its file size.

- If you want to compress a Photoshop image with an 8-bit alpha channel, use the PNG codec. JPEG compression does *not* preserve an image's alpha channel. If you choose JPEG compression for an image with an alpha channel, the alpha channel is rendered white, and it obstructs any tracks below it (**Figure 6.22**).

*Original Photoshop file (88 KB)*

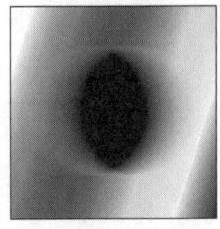

*Uncompressed (60 KB)*

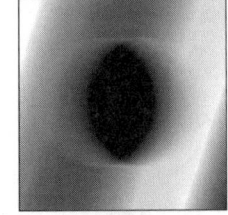

*PNG compression (8 KB)*

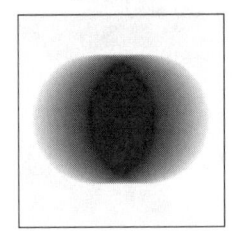

*JPEG compression (8 KB)*

**Figure 6.22** A series of photos showing a Photoshop file with an 8-bit alpha channel rendered over a gradient. The top-left picture shows the file in Photoshop. The top-right picture shows the Photoshop file over a gradient color track, uncompressed. The bottom-left picture shows the results of PNG compression, and the bottom-right picture uses JPEG compression.

# Basic Visual Tracks

## About Skin Tracks

Media skins were one of the most anticipated features of QuickTime 5, and LiveStage fully supports them. A *media skin* is a custom wrapper for your movie that lets you break out of the constricting QuickTime Player interface and make your movie any shape you want. With the advent of media skins, your movies no longer have to be rectangular; they can be ovals, hexagons, or whatever shape you like (**Figure 6.23**).

When you add a media skin to a movie, you create what is commonly called a *skinned movie*. To make a skinned movie, you must first design a window mask (**Figure 6.24**) and a drag mask (**Figure 6.25**) in a graphics application such as Totally Hip Software's WebPainter, or Adobe Photoshop. I will explain these mask types later in this chapter. For now, you need to know that a *window mask* defines which parts of the rectangular QuickTime window will be made transparent, and the *drag mask* defines the area that the viewer can select to drag the movie around the desktop.

*continues on next page*

**Figure 6.23** The "QT Viewer" pictured in this figure is a skinned movie. Skinned movies let you jump out of the standard QuickTime interface and display your content in unique ways.

**Figure 6.24** A window mask. Black areas of the window mask appear opaque; white areas are transparent.

**Figure 6.25** A drag mask. Black areas of the drag mask define regions that viewers can select to drag the movie around the screen. White areas cannot be selected; users click through them to interactive parts of the movie.

## Chapter 6

Skin tracks have a few limitations:

- You can use only one skin sample in your project. LiveStage will let you create more than one skin track or sample, but only the first one will be used.

- Both the window and drag masks must be 1-bit black-and-white images. Skin tracks do not support grayscale masks.

- Skin tracks must use still images. Moving or dynamic skins are not allowed.

- Only QuickTime Player 5 and later display skinned movies properly. If a skinned movie is opened in a Web browser or an older version of QuickTime, a black matte replaces the transparent areas of the skinned movie, and the movie is displayed in a normal rectangular window (**Figure 6.26**).

### To create a skin track:

- Choose Tracks > Create > Skin (**Figure 6.27**).

   A new skin track is created at the bottom of the Track list, and an empty skin sample is placed in the Timeline.

### ✔ Tips

- Skin tracks are created at a default size of 200 square pixels. Under most circumstances, you'll need to change the skin track's dimensions to match the dimensions of your movie.

- If you've skinned your movie, you should provide a wired Close button so viewers can close your movie. Create a sprite or Flash button, and place the following QScript action in the `Mouse Click` event handler:

   `CloseThisWindow`

*Normally transparent areas of the skinned movie are now black.*

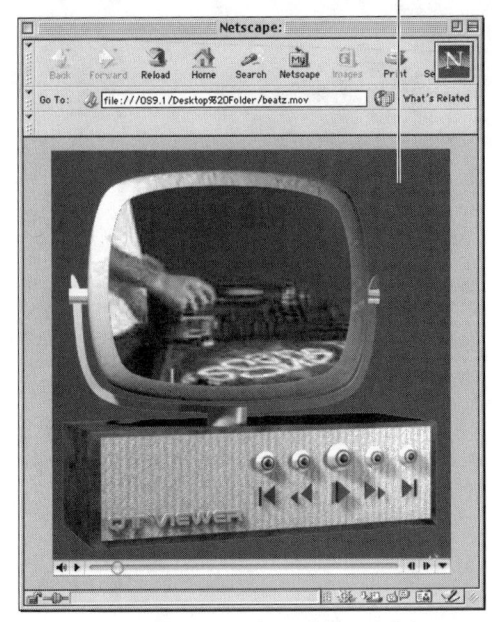

**Figure 6.26** A skinned movie played in a Web browser.

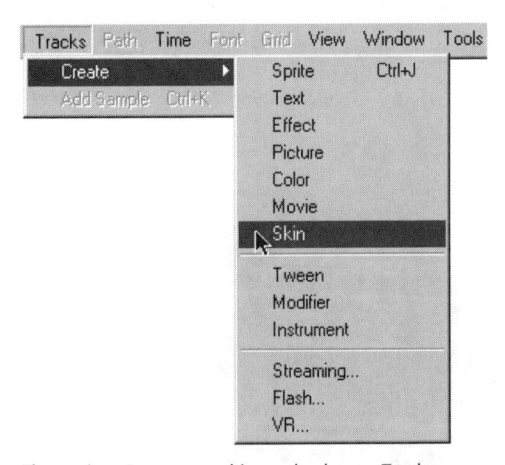

**Figure 6.27** To create a skin track, choose Tracks > Create > Skin.

Basic Visual Tracks

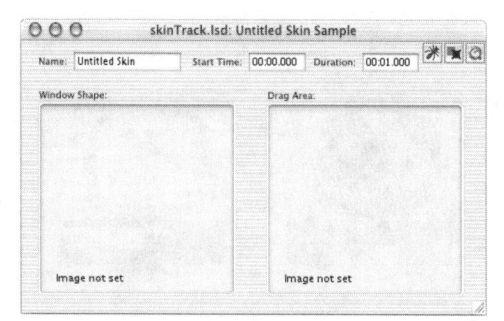

**Figure 6.28** An empty skin sample. No image has been set.

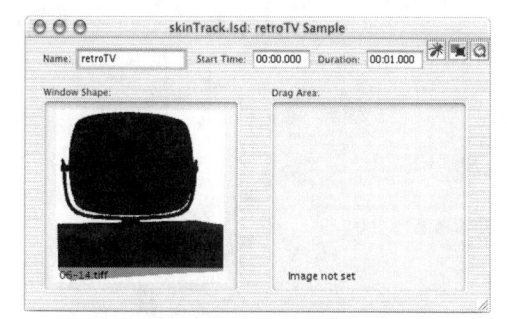

**Figure 6.29** To define which areas of your movie are transparent, drag a 1-bit black-and-white window mask into the Window Shape pane.

## Using window masks

A window mask is a 1-bit black-and-white image that defines which areas of the movie are visible in the final movie. The parts of your movie covered by the mask's black area are visible; parts covered by the white area are not visible.

### To set a window mask:

1. In the Tracks tab, double-click a skin sample.

   The skin sample opens, displaying two panes: Window Shape and Drag Area (**Figure 6.28**).

2. From the Finder (Mac), desktop (Windows), or library, drag the image you will use for your window mask to the Window Shape pane (**Figure 6.29**).

### ✔ Tip

- Window masks must have the exact same dimensions as your project. Stretched window masks sometimes create strange artifacts that mar your presentation.

ABOUT SKIN TRACKS

115

Chapter 6

## Using drag masks

A drag mask is a 1-bit black-and-white image that defines your movie's dragable regions—the areas you can select to drag the movie around your desktop. The drag mask's white parts allow mouse clicks to pass through to your movie's interactive components (buttons, sliders, and so on); the black zones serve as the dragable regions. Typically, the drag mask will be the same as your window mask, with white areas where your movie's interactive components appear.

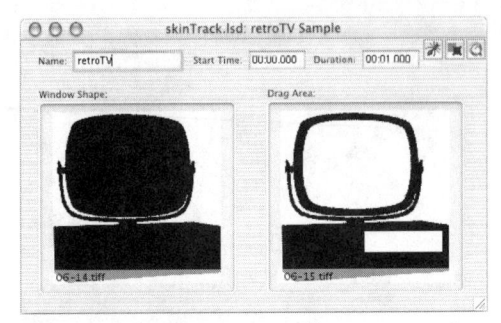

**Figure 6.30** The Drag Area pane allows you to set the drag mask for your skinned movie.

### To set a drag mask:

1. In the Tracks tab, double-click the skin sample.

   The skin sample opens.

2. From the Finder (Mac), desktop (Windows), or library, drag the image you will use for your drag mask to the Drag Area pane (**Figure 6.30**).

3. Click the Run Wired Movie button in the top-right corner of the skin sample (**Figure 6.31**).

   A skinned movie appears in the preview window (refer to Figure 6.23).

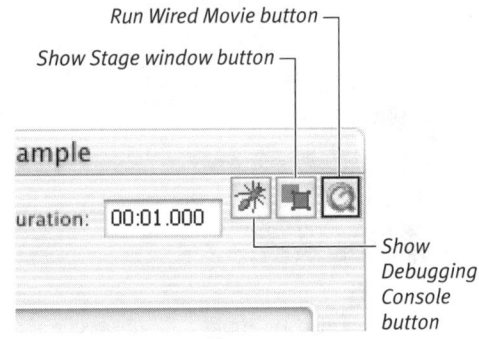

**Figure 6.31** To test your skinned movie, click the Run Wired Movie button at the top of the skin sample.

### ✔ Tip

- Make sure that the drag mask has the same dimensions as the window mask or your movie will not play correctly.

## About External Tracks

External tracks include video and sound tracks. To create the media for an external track, you must use a third-party application such as Apple's Final Cut Pro, Adobe's After Effects, or Digidesign's Pro Tools.

You cannot edit external tracks directly in LiveStage. These tracks do not have sample properties or a sample editor. Double-clicking an external track sample opens a media preview window that displays the track's content. Even though you can't edit this content, you can use QScript to control certain track properties, including volume and graphics modes.

**Figure 6.32** To preview the media content of an external track, double-click its sample in the Timeline.

### To create an external track:

◆ From the library, Finder (Mac) or desktop (Windows), drag a video or sound file to the Tracks tab.

A new external track is added to the bottom of the Track list. This technique is the only way to create an external track.

### To preview an external track:

◆ In the Tracks tab, double-click the external track's media sample.

A media preview window opens, displaying the external track's content (**Figure 6.32**).

# Chapter 6

## To change an external track sample's duration:

1. In the Timeline, position the pointer on the right edge of the external track sample (**Figure 6.33**).

   The pointer changes to a resize handle.

2. Drag until the sample is the appropriate duration (**Figure 6.34**).

## ✔ Tip

- When you change the duration of an external track, you change the rate at which it plays back. If you increase the duration of an external track, it will play back slower than normal. Conversely, if you decrease a track's duration, it will play back faster.

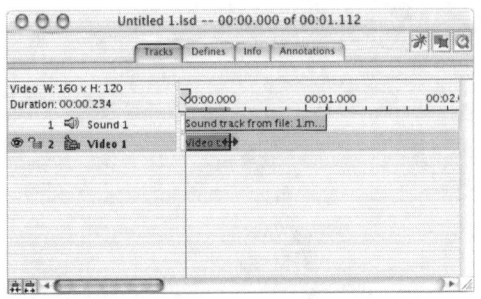

**Figure 6.33** The resize pointer appears when you move your pointer over the right end of an external track sample.

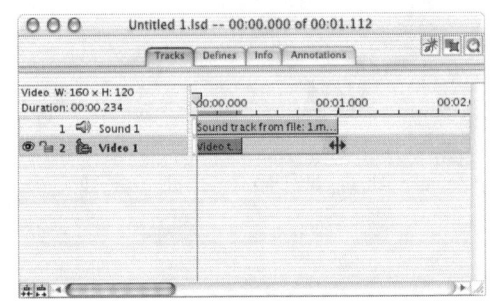

**Figure 6.34** Drag the resize pointer and stretch your external track until it is the right length.

# 7

# MOVIE TRACKS

Movie tracks let you link separate multi-track QuickTime movies in your project and manipulate them as though they are just one track. When you use a movie track to link other movies in your project, the project becomes a *container*, or *parent* movie, and the movies linked to it are called *child* movies. Together, they make a *MIAM* (Movie in a Movie) project. Because MIAM projects can contain multiple movies that can operate independently of each other, they are great for creating complex, non-linear effects.

Every MIAM project contains a parent movie, which contains one or more movie tracks. The movie tracks hold references to child movies that can be loaded into the parent movie upon request. Because the child movies are merely borrowed by—and not part of—the parent movie, they can play along their own internal Timelines. If the parent movie is stopped, the child movie may keep playing, and vice versa.

This chapter covers all aspects of using movie tracks, including embedding child movies directly in a movie track, loading child movies from a URL, and using QScript to switch between multiple child movies in the same movie track.

# About Movie Tracks

Like any other track in LiveStage, movie tracks contain samples, which in turn hold media. But unlike other tracks, movie samples can hold any type of media supported by QuickTime, from entire movies to .GIFs, MP3 files, or even plain-text files.

If you open a movie sample, you will see that it is divided into three sections (**Figure 7.1**). The top half contains several checkboxes that control child-movie playback. The panel in the bottom-left corner lists all the child movies that are in the movie sample. If you've selected a child movie in the Movies list, the preview area in the bottom-right corner displays it.

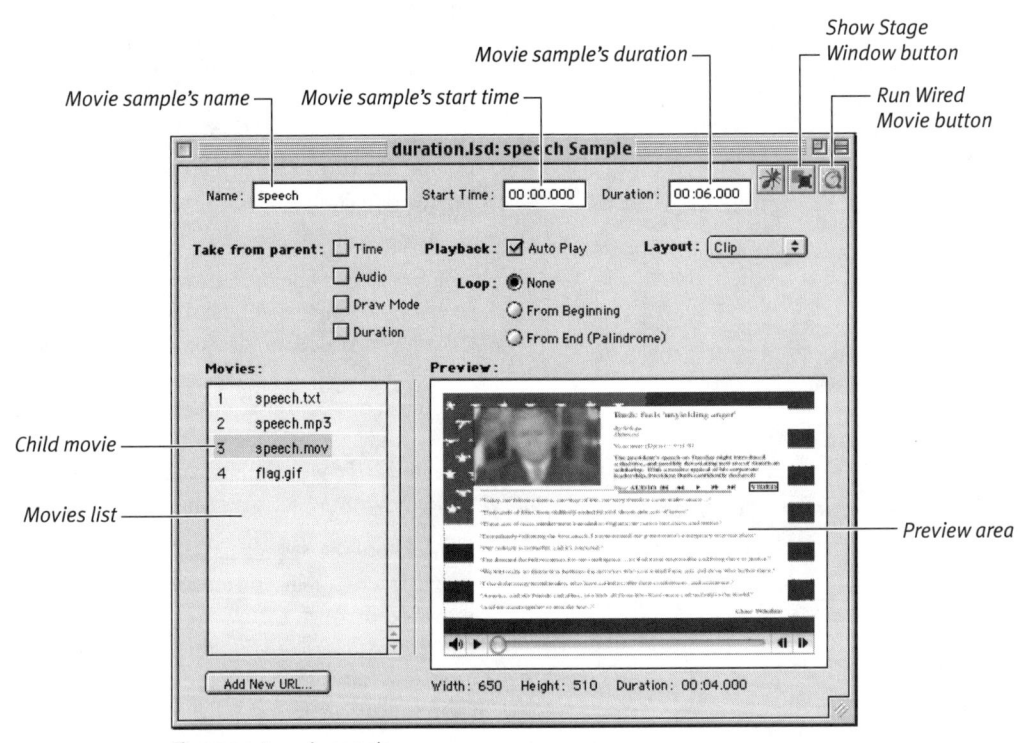

**Figure 7.1** A movie sample.

## Movie Tracks

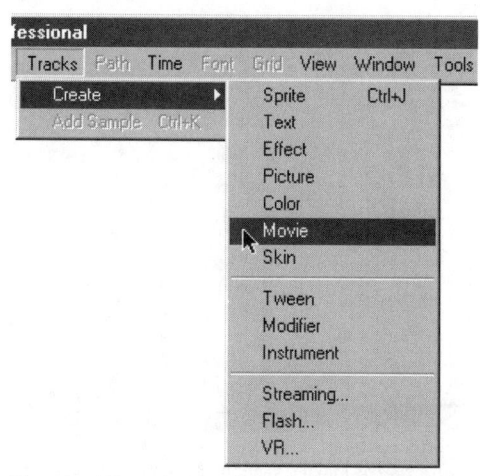

**Figure 7.2** To create a movie track, choose Tracks > Create > Movie.

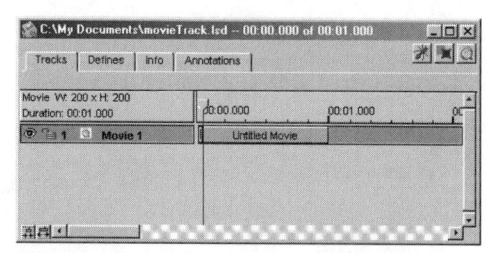

**Figure 7.3** When you create a new movie track, an untitled movie track and sample are placed in the Tracks tab.

### To create a movie track:

◆ Choose Tracks > Create > Movie (**Figure 7.2**).

A new movie track is created at the bottom of the Track list, and an empty movie sample is placed in the Tracks tab's Timeline (**Figure 7.3**).

### ✔ Tip

■ To find out whether a file can be embedded in a movie track, try dropping it on the QuickTime Player application icon. If the file opens in QuickTime, you can embed it in a movie track.

ABOUT MOVIE TRACKS

121

## About Child Movies

Creating a movie track is only the first step in making a MIAM project. Next, you must populate the track by embedding one or more child movies in it (**Figure 7.4**).

There are three ways to add a child movie to a movie track: you can embed it directly in the movie sample, load it from an Internet URL, or load it from a relative path. If you embed the child movie directly in the sample, its content becomes part of the MIAM project and is saved inside the parent movie file. This technique can make movies very large and, thus, inappropriate for Internet delivery.

When you load a child movie from an Internet URL or relative path, the child movie is never actually part of the parent movie. In fact, the child movie is loaded into the parent movie only upon request. This section explains how to use each method to add child movies to your movie tracks.

### Embedding child movies directly in a movie sample

When you embed a child movie directly in a movie sample, the child movie becomes part of the sample, just like media in other track samples. When the MIAM project is exported to a QuickTime movie file, all sample media—including child movies—are collected inside the parent movie file. As a result, the child movies add to the parent movie's file size. This problem isn't serious if the child movies are fairly small, but if they are larger, their summed file sizes quickly balloon the parent movie into a Web zeppelin that can't glide down the Internet pipeline efficiently.

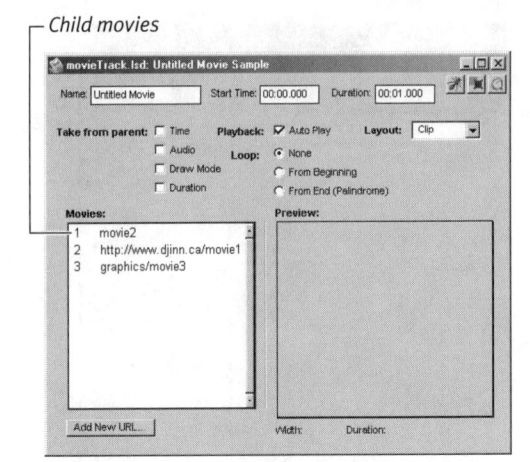

**Figure 7.4** The Movies section of the movie sample lists the child movies that are embedded in the sample. The top child movie is embedded directly in the sample; the second child is referenced by an absolute URL, and the third is referenced by a relative path.

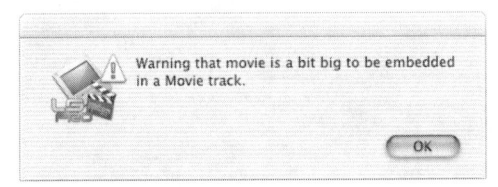

**Figure 7.5** Directly embedding child movies with file sizes of between 100 and 400 kilobytes results in this warning dialog.

# Movie Tracks

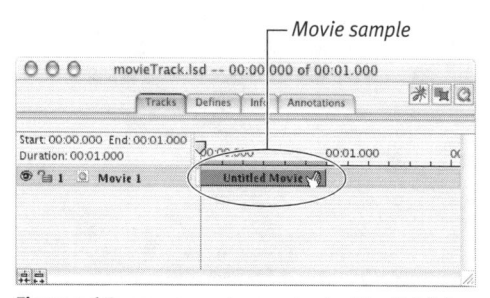

**Figure 7.6** To open a movie sample, double-click it in the Timeline.

**Figure 7.7** An open movie sample. This sample belongs to a new movie track and therefore has no movies in its Movies list.

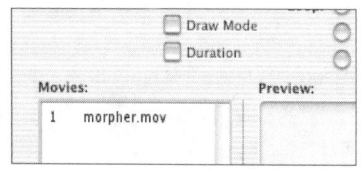

**Figure 7.8** The child movie's filename appears in the Movies list, indicating that it has been embedded in the parent movie.

As a general rule, you should not embed child movies that are larger than 100 KB. You can embed child movies with file sizes between 100 KB and 400 KB, but this practice is strongly discouraged, and attempting to do so will result in the warning dialog pictured in **Figure 7.5**. Don't even bother trying to embed a child move that's larger than 400 KB; LiveStage does not allow you to do so. If your child movie is larger than 100 KB, load it from a URL instead.

## To embed a child movie directly:

1. In the Tracks tab of the Project window, double-click the movie sample (**Figure 7.6**).

   The movie sample opens (**Figure 7.7**).

2. From the library, Finder (Mac), or desktop (Windows), drag a movie file directly into the Movies list.

   The movie becomes a child movie and is embedded in the parent movie. Its filename appears in the Movies list (**Figure 7.8**).

## ✔ Tips

- The Movies list runs down the left side of the movie-sample window and contains a list of all the child movies associated with that sample. If you've just created the movie track, there will be no child movies in this list.

- If you're having a hard time dragging a file into the Movies list, open it in QuickTime Player and resave it by choosing File > Save.

**ABOUT CHILD MOVIES**

123

## Loading child movies from a URL

A URL is an address that shows LiveStage how to find a child movie located on the Web. When you load a child movie from a URL, you supply the parent movie a reference to a child movie that's located on a Web server. The child movie is like a rented videotape plugged into a VHS player. It is never part of the parent movie; instead, it is loaded into the movie track upon request.

### To load a child movie from the Internet:

1. In the Tracks tab of the Project window, double-click the movie track's sample.

   The movie sample opens.

2. Click the Add New URL button (**Figure 7.9**).

   The Edit Movie URL dialog opens (**Figure 7.10**).

3. Enter the URL to be used as a reference to the child movie (**Figure 7.11**).

   You must be sure to enter the full path to the child movie. If the child movie is stored on an HTTP server, for example, make sure that you enter the pathname as follows:

   http://www.yourDomain.com/yourMovie.mov

   If you do not enter the http:// part of the pathname, QuickTime will not understand that it must go out and search the Internet to find the child movie; as a result, it will not be able to locate the child movie file.

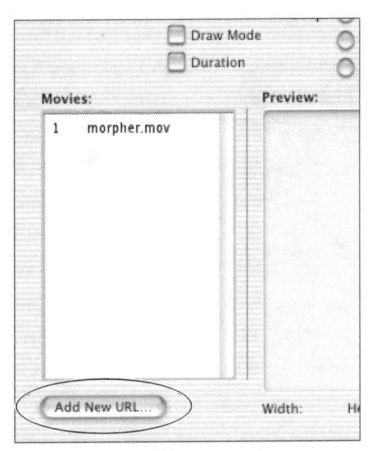

**Figure 7.9** The Add New URL button.

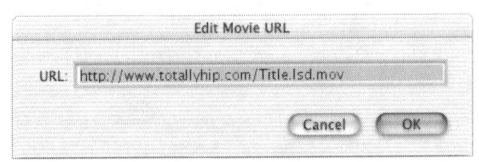

**Figure 7.10** The Edit Movie URL dialog lets you add a reference to a child movie that's stored on a Web server. This child movie is not embedded in your movie but is loaded by your movie when called.

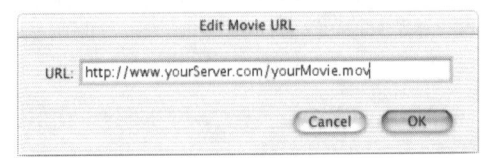

**Figure 7.11** Absolute URL references must include the http:// prefix; otherwise, LiveStage will not know that it must load your movie from a remote Web server.

Movie Tracks

4. Click OK.

   The Edit Movie URL dialog closes, and the child movie's URL is added to the movie sample's Movies list (**Figure 7.12**).

### ✔ Tip

- You can also add streaming movies off of a streaming (RTSP) server into a movie sample. Just be sure to preface the movie's URL with `rtsp://` instead of `http://`.

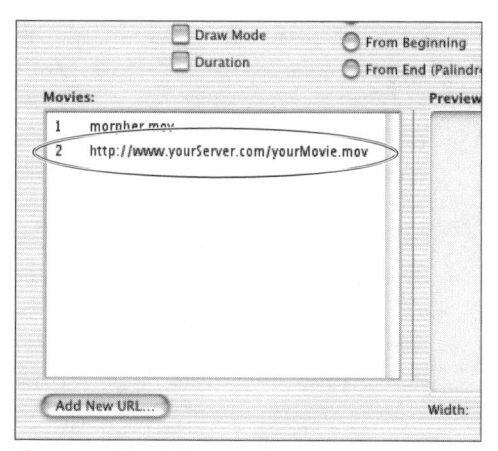

**Figure 7.12** The child movie's absolute URL is added to the Movies list.

---

## Updating CD-ROM Movies

If you are delivering your MIAM project on a CD-ROM, setting the project to download child movies from the Internet is a convenient way of keeping its content current. Perhaps your CD-ROM movie contains information that would benefit from periodic updating, such as a stock quotation or a news section. Unfortunately, after the CD-ROM is distributed, there is no way for you to change or update its content. You can get around this problem by using an absolute URL to link the CD-ROM parent movie to a child movie on the Internet. When the CD-ROM-based parent movie is opened, it reaches out to the Internet, finds the new child movie, and updates automatically.

Child movies loaded from an absolute URL also benefit MIAM projects that are distributed over the Internet. If you reference all your child movies by absolute URLs, movies saved from the Internet to a viewer's hard disk will still play correctly. When the parent movie is launched, it looks at the child movie's URL, and then searches the Internet for it. (Both examples work only if the viewer is connected to the Internet, of course.)

ABOUT CHILD MOVIES

## Loading child movies from a relative path

Relative paths in MIAM projects work much the same way as relative paths in HTML links, so if you have ever written an HTML page, you will have no problem understanding how to establish a relative path between parent and child movies.

A relative path directs the parent movie to child movies that are in the same directory as the parent movie or in a directory close to the parent movie on the same hard disk, CD-ROM, or Web server (**Table 7.1**).

Like HTML links, relative paths can include directory names. You can use a relative path to point to child movies in subdirectories of the parent movie's directory or in directories filed above the parent movie. A relative path could point to a child movie that is up one directory and then down one directory from the parent movie, like this:

../down1/childMovie.mov

In this relative path, a slash (/) separates directories and filenames, and the double dots (..) tell the parent movie to jump up one directory. For more information on creating relative paths, see Table 7.1.

Relative paths make your MIAM project portable. If you intend to upload your project to a Web server or publish it on a CD-ROM, relative paths provide a convenient way of keeping your child movies gathered together and properly organized. Just make sure that you maintain the same hierarchy of directories you used while creating the project.

Table 7.1

### Relative Pathnames

| RELATIVE URL | DESCRIPTION |
| --- | --- |
| ChildMovie.mov | The child movie is in the same directory as the parent. |
| Library/childMovie.mov | The child movie is in a directory named Library. The directory named Library is in the same directory as the parent movie. |
| ../childMovie.mov | The child movie is in a directory that's one level up from the parent movie. |
| ../Library/childMovie.mov | The child movie is in a directory named Library. The directory named Library is one level up from the parent movie. |

## Movie Tracks

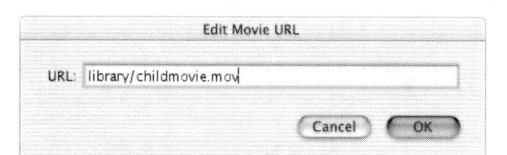

**Figure 7.13** A relative path shows the parent movie how to locate and load a child movie that's saved on the same Web server, CD-ROM, or hard disk. The path is written exactly the same way as an HTML relative link.

**Figure 7.14** The child movie resides in the same directory as the parent movie, so the relative path is `childMovie.mov`.

**Figure 7.15** The child movie is in a directory named Library. The directory named Library is in the same directory as the parent movie, so the relative path is `Library/childMovie.mov`.

### To load a child movie by using a relative path:

1. In the Tracks tab of the Project window, double-click the movie track's sample.
   The movie sample opens.

2. Click the Add New URL button.
   The Edit Movie URL dialog opens.

3. Enter the relative path that you're using to reference the child movie (**Figure 7.13**).

   The relative path must be relative to the parent movie; otherwise, the child movie will not load. If a child movie named childMovie.mov resides in the same directory as its parent movie, for example, the relative path is simply the child movie's filename (**Figure 7.14**).

   If the child movie rests in a sub-directory, named Library, of the directory containing the parent movie, the relative path is `Library/childMovie.mov` (**Figure 7.15**).

4. Click OK.
   The Edit Movie URL dialog closes, and the relative path to the child movie is added to the movie sample's Movies list.

### ✔ Tip

- When you distribute your movie (by uploading it to a server or placing it on a CD-ROM), be sure to maintain exactly the same hierarchy of directories that you used in your relative path references. If you fail to do this, your parent movie will not be able to find, load, or display the child movies.

**ABOUT CHILD MOVIES**

## Previewing a child movie

The preview area on the right side of the movie sample displays the child movie selected in the Movies list, preserving any interactivity it may contain.

### To preview a child movie:

◆ In the Movies list, select a child movie (**Figure 7.16**).

 The child movie is loaded into the preview area.

### ✔ Tips

- If you used a relative path as a reference to a child movie, the preview area will not work.

- The child movie's width and height are displayed at the bottom of the preview area. To preserve the child movie's dimensions, use these width and height values as the movie track's dimensions.

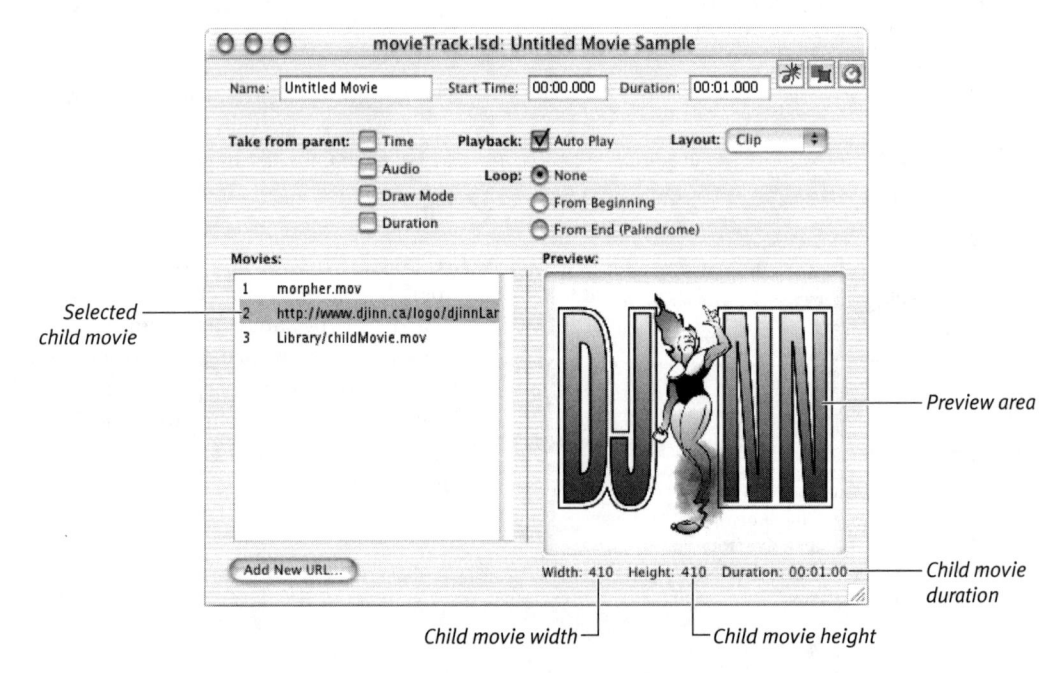

**Figure 7.16** The preview area on the right side of the movie sample displays a fully interactive preview of any child movie selected in the Movies list.

# Movie Tracks

**Figure 7.17** If you position your pointer above the bar separating the Movies list from the preview area, it changes to a resize pointer.

**Figure 7.18** Drag the bar until the preview area is as wide as needed.

## To change the width of the preview area:

1. Position your pointer above the bar separating the preview area from the Movies list (**Figure 7.17**).

   The pointer changes into the resize pointer.

2. Drag the bar to the left or right (**Figure 7.18**).

   If you drag the bar to the left, the preview area widens. If you drag the bar to the right, the preview area shrinks.

### Testing MIAM Projects

If you've embedded your child movies directly in a movie sample or used URLs to point to them, previewing your movie is not a problem. Simply click the Run Wired Movie button in the top-right corner of the Project window. The preview movie functions just as it will when compiled, allowing you to test the movie tracks and ensure that their child movies load and play properly.

If you've used relative paths to point to child movies, you can still preview your MIAM projects, but you must take extra care to make sure all your child movies are in the correct place on your hard disk. When you preview a movie by clicking the Run Wired Movie button, a temporary movie file is created in the same directory as the LiveStage project file. For the length of time that the preview is running, this temporary movie becomes the parent movie. As a result, all relative paths must lead from this temporary movie to the child movies. If they do not, the child movies will fail to load in the preview.

Fortunately, it's easy to make sure that your relative paths will always work. Simply collect each child movie in the same folder as the LiveStage project file. The path to each child movie is now nothing more than the child movie's filename. When you export the parent movie to a QuickTime file, place it in the same folder as the child movies. All relative paths will work, and you can upload the entire folder to a Web server or publish it to a CD-ROM.

ABOUT CHILD MOVIES

129

# About Slaving Child Movies

By default, a child movie's playback is unhindered by the parent movie's playback. The child movie's duration, for example, is unaffected by the parent movie's duration. In fact, a child movie can be longer than the parent movie containing it. The parent movie might be only one second long, but the child movie could be one minute or even several minutes long.

Under certain circumstances, you may want to alter this default behavior and slave the child movies to the parent. When you *slave* the child movies to the parent movie, you force them to play back with settings adopted from the parent. If you need one slider that controls the volume of every child movie that's loaded into the movie track, for example, slave the child movies' audio to their containing movie track. As you raise and lower the movie track's volume, the volume of the currently loaded child movie follows suit.

The Take from Parent section of the movie sample holds four checkboxes that let you slave a child movie to its parent: Time, Audio, Draw Mode, and Duration (**Figure 7.19**).

## Using the Time checkbox

When the Time checkbox is checked, the child movie's rate of playback is tied to that of the parent. If the parent movie plays, the child movie also plays. Similarly, if the parent movie is stopped or played in reverse, the child movie is also stopped or played in reverse. This process is often called *time slaving*.

### To time-slave a child movie:

◆ In the Take from Parent section of the movie sample, check the Time checkbox (**Figure 7.20**).

The child movie plays back at the same rate as the parent movie.

*Take from Parent section*

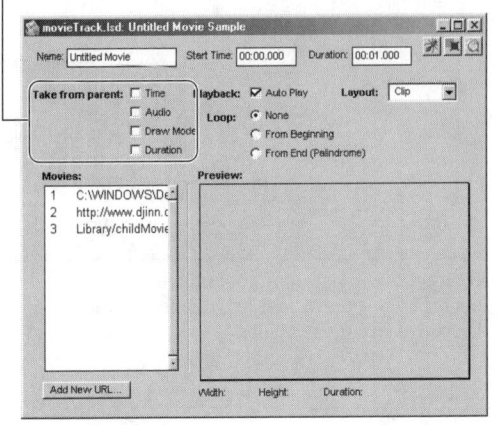

**Figure 7.19** The Take from Parent section of the movie sample lets you slave a child movie's rate of playback, audio settings, graphics mode, and duration to its parent movie.

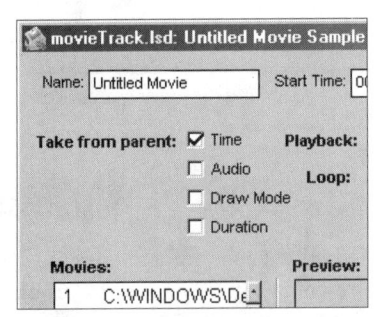

**Figure 7.20** If you check the Time checkbox, the child movie's rate of playback is governed by the parent movie. If the parent movie plays, so does the child.

## Using the Audio checkbox

When the Audio checkbox is checked, the child movie's volume and pan settings are defined by the volume and pan settings of its movie track.

### To slave a child movie's audio settings:

1. In the Take from Parent section of the movie sample, check the Audio checkbox (**Figure 7.21**).

   The child movie assumes the same volume and pan settings as the movie track containing it. The next step is to set the movie track's volume.

2. In the Tracks tab, double-click the movie track's header.

   The Track Properties window opens, displaying the Track tab (**Figure 7.22**).

3. Enter a new value in the Volume text box (**Figure 7.23**).

   Possible values range from 0 (silent) to 256 (full volume). By default, the volume value is set to 256. When the movie plays, the child movie plays at the volume you set for the movie track.

### ✔ Tip

- The volume value you assign to a movie track sets its volume relative to other tracks in the movie. If you use QuickTime to raise or lower the volume of the entire movie, this relative volume relationship is preserved; quieter tracks will always be quieter.

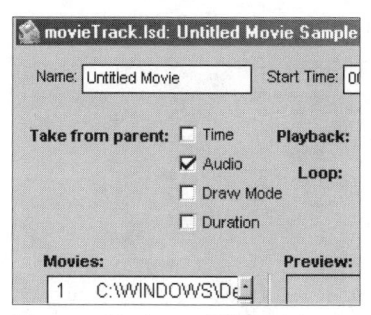

**Figure 7.21** To slave a child movie's audio to the setting of the movie track containing it, check the Audio checkbox.

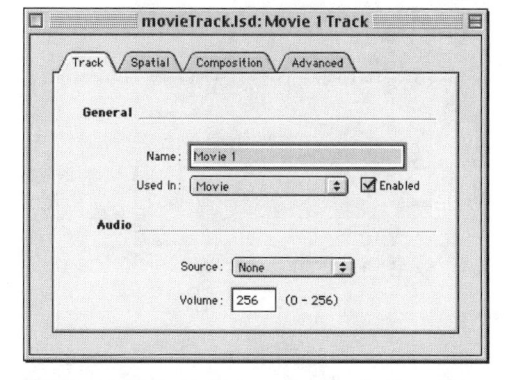

**Figure 7.22** Movie tracks have an extra Audio section in the Track tab; otherwise, their track properties are exactly the same as those of any other visual track.

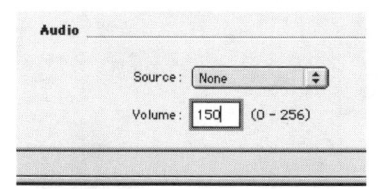

**Figure 7.23** If you checked the Audio checkbox in the movie sample's Take from Parent section, the volume you set for your movie track will affect every child movie it contains.

## Using the Draw Mode checkbox

When the Draw Mode checkbox is checked, the child movie's graphics mode reflects the graphics mode set for its parent movie track.

This option does not work with QuickTime up to the last version released when this book was written (5.0.2).

### To slave a child movie's graphics mode:

◆ In the Take from Parent section of the movie sample, check the Draw Mode checkbox (**Figure 7.24**).

The child movie's graphics mode mirrors that of its parent movie track.

### ✔ Tip

■ Selecting this option will crash QuickTime versions 4.1.2 and earlier.

## Using the Duration checkbox

When the Duration checkbox is checked, the child movie reduces or expands in duration to match the length of its parent movie sample. If the parent movie sample is shorter than the child movie, the child is condensed and consequently plays faster. Conversely, if the movie sample is longer than the child movie, the child is stretched and plays more slowly.

This option does not work with QuickTime up to the last version released when this book was written (5.0.2).

### To slave a child movie's duration:

◆ In the Take from Parent section of the movie sample, select the Duration checkbox (**Figure 7.25**).

The child movie's duration expands or contracts to match the duration of its parent movie sample.

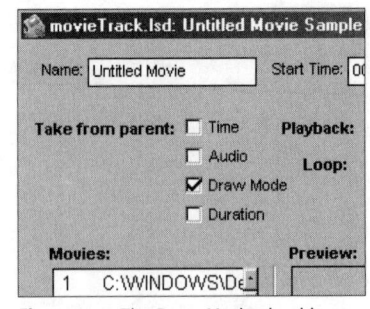

**Figure 7.24** The Draw Mode checkbox.

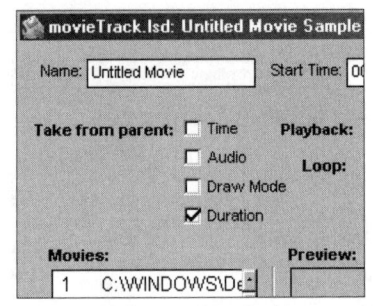

**Figure 7.25** The Duration checkbox.

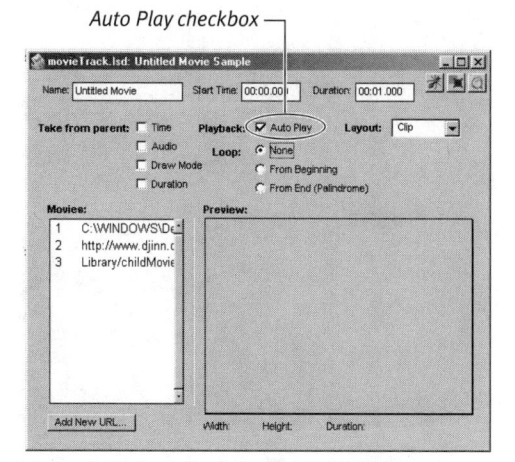

**Figure 7.26** Check the Auto Play checkbox to make your child movies start playing as soon as they are loaded by the parent movie.

# About MIAM Playback Parameters

In Chapter 5, "Setting Movie Properties," you learned how to make a movie auto start and loop. You can set a child movie to auto start and/or loop in much the same way by selecting the appropriate settings in the movie sample's Playback and Loop sections. But be warned—these sections will work only if you have *not* checked the Time checkbox in the Take from Parent section. The Time checkbox overrides these settings and slaves the child movie to its parent's playback rate.

## Using auto start

When you set a child movie to play automatically, it begins playing as soon as the parent movie loads it. This setting is particularly useful if you are using a child movie to play background music, as the background music will start immediately, even before the viewer clicks Play on the main movie.

### To auto start a child movie:

◆ In the Playback section of the movie sample, check the Auto Play checkbox (**Figure 7.26**).

The child movie plays as soon as it is loaded into the parent movie.

Chapter 7

## Setting a child movie to loop

Child movies normally play through to the end and then stop. If you set a loop value, however, the child movie continues playing indefinitely or until it is paused. A child movie can be set to loop in one of three ways:

**None.** The child movie plays to the end and stops. No looping occurs.

**From Beginning.** The child movie plays to the end and then starts replaying from the beginning, looping continuously until playback is halted.

**From End (Palindrome).** The child movie plays to the end and then plays in reverse until it reaches the beginning, where it reverses direction again. The child movie loops continuously until playback is halted.

### To loop a child movie:

◆ In the Loop section of the movie sample, choose the appropriate radio button (**Figure 7.27**).

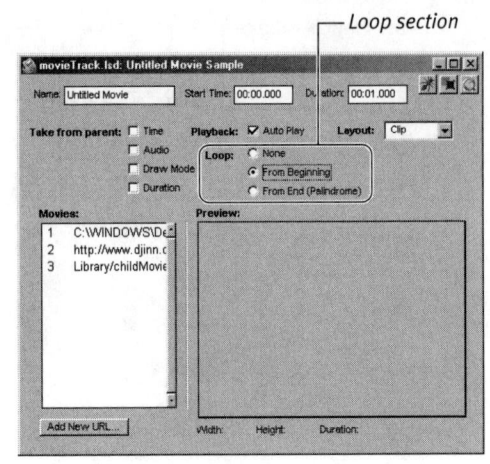

**Figure 7.27** To loop a child movie, choose a radio button in the movie sample's Loop section.

## Movie Tracks

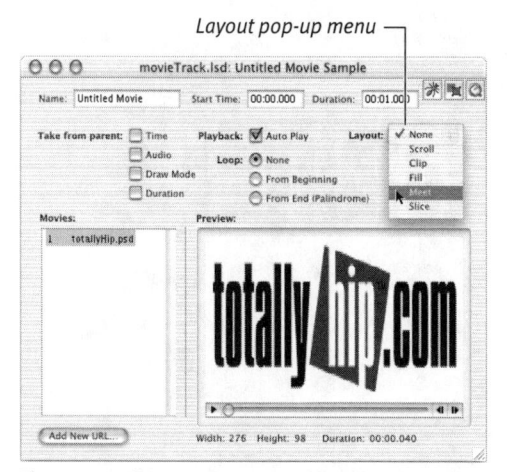

**Figure 7.28** The Layout menu settings alter the size of your child movies so that they fit within the movie track's dimensions.

**Figure 7.29** None and Fill stretch the four corners of the child movie to meet the four corners of the movie track containing it.

## About the Layout Pop-Up Menu

Some of your child movies may have different dimensions from the movie track that contains them. In this case, you need to tell the movie track how to display those improperly sized movies. To do so, choose a setting from the movie sample's Layout pop-up menu (**Figure 7.28**):

**None** and **Fill.** Both settings scale the child movie to match the dimensions of its containing movie track. Choosing one of these settings may warp the child movie's aspect ratio, causing it to appear stretched and/or compressed (**Figure 7.29**).

**Scroll.** As of QuickTime 5.0.2, the Scroll Layout setting has not been implemented. Until such time as that feature is implemented, the Scroll setting does exactly the same thing as the Clip setting.

*continues on next page*

**Clip.** The Clip setting does not resize the child at all. If the child movie is smaller than the movie track, blank space will show at the bottom and/or right edges of the child movie. If the child movie is bigger than the movie track, it will be clipped. Areas of the child movie that extend below and/or to the right of the movie track will not be visible (**Figure 7.30**).

**Meet.** The child movie is resized proportionally so that it just fits within the dimensions of the movie track, though blank spaces may be visible at the bottom and/or right edges of the child movie (**Figure 7.31**).

**Slice.** The child movie is resized proportionately so that it fills the movie track. Some areas of the child movie may be clipped off (**Figure 7.32**).

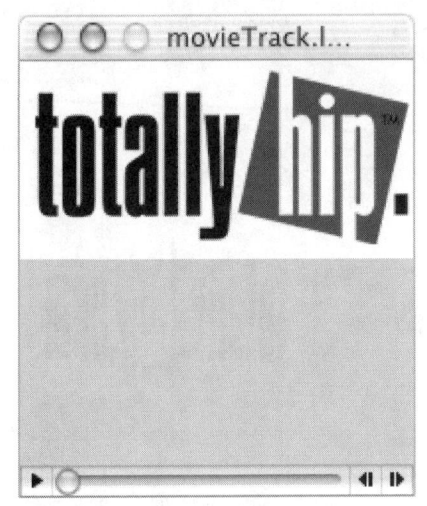

**Figure 7.30** When you choose Scroll or Clip, the child movie is cut to the dimensions of the movie track.

**Figure 7.31** When you choose Meet, the child movie is resized proportionally so that all of it fits within the movie track.

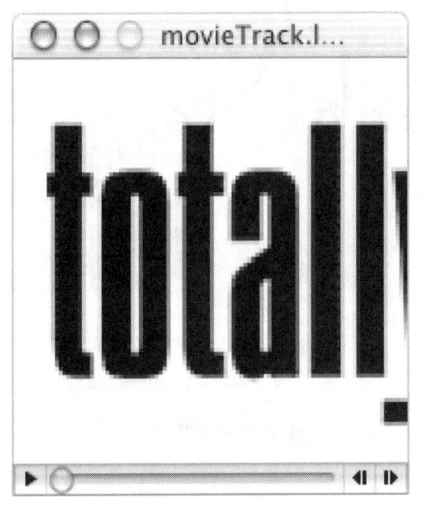

**Figure 7.32** When you choose Slice, the child movie is resized proportionally so that it fills the movie track.

# Movie Tracks

## About Loading Child Movies

When you embed more than one child movie in a movie track, by default only the top child movie is displayed. The other child movies simply lurk in the wings, waiting to be loaded by the parent. For example, movie tracks make the perfect screen for an online TV that lets viewers choose among several video files (**Figure 7.33**). By default, the TV loads the top child movie from the Movies list. When the viewer selects a new video file, that video jumps into the parent movie and replaces the default one. Loading and unloading child movies lets viewers change channels as they watch your movie.

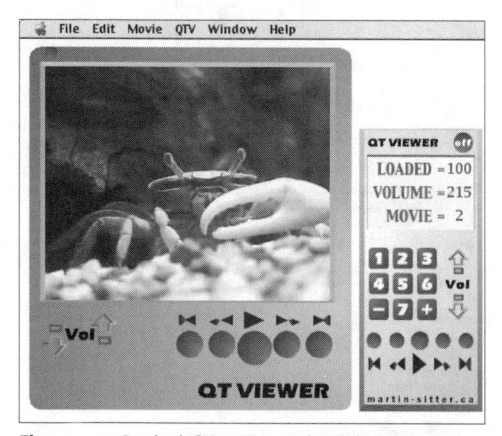

**Figure 7.33** On the left is a TV; on the right is a remote control that lets viewers switch channels and control playback. The TV screen is actually a movie track that holds seven child movies, loaded by the seven numbered buttons on the remote control.

If you look at a Movies list, you will see a series of numbers running down its left side (**Figure 7.34**). These numbers are the child movies' ID numbers. Each child movie has a distinct ID number, which you can use to load that movie with the `LoadChildMovie(ID)` QScript.

This section assumes that you have at least a basic understanding of how to make a working sprite button. If you do not know how to make a sprite button, read Chapter 10, "Sprite Tracks."

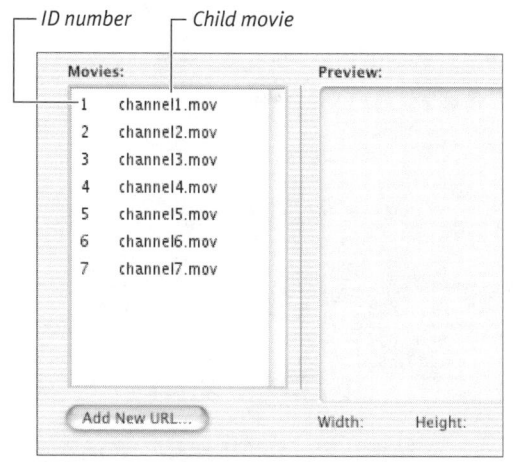

**Figure 7.34** ID numbers identify child movies in the Movies list.

## To load a child movie:

1. Create a sprite button.

   To learn how to create a sprite button, see Chapter 10, "Sprite Tracks."

2. Open the button's script editor (**Figure 7.35**).

3. Attach the following QScript to a `Mouse Click` event handler (**Figure 7.36**):

   `ChildMovieTrackNamed`
   → `("YourMovieTrack").`
   → `LoadChildMovie(ID)`

   "YourMovieTrack" is the name of the movie track containing the child movies. ID is the ID number of the child movie you want to load.

   When the sprite button is clicked, the child movie with the specified ID number replaces the currently loaded child movie.

### ✔ Tip

- Although you attached the `LoadChildMovie(ID)` to a `Mouse Click` event handler in the preceding exercise, you can place it in any event handler according to your needs.

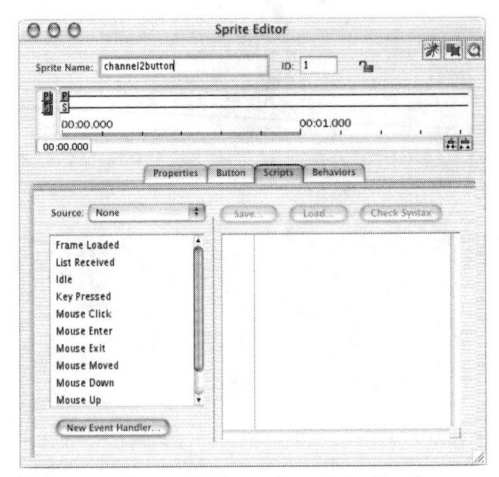

**Figure 7.35** Pictured is the sprite script editor for a sprite button. To load a new child movie, you must write a QScript in a scriptable track.

*Loads child movie of ID number 2*
*This child movie is loaded*

**Figure 7.36** When the sprite button is clicked, the QScript is executed. The movie track named "yourMovieTrack" loads the second child movie contained in its Movies list.

## Child Movie Target Specifiers

You can use the following QScripts to target child movies:

ChildMovieTrackNamed("name"). When you use this target specifier, the parent movie first locates the named movie track and then targets whatever child movie is currently loaded into that movie track: Please note that the name you enter is the name of the movie track, not the child movie. To find the movie track's name, look at its track header in the Track list. Example:

ChildMovieTrackNamed("movieTrack1").StartPlaying

ChildMovieTrackOfIndex(index). This target specifier works exactly the same way as the preceding one but uses the movie track's index number instead of its name. The movie track's index number is located in its track header. Example:

ChildMovieTrackOfIndex(2).GoToTime(00:06.300)

ChildMovieNamed("name"). The parent movie searches through all currently loaded child movies and targets the one with the tag name matching the name that you enter as a target. For this target specifier to work, you must supply tag names for your child movies. (To learn more about tag names, see Chapter 5, "Setting Movie Properties.") Example:

ChildMovieNamed("myChild").SetRateTo(3)

ChildMovieOfID(ID). The parent movie searches through all currently loaded child movies and targets the one with the tag ID matching the one you enter as a target. For this target specifier to work, you must supply tag IDs for your child movies. Example:

ChildMovieOfID(ID).StartPlaying

# TEXT TRACKS

Most people are drawn to QuickTime's immense power in displaying video and sound, and as a result, they often overlook text tracks. For those who take the time to learn how to use text tracks, a whole new dimension of QuickTime authoring opens.

Text tracks are perfectly suited for displaying character-based information. You can use them to create sentences, such as the subtitles that run across the bottom of a video, or even entire pages of paragraphed text.

Text tracks are also scriptable and can respond to viewer interaction. Interactive sections of text tracks are called *hotspots*, and they function just like hyperlinks in an HTML page. You can use them to link to other documents or even wire (script) them to control the playback of your movie.

This chapter covers formatting text, animating text to make it scroll, creating hotspots, and using chapter tracks.

# Chapter 8

## To create a text track:

1. In the Project window, select the Tracks tab (**Figure 8.1**).

    At the top of the screen, the Tracks menu becomes active.

2. Choose Tracks > Create > Text (**Figure 8.2**).

    A new text track is created, and a default text sample is placed in the Timeline.

The text field functions just like any other simple text editor. You can enter text with multiple spaces between characters, as well as carriage returns and tabs. If a line of text extends beyond the boundary of the text track, it will wrap around to the next line; otherwise, the text in your final movie will look just like it does in the text field.

## To enter text:

1. In the Tracks tab, double-click a text sample (**Figure 8.3**).

    The text sample opens (**Figure 8.4**), with a blinking insertion point in the text field.

2. Type your text in the text field (**Figure 8.5**).

## To change the size of the text field:

1. In an open text sample, position the pointer over the bar between the text field and the script editor (**Figure 8.6**).

    The pointer changes to a resize pointer.

2. Drag the bar until the text field is the appropriate size.

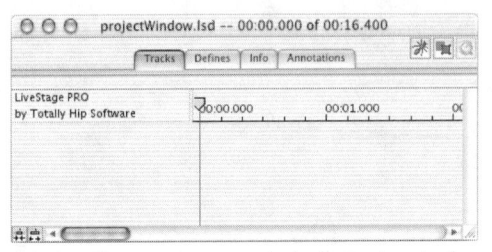

**Figure 8.1** You create text tracks in the Tracks tab of the Project window.

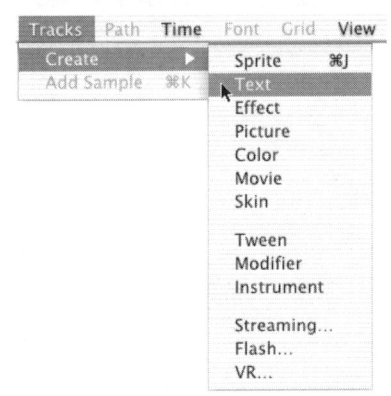

**Figure 8.2** Choose Tracks > Create > Text to create a text track.

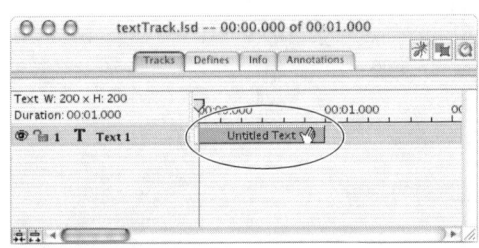

**Figure 8.3** To open a text sample, double-click it in the Timeline.

**TEXT TRACKS**

142

Text Tracks

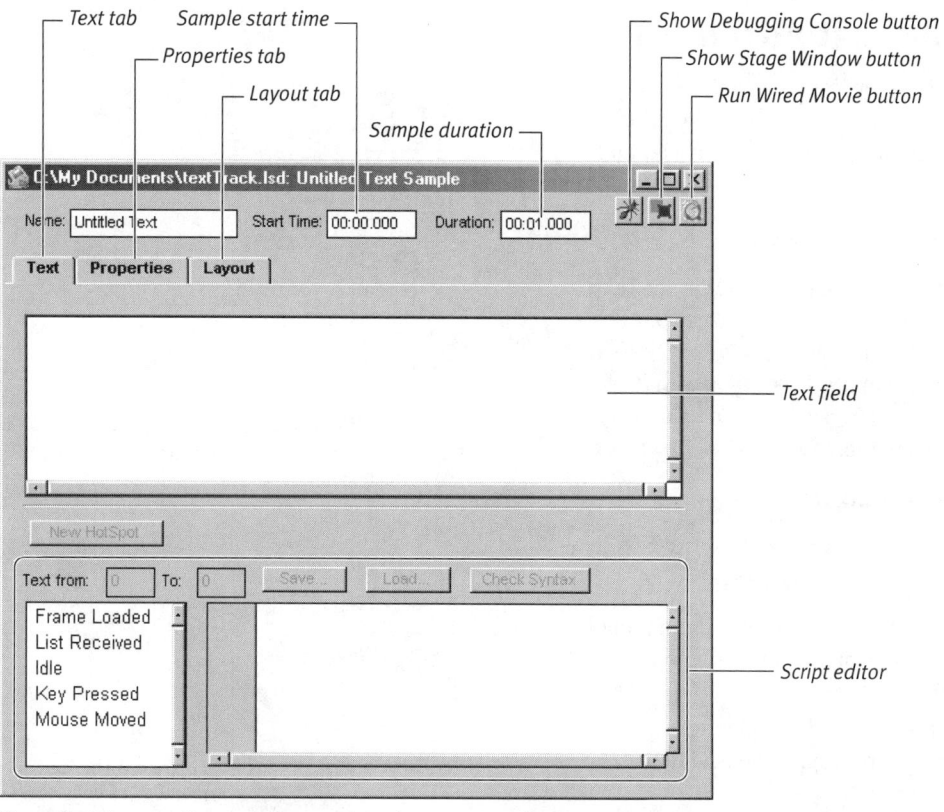

Figure 8.4 labels (clockwise from top-left):
- Text tab
- Sample start time
- Properties tab
- Layout tab
- Sample duration
- Show Debugging Console button
- Show Stage Window button
- Run Wired Movie button
- Text field
- Script editor

**Figure 8.4** When you first open a text sample, the Text tab is displayed. The Text tab houses the text field, which is where you enter all the text this sample will display.

**Figure 8.5** The text field works much like any simple text editor.

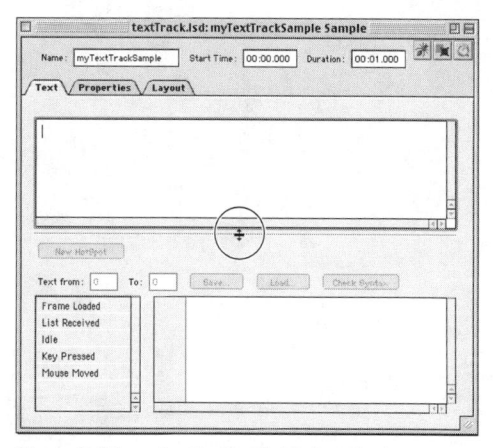

**Figure 8.6** To resize the text field, drag the bar between the text field and the script editor.

143

# About Text Attributes

Text tracks can be styled and formatted. You can set text size, font, style, color, and justification, just as you can in a regular text editor.

## Setting font size

By default, the text you enter in the text field is displayed at a font size of 9. At this extremely small size, text is near the lower end of readability. Unless you want to force your viewers to reach for their glasses, you will need to increase the size of your text.

### To set text size:

1. In an open text sample, select text in the text field (**Figure 8.7**).
2. Choose Font > Size, and choose a new text size from the Size submenu (**Figure 8.8**).

   In the text field, the highlighted text changes to display the new text size (**Figure 8.9**).

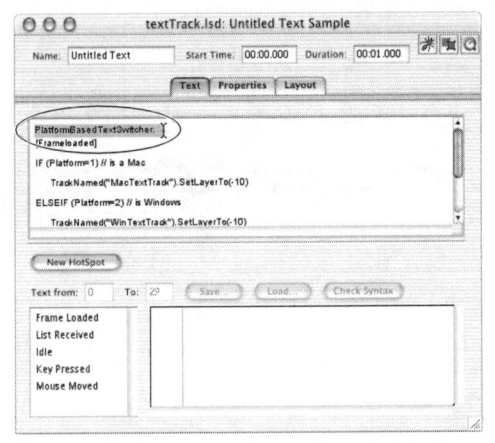

**Figure 8.7** To change text size, start by selecting the text in the text field.

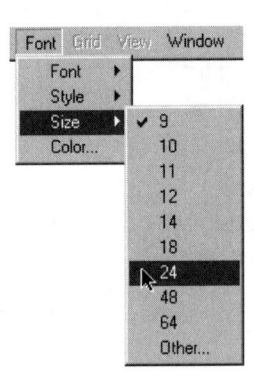

**Figure 8.8** The Font menu gives you access to many preset text sizes. If you need to set a more precise text size, choose Other.

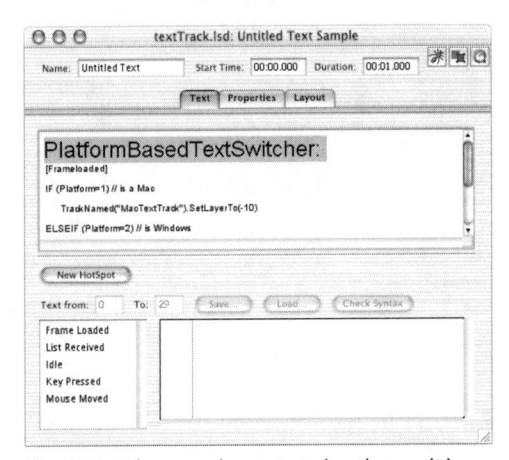

**Figure 8.9** When you change text size, the result is visible immediately in the text field.

# Text Tracks

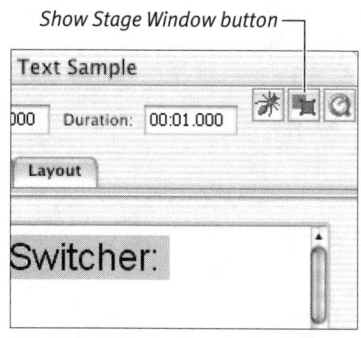

**Figure 8.10** To get a true feeling for your resized text, open the Stage window.

3. In the top-right corner of the open text sample, click the Show Stage Window button (**Figure 8.10**).

   The stage opens, displaying your text exactly as it will appear in the final movie (**Figure 8.11**).

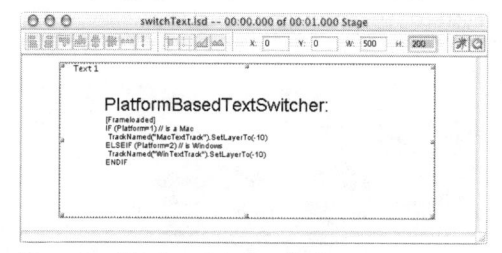

**Figure 8.11** The Stage window displays your text accurately, letting you see how your resized text looks.

## Text-Size Traumas

Windows displays fonts at 96 dots per inch (dpi), whereas the Macintosh displays fonts at 72 dpi. This difference has drastic implications for how your font is displayed, because in some (but not all) instances your text will appear up to 33 percent larger in Windows than it does on the Macintosh.

If you're using a text track to display movie credits or subtitles across the bottom of a video, you can compensate for this problem by making the text track a bit larger than the text. This technique allows the text to shrink or expand as needed. If you have access to both a Macintosh and a Windows computer, test your movie on both to make sure that the text displays properly and is not too big to fit in the text track (Windows) or too small to read (Mac).

Sometimes, you need to exercise strict control over your text display. In this case, you must create two separate text tracks: one formatted for Windows and another for Macintosh users. With a small QScript control statement, you can check to see what platform the viewer is using and then enable or disable the correct text track. To learn how to use a control statement, see Chapter 13, "Advanced QScript."

145

# Chapter 8

## Setting a font face

Selecting a font face is a bit of a black art in QuickTime, as you cannot be 100 percent certain that your chosen font will display properly on the viewer's computer. To keep your files as small as possible, QuickTime does not embed fonts directly in movies; instead, it renders your text tracks at run time, using fonts already installed on the viewer's computer.

If the viewer has not installed the font you've used for your text track, QuickTime will display the track in a standard default font. To be safe, use Times, Courier, Helvetica, or Arial, which typically are installed on every computer.

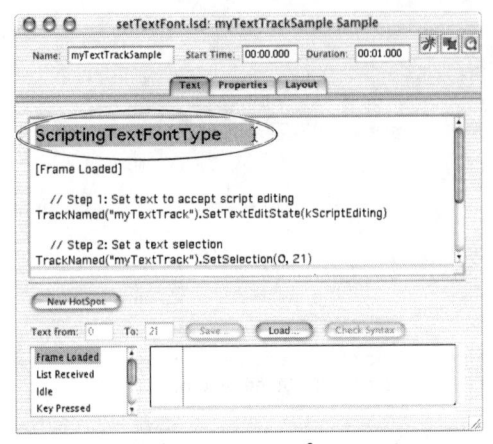

**Figure 8.12** Any time you want to format text, you must start by making a text selection.

### To set a font face:

1. In an open text sample, select text in the text field (**Figure 8.12**).

2. Choose Font > Font, and from the submenu, choose a new font (**Figure 8.13**).

   The Font submenu lists the fonts installed on your computer.

   In the text field, the highlighted text changes to display the selected font (**Figure 8.14**).

3. In the top-right corner of the open text sample, click the Show Stage Window button.

   The stage opens, displaying your text exactly as it will appear in the final movie (**Figure 8.15**).

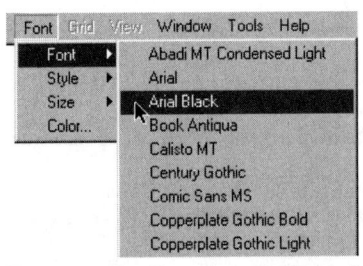

**Figure 8.13** Your Font menu might include fonts that are not available to every computer displaying your movie. If the viewer's computer does not have the font you've selected, QuickTime will display the text in a default font.

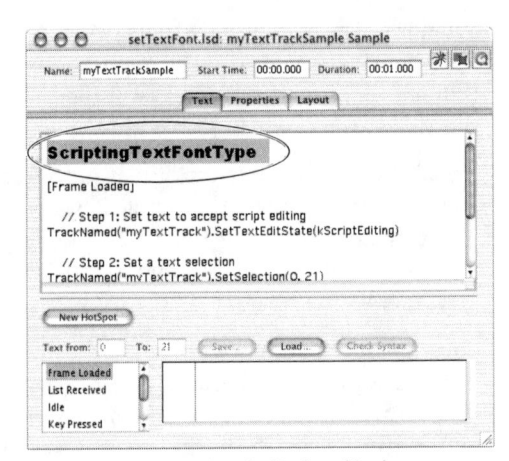

**Figure 8.14** The new font is displayed in the text field, and...

ABOUT TEXT ATTRIBUTES

146

# Text Tracks

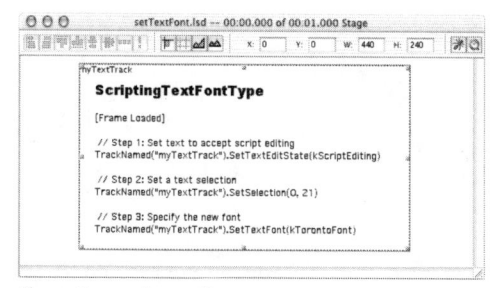

**Figure 8.15** ...also on the stage.

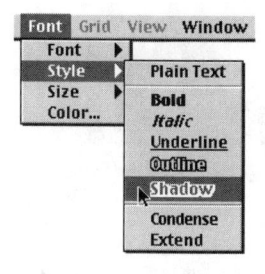

**Figure 8.16** The Font menu's Style submenu.

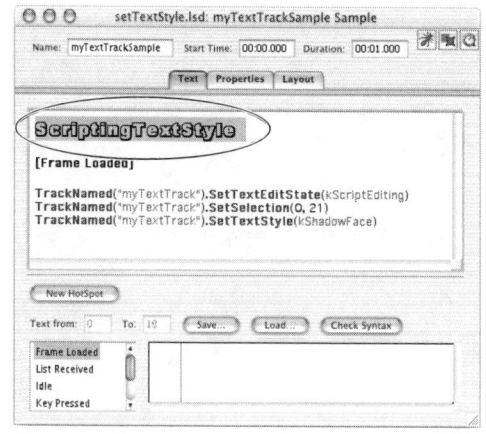

**Figure 8.17** The text field updates to display the selected style.

## Setting text style and color

Unlike font size or font type, which are somewhat dependent on the viewer's computer setup, text style and color may be used with impunity. If you set your text to be green, bold, and underlined, for example, it will appear that way on all computer systems.

### To set text style:

1. In an open text sample, select text in the text field.

2. Choose Font > Style, and choose a new text style from the Style submenu (**Figure 8.16**).

   In the text field, the highlighted text changes to display the new text style (**Figure 8.17**).

**ABOUT TEXT ATTRIBUTES**

147

Chapter 8

**To set text color:**

1. In an open text sample, select text in the text field.

2. Choose Font > Color (**Figure 8.18**).
   The Color Picker opens.

3. Choose a new color for your font, and click OK (**Figure 8.19**).
   The Color Picker closes. In the text field, the highlighted text changes to display the new color setting (**Figure 8.20**).

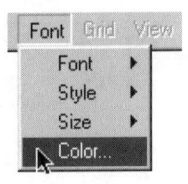

**Figure 8.18** If you have selected some text in the text field, you can change its color by choosing Font > Color.

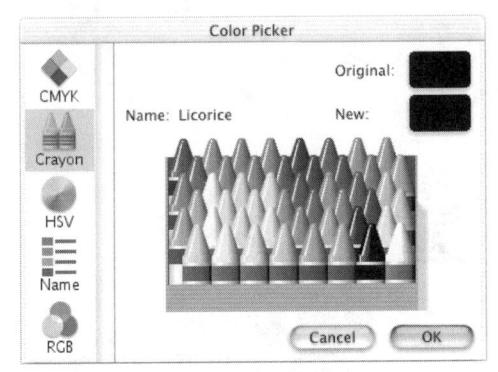

**Figure 8.19** The Color Picker. Pictured is the Crayon Color Picker, which is available only to Macintosh users.

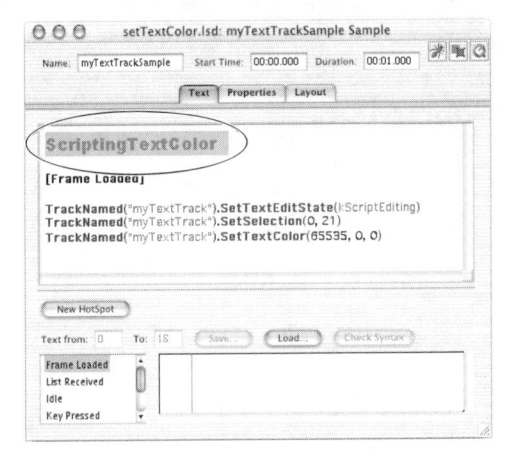

**Figure 8.20** In the text field, the selected text changes color.

ABOUT TEXT ATTRIBUTES

148

# Text Tracks

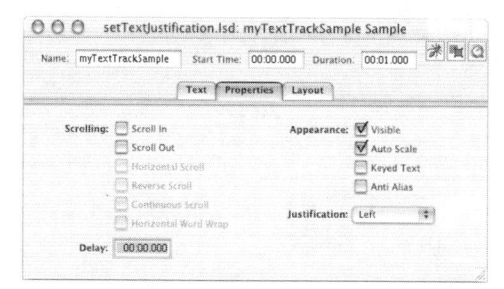

**Figure 8.21** The text sample's Properties tab.

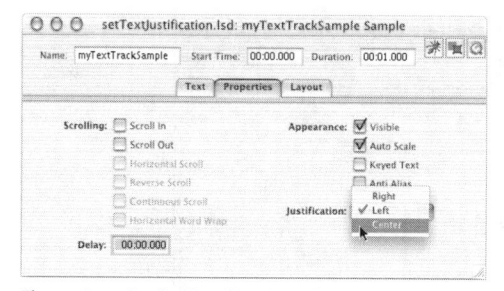

**Figure 8.22** Setting justification affects all the text in the sample.

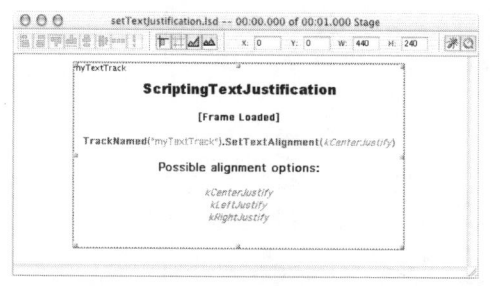

**Figure 8.23** In the Stage window, you can see how your justified text looks.

## Setting text justification

The Justification pop-up menu sits in the bottom-right corner of the text sample's Properties tab; you can use it to left-align, center, or right-align paragraphs of text. By default, the Justification pop-up menu is set to Left, meaning that each line of text is aligned to the left edge of the paragraph. (This paragraph is an example of left alignment.)

Unlike all the other text attributes discussed in this chapter, the text justification setting applies to the entire text sample. You cannot set one section of a sample's text to be centered and another section of the same text to be left-aligned.

### To justify text:

1. In the open text sample, select the Properties tab (**Figure 8.21**).

2. From the Justification pop-up menu, choose a justification option (**Figure 8.22**).

    This menu offers three justification choices: Right, Left, and Center.

3. In the top-right corner of the text sample, click the Show Stage Window button.

    The stage displays your text with the new justification setting (**Figure 8.23**).

**ABOUT TEXT ATTRIBUTES**

149

## About Text Margins

A text box serves the same purpose as the margins settings of a standard word processing program. When you set a text box, you determine how much space lies between your text and the edges of the text track (**Figure 8.24**).

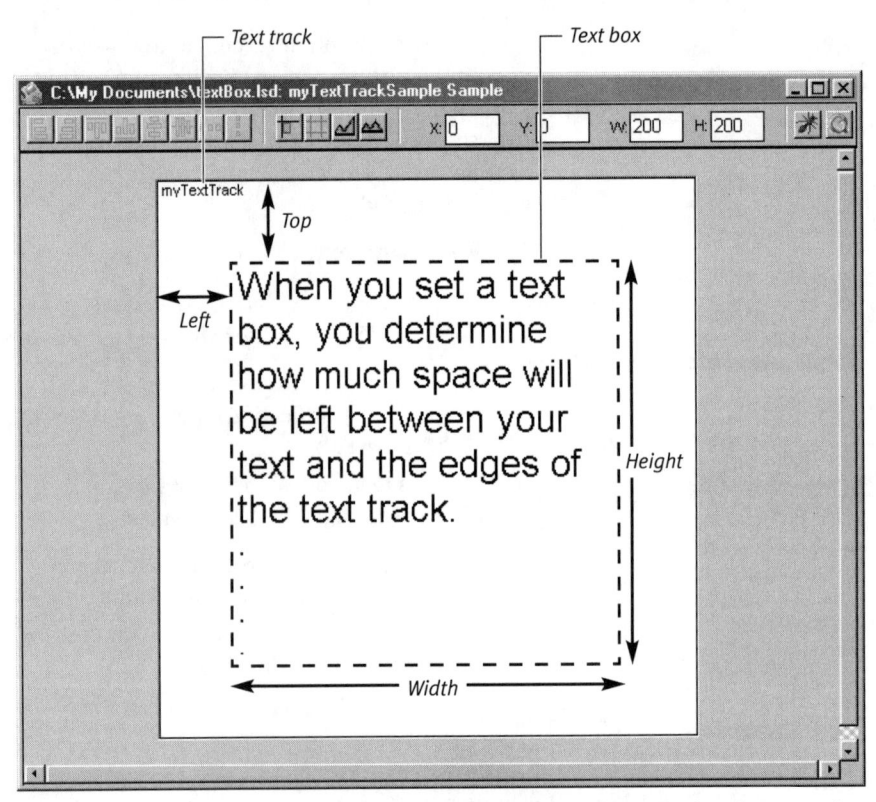

**Figure 8.24** A text box constrains your text to a rectangular area that's smaller than the text track that contains it.

The background box, on the other hand, determines how much of the overall text track is displayed in the final movie. Any parts of the text track that fall outside the track's background box will not be visible (**Figure 8.25**). If the background box is smaller than the text box, your text might be clipped during playback (**Figure 8.26**).

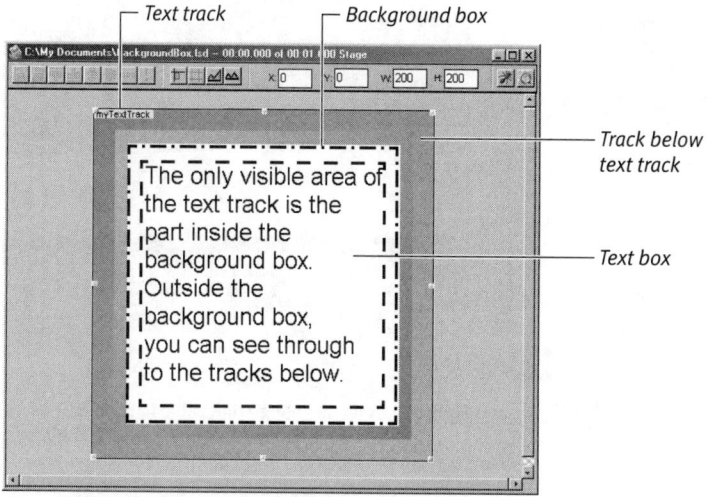

**Figure 8.25** The background box constricts a text track's display area to a space smaller than the track's dimensions.

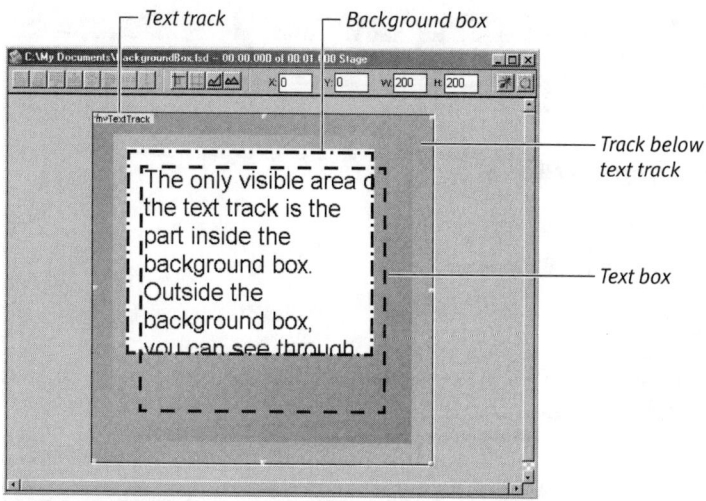

**Figure 8.26** If the background box is smaller than the text box, your text will be clipped.

# Chapter 8

Text and background boxes have four options, located in the text sample's Layout tab:

**Left.** Sets the amount of pixels between the left edge of the text track and the left edge of the text or background box.

**Width.** Sets the width of the text or background box in pixels.

**Top.** Sets the amount of pixels between the top edge of the text track and the top edge of the text or background box.

**Height.** Sets the height of the text or background box in pixels.

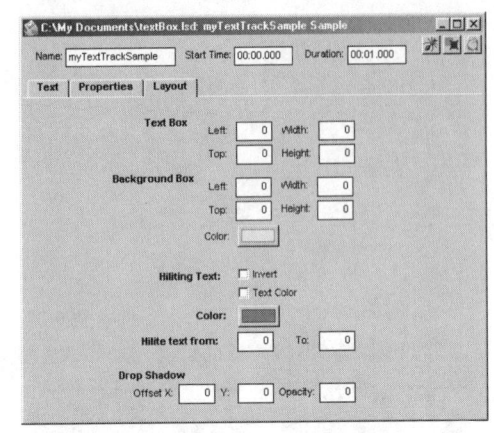

**Figure 8.27** The text sample's Layout tab.

## To set a text box:

1. In the open text sample, select the Layout tab (**Figure 8.27**).

2. In the Text Box section, enter new values in the Left, Width, Top, and Height text boxes (**Figure 8.28**).

3. In the top-right corner of the text sample, click the Show Stage Window button.

   The stage displays your text with a margin between it and the text track's boundary (**Figure 8.29**).

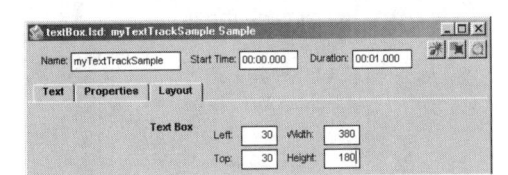

**Figure 8.28** If you change one value in the Text Box section, make sure that you change them all. The width and height values are particularly important; if you don't set these values, the text box will not work.

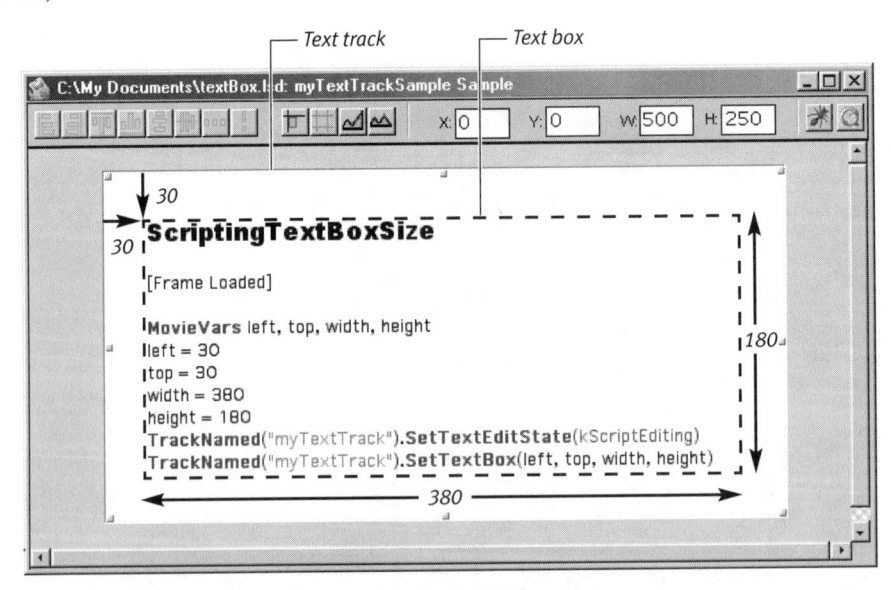

**Figure 8.29** The text appears with a margin in the text track.

# Text Tracks

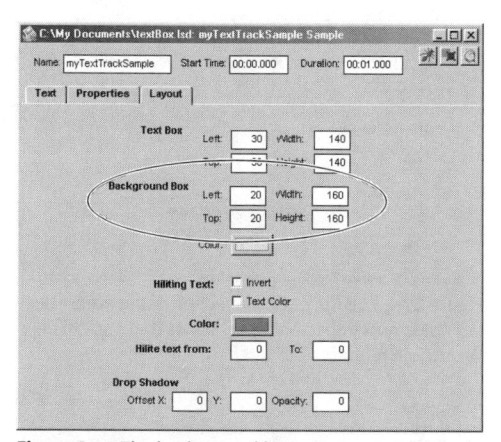

**Figure 8.30** The background box crops your text track to a rectangle smaller than the footprint of the text track itself. Like the text box, the background box must have set width and height values.

**Figure 8.31** You can test your background-box settings by running a preview movie.

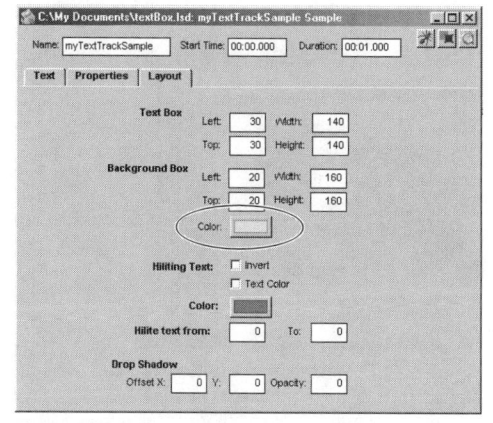

**Figure 8.32** Text tracks do not have to be white. The Background Box section contains a Color box, which you use to set the text track's background color.

## To set a background box:

1. In the open text sample, select the Layout tab.

2. In the Background Box section, enter new values in the Left, Width, Top, and Height text boxes (**Figure 8.30**).

3. Choose File > Run Wired Movie (Command/Ctrl-R), or click the Run Wired Movie button in the top right corner of the text sample.

   The preview movie displays your text with the new background-box setting (**Figure 8.31**).

## To set the background-box color:

1. In the open text sample, select the Layout tab.

2. In the Background Box section, click the Color box (**Figure 8.32**).

   The Color Picker opens.

3. Choose a new background color for your text, and click OK.

   The Color Picker closes.

4. In the top-right corner of the text sample, click the Show Stage Window button.

   The stage displays your text with the new background color (**Figure 8.33**).

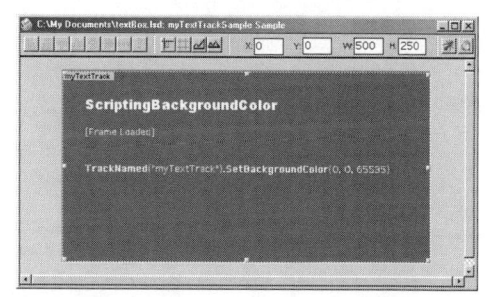

**Figure 8.33** The new background color is displayed on the stage.

**ABOUT TEXT MARGINS**

# About Text Appearance

The Appearance section of the text sample's Properties tab holds four options that define how QuickTime should render your text (**Figure 8.34**):

**Visible.** Visible text, obviously, is text you can see. By default, the Visible checkbox is checked, and the sample's text is visible. If the visibility checkbox is not checked, the sample's text will be invisible, but all the sample's QScripts will still execute.

**Auto Scale.** When the Auto Scale checkbox is checked, every time the movie or text track is resized, the sample's text gets bigger or smaller (**Figure 8.35**). If this checkbox is not checked, the text stays its normal size (**Figure 8.36**).

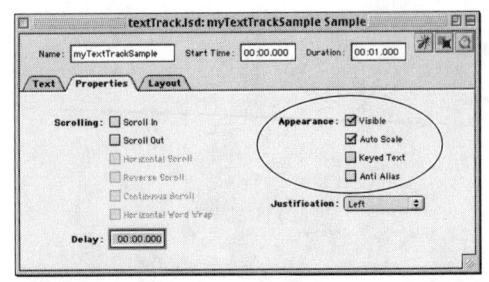

**Figure 8.34** The Appearance section of the Properties tab holds four important checkboxes that control how QuickTime renders your text.

**Figure 8.35** The movie on the bottom is played at twice its original size. In this example, the Auto Scale checkbox is checked, so the text becomes bigger.

154

# Text Tracks

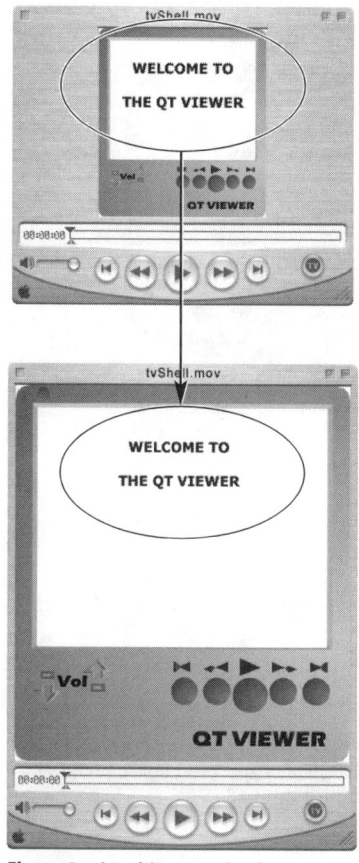

**Figure 8.36** In this example, the Auto Scale checkbox has not been checked. The text stays its normal size and does not grow with the movie.

**Figure 8.37** Keyed text has no background, allowing the tracks below to show through.

**Keyed Text.** This checkbox, when checked, causes the text track's background to disappear. If you are designing text that will sit on top of other images, you will want to check this checkbox.

Suppose that you've created a set of movie credits that will overlap a video intro (**Figure 8.37**). If you check the Keyed Text checkbox, you will be able to see the video playing below the text.

By default, this checkbox is unchecked. Keyed text is very processor-intensive, and unless you really need it to achieve a certain effect for your movie, you should leave this checkbox unchecked.

**Anti Alias.** Antialiased text looks smoother, or softer, than normal text. To antialias text, QuickTime mixes some of the background color into the edges of the text (**Figure 8.38**). Antialiasing makes the edges of large fonts look particularly sharp, but small fonts may look blurry.

Like keyed text, antialiased text is very processor-intensive. By default, the Anti Alias checkbox is unchecked. If your fonts look rough or jagged, check this checkbox; otherwise, leave it unchecked.

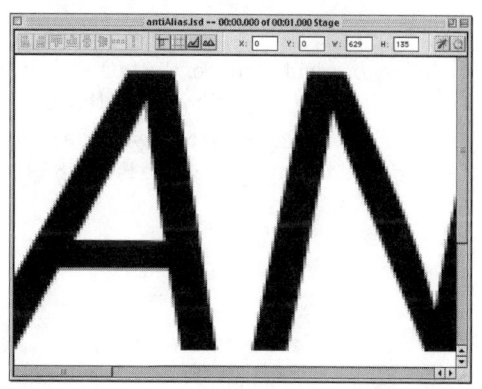

**Figure 8.38** An extreme close-up of antialiased text on the stage, illustrating how the text's edges are blended with the background.

**ABOUT TEXT APPEARANCE**

155

# About Text Effects

You can use two simple text effects to make words stand out on the page: drop shadows and highlights.

## Using drop shadows

A *drop shadow* is a lighting effect that makes the text look like it is hovering above the page (**Figure 8.39**).

### To add a drop shadow:

1. In the open text sample, select the Layout tab.

2. In the Drop Shadow section, enter new values in the Offset X and Y text boxes (**Figure 8.40**).

   Offset is measured in pixels. The Offset X value moves the drop shadow to the right of the original text; the Y value moves the drop shadow below the text.

3. In the Opacity text box, enter a new drop-shadow opacity value (**Figure 8.41**).

   Drop-shadow opacity is measured on a scale from 0 to 256, in which 0 is fully transparent (not visible) and 256 is fully opaque (black). Drop-shadow opacity values typically range from 80 to 150, but feel free to use any setting to create the effect you are after.

4. In the top-right corner of the text sample, click the Show Stage Window button.

   The stage displays your text with the new drop shadow settings (refer to Figure 8.39).

**Figure 8.39** Text with a drop shadow.

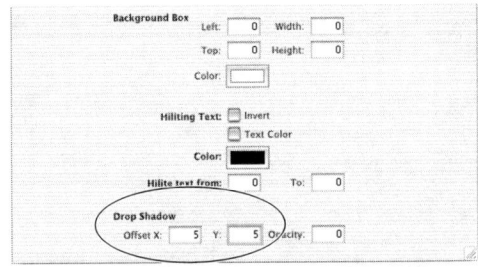

**Figure 8.40** The Offset X and Y text boxes set how far below the text the drop shadow appears to be.

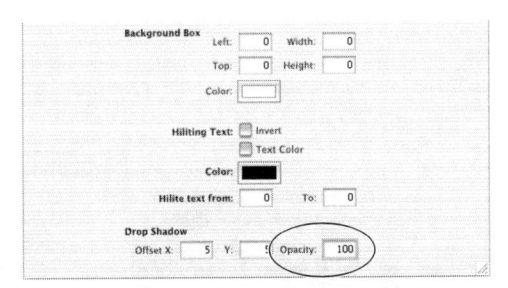

**Figure 8.41** Set the darkness of your drop shadow by entering a value between 0 and 256 in the Opacity text box.

## Using highlights

Highlighted text mimics the effect created by dragging a highlight pen over a row of text on a sheet of paper. Your highlights can be yellow, green, blue, or any other color. By clicking the Color box in the Hiliting Text section of the Layout tab, you can make text highlights any color you want (**Figure 8.42**).

## Determining a text range

Unlike a drop shadow, which affects every character in the text sample, a highlight can be applied to just a few of the sample's characters. To set a highlight, you must first determine the range of text the highlight will cover.

### To determine a text range:

1. In an open text sample, select the Text tab.

2. In the text field, select some text (**Figure 8.43**).

   Below the text field, the numbers in the Text From and To text boxes are updated to reflect the start and end values of the selected text segment. This is the text range you will use for your highlight.

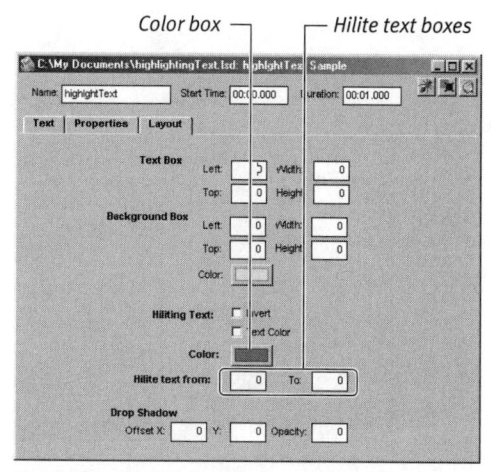

**Figure 8.42** The Hiliting Text section contains options for highlighting a selection of the text sample's text.

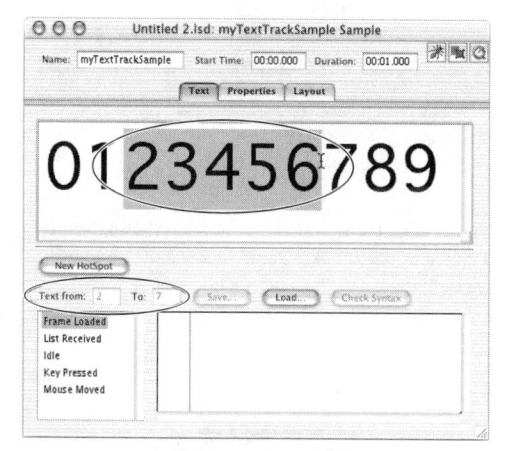

**Figure 8.43** Some text selected in the text field. The start and end points of the selection are displayed in the Text From and To text boxes.

Chapter 8

## Highlighting a text range

After you determine a range of text for your highlight to cover, the next step is setting the highlight.

### To highlight a text range:

1. Determine the start and end values of the text range, as described in the preceding section.

2. In the open text sample, select the Layout tab (**Figure 8.44**).

3. In the Hiliting Text section, enter the values culled from step 1 in the Hilite Text From and To text boxes (**Figure 8.45**).

4. Click the Show Stage Window button.

    The stage displays your text with the specified range highlighted (**Figure 8.46**).

### ✔ Tip

- The Hiliting Text section's Text Color checkbox provides a far more subtle form of highlighting. If you check this checkbox, instead of drawing a colored rectangular bar over text, LiveStage changes the color of the text characters themselves.

### To change the highlight color:

1. In the open text sample, select the Layout tab.

2. In the Hiliting Text section, click the Color box (**Figure 8.47**).

    The Color Picker opens.

3. Choose a color for the highlight, and click OK.

    The Color Picker closes, and the new highlight color is applied to your highlighted text track.

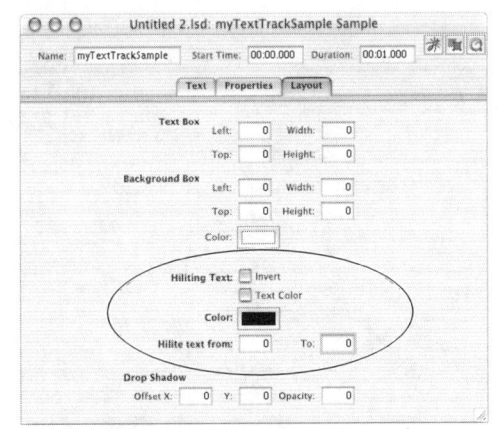

**Figure 8.44** The Hiliting Text section sits halfway down the Layout tab.

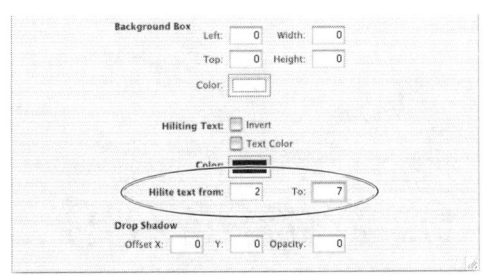

**Figure 8.45** The numbers you enter in the Hilite Text From and To text boxes set the text selection to be highlighted with the color of your choice.

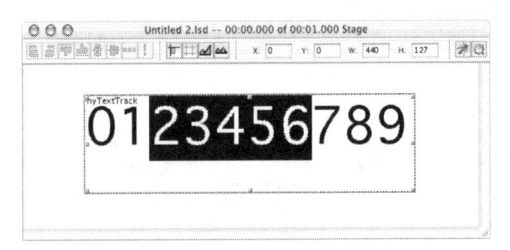

**Figure 8.46** Highlighted text on the stage.

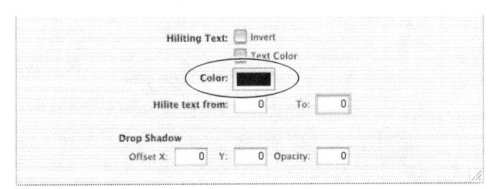

**Figure 8.47** Click the Hiliting Text section's Color box to set the highlight color.

ABOUT TEXT EFFECTS

158

Text Tracks

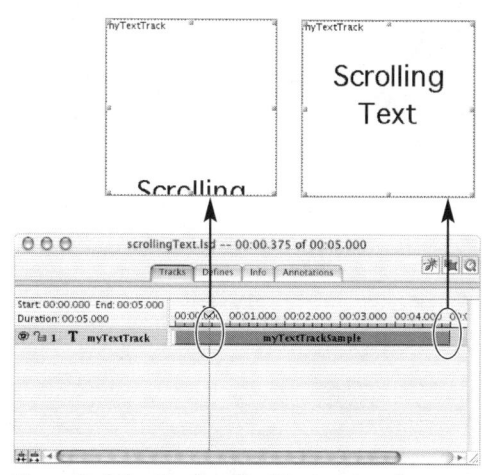

**Figure 8.48** The time length of the text sample determines how long the text takes to scroll onto the screen. At the beginning of the sample, the text is fully off-screen. At the end of the sample, the text has completed scrolling and is fully on-screen.

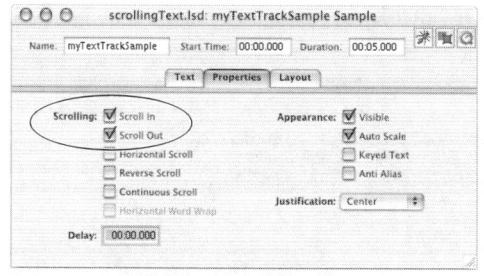

**Figure 8.49** The Scrolling section contains several methods for animating text. To set text to scroll, check the Scroll In and/or Scroll Out checkboxes.

# About Animated Text

The Scrolling section of the text sample's Properties tab lets you animate your text to scroll on and off the screen. Scrolling text adds eye-catching motion to your movie. Imagine you are in a cinema, watching the end credits for your favorite film. Nine times out of 10, credits will scroll from the bottom of the screen toward the top. The text sample's Scrolling section lets you create a similar effect with just two clicks.

## Using scrolling text

If you set your text to scroll, its rate of scrolling is tied directly to movie playback. If the movie plays, the scrolling text plays. If the movie is stopped or played in reverse, the scrolling text is also stopped or played in reverse.

The time length of the text sample dictates how long it takes for the text to scroll. If the text sample is 5 seconds long, and you have set your text only to scroll in, it will take 5 seconds for all the text to scroll onto the screen (**Figure 8.48**). Where the sample begins in the movie's Timeline, the text is completely off-screen. Half way through the sample, the text is halfway on-screen. At the end of the sample, the text is fully on-screen.

If you set the text to scroll in and out, it scrolls in over the first half of the sample and scrolls out over the last half. In a 5-second sample, the text would take 2.5 seconds to scroll on-screen and 2.5 seconds to scroll off.

### To scroll text in or out:

1. In the open text sample, select the Properties tab.

2. In the Scrolling section, check Scroll In and/or Scroll Out (**Figure 8.49**).

   When the movie plays, the text scrolls on and/or off the screen.

159

Chapter 8

## Setting a scroll delay

Moving text can be hard to read. With this fact in mind, you can set a scroll delay to stop the text momentarily so that viewers can see what it says.

The amount of time you select for the delay is subtracted from the total time length of the sample. The remaining time is given to the scroll functions. The easiest way to understand this arrangement is to look at an example. In a 5-second text sample set to scroll both in and out, text normally takes 2.5 seconds to scroll in and 2.5 seconds to scroll out. If you set a scroll delay of 3 seconds, that leaves only 1 second for the text to scroll in and 1 second for it to scroll out (**Figure 8.50**).

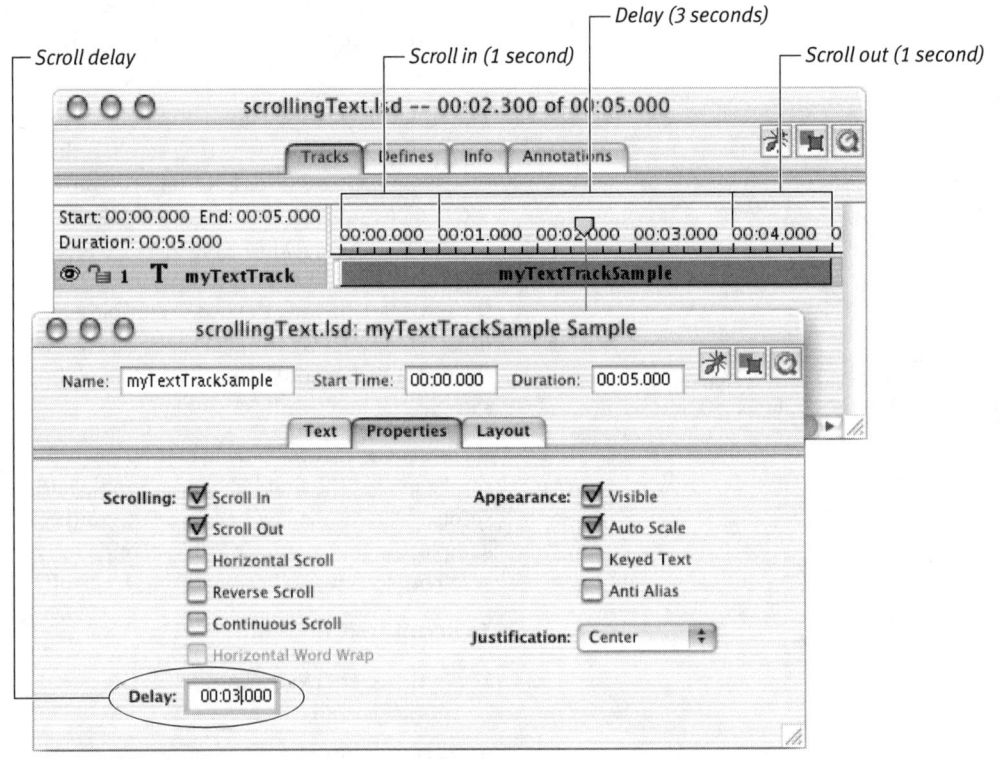

**Figure 8.50** The Delay text box in the bottom-left corner of the text sample's Properties tab (foreground) causes the text to stop scrolling for the specified amount of time. In this figure, the text sample is 5 seconds long, and its text is set to scroll in and out, with a 3-second delay. If you look at the text sample in the Timeline (background), you see that the text scrolls in over the first second, pauses for 3 seconds, and scrolls out over the last second.

# Text Tracks

## To set a scroll delay:

1. In an open text sample, select the Properties tab.

2. Enter a delay value in the Delay text box (refer to Figure 8.50).

    During playback, the scrolling text pauses for the specified period of time.

## ✔ Tips

- The delay value must be set in the LiveStage timescale of 600 ticks per second. (To learn more about the LiveStage timescale, see Chapter 1, "The Tracks Tab"). To set a delay of 3.5 seconds, for example, enter `00:03.300` in the Delay text box.

- If your scroll delay is set to a time value greater than the length of the text sample, your text will not scroll.

---

### More Ways to Scroll

Three additional scrolling options may prove useful:

**Horizontal Scroll.** By default, text scrolls from top to bottom. If you check the Horizontal Scroll checkbox, your text will scroll from right to left. Horizontal Scroll turns all paragraphs into a single line of text and scrolls them like a banner across the screen. If you would like to preserve the structure of your paragraph, you must also check the Horizontal Word Wrap checkbox, which becomes active only after you have selected Horizontal Scroll.

**Reverse Scroll.** As its name implies, the Reverse Scroll checkbox causes your text to scroll in reverse. Text will enter from the top of the screen and scroll off the bottom. If you've also checked the Horizontal Scroll checkbox, the text scrolls from left to right across the screen.

**Continuous Scroll.** If one text track holds two or more back-to-back text samples, selecting continuous scroll causes the second text sample to push out the text from the first sample. The text from the first sample scrolls off screen as the text from the second sample scrolls on. While scrolling, text from both samples is on the screen at the same time.

---

ABOUT ANIMATED TEXT

161

# Chapter 8

## About Hotspots

Text hotspots are interactive links that you create from words within a text sample. Using the pointer, the viewer can interact with text hotspots to control the movie. You can make a text hotspot that opens a Web page, jumps the current movie forward along its Timeline, or toggles the movie's audio. In fact, you can make hotspots do almost anything you want; they are among the most scriptable objects in LiveStage.

A text sample can hold multiple hotspots, which are perfect for building a JavaScript-style multiple-link menu bar (**Figure 8.51**) or for creating multiple hyperlinks within one text paragraph.

### To create a hotspot:

1. In the open text sample, select the Text tab.

2. In the text field, select the text that will be used as a hotspot.

3. Click the New HotSpot button (**Figure 8.52**).

   The selected text becomes a hotspot and is surrounded by a light gray box. Also, several new mouse events are added to the Event Handler list (**Figure 8.53**).

### ✔ Tip

- Hotspots cannot overlap. If text is part of one hotspot, you cannot make it part of another hotspot.

**Figure 8.51** A text track with multiple hotspots (the directory names beside the folders) has been used to make a JavaScript-style menu bar.

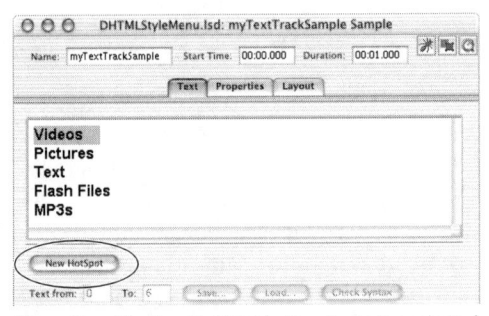

**Figure 8.52** The New HotSpot button turns the selected text into a hotspot.

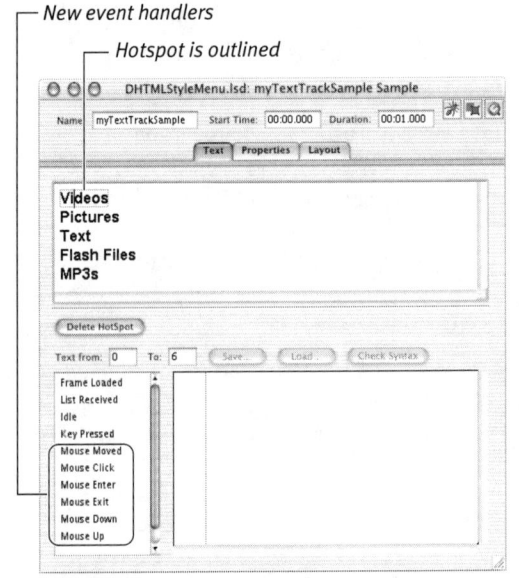

**Figure 8.53** In the text field, you can recognize a hotspot by the light gray outline surrounding it. When you create a hotspot, additional event handlers are added to the Event Handler list.

Text Tracks

— Text From and To text boxes
— Insertion point

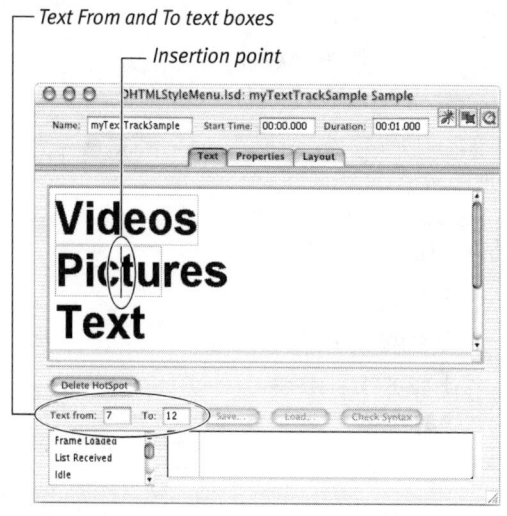

**Figure 8.54** If your hotspot isn't big enough, you can change its length using the Text From and To text boxes.

**Figure 8.55** When the hotspot is clicked, the movie jumps to the specified point of its Timeline (1.5 seconds).

## To change hotspot length:

1. In the text field, click inside a hotspot.
   The Text from and To text boxes of the Text tab become active (**Figure 8.54**).

2. Enter new values in the Text From and/or To text boxes.
   The hotspot expands or shrinks to encompass the specified text.

## To script a hotspot:

1. In the text field, click inside a hotspot.
   All hotspots have five mouse-activated events (Mouse Click, Mouse Enter, etc.). After you click the pointer inside a text hotspot, these events appear in the Event Handler list.

2. In the Event Handler list, select a mouse event.

3. In the script edit field, write your QScript (**Figure 8.55**).

ABOUT HOTSPOTS

163

Chapter 8

## To delete a hotspot:

1. In the text field, click inside a hotspot. The New HotSpot button changes to the Delete HotSpot button (**Figure 8.56**).

2. Click the Delete HotSpot button.
   The selected hotspot is deleted. Any event handler attached to that hotspot is also deleted.

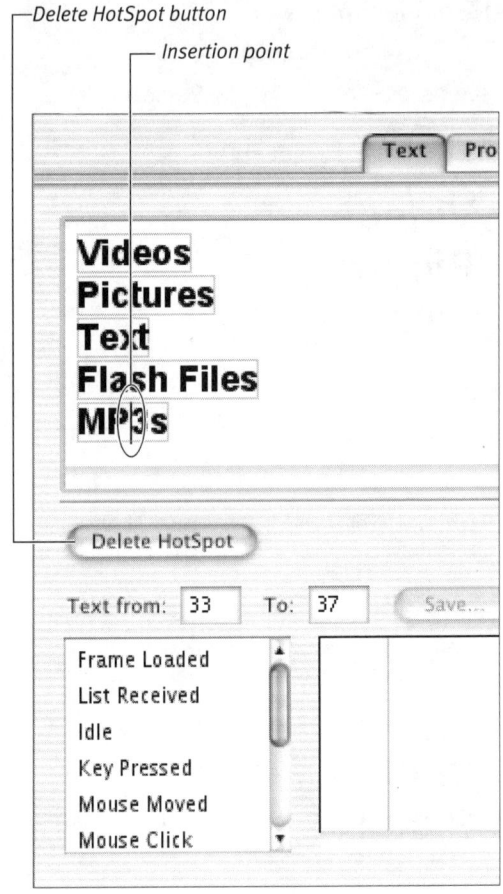

**Figure 8.56** To delete a hotspot, select it and then click the Delete HotSpot button.

ABOUT HOTSPOTS

164

## About Formatting Hotspots

LiveStage renders hotspots in blue and underlines them, following classic hypertext conventions. Depending on the design, layout, and visual tone of your project, you might not want a blue, underlined hotspot. To change a hotspot's color or take away that underline, you must write a QScript (**Figure 8.57**).

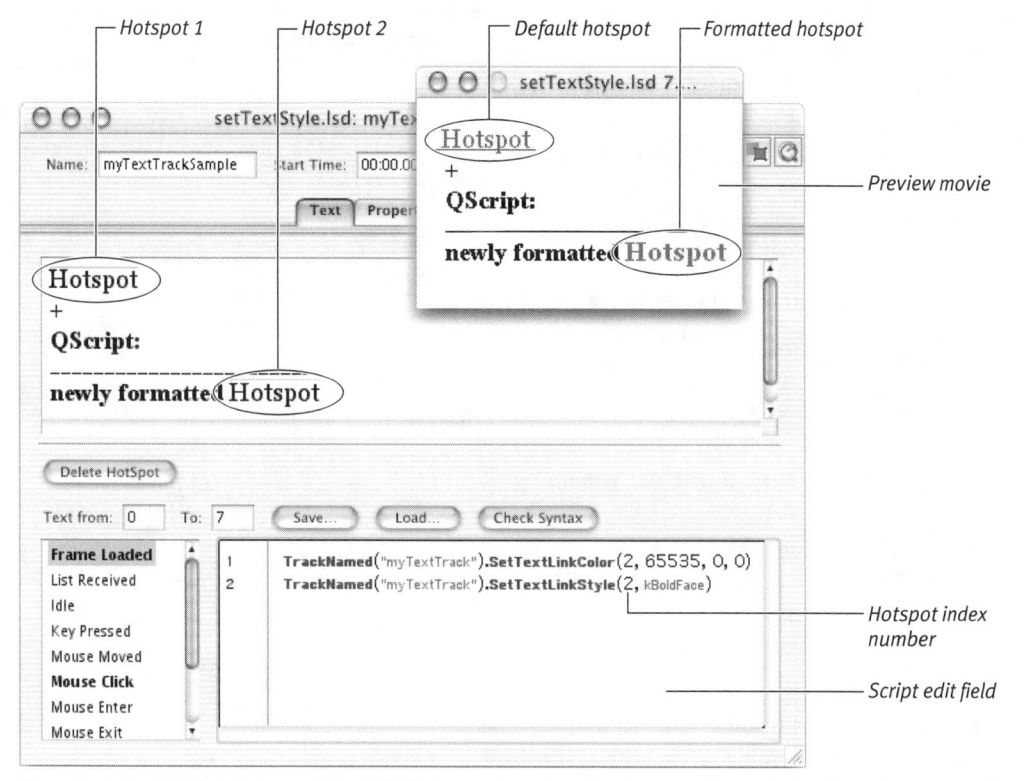

**Figure 8.57** The QScripts in the script edit field change the color of, and remove the underline from, the hotspot of index number 2 (the second one). In the preview movie (foreground), the second hotspot is bold and red, instead of blue and underlined like the unformatted default hotspot.

## Chapter 8

All QScripts must be placed in the correct event handler, including the scripts you write to format a hotspot. Because text is formatted as the text sample loads, you should place the formatting QScript in the Frame Loaded event handler. As the text loads, the Frame Loaded event handler is executed, and the hotspot displays properly.

### To change hotspot color:

1. In the text sample's script editor, select the Frame Loaded event handler (**Figure 8.58**).

2. In the script edit field, enter the following QScript (**Figure 8.59**):
   SetTextLinkColor(hotspot_index,
   → red, green, blue)
   
   For LiveStage to understand this command, you must specify the hotspot's index number, as well as the color that will be used to format that hotspot.

3. Replace hotspot_index with the index number of the hotspot that you want to format.
   
   The first hotspot in the text sample is number 1, the second is number 2, etc.

4. Replace red, green, blue with red, green, and blue values.
   
   Red, green, and blue values range from 0 to 65535. To learn more about selecting proper color values, see the sidebar "Text-Color Values" in this section.

5. Preview your text track by clicking the Run Wired Movie button in the top-right corner of the text sample.
   
   In the preview movie, the hotspot is formatted with the new color.

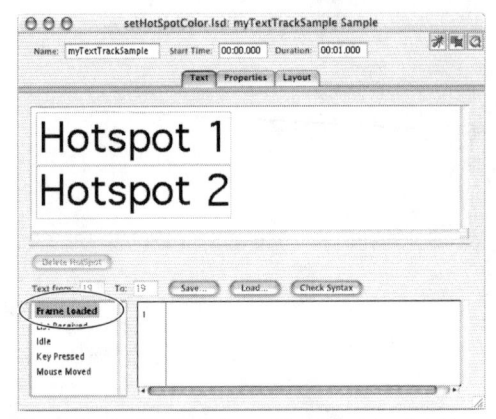

**Figure 8.58** All hotspot formatting QScripts should be placed in Frame Loaded event handlers. As the text sample loads, the Frame Loaded event handler is executed, and the hotspot is formatted properly.

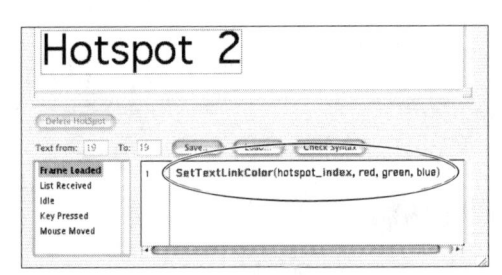

**Figure 8.59** This QScript sets hotspot color.

166

**Table 8.1**

| Color Conversions | |
|---|---|
| COLOR | RED, GREEN, BLUE VALUE |
| Black | 0, 0, 0 |
| White | 65535, 65535, 65535 |
| Red | 65535, 0, 0 |
| Green | 0, 65535, 0 |
| Blue | 0, 0, 65535 |
| Orange | 65535, 32768, 0 |
| Yellow | 65535, 65535, 0 |
| Pink | 65535, 0, 65535 |
| Purple | 49150, 16380, 65535 |

## ✔ Tips

- A hotspot is not activated until you have written an event handler for it. Empty hotspots look like all other text in the final movie—neither blue nor underlined.

- If your text sample contains multiple hotspots, you must define each hotspot's color individually. If the sample has 10 hotspots, you must write 10 versions of the QScript discussed in the preceding section—one for each hotspot.

### Text-Color Values

In text tracks, each color channel is represented by 16-bits, which means that each channel can be assigned one of 65535 different shades. Not many graphics cards or monitors can display that many colors, but when computer color moves beyond 8-bits per channel, QuickTime will be ready.

This vast range can be confusing when you're trying to determine what values to enter for the red, green, and blue color channels of the SetTextLinkColor(hotspot_index, red, green, blue) QScript. All you need to remember is this: The red, green, and blue color channels can each hold a value between 0 and 65535. In this range, 0 is as dark as the color can go, and 65535 is as bright as the color can get. If you want a track to be fully red, you would replace the red, green, and blue color values with 65535, 0, and 0, respectively. **Table 8.1** shows some common colors and their corresponding color-channel values.

# Chapter 8

## To change hotspot style:

1. In the Text tab's script editor, select the Frame Loaded event handler.

2. In the script edit field, enter the following QScript (**Figure 8.60**):

   SetTextLinkStyle(hotspot_index,
   → style).

   For LiveStage to understand this command, you must specify the hotspot's index number, as well as the style that will be used to format the hotspot.

3. Replace hotspot_index with the appropriate hotspot index number (**Figure 8.61**).

   The first hotspot in the text sample is number 1, the second is number 2, etc.

4. If the QScript Reference Window is not open, choose Window > Show QScript Reference to open it.

   The QScript Reference window holds a list of available text styles (**Figure 8.62**).

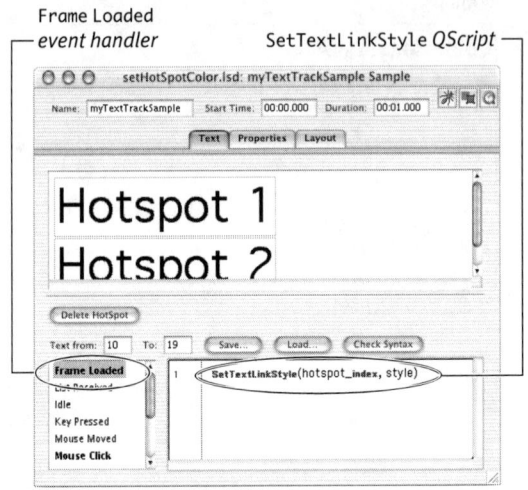

**Figure 8.60** This QScript changes hotspot style and removes the default underline.

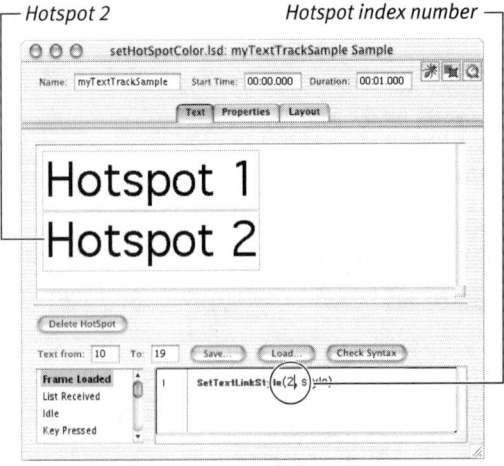

**Figure 8.61** For your QScript to figure out which hotspot to target, you must specify the hotspot's index number.

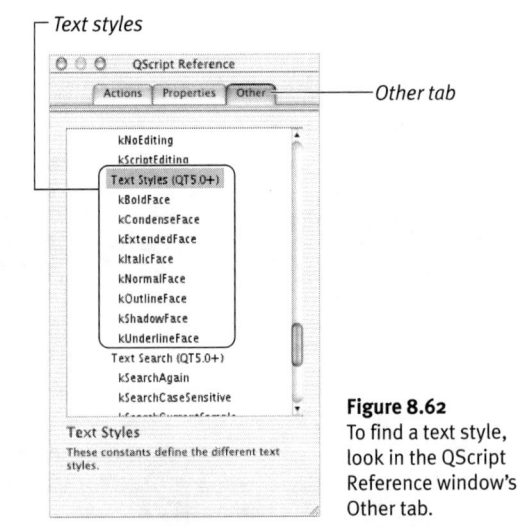

**Figure 8.62** To find a text style, look in the QScript Reference window's Other tab.

168

Text Tracks

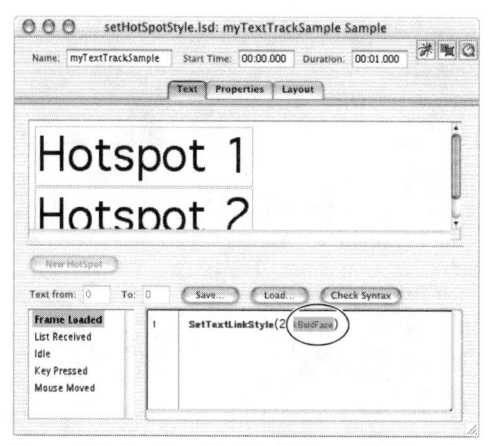

**Figure 8.63** Complete the QScript by supplying a hotspot style.

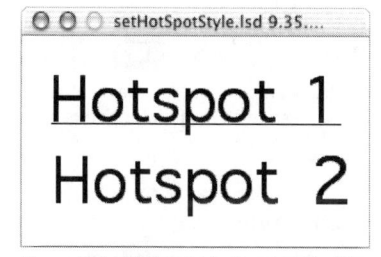

**Figure 8.64** Hotspot 1 is formatted with the default underline. Hotspot 2 is bold and has had the underline removed.

5. From the QScript Reference window's Other tab, scroll down until you see the Text Track (QT5.0+) section.

6. Click the expansion arrow (Mac) or box (Windows) beside the Text Track (QT 5.0+) section.

   The Text Track section opens to reveal many formatting options that work with text tracks.

7. In the text sample's text field, replace style with a formatting option from the QScript Reference window's Text Styles section (**Figure 8.63**).

   You can type the formatting option or drag it from the QScript Reference window to the script edit field.

8. Preview your text track by clicking the Run Wired Movie button in the top-right corner of the text sample.

   In the preview movie, the hotspot is formatted with this new style (**Figure 8.64**).

## ✔ Tip

- If your text sample contains multiple hotspots, you must define the text style for each one individually. If the sample has 10 hotspots, you must write 10 versions of the QScript discussed in the preceding section—one for each hotspot.

---

### No Target Specifier?

If no target object is specified, QScript track actions automatically target their own tracks. The QScripts that set hotspot color and style are track actions. As a result, you can leave off the target specifier, and the scripts will still work.

When placed in the `Frame Loaded` event handler of a text sample in the track named "myTextTrack", each of the following QScripts turns the second hotspot red:

```
TrackNamed("myTextTrack").SetTextLinkColor(2, 65535, 0, 0)
SetTextLinkColor(2, 65535, 0, 0)
```

ABOUT FORMATTING HOTSPOTS

169

# Chapter 8

# About Advanced Hotspot Editing

A typical hyperlink has three pointer states: Normal, Mouse Over, and Mouse Click. As the viewer moves the pointer over the hyperlink, the pointer changes to an open hand, and the hyperlink changes color. When the viewer clicks the hyperlink, the pointer changes to a closed hand, and the hyperlink once again changes color to let the viewer know that it has been clicked.

In QuickTime, hotspots don't act this way by default. To simulate a classic hyperlink effect, complete with changing pointers and colors, you'll have to do a bit of work.

## Changing hotspot color dynamically

The first step in creating a classic hyperlink effect is to make the hotspot change colors as the user interacts with it. This example demonstrates only how to change a hotspot's Mouse Enter color. To change its Mouse Down, Mouse Up, Mouse Click, or Mouse Exit color, simply repeat the following steps, but select the appropriate event in the Event Handler list.

### To simulate a rollover color:

1. In the Text tab's script editor, select the Mouse Enter event handler (**Figure 8.65**).

2. Enter the following QScript in the script edit field:
   SetTextLinkColor(hotspot_index, red, → green, blue)

3. Replace hotspot_index with the index number of the hotspot that you want to format (**Figure 8.66**).

   The first hotspot in the text sample is number 1, the second is number 2, and so on.

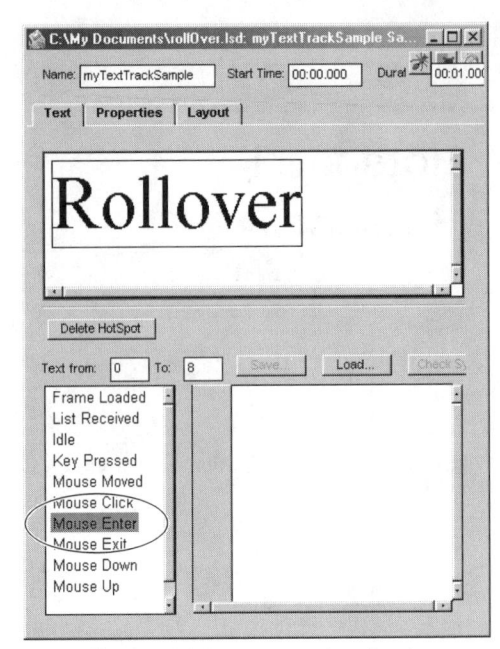

**Figure 8.65** The Mouse Enter event handler changes the hotspot's color as soon as the pointer enters the hotspot.

*Hotspot index number*

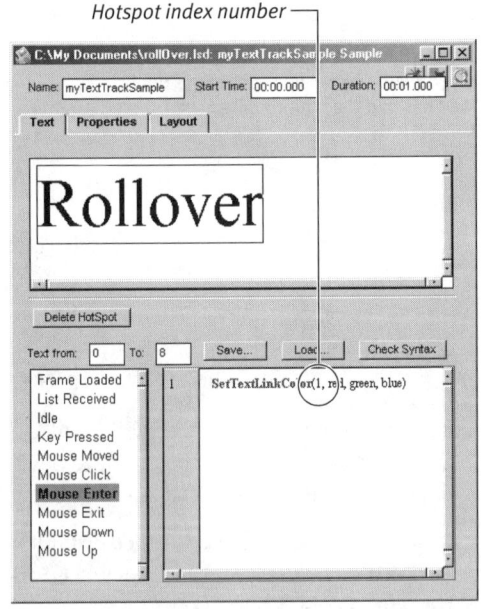

**Figure 8.66** For your QScript to figure out which hotspot to target, you must specify the hotspot's index number.

# Text Tracks

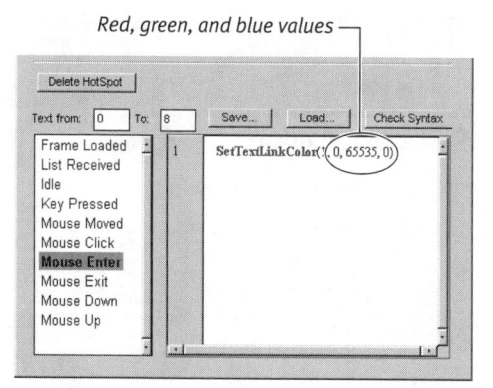

**Figure 8.67** You can set red, green, and blue values by using numbers that range from 0 to 65535.

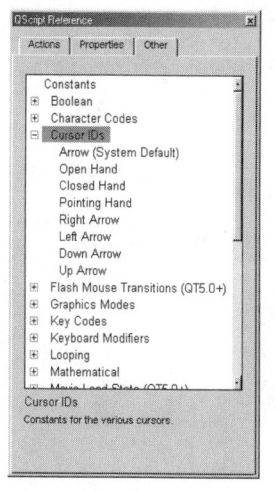

**Figure 8.68** To find a pointer type, look in the QScript Reference window's Other tab, below Cursor IDs.

4. Enter new red, green, and blue values (**Figure 8.67**).

5. Preview your rollover effect by clicking the Run Wired Movie button in the top-right corner of the text sample.

   In the preview movie, the hotspot changes color when you move the pointer over it.

## Changing pointers dynamically

The last step in making a classic hyperlink rollover is changing the pointer into a hand that grabs the hyperlink as the viewer clicks it. The QScript Reference Window's Other tab contains a list of pointer IDs, including several hand-shaped pointers (**Figure 8.68**).

# Chapter 8

## To change pointer style:

1. In the Text tab's script editor, select the Mouse Enter event handler from the Event Handler list.

2. Enter the following QScript in the script edit field (**Figure 8.69**):

   SetCursor(kQTCursorOpenHand)

   When the pointer moves over the hotspot, this QScript changes the pointer to an open hand.

3. In the Event Handler list, select the Mouse Down event handler.

4. Enter the following QScript in the script edit field:

   SetCursor(kQTCursorClosedHand)

5. In the Event Handler list, select the Mouse Up event handler.

6. Enter the following QScript in the script edit field:

   SetCursor(kQTCursorOpenHand)

7. In the Event Handler list, select the Mouse Exit event handler.

8. Enter the following QScript in the script edit field:

   SetCursor(kQTCursorArrow)

   When the pointer is moved out of the hotspot, this QScript changes it back to the default arrow pointer.

9. Preview the changing pointer effect by clicking the Run Wired Movie button in the top-right corner of the text sample.

   In the preview movie, the hotspot functions like a classic hyperlink, complete with open and closed hand pointers that grab the hotspot (**Figure 8.70**).

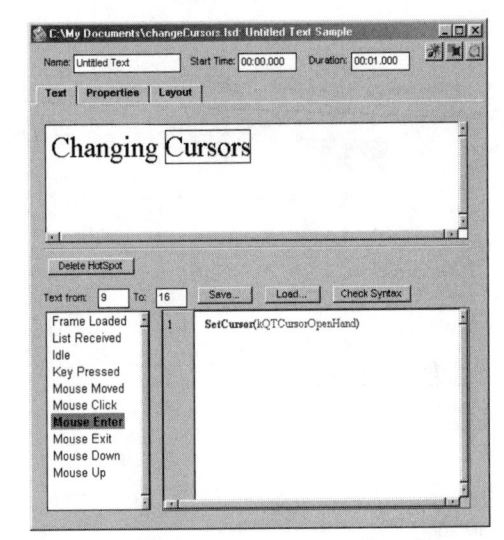

**Figure 8.69** This QScript uses a preset ID to change the pointer into an open hand as the pointer is moved over the hotspot.

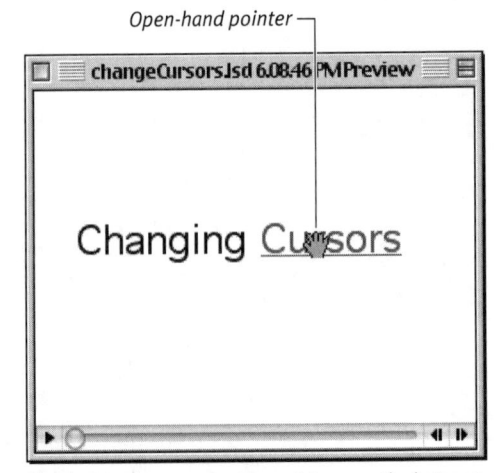

**Figure 8.70** As you move the pointer over the hotspot, it changes into an open hand.

Text Tracks

## About Chapter Tracks

QuickTime supports a special type of text track called a *chapter track*, which divides your movie into named sections that can be selected in the QuickTime controller's chapter list (**Figure 8.71**). The chapter list lets a viewer select a topic and jump directly to that section of the movie.

At its base, a chapter track is just a text track, but one with many samples. Each sample in the text track becomes a separate chapter in the chapter track, with the sample's length defining the length of the chapter.

For a chapter track to be enabled, it must be assigned to a second track, called an *owner track*. By assigning the text track to an owner track, you turn it into a chapter track, and its chapter list is displayed in the QuickTime controller.

When it comes to selecting an owner track, you typically choose the movie's main audio or video track, though you can select any track you want. Just remember one thing: If the chapter track's owner is disabled, so is the chapter track (To learn more about enabling tracks, see Chapter 3, "Setting Track Properties.") As a result, you should assign chapter tracks only to owner tracks that will be enabled for the entire movie.

*QuickTime Player chapter list*

*QuickTime plug-in chapter list*

**Figure 8.71** All chapter labels appear in a list on the right side of the QuickTime control bar.

## To create a chapter track:

1. Choose Tracks > Create > Text.

   A new text track is created, and an empty text sample is placed in the Timeline. This empty text sample will become the first chapter of the chapter track.

2. Double-click the text sample to open it.

3. In the text field, enter the name of the first chapter in your project (**Figure 8.72**).

4. In the Timeline, stretch the text sample so that it covers the full time length of the project's first chapter.

   Each chapter's length is determined by the length of its corresponding text sample.

5. Choose Tracks > Add Sample (Command/Ctrl-K) (**Figure 8.73**).

   In the Timeline, a new sample is added behind the text track's last sample.

6. Repeat steps 2 to 5 until you have created a text sample for every chapter in your project (**Figure 8.74**).

7. Double-click the text track's header (**Figure 8.75**).

   The Track Properties window opens.

   In the next few steps, you will select an owner track. The chapter track must be attached to an owner track; otherwise, the chapter list will not be enabled in the final movie.

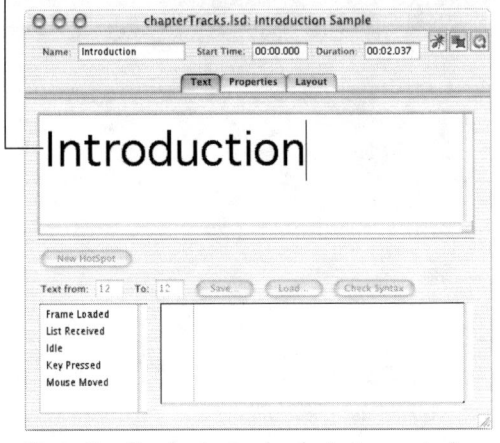

**Figure 8.72** For chapter tracks, the text you enter in the text field becomes the name of the chapter.

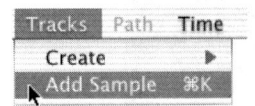

**Figure 8.73** For your movie to have multiple chapters, you must add multiple text samples to the chapter track.

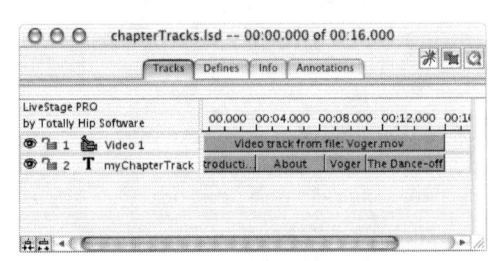

**Figure 8.74** This chapter track has four samples and, therefore, four chapters.

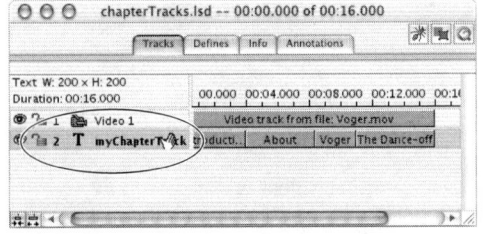

**Figure 8.75** To open the Track Properties window, double-click the chapter track's header in the Track list.

## Text Tracks

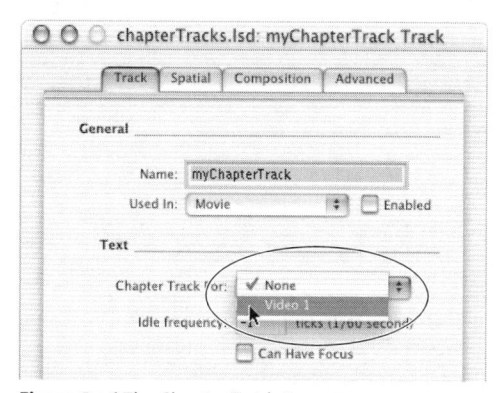

**Figure 8.76** The Chapter Track For pop-up menu specifies a second project track that will be the target for your chapter track.

**Figure 8.77** If you uncheck the Enabled checkbox, the text track will not be visible in your movie, but its chapters will still show up in the QuickTime controller's chapter list.

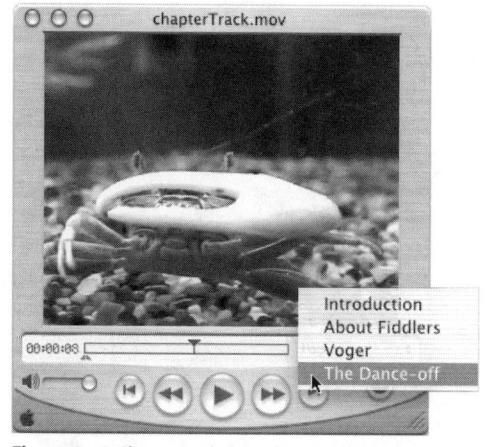

**Figure 8.78** Choose a chapter from this menu, and QuickTime jumps to the beginning of the chapter.

8. From the Chapter Track For pop-up menu, choose a track (**Figure 8.76**).

   The text track is transformed into a chapter track. Each sample becomes a chapter label and is displayed in the QuickTime controller's chapter list.

9. With the Track Properties window still open to the Track tab, uncheck the Enabled checkbox (**Figure 8.77**).

   The text track is turned off and is not visible in the final movie. Don't worry—the chapters will still show up in the QuickTime controller, but the text track itself will not be visible.

10. Choose File > Export Wired Movie.

    For more detailed instructions on exporting movies, see Chapter 5, "Setting Movie Properties."

11. Open the movie in QuickTime Player.

    The chapter list is visible in the right corner of the QuickTime control bar.

12. Choose a chapter (**Figure 8.78**).

    QuickTime Player jumps to the selected chapter.

### ✔ Tips

- In the QuickTime plug-in, if your movie isn't wide enough to display the chapter list's chapters, the chapter list is disabled.

- If your movie has alternate language tracks, create multiple chapter tracks in different languages, and set the appropriate alternate language track as the owner. (To learn more about alternate language tracks, see Chapter 5, "Setting Movie Properties.") If the owner language track is called for, its chapter track is also called, and the QuickTime controller's chapter list changes accordingly.

**ABOUT CHAPTER TRACKS**

175

# Streaming, Flash, and VR Tracks

Streaming, Flash, and VR files are created outside LiveStage in third-party applications such as Apple's QuickTime Player Pro (streaming), Macromedia's Flash or Electricrain's Swift 3D (Flash), and Apple's QuickTime VR Authoring Studio (VR).

All three of these track types compress complex media files into one easy-to-use sample. Streaming and VR files are often made of two or more tracks, and Flash files can have several scenes and layers (**Figure 9.1**). When imported into your project, however, each of these complex files takes up just one track in the Timeline, making them extremely easy to work with (**Figure 9.2**).

This chapter covers everything you need to know to incorporate streaming, Flash, and VR files into your LiveStage project, including working with live streams, QScripting Flash tracks, and using multi-node VR scenes.

Chapter 9

*Streaming file*

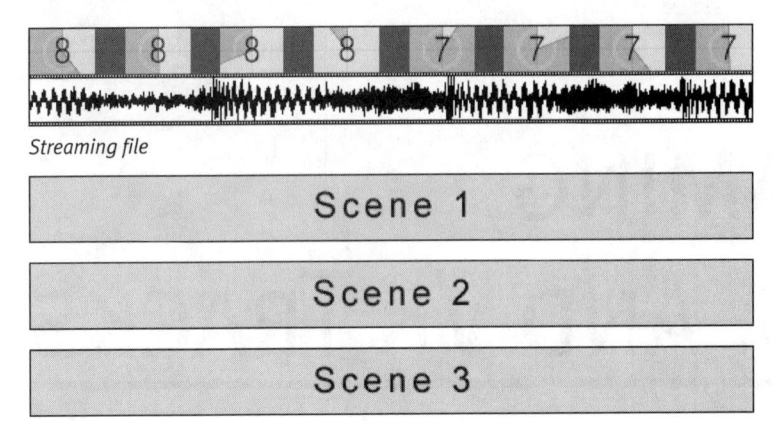

*Flash file*

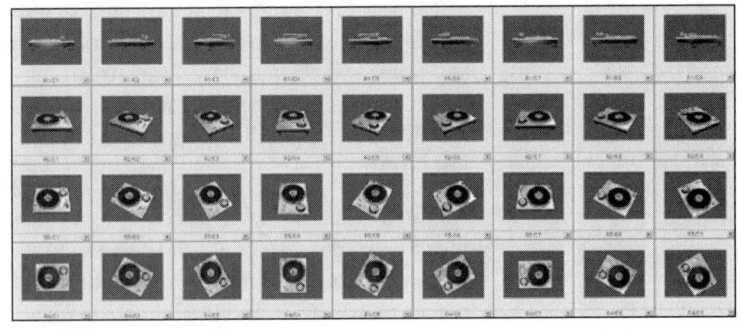

*VR file*

**Figure 9.1** Streaming, Flash, and VR tracks take complex media files...

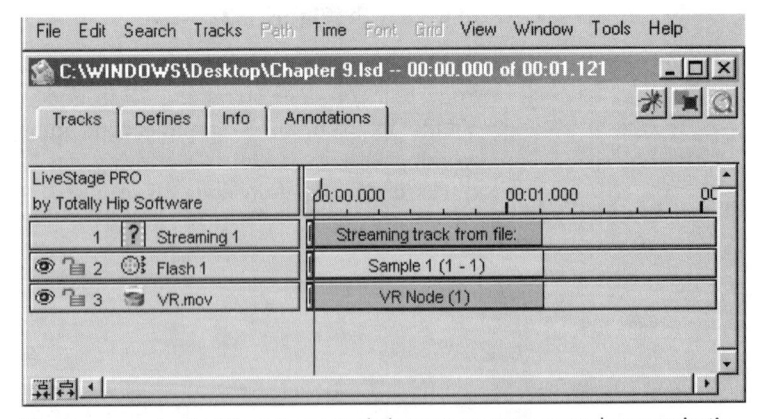

**Figure 9.2** ...and collect them in one track that you can move around your project's Timeline easily.

## About Streaming Tracks

When you make a standard QuickTime movie, the content progressively downloads to the viewer's computer as she watches the movie. For most files, this system works perfectly. If you're delivering large files, however, such as a promotional film trailer or a recorded DJ set, your file will eat up space on the viewer's hard disk. In this case, you'll want to package your media in a track that doesn't download to the viewer's hard disk: a streaming track.

It is beyond the scope of this book to teach you how to create a streaming movie. For more information on creating a streaming movie, see Peachpit's *QuickTime for Macintosh and Windows: Visual QuickStart Guide*, by Judith Stern and Robert Lettieri.

If you've already created a streaming movie and placed it on an RTSP server (a special server used for streaming content), you must create a pointer movie that sits on your hard disk and points to the streaming file. When you import the pointer movie into your project, it shows LiveStage exactly where to find the server containing your streaming file.

To create a pointer movie, you must use QuickTime Pro. The free version of QuickTime does not let you save files, which is an essential step in the process. If creating wired movies is more than just a hobby to you, you should seriously consider upgrading to QuickTime Pro. It's a perfect companion to LiveStage, and at $29.99 is probably one of the biggest software bargains on the market. To purchase QuickTime Pro, visit http://www.apple.com/quicktime/.

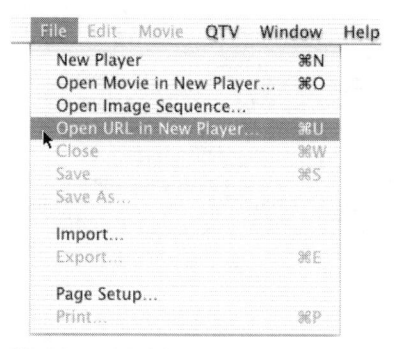

**Figure 9.3** In QuickTime Player, you can open a streaming movie straight from its RTSP server by choosing File > Open URL in New Player.

### To create a pointer movie:

1. Open QuickTime Player.

2. Choose File > Open URL in New Player (**Figure 9.3**).

   The Open URL dialog appears.

*continues on next page*

Chapter 9

3. Enter the streaming file's URL
   (**Figure 9.4**).
   Make sure that you enter RTSP:// before the name of the streaming server; otherwise, QuickTime will not know where to find the streaming file.

4. Click OK.
   The Open URL dialog closes.

5. Choose File > Save.
   The Save dialog opens.

6. Navigate to the place on your hard disk where you want to save this file.

7. In the Save As text box, enter a new file name for the movie (**Figure 9.5**).

8. Click Save.
   The pointer movie is saved to your hard disk (**Figure 9.6**). If you open this pointer movie in LiveStage, it accesses your streaming file when the movie is played.

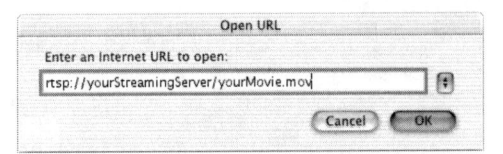

**Figure 9.4** In the Open URL dialog, enter the full URL (including rtsp://) of the streaming movie that you would like to open in QuickTime Player.

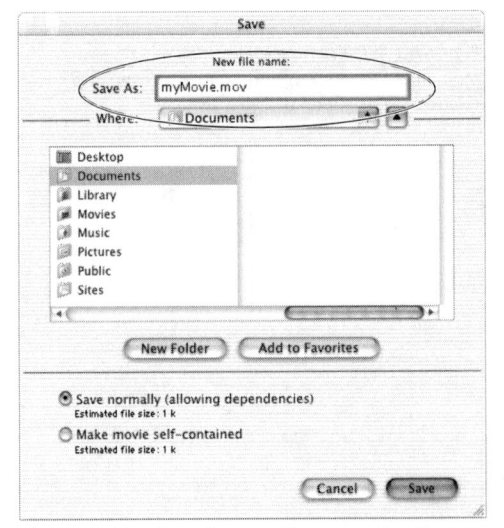

**Figure 9.5** Give the pointer movie a recognizable name so that you can identify it quickly on your hard disk.

**Figure 9.6** A pointer movie is saved to your hard disk. If you open this pointer movie, it reaches out to the Internet, finds your streaming file, and plays it.

ABOUT STREAMING TRACKS

180

## Streaming, Flash, and VR Tracks

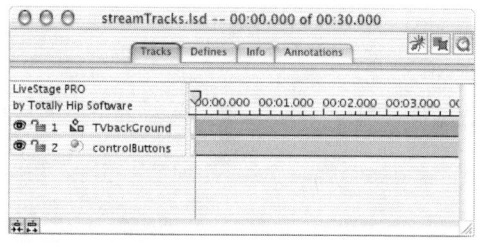

**Figure 9.7** The Tracks tab.

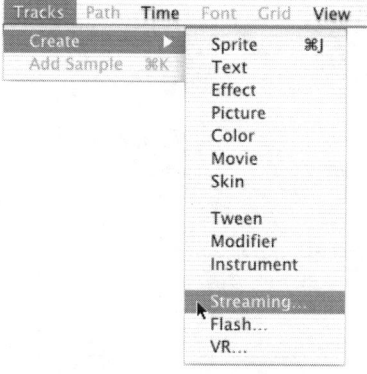

**Figure 9.8** To add a streaming track to your LiveStage project, choose Tracks > Create > Streaming.

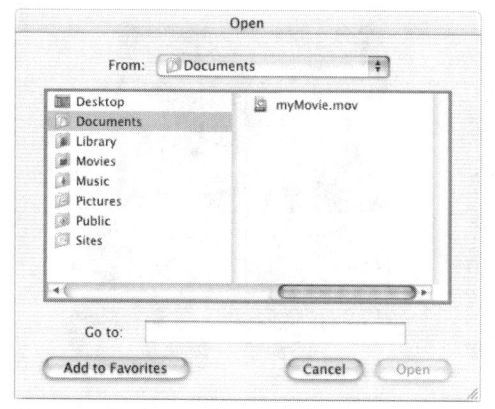

**Figure 9.9** Navigate to the movie that contains your streaming file.

### To add a streaming file:

1. In the Project window, select the Tracks tab (**Figure 9.7**).

2. Choose Tracks > Create > Streaming (**Figure 9.8**).
   
   The Open dialog appears (**Figure 9.9**).

3. Select a pointer movie on your hard disk and click Open.
   
   At the bottom of the Tracks tab's Track list, a streaming track is created (**Figure 9.10**).

### ✔ Tips

- To speed the import process, drag a pointer movie into the Tracks tab from the library, Finder (Mac) or desktop (Windows).

- After you've created a streaming track, you can preview it inside LiveStage by simply double-clicking it in the Timeline.

**Figure 9.10** Your streaming file is added to the bottom of the Track list.

**ABOUT STREAMING TRACKS**

181

## Chapter 9

## Using streaming tracks

Streaming tracks can be very long. In fact, in the case of a live stream (such as one from a radio or TV station), the stream has an infinite duration, which means that it has no end.

If you're using LiveStage to mix a streaming track with other media content, there's a very good chance that the streaming track will be much longer than your other tracks (**Figure 9.11**). This difference can create some real problems. Let's say that you've created a TV shell to play a streaming video. The shell itself is made of a picture track containing a background image; a sprite track holding the play and volume controls; and, of course, a streaming track (**Figure 9.12**). To ensure that your movie displays correctly from beginning to end, you must set the picture and sprite tracks to be equal in length to the streaming track. If they're not, the movie will continue to play along the stream, past the end of the sprite and picture tracks, and the TV shell disappears (**Figure 9.13**). Although the stream continues to play, the area that previously contained the TV shell goes blank, and your presentation's integrity is destroyed.

To fix this problem, you must stretch all your tracks to match the duration of the streaming track. If your streaming track is a live feed, it theoretically has no end. To compensate, you will have to provide your other tracks an infinite duration.

### To set an infinite duration:

1. In the Tracks tab, double-click the sample of a sprite, text, color, picture, or movie track.
   The sample opens (**Figure 9.14**).

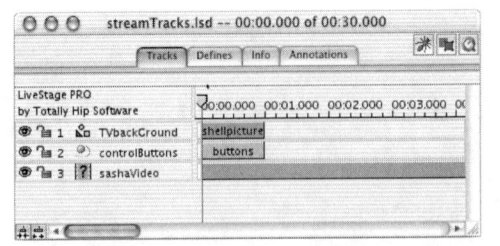

**Figure 9.11** In most cases, streaming tracks stretch out beyond the end of your project's other tracks. To make sure that your movie plays correctly, you must change the length of the other tracks to match the streaming track's length.

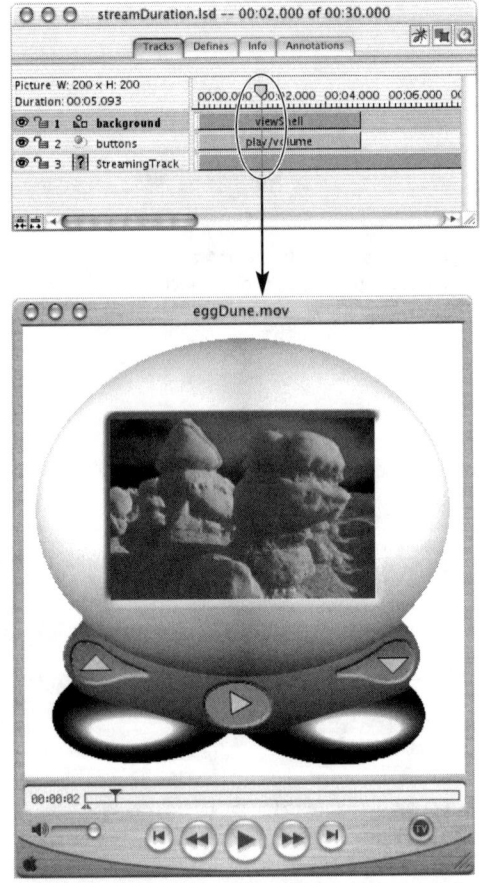

**Figure 9.12** A streaming video player, at two seconds into the movie. The project file (top) has a picture, sprite, and streaming track that combine to make a movie (bottom).

# Streaming, Flash, and VR Tracks

**Figure 9.13** If the movie plays past the picture and sprite tracks, the streaming video player's shell disappears.

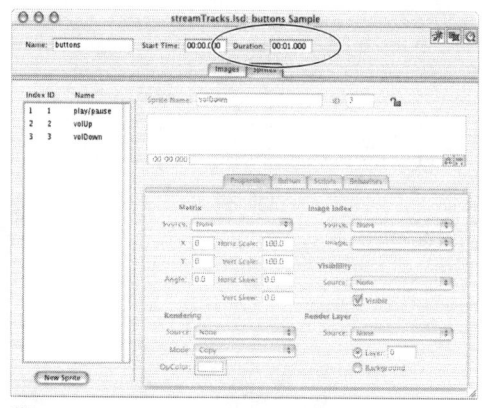

**Figure 9.14** An open sprite sample. The sample's duration is defined by the Duration text box.

**2.** In the Duration text box, type an asterisk (*) (**Figure 9.15**).

The text box does not accept letters, so you cannot type infinite. As a result, you must enter an asterisk (Shift-8).

**3.** Select the Tracks tab.

The sample expands to fill the Timeline (**Figure 9.16**).

## ✔ Tips

- To find the duration of a streaming track, select its header in the Track list and then look at the Selection Properties panel (above the Track list). The streaming track's duration is listed at the bottom of this panel.

- Do not try to resize your streaming track to match the length of the movie's other tracks. The length of a streaming track is hard-wired into it. Although you can resize a streaming track by dragging its left edge in the Timeline, doing so has no effect on the stream's duration, and your movie will still play beyond its other tracks.

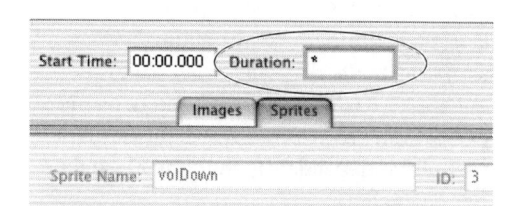

**Figure 9.15** Typing an asterisk (*) in the Duration text box assigns the track an infinite duration.

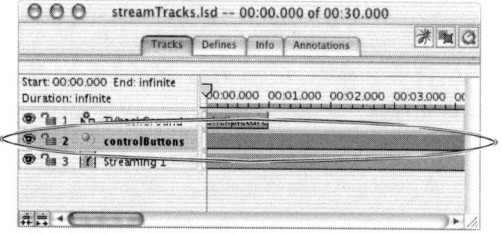

**Figure 9.16** Back in the Tracks tab, the track stretches beyond the right edge of the Timeline.

**ABOUT STREAMING TRACKS**

183

## About Flash Tracks

Flash creates small, scalable vector files that you can import straight into your LiveStage projects. Unlike a traditional bitmapped image, in which every pixel represents a chunk of data in the file, Flash vectors are stored as mathematical formulas that are drawn when the Flash file is opened. This arrangement leads to much smaller files and also has a bonus: you can reduce or enlarge a Flash file without destroying its image quality. Because the Flash file is drawn mathematically every time it is opened, if it is scaled to a larger dimension, it is simply drawn larger.

Flash and LiveStage make a perfect match, as both are designed to create interactive, low-bandwidth movies for the Internet. Whether you need a few buttons to control movie playback, a small animation to add some action, or perhaps even an entire backdrop for your movie, you won't go wrong using Flash.

### Adding Flash files

The typical Flash file is composed of several layers containing graphics, audio, and/or scripting. Some Flash files even have different scenes that viewers can jump to as they explore the project or separate movie clips that play independently from the Flash file's main Timeline.

Fortunately, when you add a Flash file into LiveStage, all of its layers, scenes, and movie clips are collected in one sample in the project's Timeline. This system makes it easy for you to arrange the Flash file to fit with the rest of your project's content, as all you have to worry about is that one little sample.

# Streaming, Flash, and VR Tracks

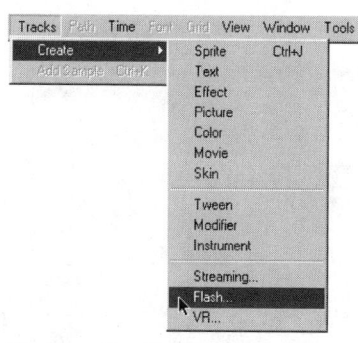

**Figure 9.17** To add a Flash track to your project, choose Tracks > Create > Flash.

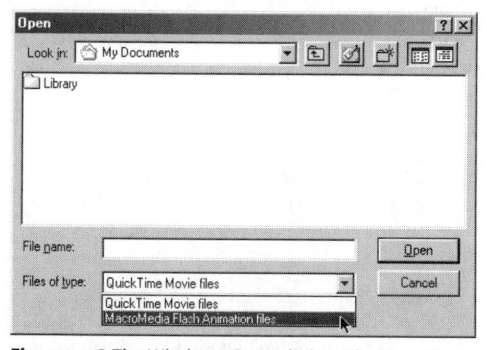

**Figure 9.18** The Windows Open dialog. If you can't see your Flash files in the file list, choose Macromedia Flash Animation Files from the Files of Type pop-up menu at the bottom of the Open dialog.

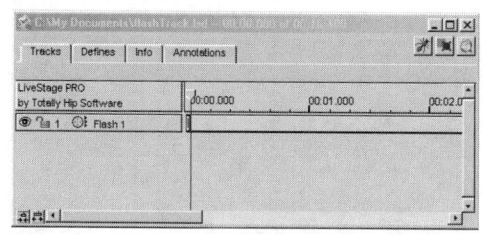

**Figure 9.19** A newly added Flash track in the Tracks tab.

## To add a Flash file:

1. In the Project window, select the Tracks tab.

2. Choose Tracks > Create > Flash (**Figure 9.17**).

   The Open dialog appears (**Figure 9.18**).

3. Select a Flash file on your hard disk.

4. Click Open.

   A Flash track is added to the bottom of the Tracks tab's Track list. A sample containing the Flash file's media is placed in the Timeline (**Figure 9.19**).

## ✔ Tips

- Only Flash 4 files are fully supported by QuickTime 5. If you're using Flash 5, you must make all Flash files compatible with Flash 4 before bringing them into LiveStage. From inside Flash 5, choose File > Publish Settings > Flash tab > Version > Flash 4. When you publish your Flash file, Flash ensures that the file is compatible with Flash 4 (to learn more about publishing Flash files, see Peachpit's *Macromedia Flash for Windows and Macintosh: Visual QuickStart Guide*, by Katherine Ulrich).

- To speed the import process, drag a Flash file into the Tracks tab from the library, Finder (Mac) or desktop (Windows).

**ABOUT FLASH TRACKS**

185

Chapter 9

## Understanding sample duration

A Flash sample can be stretched or reduced in the Timeline with little effect on the Flash file's functionality. Its rate of playback will be affected, however. When you stretch a Flash sample, you slow the rate at which the Flash file plays (see the sidebar "Stretching Flash Files" in this section). Conversely, when you reduce a Flash sample, you speed it up.

If your Flash file has only one frame, you can safely stretch it to match the length of your project. This technique is particularly handy for making Flash movie controllers. If you create a one-frame Flash file containing play, pause, and volume buttons, you can stretch that one frame to cover the entire length of the movie. No matter where you are in the movie's Timeline, the Flash buttons are there, obediently awaiting your instructions.

### To change a Flash track's duration:

1. In the Tracks tab, double-click the Flash track's header.

   The Track Properties window opens, displaying the Track tab with a Flash section at the bottom (**Figure 9.20**).

2. In the Flash section, enter a new duration in the Duration text box (**Figure 9.21**).

   In the Timeline, the Flash track resizes to match its new duration (**Figure 9.22**).

### ✔ Tips

- You can also change the Flash track's duration by grabbing its right edge and dragging it along the Timeline.

- To give your Flash track an infinite duration, enter an asterisk (*) in the Duration text box.

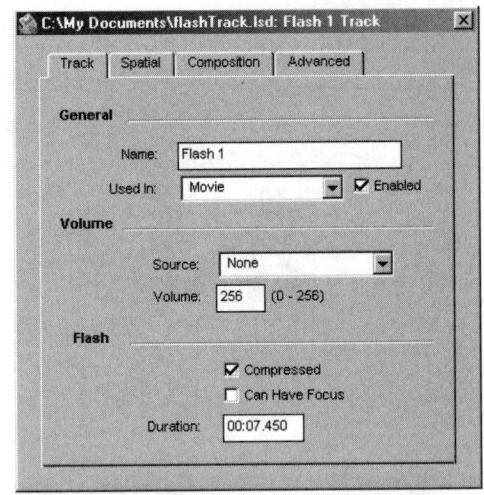

**Figure 9.20** The Track Properties window, with the Track tab open.

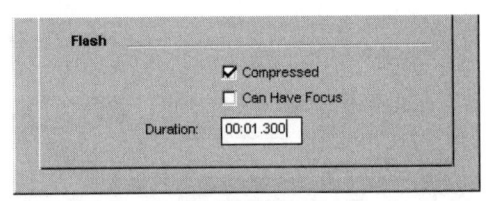

**Figure 9.21** The Duration text box lets you adjust the length of your Flash tracks precisely. In this case, the Flash file will be resized to 1.5 seconds.

*Flash sample is now 1.5 seconds long*

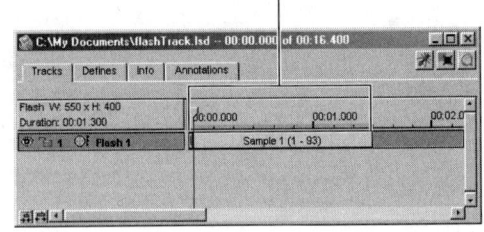

**Figure 9.22** The Flash file is resized to match the duration defined in the Track Properties window.

## Streaming, Flash, and VR Tracks

**To change a Flash track's volume:**

1. In the Tracks tab, double-click the Flash track's header.

   The Track Properties window opens, displaying the Track tab with a Flash section at the bottom.

2. In the Volume section, enter a new track volume in the Volume text box (**Figure 9.23**).

   You can enter any number between 0 and 256, with 0 representing off and 256 indicating full volume.

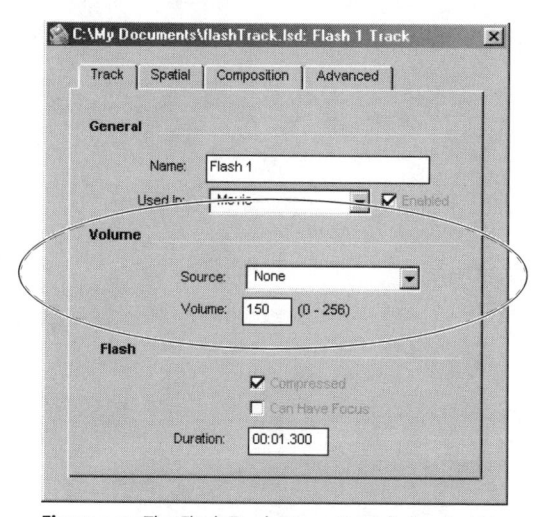

**Figure 9.23** The Flash Track Properties window holds a Volume section. If your Flash file has audio in it, use this window to adjust its default volume.

### Stretching Flash Files

When you change the duration of a Flash file, you also change the rate at which it plays back. Imagine that your Flash file is a 12-frame animation of a corporate logo that takes one second to play. Under normal circumstances, this animation plays back at 12 frames per second. When you bring the animation into LiveStage, however, you discover that the Flash file must be stretched to six seconds in length to mesh with the rest of your project's content. The Flash file still has only 12 frames, but now they play over six seconds instead of one. At this rate, the Flash file plays back at two frames per second (12 frames divided by six seconds) and appears to move very slowly.

### Flash and Text

To conserve file size, QuickTime doesn't embed text tracks' fonts directly in the movie (see Chapter 8, "Text Tracks"). If the viewer doesn't have one or more of the movie's fonts installed on his computer, different fonts are substituted, and your text looks different from what you intended. To make matters worse, Macintosh computers display fonts at 72 dots per inch, whereas Windows systems display them at 96 dpi, so your fonts look bigger on PCs than on Macs.

Flash files do not suffer from these issues. Text in a Flash file looks exactly as you intended across all platforms. If you need text in your movie to look the same regardless of the viewer's computer platform, use a Flash file. Because Flash files are very small, using a Flash file for your text will add very little to the project's overall file size.

# Chapter 9

## Exploring a Flash sample

Each Flash sample holds a complete Flash file. If the Flash file has multiple frames, each frame is represented in a Timeline across the top of the Flash sample (**Figure 9.24**). If you click one of the sample Timeline's frames, a red indicator highlights the selected frame. Frames with a small gray dot contain buttons, and frames with a small black dot contain QScripts.

The bottom of the Flash sample holds a script editor. (To learn more about the script editor, see Chapter 4, "The Script Editor.") On the right side is the script edit field, and on the left side is the Object/Event Handler list.

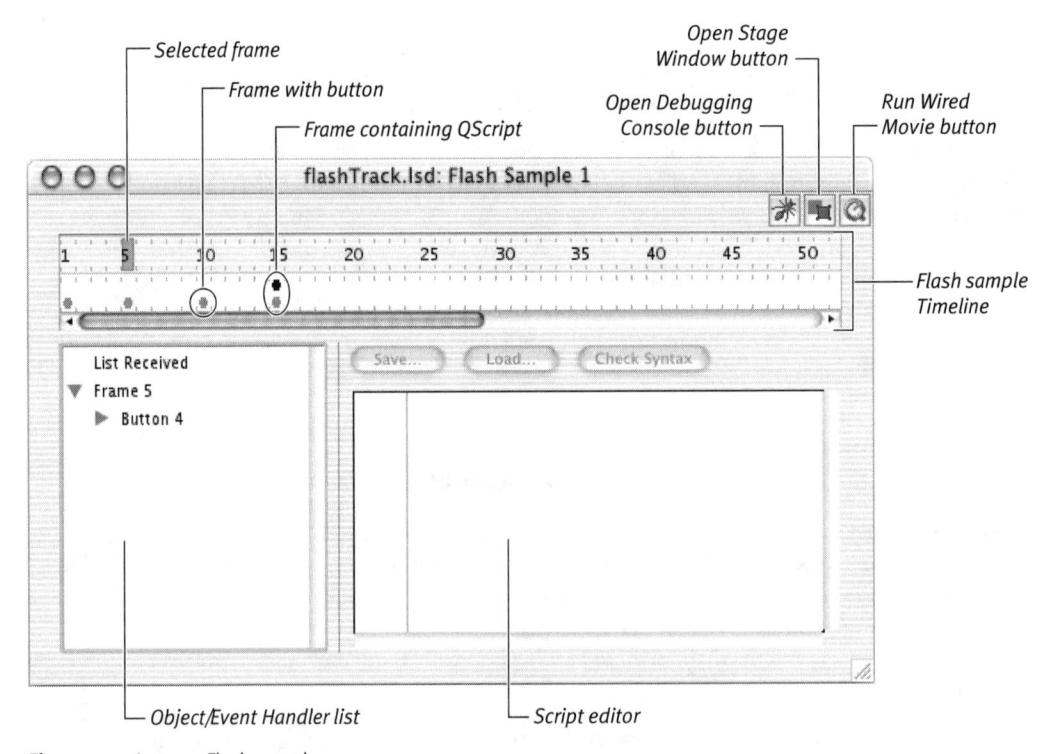

**Figure 9.24** An open Flash sample.

The Object/Event Handler list works just like the Event Handler list of a standard script editor but serves one additional purpose. If you select a frame containing buttons from the Flash sample's Timeline, each button is also displayed in the Object/Event Handler list (**Figure 9.25**).

## To select a frame from a Flash sample's Timeline:

1. In the Tracks tab, double-click a Flash sample to open it.

2. In the Flash sample's Timeline, select a frame.

   A red indicator highlights the selected frame (refer to Figure 9.25).

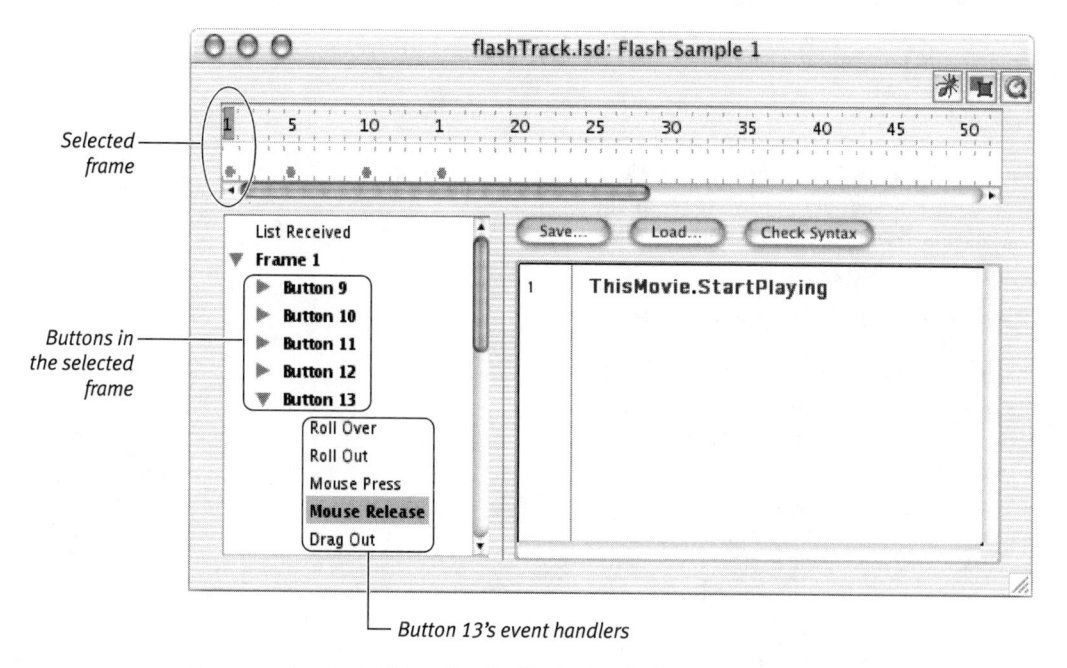

**Figure 9.25** The Object/Event Handler list displays both buttons and event handlers.

# About Scripting Flash Tracks

Like LiveStage, Flash files use frame and object events to trigger scripted actions. A Flash frame event is similar to the Frame Loaded event handler in LiveStage; when the frame loads, an action is executed. These actions typically tell the Flash file how to run, such as a script that stops the Flash file or makes it loop continuously over the first five frames.

Object events occur when the viewer interacts with a Flash button. Like text track hotspots, Flash buttons are movie objects that can react to the pointer and control your movie. Flash buttons can launch Web pages, raise or lower movie volume, and more. The button itself is simply a movie object; you must give it action.

If you've already wired your Flash files by using Flash scripts, you can import the files into LiveStage, and the scripts will work. If you haven't already scripted your Flash files, use the Flash sample's script editor to add interactivity with QScript.

## Scripting Flash frame events

Each frame in the Flash sample Timeline has its own frame event, which you can script even if the frame lacks buttons (**Figure 9.26**). Frame events execute as the movie plays. Because frame events don't require any viewer interaction to execute, they are ideally suited to control internal movie navigation structures, such as QScripts that make the movie play or pause automatically.

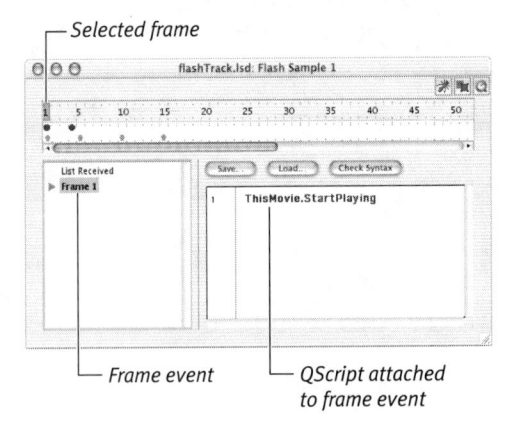

**Figure 9.26** Every frame of the Flash sample's Timeline has a frame event.

## Streaming, Flash, and VR Tracks

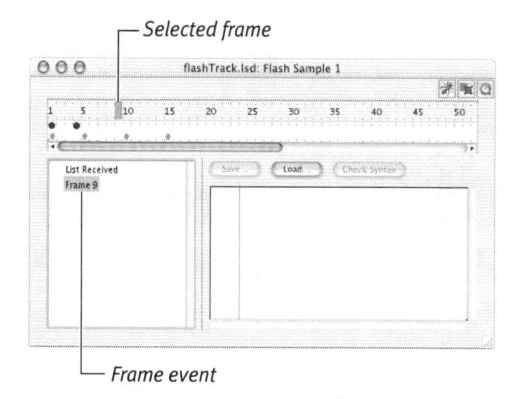

**Figure 9.27** Before you can script a Flash frame event, you must select it in the Object/Event Handler list.

*Selected frame*
*Frame event*

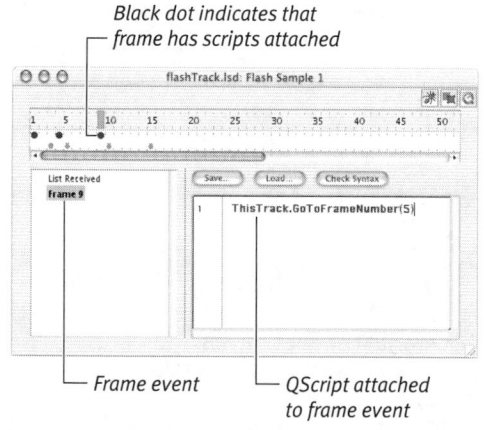

**Figure 9.28** This QScript is attached to the frame event and will be executed when QuickTime loads the frame.

*Black dot indicates that frame has scripts attached*
*Frame event*
*QScript attached to frame event*

### To QScript a Flash frame event:

1. In the Tracks tab, double-click a Flash sample to open it.

2. In the Flash sample's Timeline, select the frame that you want to script.

3. At the top of the Object/Event Handler list, click the frame event to select it (**Figure 9.27**).

   The number next to the frame event indicates the selected frame.

4. In the script edit field, write your QScript (**Figure 9.28**).

   A black dot appears in the Flash sample's Timeline, indicating that a script has been attached to the selected frame. When the movie loads the Flash frame, the QScript is executed.

### ✔ Tips

- QuickTime drops frames as it plays, and in rare circumstances, it leaps right over your Flash frame events. If you are scripting a Flash frame, you can prevent this situation by setting All Frames playback, though your audio will be disabled. To learn more about All Frames playback, see Chapter 5, "Setting Movie Properties."

- Flash labels let you define names for certain frames of the Flash file. If you used labels in your Flash files, those label names appear beside the frame events at the top of the Object/Event Handler list.

# Chapter 9

## Scripting Flash object events

As mentioned earlier in this chapter, Flash buttons are objects, and interacting with a Flash button triggers an object event handler. Flash buttons use all the standard event handlers you've come to recognize in LiveStage, plus a few extras. There is, however, one small catch: Flash object events have different names from their LiveStage counterparts. But don't let the differences confuse you; translating them is easy (**Table 9.1**).

### To script a Flash button:

1. In the Tracks tab, double-click a Flash sample to open it.

2. In the Flash sample's Timeline, select a frame containing one or more buttons (**Figure 9.29**).

   An expansion arrow appears beside the frame event.

3. Click the expansion arrow beside the frame event.

   The frame's buttons appear in the Object/Event Handler list (**Figure 9.30**).

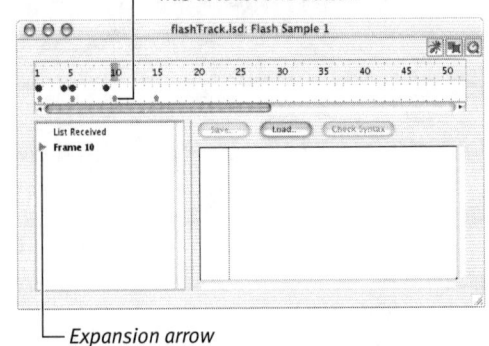

**Figure 9.29** When you select a frame containing buttons, an expansion arrow appears beside the frame event.

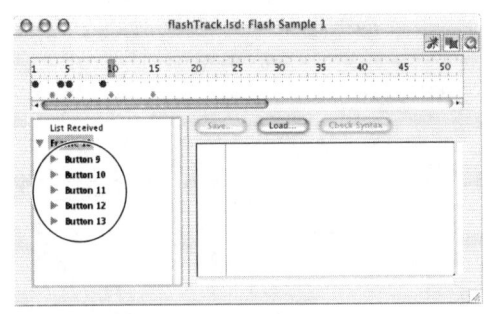

**Figure 9.30** The frame's buttons.

**Table 9.1**

### LiveStage Object Events vs. Flash Object Events

| LIVESTAGE OBJECT EVENT | FLASH OBJECT EVENT | DESCRIPTION |
| --- | --- | --- |
| Mouse Enter | Roll Over | The pointer moves over a button |
| Mouse Exit | Roll Out | The pointer moves off a button |
| Mouse Down | Mouse Press | With the pointer over a button, the viewer presses the mouse button |
| Mouse Up/Mouse Click | Mouse Release | With the pointer over a button, the viewer releases the mouse button |

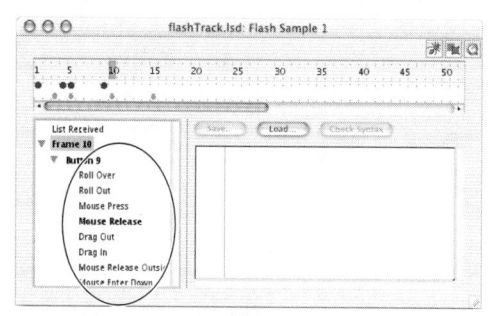

**Figure 9.31** Every button has its own list of event handlers, which are exposed when you click the expansion arrow beside the button's name in the Object/Event Handler list.

**4.** Click the expansion arrow beside the button that you want to script.

The button's events appear below it in the Object/Event Handler list (**Figure 9.31**).

**5.** Select an event.

**6.** Enter a QScript in the script edit field (**Figure 9.32**).

In the compiled movie, the QScript is triggered when a viewer clicks the scripted button.

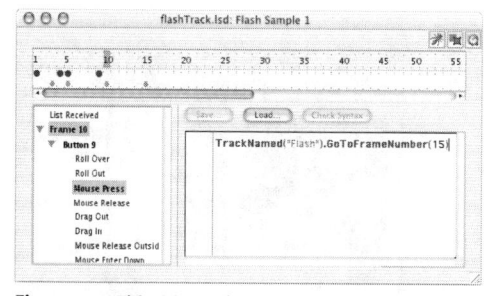

**Figure 9.32** This QScript has been attached to the Mouse Press event handler. When the viewer clicks this button, the track named Flash jumps to frame 15.

# Chapter 9

## About Flash Buttons

Imagine that you've created a Flash controller with three buttons: a Rewind button, a Play/Pause button, and a Fast Forward button. When you import the Flash file into LiveStage and look at the buttons in the Object/Event Handler list, you find it hard to distinguish which button is which (**Figure 9.33**). Although each button is numbered in the Object/Event Handler list, those numbers do very little to distinguish one button from the next.

Fortunately, you can use two techniques to identify your Flash buttons. The easiest is to open the Stage window and double-click a button on the stage. This action causes the Flash file to pop open, with the button's event handlers displayed in the Object/Event Handler list. The second method involves using Flash's `FSCommand` to attach a label to the button as you create the Flash file.

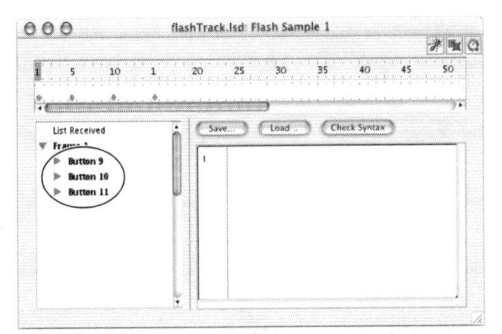

**Figure 9.33** All buttons look the same in the Object/Event Handler list, making it hard to figure out which button is which.

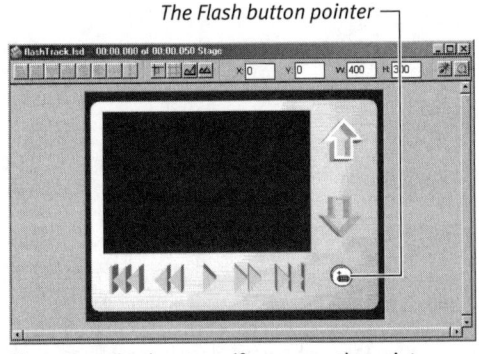

**Figure 9.34** On the stage, if you move the pointer over a Flash button, it changes into a button pointer.

### Opening Flash buttons from the stage

Opening a Flash button from the stage offers a convenient, sure-fire method of attaching the right QScript to the right button. When you double-click a Flash button on the stage, the Flash sample opens, with the clicked button's event handlers displayed in the Object/Event Handler list. It is now a simple matter to select an event and wire a QScript into it.

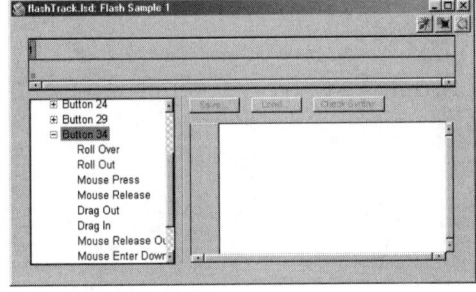

**Figure 9.35** An open Flash sample. In the Object/Event Handler list, the button that was clicked is expanded to show its event handlers.

#### To open a Flash button from the stage:

1. If the Stage window is not already open, choose Window > Show Stage Window.

2. Place the pointer over a Flash button.
   The default arrow pointer changes into a button pointer (**Figure 9.34**).

3. Double-click the Flash button.
   The Flash sample opens, with the button you selected expanded in the Object/Event Handler list (**Figure 9.35**).

194

## Using the Flash FSCommand

Although clicking a button on the stage certainly offers convenience, if the stage has multiple buttons, you may find it easier to use the Macromedia Flash application to label your buttons with an *FSCommand*. The *FSCommand* action lets Flash files communicate with other application programs, including LiveStage. If you attach an *FSCommand* to a Flash button and then import the Flash file into your project, the *FSCommand* is visible in the Flash sample's script edit field (**Figure 9.36**). In the frenzy of a QScript session, this arrangement makes it easy for you to determine which Flash button is which.

This example assumes that you are familiar with creating and scripting Flash buttons in Macromedia Flash 5. For more information on using Flash, see Peachpit's *Macromedia Flash for Windows and Macintosh: Visual QuickStart Guide*, by Katherine Ulrich.

*Flash Object Actions panel*

*Flash sample*

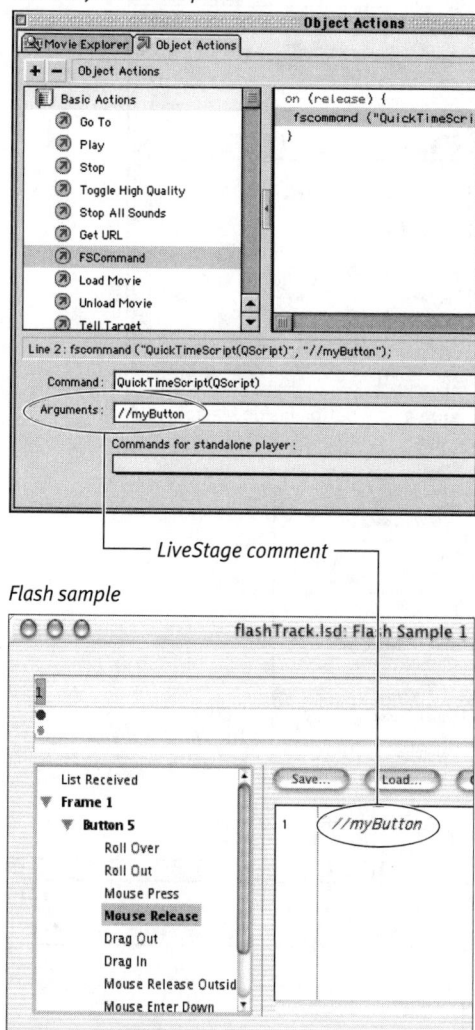

**Figure 9.36** When attached to a button event, the text that you enter in the Arguments text box of a Flash *FSCommand* also appears in LiveStage, in the Flash sample's script editor.

Chapter 9

## To label a Flash button with an FSCommand:

1. Open Flash and create a button.

2. In the main Timeline in Flash, click the button to select it.

   A thin blue rectangle appears around the button (**Figure 9.37**).

3. Choose Window > Actions (**Figure 9.38**). The Object Actions panel opens.

4. In the Basic Actions folder, double-click FSCommand.

   The FSCommand action appears in the Actions list, attached to the button's Mouse Release event (**Figure 9.39**).

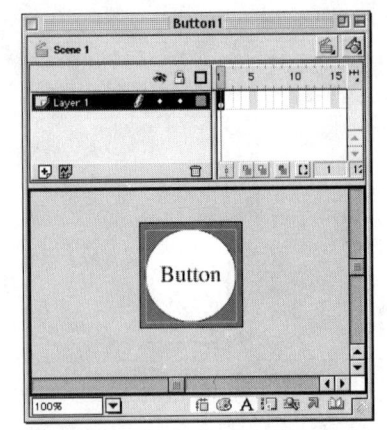

**Figure 9.37** A button inside Macromedia Flash 5.

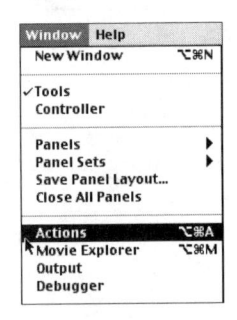

**Figure 9.38** The Window menu in Flash 5.

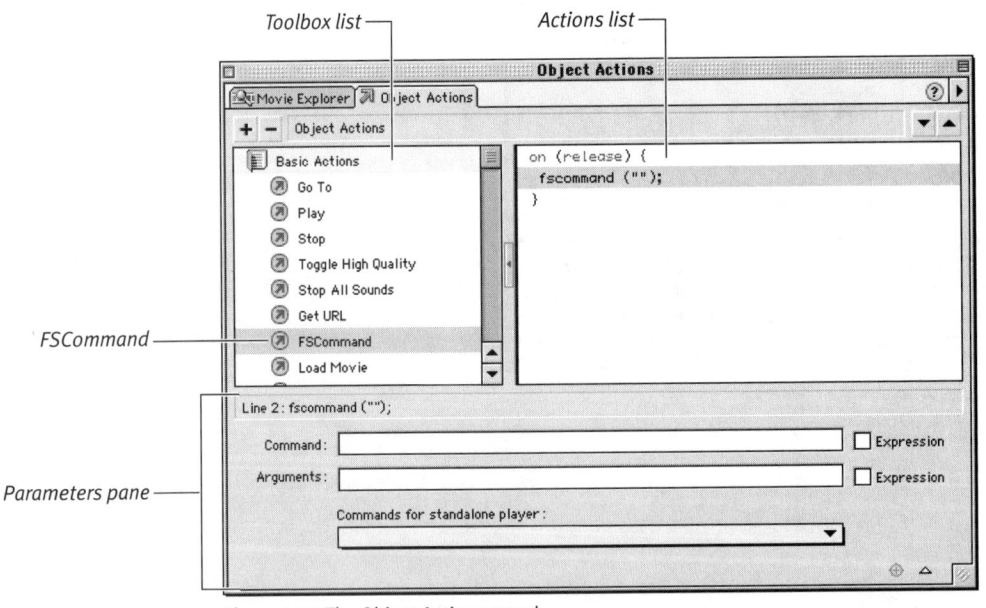

**Figure 9.39** The Object Actions panel.

196

# Streaming, Flash, and VR Tracks

**5.** In the Command text box, type the following:

`QuickTimeScript(QScript)`

You must type this command exactly as shown; otherwise, the Flash file will not be able to communicate with LiveStage, and the button label will not be passed on.

**6.** In the Arguments text box, type the following (**Figure 9.40**):

`//myButton`

You can replace `myButton` with any name you want. Just be careful to leave the double slashes (`//`) in front of the name; otherwise, you will have problems later when you try to compile your LiveStage project. (The double slashes create a LiveStage comment, which the compiled movie ignores.)

*continues on next page*

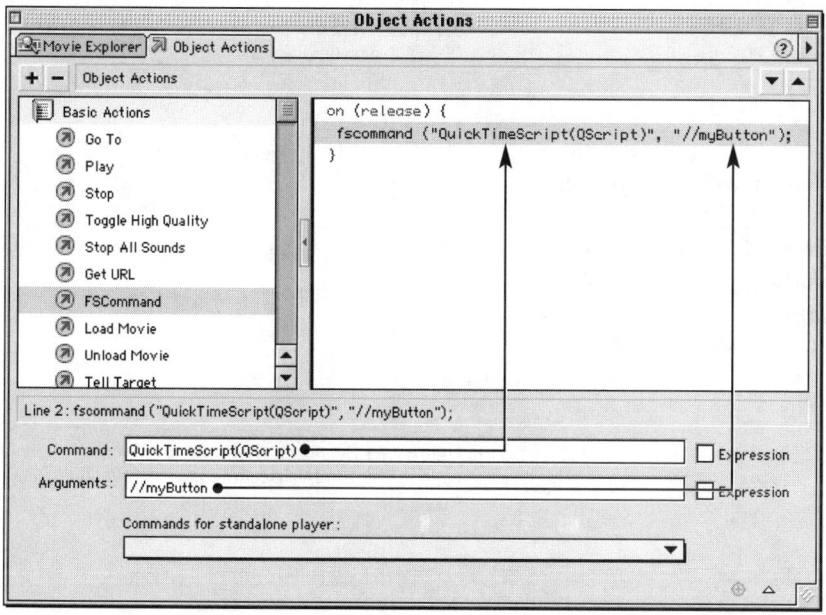

**Figure 9.40** The command and arguments that you enter in the Parameters pane are both attached to the `FSCommand`.

## About Flash Buttons

197

# Chapter 9

7. Publish the Flash file, and drag it into the Tracks tab of the Project window.

8. In the Tracks tab, double-click the Flash sample to open it (**Figure 9.41**).

9. In the Flash sample's Timeline, select the frame containing the button.

    The frame is highlighted with a red indicator mark.

10. In the Object/Event Handler list, click the expansion arrow next to the frame event (**Figure 9.42**).

    The button appears below the frame event in the Object/Event Handler list.

11. Click the expansion arrow next to the button.

    The button's event handlers appear below it in the Object/Event Handler list.

12. Select the `Mouse Release` event handler.

    In the script edit field, a QScript comment appears, displaying the button's name (**Figure 9.43**).

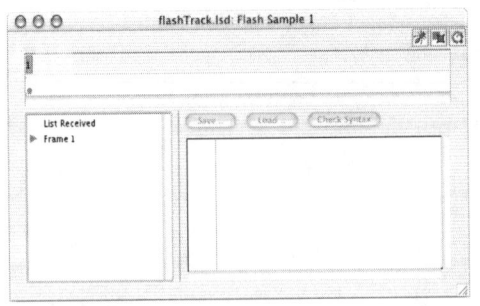

**Figure 9.41** An open Flash sample.

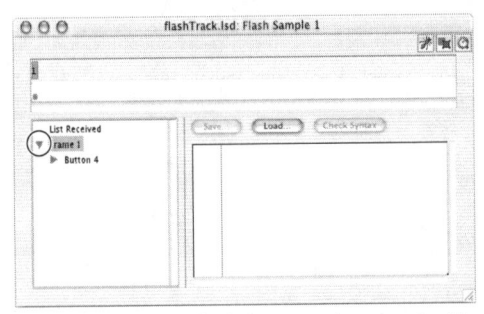

**Figure 9.42** When clicked, the expansion arrow beside the frame event displays all the frame's buttons in the Object/Event Handler list.

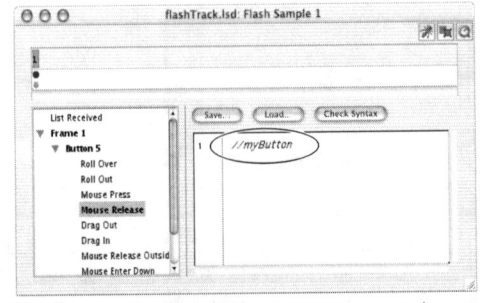

**Figure 9.43** The argument from the `FSCommand` shows up in the button's `Mouse Release` event handler.

## ✔ Tip

- You can write any QScript you want in an `FSCommand`, and it will show up when the Flash file is brought into LiveStage. Although the preceding example used a comment, nothing stops you from using an `FSComand` to wire more-complex QScript actions directly into your Flash files.

**ABOUT FLASH BUTTONS**

198

# Streaming, Flash, and VR Tracks

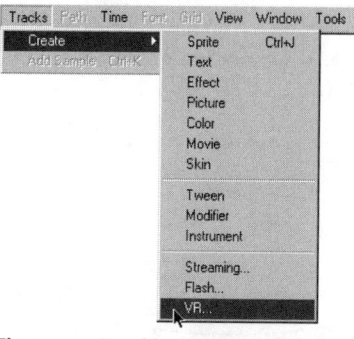

**Figure 9.44** To add a VR file to LiveStage, choose > Tracks > Create > VR.

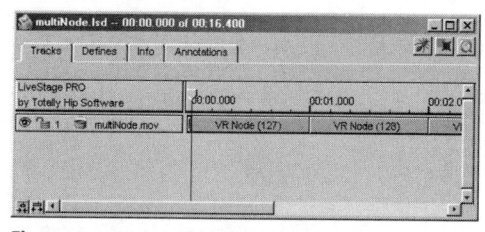

**Figure 9.45** A new VR track is added in the Tracks tab.

## About VR Tracks

VR tracks create immersive 3D environments that come in two flavors: panoramas and objects. A *VR panorama* is a 360-degree photograph that the viewer can grab and spin around to see every vista (an effect not dissimilar to standing in one spot and spinning). A *VR object* is a series of photos of one object taken from different angles. These photos are stitched together to form the illusion of being one 3D object that the viewer can grab and spin around.

You cannot create VR tracks inside LiveStage. To create a VR track, you need to use a third-party application, such as Apple's QuickTime VR Authoring Studio, or one of the free applications offered in the Developer's Tools section of Apple's Web site:

http://developer.apple.com/quicktime/quicktimeintro/tools/

### To add a VR file:

1. In the Project window, select the Tracks tab.

2. Choose Tracks > Create > VR (**Figure 9.44**).

    The Open dialog appears.

3. Select a VR file on your hard disk.

4. Click Open.

    A VR track is added at the bottom of the Tracks tab's Track list (**Figure 9.45**).

199

Chapter 9

When it comes to duration, panoramic VR files are somewhat flexible and can be enlarged or reduced to cover more or less of the project's Timeline. Object VRs, on the other hand, are inflexible; you cannot change their duration.

## To change the duration of a panoramic VR:

1. In the Tracks tab, double-click the VR track's header in the Track list.

    The Track Properties window opens, displaying the Track tab (**Figure 9.46**). The bottom of the Track tab holds a VR section, which contains a Duration text box.

2. In the Duration text box, enter a new duration for your VR panorama.

    In the Timeline, the VR track expands or contracts to match this new duration (**Figure 9.47**).

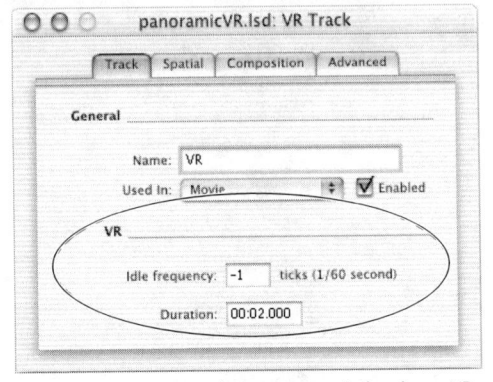

**Figure 9.46** The VR Track Properties window has a VR section with a Duration text box.

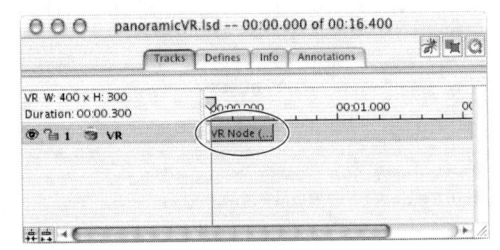

**Figure 9.47** In the Timeline, the VR track expands or contracts to match its new duration.

200

## About VR Tracks and QScript

VR tracks are fully scriptable and may contain interactive hotspots. VR hotspots typically link multiple VRs in a multi-node panorama that the viewer can "walk" through, such as a series of galleries in a museum. These hotspots can have other uses, however. You could, for example, create a VR panorama of a single museum gallery in which every painting is a hotspot. When the viewer clicks a painting, a new movie opens, displaying a high-resolution image of the painting, complete with audio narration about its history.

Like all scriptable tracks in LiveStage, VR tracks use both track and object events. Track events do not depend upon user interaction, but object events do. To use a track event, the VR track can be devoid of hotspots, but to use an object event, you will need to use a third-party application (such as Apple's QuickTime VR Authoring Studio) to make hotspots for your VR file. Currently, you cannot create hotspots in LiveStage.

### Scripting VR track events

The only two VR track events are `Frame Loaded` and `Idle`. QScripts attached to the `Frame Loaded` event are executed as soon as the VR sample is loaded into LiveStage. The `Idle` event executes a certain number of times per second. By changing a VR track's idle frequency, you can slow or speed the rate at which `Idle` events execute, which is particularly useful for animating the rotation of a VR object or panorama.

Chapter 9

## To script a VR track event:

1. In the Tracks tab, double-click a VR sample to open it.

2. In the Hotspot list, select Node Handlers (**Figure 9.48**).

   On the right side of the VR sample, the Scripts tab opens to reveal a script editor.

3. In the Event Handler list, select a track event.

4. In the script edit field, write a QScript (**Figure 9.49**).

   When the compiled movie plays, the track event executes automatically.

If you've scripted an `Idle` event, you must perform one last step to turn it on. By default, the VR track's idle frequency is –1 (off). For the `Idle` event to work, the idle frequency must be a positive integer; you must change it from its default setting so that the `Idle` event can execute.

## To change VR idle frequency:

1. In the Tracks tab, double-click the VR track's header in the Track list.

   The Track Properties window opens, displaying the Track tab. The bottom of the Track tab holds a section labeled VR, which contains the Idle Frequency text box.

2. Enter a new value in the Idle Frequency text box (**Figure 9.50**).

   The `Idle` event now executes at the rate you've specified. Idle frequency is measured in ticks per second; 1 tick is equal to 1/60 second. To learn more about idle frequency, see Chapter 4, "The Script Editor."

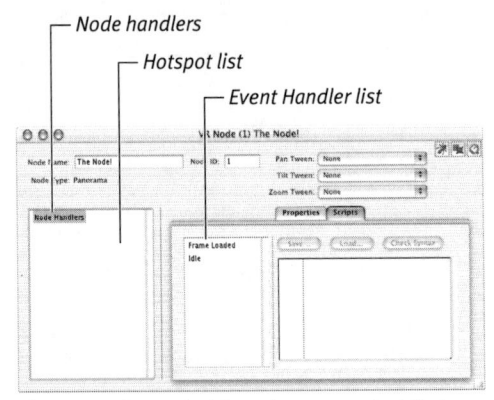

**Figure 9.48** To access VR track events, select Node Handlers in the Hotspot list.

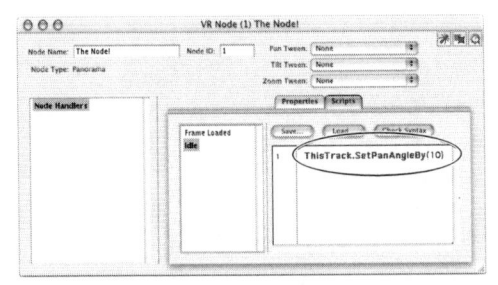

**Figure 9.49** Because it is attached to the VR track's `Idle` event, this QScript makes the VR rotate clockwise continuously in 10-degree increments.

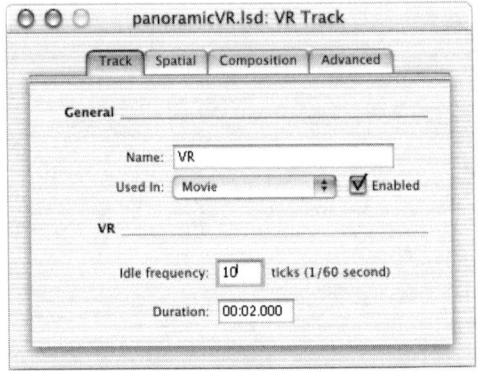

**Figure 9.50** The Idle Frequency text box controls how often the `Idle` event executes. By default, the VR track's idle frequency is set to –1 (off), and no `Idle` events execute.

202

# Streaming, Flash, and VR Tracks

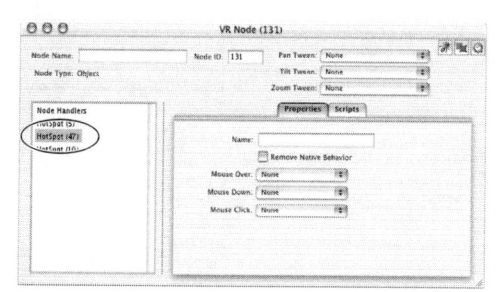

**Figure 9.51** To script a VR hotspot, start by selecting it in the VR sample's Hotspot list.

— Selected hotspot  — Event Handler list  — Script edit field

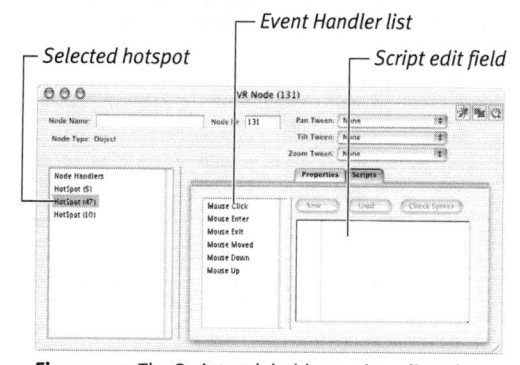

**Figure 9.52** The Scripts tab holds a script editor that you use to attach scripts to the selected hotspot.

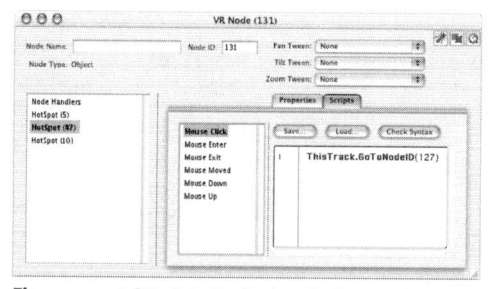

**Figure 9.53** A QScript attached to the hotspot's Mouse Click event handler. When the viewer clicks this hotspot, the movie displays the VR node that's listed in the QScript.

## Scripting VR object events

Object events are triggered when the viewer interacts with a VR hotspot. The standard object events are available to VR hotspots, including Mouse Click, Mouse Enter, and Mouse Exit.

### To script a VR object event:

1. In the Tracks tab, double-click a VR sample to open it.

2. In the Hotspot list, select the hotspot that you want to script (**Figure 9.51**).
   On the right side of the VR sample, the Properties tab becomes active.

3. Select the Scripts tab (**Figure 9.52**).
   The Scripts tab opens to reveal a script editor. The right side of the script editor holds the script edit field; the left side houses the Event Handler list. Because you are scripting an object, only object events appear in the Event Handler list.

4. In the Event Handler list, select an object event.

5. Enter a QScript in the script edit field (**Figure 9.53**).
   When the viewer clicks the VR hotspot in your compiled movie, an object event is executed.

ABOUT VR TRACKS AND QSCRIPT

203

# Chapter 9

## About VR Hotspots

You can make it easier for viewers to find your VR hotspots by using custom pointers that change as the pointer enters and interacts with the hotspot. LiveStage comes stocked with several custom pointers that you can use.

### To change the VR pointer:

1. In the Tracks tab, double-click a VR sample to open it.

2. In the Hotspot list, select a hotspot (**Figure 9.54**).

   The Properties tab becomes active. In its center are three pop-up menus: Mouse Over, Mouse Down, and Mouse Click. Each pop-up menu holds a list of alternative pointers.

3. Choose an alternative pointer from one or more of the pop-up menus (**Figure 9.55**).

   As the viewer interacts with the hotspot, the pointer changes form.

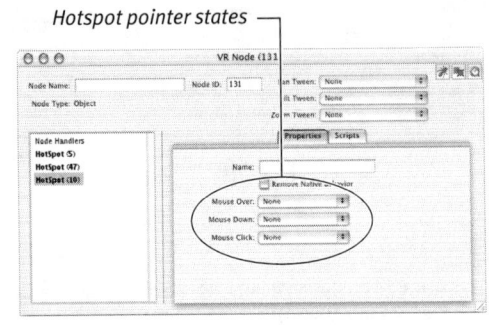

**Figure 9.54** When you select a hotspot in the Hotspot list, the Properties tab opens. The Properties tab holds properties that are unique to the selected hotspot, such as its name and pointer states.

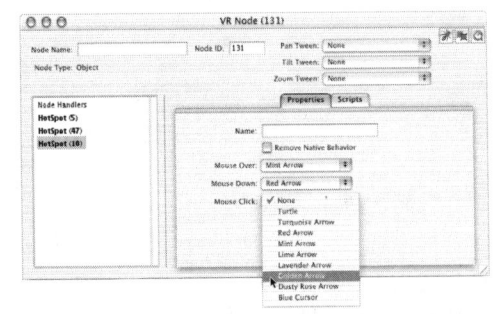

**Figure 9.55** The pointer pop-up menus let you choose among several VR pointers packaged in LiveStage.

# Streaming, Flash, and VR Tracks

— Hotspot name    — Pointer over hotspot

**Figure 9.56** If you name your hotspots, the name appears in the QuickTime controller (in both QuickTime Player and the QuickTime plug-in).

Another easy way to identify your hotspots is to give them names. When the pointer enters a named hotspot, the name appears in the QuickTime VR controller (**Figure 9.56**).

## To name a hotspot:

1. In the Tracks tab, double-click a VR sample to open it.

2. In the Hotspot list, select a hotspot.
   The Properties tab becomes active (**Figure 9.57**).

3. Enter a name in the Name text box.
   When the movie is opened in QuickTime, the hotspot's name is displayed in the QuickTime VR controller (refer to Figure 9.56).

— Selected hotspot    — Name text box

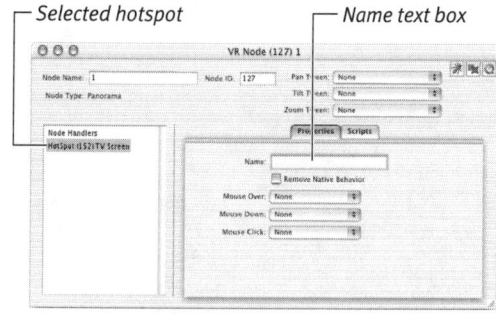

**Figure 9.57** To name a hotspot, use the Name text box at the top of the Properties tab.

**ABOUT VR HOTSPOTS**

205

# About Multi-Node VRs

A *multi-node VR* is a series of panoramas and/or objects that are linked to create a VR scene. Realtors, for example, sometimes use multi-node VRs to let potential home buyers take a virtual tour of a house. In such a multi-node VR, each room is a node in the scene, and the doorways between the rooms are hotspots that link the nodes.

When you bring a multi-node VR into LiveStage, each node is represented as a separate sample in the Timeline (**Figure 9.58**). If you've used a program such as QuickTime VR Authoring Studio, chances are good that you've already created internal links between the scene's nodes. Using LiveStage, you can rewire your VR scene so that the hotspots link to different nodes from those in the original VR file, which is very handy if you made a mistake while creating a scene. You can also use LiveStage to attach a host of other actions to your hotspots, creating complex, highly immersive, and exciting multi-node panoramas for your viewers to explore.

## Removing hotspot behaviors

In a multi-node VR scene, you click a hotspot to jump to a different node in the scene. The hotspot action that causes this jump is called a *hotspot behavior*.

Before you attach new QScripts to a multi-node VR scene in LiveStage, you should remove all the scene's native (existing) hotspot behaviors. If you do not remove the native behaviors, they will compete with the new QScripts, and your movie may not react as you wanted.

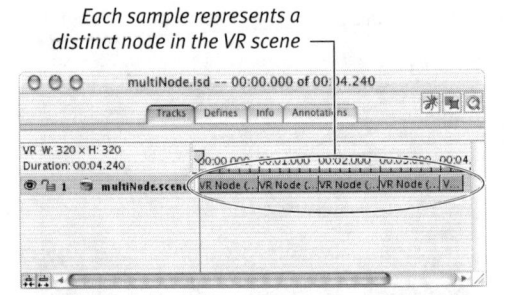

**Figure 9.58** A multi-node VR scene takes up just one track in your project.

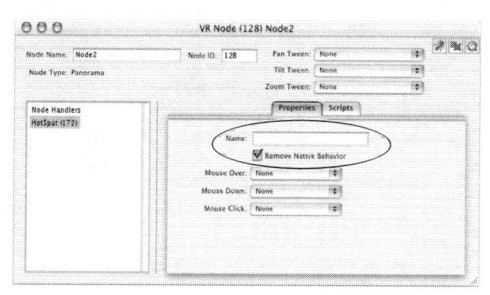

**Figure 9.59** The Remove Native Behavior checkbox tells LiveStage to disregard any scripts or behaviors previously attached to the VR hotspot.

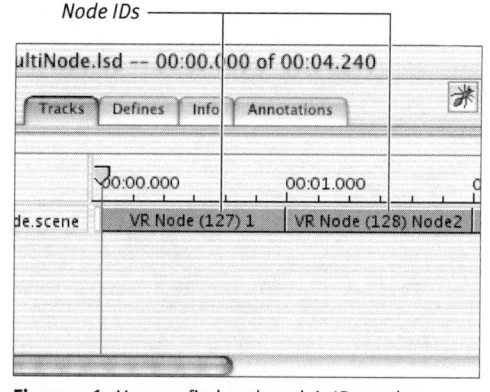

**Figure 9.60** You can find each node's ID number simply by looking at its sample in the Timeline.

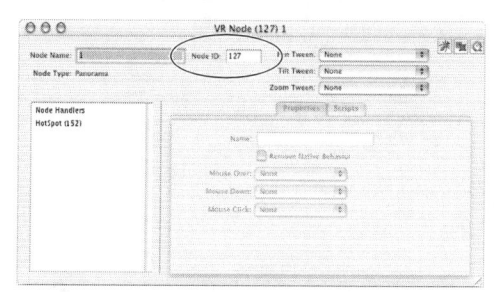

**Figure 9.61** If you open a VR sample, the node ID also appears at the top of the sample in the Node ID text box.

### To remove existing hotspot behaviors:

1. Drag a multi-node VR scene into the Tracks tab of the Project window.

2. In the Tracks tab's Timeline, double-click one of the VR samples to open it.

3. Select a hotspot in the Hotspot list. The Properties tab becomes active.

4. In the Properties tab, check the Remove Native Behavior checkbox (**Figure 9.59**).

   LiveStage ignores all behaviors previously attached to the hotspot.

## Linking VR nodes

Each node has an identifying number called a *node ID*. This node ID is used when linking the nodes of a VR scene.

### To determine a node ID:

◆ In the Tracks tab's Timeline, look at the node's sample.

   Each node's ID is displayed with its sample in the Timeline (**Figure 9.60**).

   *or*

   In the Timeline, double-click a VR sample. The sample opens, revealing the Node ID text box (**Figure 9.61**).

## To link two nodes:

1. Determine which hotspot should link to which node.

2. Open the script editor for the hotspot (refer to "Scripting VR object events" earlier in this chapter).

3. In the Event Handler list, select Mouse Click.

4. Enter the following QScript for the Mouse Click event (**Figure 9.62**):
   ThisTrack.GoToNodeID(ID)

5. Replace ID with the ID of the node that you want to link to.

   To determine the ID of the node that you want to link to, see "To determine a node ID" on the previous page.

   In the compiled movie, the hotspot activates the specified node when the viewer clicks the hotspot.

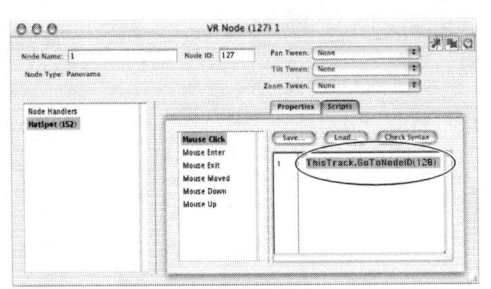

**Figure 9.62** This QScript links the current VR hotspot to the node with ID number 128.

# 10

# SPRITE TRACKS

LiveStage makes interactive QuickTime movies optimized for Web delivery. Think about what that sentence means:

**Interactive.** Viewers can interact with objects, such as buttons.

**Movies.** The project features motion, animation, and style. It is visually engaging.

**Web delivery.** The final compiled movie is file-size-optimized to slide down the thinnest possible Internet pipe at the fastest possible speed.

Sprite tracks satisfy all these qualifications. At their core, sprite tracks are nothing more than containers for sprites. The sprites themselves provide the entertainment, and the interaction.

Think of sprites as being characters in a play, acting on the stage of the sprite track. They are autonomous, individual visual objects that live in a tiny world defined by their sprite tracks. Inside that sprite track, sprites can move around, react to other sprites, and even interact with the viewer.

# Chapter 10

Although sprite tracks are scriptable, this chapter does not cover using QScript. To learn more about QScript, see Chapter 4, "The Script Editor," or Chapter 13, "Advanced QScript." To learn how to make sprites that will react to those QScripts, read on.

## To create a sprite track:

1. In the Project window, select the Tracks tab.

   The Tracks menu becomes active.

2. Choose Tracks > Create > Sprite, or press Command/Ctrl-J (**Figure 10.1**).

   A new sprite track is created, and an empty sprite sample is placed in the Timeline (**Figure 10.2**).

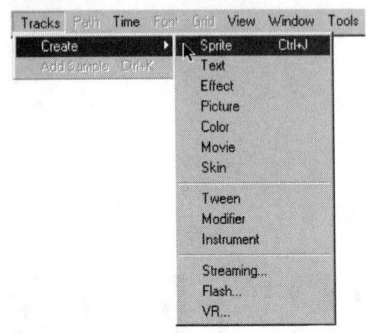

**Figure 10.1** To create a sprite track, choose Tracks > Create > Sprite.

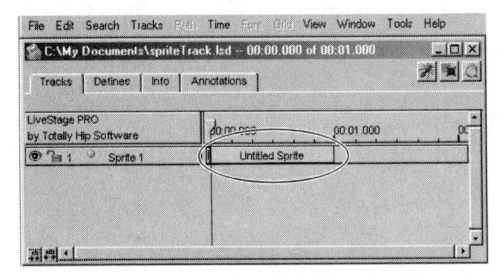

**Figure 10.2** When you create a sprite track, a default sprite sample is placed in the Timeline.

# About Sprite Images

If sprites are characters in a play, images are the actors that play those characters on the stage. In other words, an image functions as a sprite's face; it is the picture you see when you look at the sprite on the stage.

## Adding sprite images

Sprite samples can hold many images. In fact, LiveStage devotes one entire tab of the sprite sample to a special environment where you can collect images: the Images tab (**Figure 10.3**). This tab is like a dressing room for the actors, providing a reservoir of images you can dip into as you create sprites.

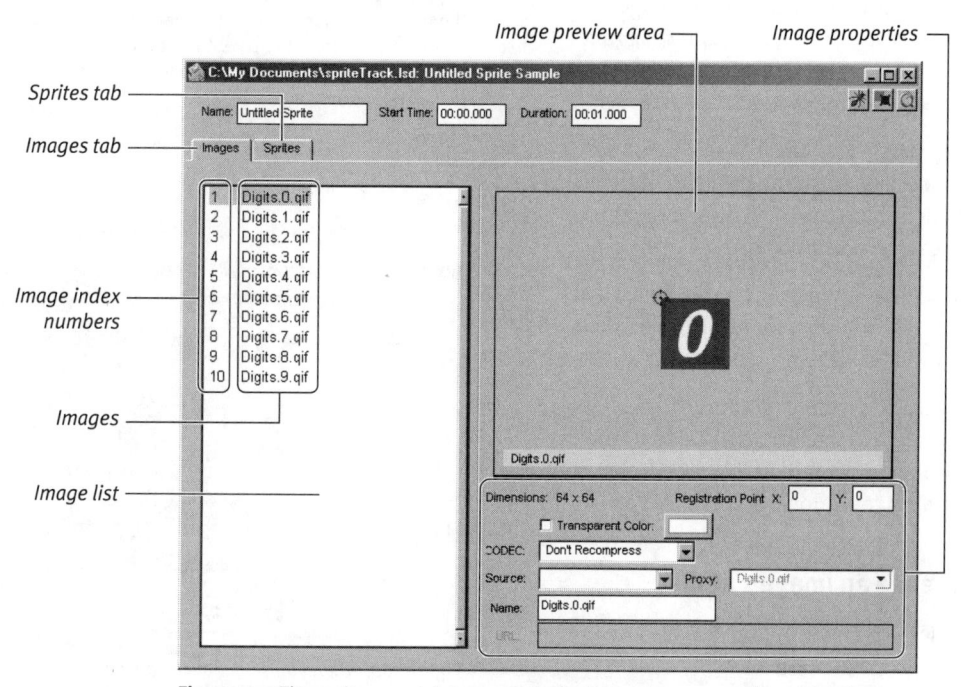

**Figure 10.3** The sprite sample's Images tab. Sprite tracks can contain multiple images. The Images tab serves as a storage bin. The left side holds all the images available to the sample's sprites. The right side contains image properties, such as the image's name and the position of its registration point.

## Chapter 10

### To add images to a sprite sample:

1. In the Tracks tab, double-click a sprite sample to open it.

    The sprite sample opens with the Images tab displayed (refer to Figure 10.3). The left side of the Images tab is home to the sample's Image list, which remains empty until you add images to it.

2. Drag an image into the Image list from the library, Finder (Mac), or desktop (Windows).

    The image's file name appears in the Image list (**Figure 10.4**), and the image is displayed in the image preview area on the right side of the tab.

### ✔ Tips

- Add multiple images to the Image list at one time by selecting and dragging them from the library, Finder (Mac), or desktop (Windows) to the Image list.

- To change an image's position in the Image list, drag it up or down in the list. When you release the mouse button, the image jumps to its new position.

- To delete an image from the Image list, select it and then press the Delete key on your keyboard.

- When you compile your movie, each image from the Image list is included in the file, adding to the movie's file size. Delete any images your movie doesn't use to keep the file as small as possible.

### To change an image's name:

1. Select an image in the Images tab's Image list (**Figure 10.5**).

2. In the Name text box, enter a new name for the selected image.

    The image's name changes in the Image list.

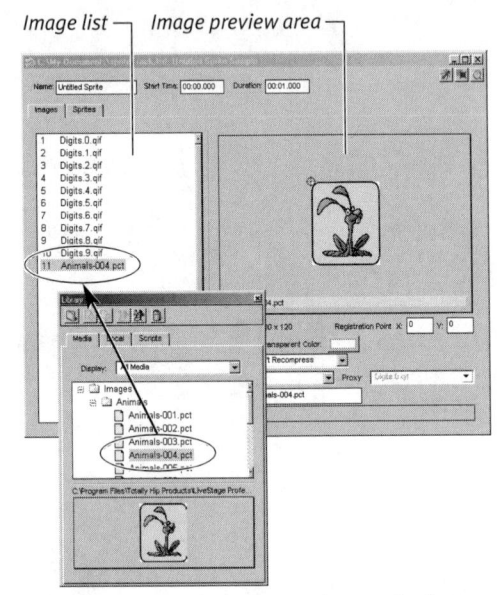

**Figure 10.4** To add images to a sprite sample, drag them into the Image list. In this example, I'm dragging a rabbit image from the LiveStage library into the Image list. You can see the image in the image preview area.

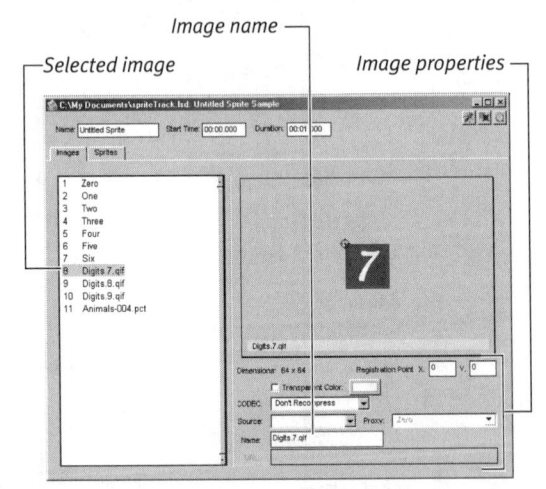

**Figure 10.5** When you select an image in the Image list, the section to its right displays the image's properties, including its name.

# Sprite Tracks

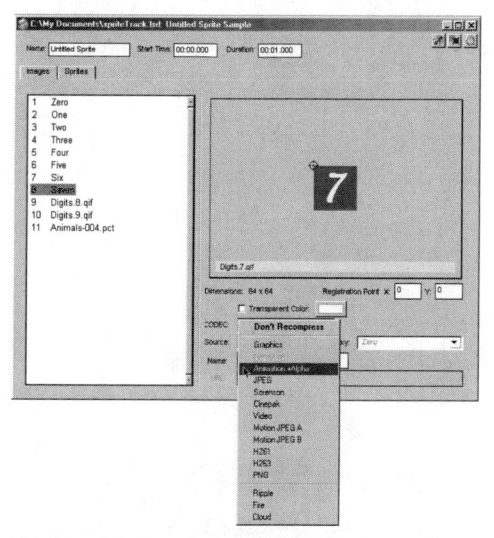

**Figure 10.6** Each sprite image can be compressed separately from other images in the sample. To compress a sprite image, select it in the Image list and then choose a compression codec from the CODEC pop-up menu.

## Compressing sprite images

Sprite samples accept images in many formats, including uncompressed Photoshop images, which offer excellent quality but produce large files. If you plan to distribute your movie over the Internet, you must compress all uncompressed images to reduce file size for speedy downloads. You can decrease a sprite image's file size dramatically by using one of the QuickTime compression codecs in the Images tab's image properties section.

### To compress a sprite image:

1. In the Images tab, select an image to compress.

    The image is highlighted and displayed in the image preview area.

2. From the CODEC pop-up menu, choose a compression codec (**Figure 10.6**).

    When LiveStage compiles your project into a finished movie, it uses the selected codec to compress the sprite image. You can choose any codec, but only three of them are well-suited for compressing sprite images: Animation, JPEG, and PNG.

### ✔ Tip

- If your image has already been compressed in GIF, JPEG, or PNG format, do not recompress it. Whenever you compress an image file, compression artifacts occur, and these artifacts degrade the file's visual quality. If you recompress a compressed image, the compression artifacts magnify and become more noticeable. Even worse, recompressing an image sometimes increases its file size.

ABOUT SPRITE IMAGES

213

# About Sprites

Just as a sprite sample can hold multiple images, it can contain several sprites, which are collected in the sprite sample's Sprites tab (**Figure 10.7**).

As you create sprites, each one is added to the Sprite list on the left side of the Sprites tab. Selecting a sprite in this list causes the Sprite tab's four subtabs to become active. These subtabs hold various editors that you use to wire (QScript) sprites and/or manipulate their properties, such as a sprite's name or the image that provides its face.

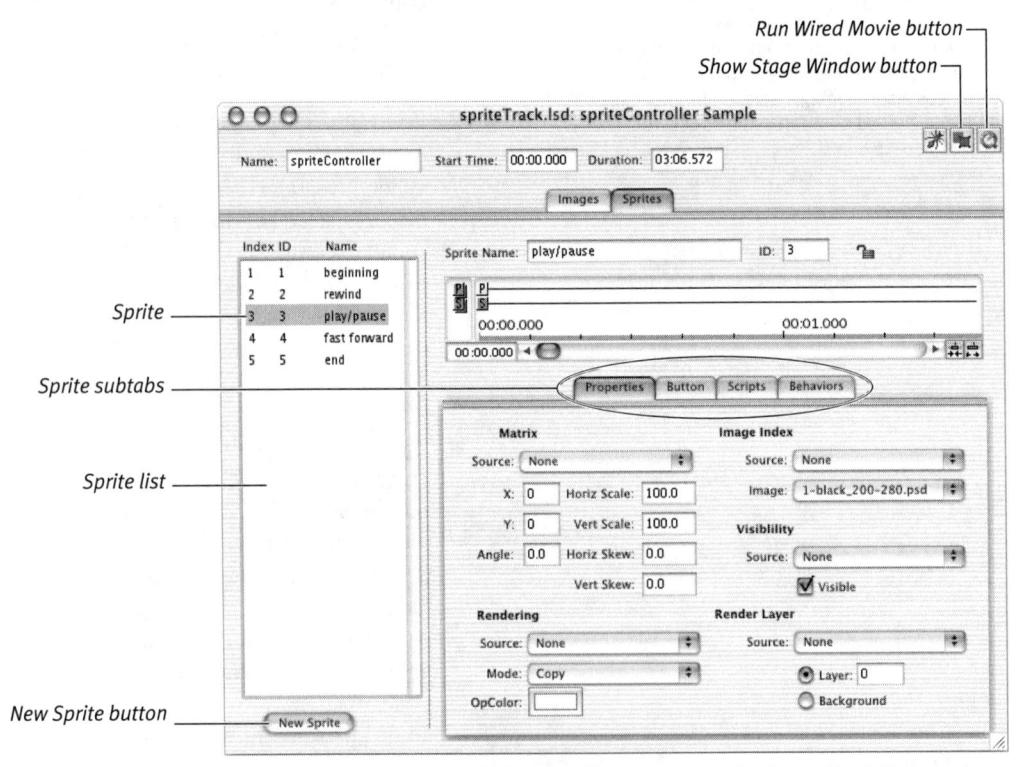

**Figure 10.7** You use the Sprites tab to organize, arrange, and script sprites in the sample. When you select a sprite in the Sprite list on the left side of the Sprites tab, the subtabs on the right become active. You use these tabs to set sprite properties and also to attach behaviors and QScripts to the sample's sprites.

# Sprite Tracks

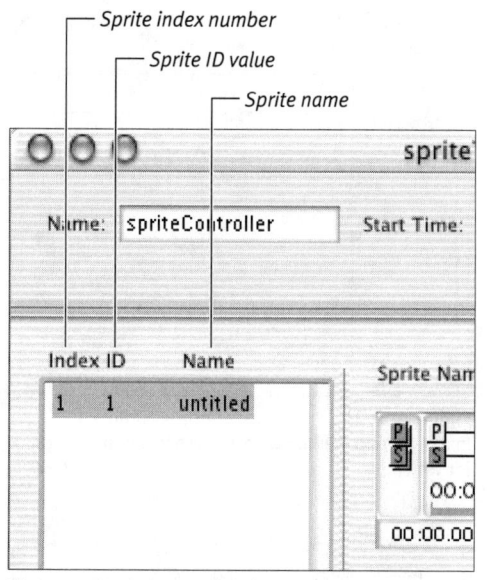

**Figure 10.8** When you click the New Sprite button, a sprite is added to the Sprite list. To the left of the sprite's name are two numbers. The first is the sprite's index number, and the second is its ID value. Later, when you start wiring your projects, you can use these two numbers to target sprites via QScript.

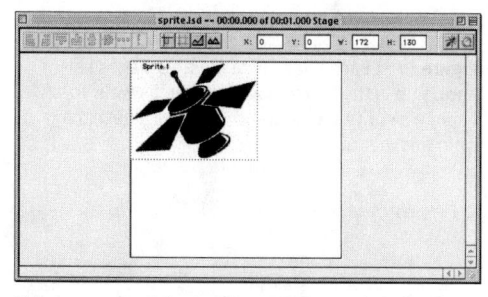

**Figure 10.9** By default, new sprites are placed in the top-left corner of the Sprite track.

## To create a sprite:

1. In the Timeline, double-click a sprite sample to open it.

2. Select the Sprites tab (refer to Figure 10.7).

   When created, a sprite sample has no sprites, and the Sprite list is empty.

3. At the bottom of the Sprite list, click the New Sprite button.

   A new, unnamed sprite is created and placed in the Sprite list (**Figure 10.8**).

4. In the top-right corner of the sprite sample, click the Show Stage Window button.

   The stage opens, displaying the new sprite (**Figure 10.9**).

### ✔ Tips

- If you need several sprites, click the New Sprite button several times. For each click, a new sprite appears in the Sprite list.

- To delete a sprite, select it in the Sprite list and then press the Delete key on your keyboard.

- If the Stage window is open and on top of all the other windows, you can create sprites by dragging images from the library, Finder (Mac), or desktop (Windows) and dropping them directly on a sprite track. The newly created sprites are placed exactly where you drop them.

**ABOUT SPRITES**

215

# Chapter 10

## Changing a sprite image

By default, when you create a sprite, it is assigned the currently selected image in the Image tab's Image list. The Properties subtab lets you change this assigned image.

### To change a sprite image:

1. In the Timeline, double-click a sprite sample to open it.

2. In the Sprites tab, select a sprite in the Sprite list.

3. Click the Properties subtab to open it (**Figure 10.10**).

4. In the Image Index section, use the Image pop-up menu to choose an image for the sprite (**Figure 10.11**).

   The selected image replaces the old image and is displayed on the stage when you click the Show Stage Window button.

## Naming sprites

You don't have to name your sprites, but doing so will help you spot one in a crowd, which is handy if your sample contains a crowd of sprites. If you're creating a movie controller with a bunch of buttons, for example, giving sprites distinct names helps you identify them quickly. Later, as you begin targeting sprites via QScript, these individual names ensure that the right sprite receives the right directions.

### To name a sprite:

1. In the Timeline, double-click a sprite sample to open it.

2. In the Sprites tab, select a sprite in the Sprite list.

3. In the Sprite Name text box at the top of the Sprites tab, enter a name for the selected sprite (**Figure 10.12**).

   In the Sprite list, the sprite's name changes.

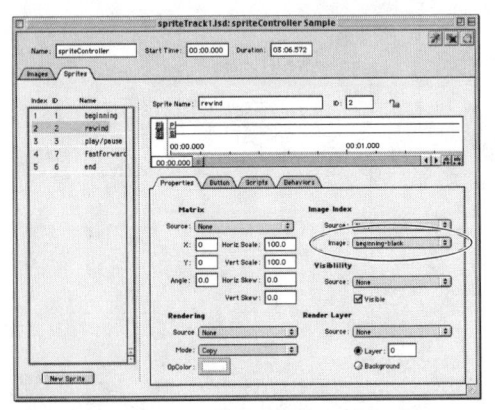

**Figure 10.10** The Properties subtab contains an Image pop-up menu, which you use to set the image for whichever sprite is selected in the Sprite list.

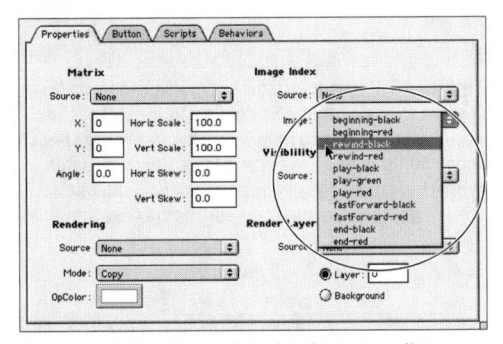

**Figure 10.11** Each image listed in the Images list shows up in the Image pop-up menu as well. To change a sprite's appearance, choose a new image from this menu.

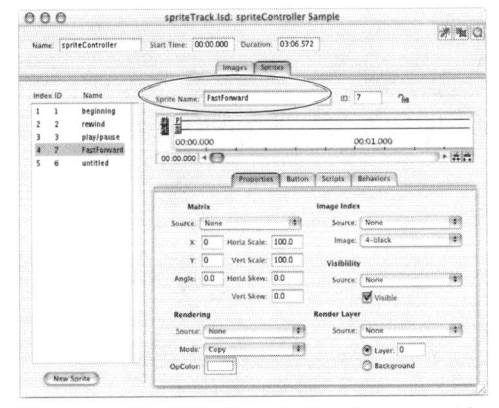

**Figure 10.12** The Sprite Name text box lets you attach meaningful names to your sprites, helping you identify them easily in the Sprite list.

## About Sprite Layout Properties

A sprite track functions as its own self-contained little world. Each sprite within the track is a separate entity that can be repositioned, scaled in size, or even rotated to a different angle. As the creator of that sprite world, you are free to arrange your sprites as you desire; they are only too happy to do your bidding.

The Properties subtab contains a Matrix section that you can use to move, stretch, skew, or even rotate sprites into exact positions (**Figure 10.13**). As you add sprites to the Sprite list, back on the stage, the new sprites are placed on top of the older ones. This layering effect is called the *sprite stacking order*, and you can change it by using the Properties subtab's Render Layer section. The Layer option in that section allows you to move an individual sprite above or below its brothers and sisters on the stage.

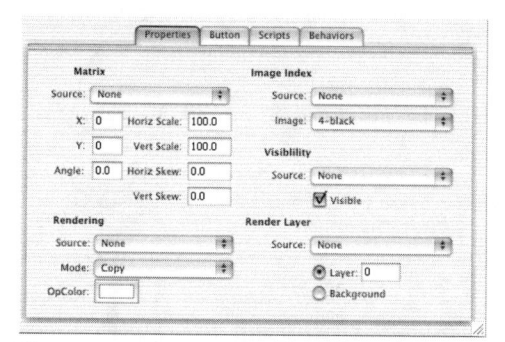

**Figure 10.13** The Matrix section holds settings that you use to position a sprite within its sprite track, as well as settings that you use to change a sprite's dimensions and rotational angle.

# Understanding registration points

Before you do any arranging, it helps to understand exactly how LiveStage keeps track of sprites. Each image listed in the Images tab has a *registration point*, which is sort of like a magnet on the back of a refrigerator decoration. If you move the magnet to a different place on the fridge, the whole decoration follows.

Now imagine that the front of the fridge is covered by a graph. The position of the magnet on the graph would make a perfect registration point, which you could use to track and set the decoration's position on the fridge.

By default, an image's registration point is its top-left corner. If need be, you can move that registration point to a different part of the image. This flexibility gives you the power to create some interesting effects. If you place the `Rotate(angle)` QScript in a sprite's `Idle` event handler, for example, the sprite will spin. (For more information on scripting sprites, see "About Scripting Sprites" later in this chapter.) As it spins, the sprite circles around its registration point. If the registration point is set to the top-left corner, the sprite orbits its registration point like a fairy around a flower (**Figure 10.14**). If you move the registration point to the center of the sprite, the sprite revolves like a record on a turntable.

**Figure 10.14** The image registration point dictates how a sprite is positioned and rotated. If the registration point is left in its default position (top-left corner of the image), the sprite rotates in a large circle around its top-left corner (illustration by Adelaide Evans).

Sprite Tracks

*Selected image* — *Image registration point*

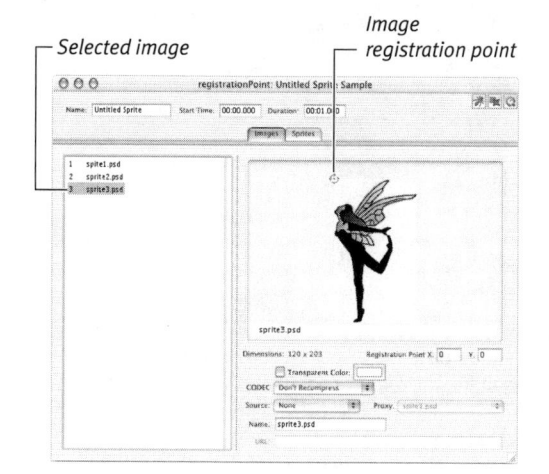

**Figure 10.15** The image preview area shows the image currently selected in the Image list (illustration by Adelaide Evans).

*New registration point*

**Figure 10.16** To change an image's registration point, enter new values in the Registration Point text boxes (illustration by Adelaide Evans).

## To reposition an image registration point:

1. In the Timeline, double-click a sprite sample to open it.

2. Select the Images tab.

3. In the Image list, select the image whose registration point you want to alter (**Figure 10.15**).

   The image is displayed in the image preview area, with a small red target finder centered on its top-left corner. This target finder represents the image's registration point.

4. Enter new coordinates in the Registration Point X and/or Y text boxes below the image preview area (**Figure 10.16**).

   The target finder moves to indicate the registration point's newly defined position.

## ✔ Tip

- If pixel-accurate placement of the registration point isn't needed, just click the image in the image preview area. Its registration point leaps to the position that you clicked.

**ABOUT SPRITE LAYOUT PROPERTIES**

219

## Positioning sprites

A sprite's position inside the sprite track is defined by its image's registration point. If the image's registration point is at its top-left corner (the default position), the sprite's coordinates are equal to the position of its top-left corner. If you change the sprite's coordinate position, the registration point moves, dragging the sprite along for the ride.

To change the sprite's coordinate position, use the Sprites tab's Properties sub-tab. Here, in the top-left corner, you will find a Matrix section with X and Y text boxes that you use to define sprite coordinates (**Figure 10.17**). To reposition a sprite, change the values in these text boxes.

By default, the Matrix section's X and Y text boxes are both set to 0, which is equal to the top-left corner of the sprite track (0,0). Like any coordinate plane in LiveStage, if you increase the value of the X text box, the sprite moves to the right. Increase the value of the Y text box, and the sprite moves down. If you set the value of both these text boxes to 50, on the stage the sprite moves right 50 pixels and down 50 pixels (**Figure 10.18**).

You can enter both positive and negative values in the X and Y text boxes. Negative values move the sprite beyond the top and/or left boundary of the sprite track. When a sprite moves beyond the boundary of its containing sprite track, it enters the track's wings and will not be visible when your compiled movie is played. Depending on the position of the sprite's registration point, negative X and/or Y matrix values may hide your sprite from view.

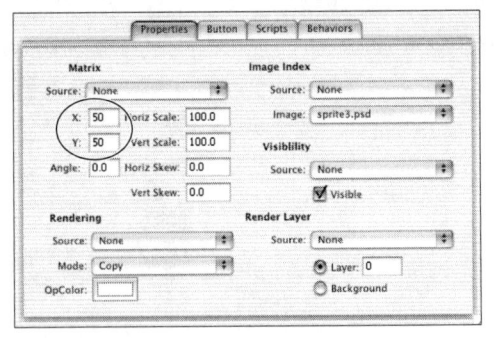

**Figure 10.17** The Matrix section of the Properties subtab. The X and Y coordinates that you set here...

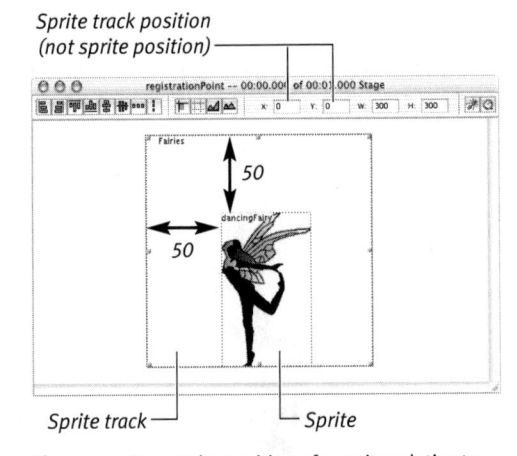

**Figure 10.18** ...set the position of a sprite relative to the top-left corner of the sprite track, as shown here (illustration by Adelaide Evans).

### The Source Pop-Up Menu

If you've noticed the Source pop-up menus scattered throughout the sprite sample, you're probably wondering what they do. Source pop-up menus set data tracks (tween and modifier tracks) as a source to animate certain sprite properties, such as a sprite's image or its position in the sprite track. Data tracks speed the creation of animations that would be tedious to program by hand. To learn more about using data tracks to create animations, see Chapter 11, "Animations and Manipulations."

# Sprite Tracks

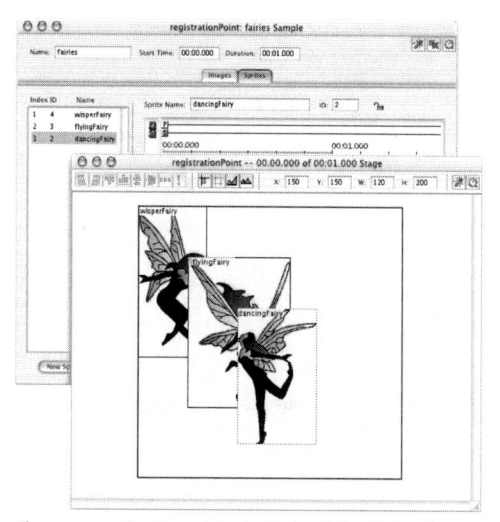

**Figure 10.19** Sprites at the bottom of the Sprite list appear on top of the other sprites on the stage (illustrations by Adelaide Evans).

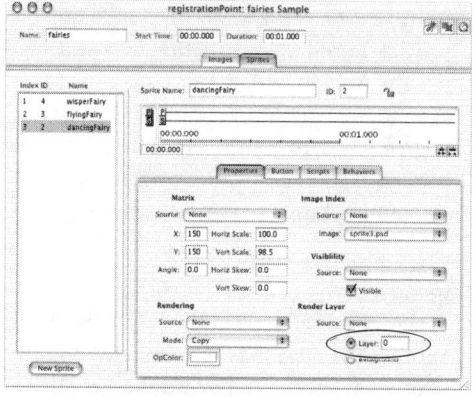

**Figure 10.20** Each sprite has an assigned layer position in the sprite track. To move a sprite above or below its sisters in the Sprite list, use the Render Layer section's Layer option.

### To position a sprite:

1. In the Timeline, double-click a sprite sample to open it.
2. In the Sprite list, select the sprite that you want to reposition.
3. Select the Properties subtab.
4. In the Matrix section, enter new coordinates in the X and Y text boxes (refer to Figure 10.17).

    On the stage, the sprite moves to its new position.

### ✔ Tip

- The easiest way to arrange your sprites is to open the Stage window and drag them around. To learn more about using the stage to arrange movie objects, see Chapter 2, "The Stage and Library."

## Changing layers

As you create new sprites, each one is added to the bottom of the Sprite list. On the stage, sprites at the bottom of the Sprite list are placed on top of sprites higher up the list. Thus, as you add new sprites, they are placed on top of the older ones (**Figure 10.19**).

To move sprites above or below other sprites in the Sprite list, you need to use the Render Layer section of the sprite sample's Properties subtab (**Figure 10.20**). The Layer option in this section accepts both positive and negative values. Positive values move sprites deeper into the sprite track, making them appear to be behind the other sprites; negative layer values move sprites above the others.

# Chapter 10

### To set sprite layer values:

1. In the Sprites tab, select the sprite in the Sprite list that you want to reposition.

2. Click the Properties subtab to open it.

3. In the Render Layer section, enter a new value in the Layer text box (**Figure 10.21**).

   If you lower the Layer value, the sprite moves up in the visual stacking order inside the sprite track; increasing the Layer value does the opposite.

### ✔ Tips

- If two or more sprites have the same layer value, you can also change their position in the sprite stacking order by dragging them up or down in the Sprite list.

- A sprite's layer value takes precedence over its position in the Sprite list. If Sprite A has a Layer value of -100 and Sprite B has a Layer value of 0, Sprite A will *always* be drawn on top of Sprite B, even if Sprite B is lower in the Sprite list.

- If you select the Background radio button in the Render Layer section, the sprite is pasted to the back of the sprite track. No other sprite can be placed behind it, regardless of its layer value. If more than one sprite is pasted to the background, their visual stacking order is determined by their positions in the Sprite list.

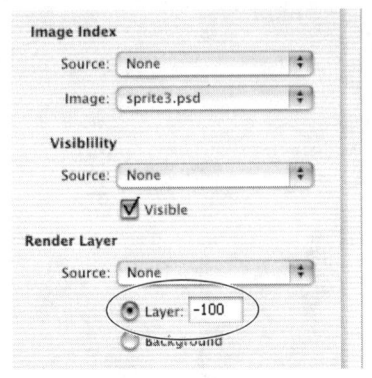

**Figure 10.21** Layer values can be positive or negative. Sprites with lower layer values are placed on top of sprites with higher layer values.

### Other Sprite Properties

The sprite sample's Properties subtab holds several other properties that you may find useful as you move sprites around your project. In the Matrix section, you can use the Angle text box to rotate a sprite around its registration point by a specific degree. The Horiz and Vert Skew text boxes are good for warping your sprites into nonrectangular parallelograms.

The Rendering section's Mode pop-up menu lets you change the graphics mode of the sprite selected in the Sprite list. If a sprite is to be placed (or animated) on top of other sprites, you may want to use this section to set the Transparent graphics mode, which makes the sprite's background color see-through. For a more general discussion of how to use graphics modes (including Transparent mode), see Chapter 3, "Setting Track Properties."

The Visibility section holds the Visible checkbox, which lets you toggle sprite visibility. Visible sprites appear on the stage; invisible sprites don't appear, but viewers can still interact with them.

# Sprite Tracks

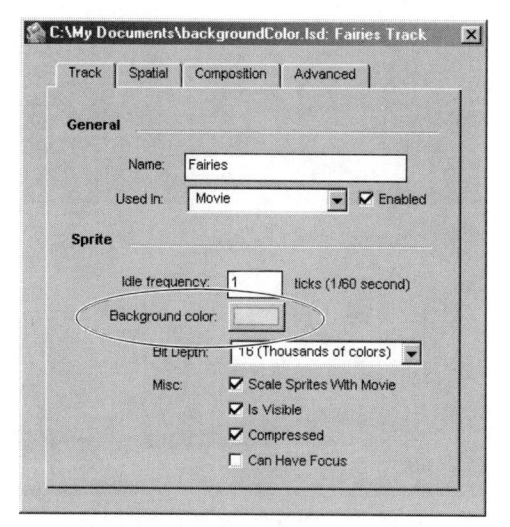

**Figure 10.22** The Background Color box lets you choose a background color for the sprite track.

**Figure 10.23** This sprite track's background has been changed to dark gray, which contrasts sharply with the sprite's white background (illustration by Adelaide Evans).

## About Sprite Backgrounds

You can fill a sprite track with as many images and sprites as you want, making it possible to design entire movies from just one sprite track. Most of your movies, however, will consist of a combination of sprite tracks (to provide interactivity) layered on top of other tracks that provide backgrounds and video. In these cases, you'll want to change the sprite track's background so that it blends in with the other tracks, perhaps even making it transparent so that viewers can see through the sprite track to whatever lies below.

## Setting background color

New sprite tracks are created with a white background. Most of the time, your movie's background will not be white, and you'll need to change the sprite track's background color so that it blends in with its surroundings.

### To set a sprite track's background color:

1. In the Tracks tab of the Project window, double-click the sprite track's header in the Track list.

   The Track Properties window opens, displaying the Track tab.

2. In the Sprite section, click the Background Color box (**Figure 10.22**).

   The Color Picker opens.

3. Choose a new background color for your sprite track.

4. Click OK to close the Color Picker.

5. In the top-right corner of the Project window, click the Show Stage Window button.

   The Stage window opens, displaying your sprite track with its new background color (**Figure 10.23**).

**ABOUT SPRITE BACKGROUNDS**

223

## Setting a transparent background

In certain cases, you'll want to drop out the sprite track's background, making it invisible. Imagine that you have an animation consisting of a cute little fairy fluttering along the beach (why not?). The animation's background is a picture of a beach. On top of that picture sits a sprite track containing a sprite fairy. But you'll have a problem when you compile your final movie: The white rectangle of the sprite track obscures your view of the picture track below. To make the image look, ahem, realistic, you need to drop out the sprite track's background color.

### To set a transparent background:

1. Set a background color for the sprite track, as described in "Setting background color" earlier in this chapter.

   Select a background color that does not appear in any of the sprite track's images. This choice is important, because if a sprite uses the same color as the sprite track's background, when the background color is made transparent, some areas of the sprite also become transparent.

2. In the Track Properties window, select the Composition tab (**Figure 10.24**).

3. From the Mode pop-up menu in the Drawing section, choose Transparent (**Figure 10.25**).

4. Click the OpColor box to open the Color Picker.

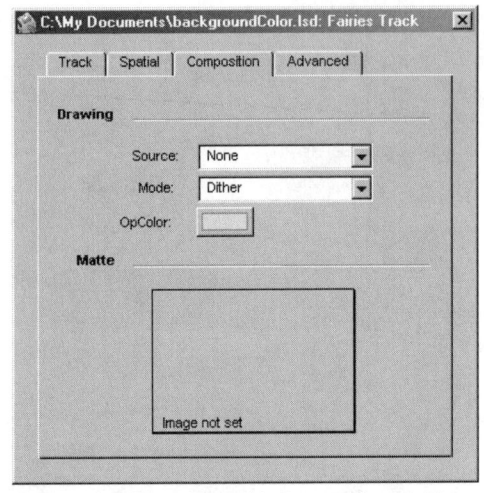

**Figure 10.24** The sprite track's Composition tab. The Drawing section has a Mode pop-up menu containing graphics modes that change the sprite track's color.

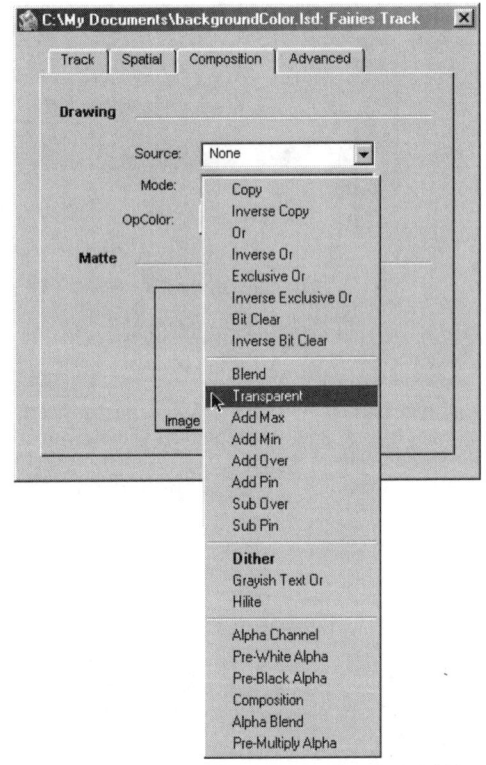

**Figure 10.25** Transparent graphics mode tells QuickTime to make the color in the OpColor box transparent.

**Figure 10.26** The sprite track is now transparent, allowing you to see through it to the track below (illustration by Adelaide Evans).

5. Choose the same color that you set as the background color for your sprite track in step 1.

    The sprite track's selected color becomes transparent on the stage and in the compiled movie.

6. Click OK to close the Color Picker.

7. In the top-right corner of the Project window, click the Show Stage Window button.

    The Stage window opens. You can now see through the sprite track to the track below (**Figure 10.26**).

### ✔ Tips

- Many other graphics modes are available in the Mode pop-up menu. To learn more about graphics modes, see Chapter 3, "Setting Track Properties."

- On the Macintosh, if you open the Color Picker and press the Option key, the pointer turns into an eye-dropper. Click the eye-dropper on any part of your monitor's screen. The color at the tip of the eye-dropper is sampled into the Color Picker.

# Chapter 10

## About Behaviors

For even the most experienced LiveStage author, behaviors provide a quick and convenient method of adding interactivity to QuickTime movies. But you don't have to be an expert to use a behavior. In fact, behaviors are designed with new LiveStage users in mind.

A *behavior* is a pre-made QScript that you simply drag from the library and drop into a sprite sample's Behaviors subtab. Behaviors can make sprites wiggle and shake, move across the stage, rotate, or even bounce off the edges of their sprite tracks. Why spend hours scripting when behaviors will do the work for you?

The standard LiveStage installation collects dozens of behaviors in a folder in the Scripts tab of the Library window. If the behavior you need is not in that folder, grab your LiveStage program CD-ROM, open its Behaviors folder, and check out the included third-party behaviors. You can also download many more behaviors free from the Resources section of the LiveStage Developer Network: http://www.totallyhip.com/lsdn/.

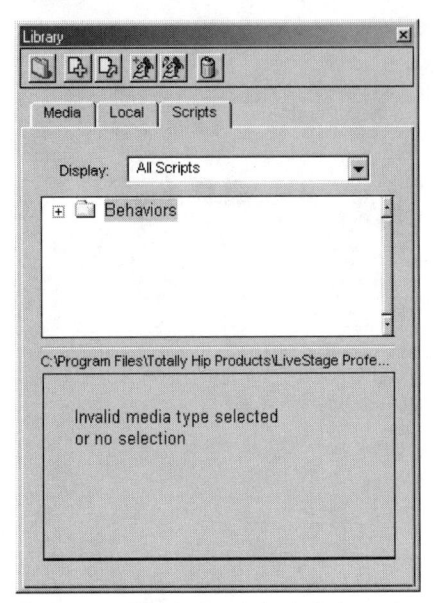

**Figure 10.27** The Library window's Scripts tab holds the Behaviors folder.

### To open the Behaviors folder:

1. Choose Window > Show Library Window.
   The Library window opens.

2. Select the Scripts tab (**Figure 10.27**).
   The Scripts tab displays several folders, including the Behaviors folder.

3. Click the expansion arrow next to the Behaviors folder (**Figure 10.28**).
   The Behaviors folder opens, revealing all the behaviors currently installed in LiveStage.

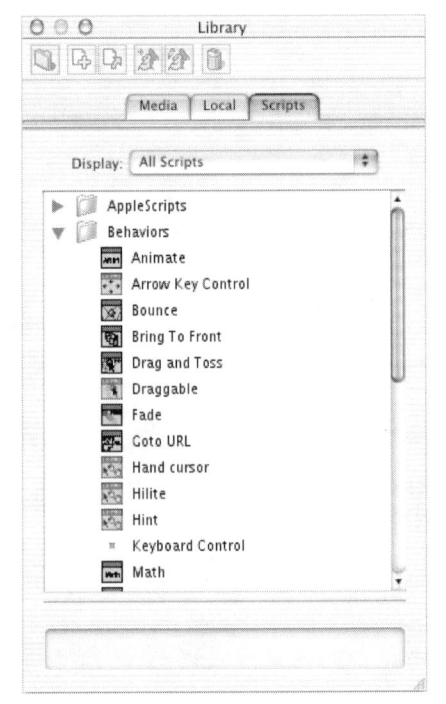

**Figure 10.28** Behaviors instantly add action and interactivity to your projects. The library comes stocked with dozens of behaviors.

# Sprite Tracks

## Using behaviors

Each behavior is designed to do one thing and to do it well. To find out what that thing is, select a behavior and check out its description in the preview area at the bottom of the Library window (**Figure 10.29**).

To attach a behavior to a sprite, you simply drag it from the library into the Sprites tab's Behaviors subtab (**Figure 10.30**). If you look at the Behaviors subtab, you'll notice it contains a lot of space, which is handy because you can attach several behaviors to each sprite.

Behaviors work in a modular fashion, letting you snap together complex QScript actions without writing a single line of QScript. Suppose that you need a sprite to launch a Web page when the sprite is clicked. No problem—just drag the GoTo URL behavior into the Behaviors subtab. To let viewers know that they can interact with the sprite, you should also drag the Hand Cursor behavior into the Behaviors subtab. Continue stacking behaviors onto the sprite until it does exactly what you want it to.

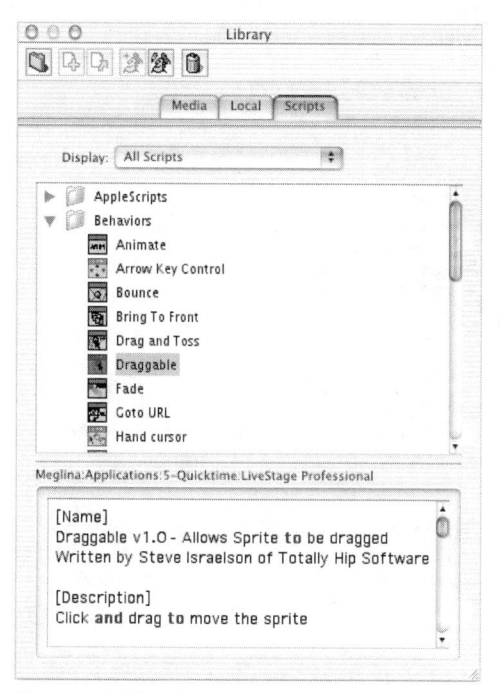

**Figure 10.29** The Library window's preview area shows a description of the selected behavior.

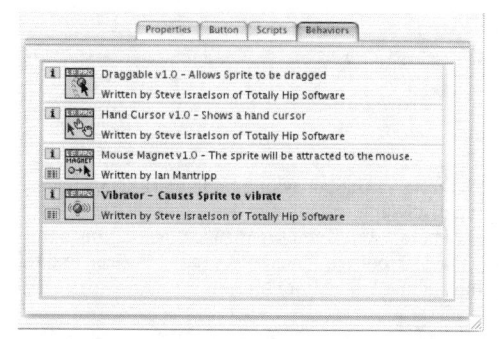

**Figure 10.30** The Behaviors subtab lets you add behaviors to your sprites.

### To assign a sprite behavior:

1. In the Timeline, double-click a sprite sample to open it.

2. Select a sprite in the Sprite list.

    The sprite that you select is the one to which the behavior will be attached. If the Sprite list contains several sprites, make sure that you select the right one; otherwise, your movie will not behave as you intend.

3. Click the Behaviors subtab to open it (refer to Figure 10.30).

*continues on next page*

4. Drag a behavior from the library's Behaviors folder into the sprite sample's Behaviors subtab.

   The behavior appears in the Behaviors subtab's Behavior list (**Figure 10.31**).

   Look closely at the bottom-left corner of the behavior. If you see a small icon containing lines of text (the Parameters icon), this behavior has parameters that you may need to set.

5. Click the Parameters icon.

   A Parameters list opens below the behavior (**Figure 10.32**).

6. Adjust any parameters that need to be set.

   If, for example, you used the `Vibrate` behavior, you could use the settings from Figure 10.32 to make the sprite move five pixels per vibration.

7. In the top-right corner of the sprite sample, click the Run Wired Movie button.

   In the preview movie, your sprite behaves exactly as told.

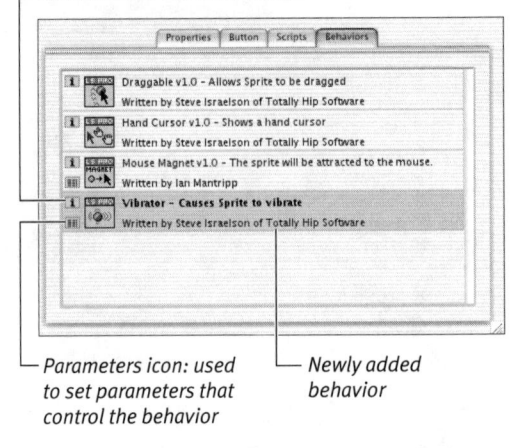

**Figure 10.31** You can stack behaviors onto a sprite until the sprite does exactly what you need it to do. When you drag a new behavior into the Behaviors subtab, it is added at the bottom of the Behaviors list.

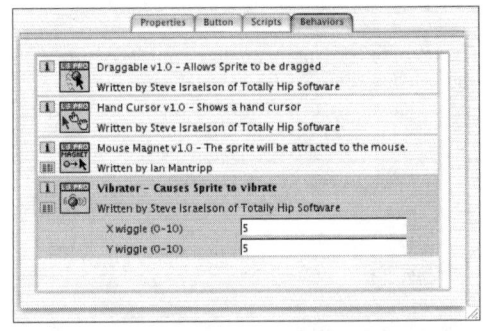

**Figure 10.32** The behavior's parameters define how the behavior functions. Not every behavior uses parameters, but if you see the Parameters icon in the behavior's bottom-left corner, expand the icon and set the parameters appropriately.

### Make Your Own Behaviors

Behaviors are easy to make. If you use a few scripts continuously, consider making those scripts into behaviors and stocking them in the library. Then, whenever you need one of those scripts, all you have to do is grab the correct behavior and drag it into the Behaviors subtab.

Perhaps you've created a killer QScript that you want to share with the LiveStage community. Turn the script into a behavior, and post it on your Web site. You won't have to wait long before someone comes by to check it out. To learn more about creating your own behaviors, see the behaviors chapter of the LiveStage Professional user manual.

# Sprite Tracks

## Installing behaviors

Dedicated LiveStage developers continually create new behaviors and post them on the Internet, free to whoever needs them. If you can't make your sprites do what you want, I guarantee that someone else can—and probably has even designed a behavior for that purpose. So the next time you have trouble making your sprite behave, fire up your favorite search engine and comb the Web until you find the behavior you need. After you've downloaded a behavior, make sure that you install it in the LiveStage library so that it's available for use every time you launch the program.

### To install a behavior:

1. Choose Window > Show Library Window.
   The Library window opens.
2. Select the Scripts subtab to open it.
3. Select the Behaviors folder.
4. At the top of the Library window, click the Add a Copy of a File button (**Figure 10.33**).
   The Choose a File dialog appears.
5. Navigate to the new behavior on your hard disk, and click Choose (Mac) or Open (Windows) (**Figure 10.34**).
   The behavior is added to the library's Behaviors folder and is available for use each time you open LiveStage.

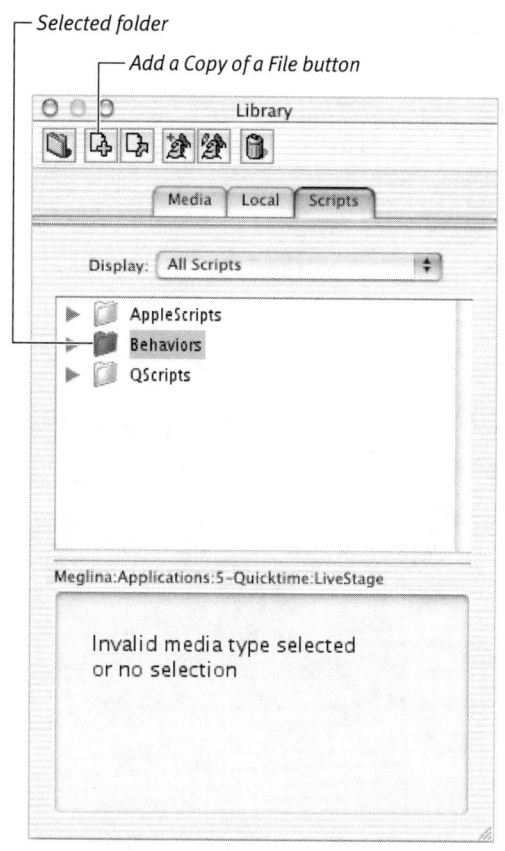

**Figure 10.33** To install a behavior in the library's Behaviors folder, start by selecting the folder. After you've selected the Behaviors folder, the buttons across the top of the Library window become active.

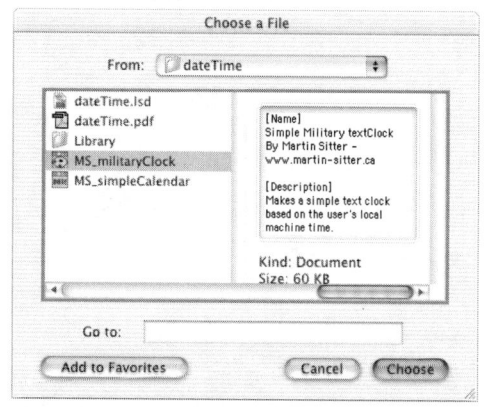

**Figure 10.34** Use the Choose a File dialog to locate a behavior on your hard disk.

**ABOUT BEHAVIORS**

229

## About Sprite Buttons

Due to their interactive capabilities, sprites make perfect buttons. If you're looking to achieve that classic JavaScript rollover effect (in which a button's image changes as the pointer moves over it), look no further than the sprite track. Each sprite has a dedicated Button subtab that effortlessly turns any sprite into a full-functioning, JavaScript-style button. All you need to do is add three button images to the sprite sample's Image list: a normal button image, an over image, and a clicked image. In the Button subtab, you specify which image is used for which state. LiveStage wires your button automatically.

Before you attempt to make a LiveStage button, you must use a graphics program to create a normal button image, as well as an over and a down button image (**Figure 10.35**). Armed with these three images, open LiveStage and begin making buttons.

First, drag your button images into the sprite sample's Image list. Then you'll need to create a sprite and open the Button subtab to define its button states (**Figure 10.36**).

The Button subtab has four sections, each corresponding to a particular button state. To change the image associated with each state, choose a new image from the Image pop-up menu. Similarly, change the pointer by making choices from the Cursor pop-up menu.

*Normal button state*

*Mouse over*

*Mouse down*

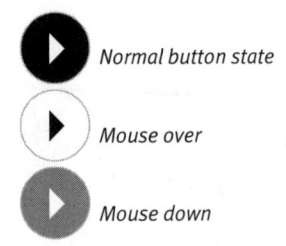

**Figure 10.35** Three button images are used to make one button with three rollover states: normal, mouse over, and mouse down.

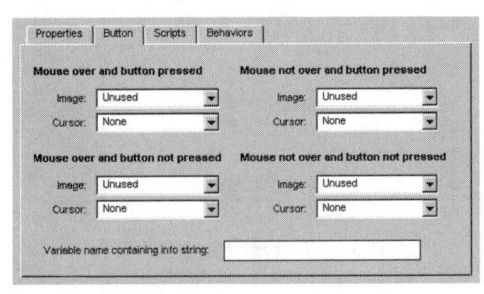

**Figure 10.36** The Button subtab defines rollover states for a sprite button.

# Sprite Tracks

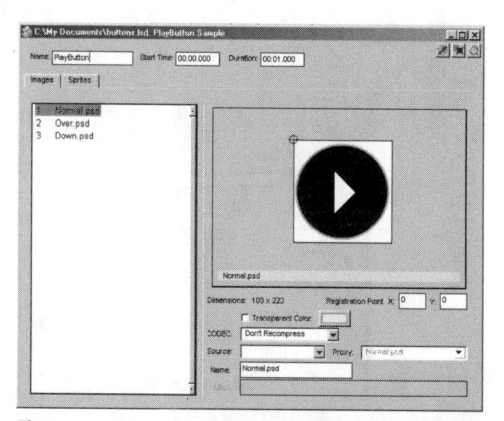

**Figure 10.37** To make a button, begin by stocking the sprite sample's Image list with the three button images that you need to create the rollover effect.

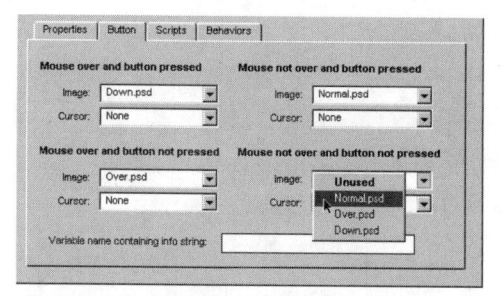

**Figure 10.38** In the Button subtab, use the Image pop-up menus to set the images for each button state.

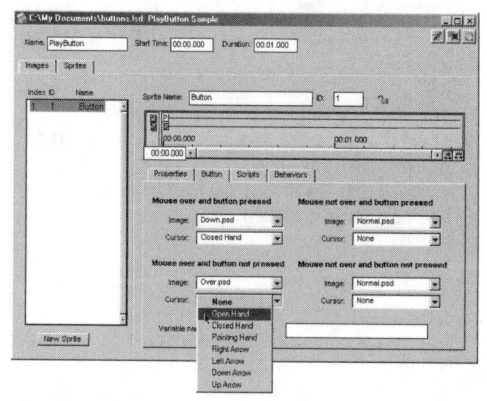

**Figure 10.39** To finish your button, set the Cursor pop-up menus so that the pointer changes as it interacts with the button.

## To make a LiveStage button:

1. In the Timeline, double-click a sprite sample to open it.

2. Click the Images tab to open it.

3. From the libray, Finder (Mac), or desktop (Windows), select your button images, and drag them into the Images tab's Image list (**Figure 10.37**).

    The three images appear in the Image list.

4. Select the Sprites tab to open it.

5. Below the Sprite list, click the New Sprite button.

    A new sprite is added to the Sprite list. This sprite will become your button.

6. Click the Button subtab to open it (refer to Figure 10.36).

7. In each of the Button subtab's sections, choose the correct button image from the Image pop-up menu (**Figure 10.38**).

    You've probably noticed that four Image pop-up menus are available, but you have only three button images. The two sections on the right side of the Button subtab define the button's state while the pointer is *not* over the button. Under most circumstances, both of these sections use the normal button image.

8. In each section, choose an appropriate pointer type from the Cursor pop-up menu (**Figure 10.39**).

9. In the top-right corner of the sprite sample, click the Run Wired Movie button.

    In the preview movie, the pointer and button change form as specified.

## ✔ Tip

- With a combination of buttons and behaviors, you can create highly interactive movies without writing a single line of QScript. To learn more about behaviors, refer to "About Behaviors" earlier in this chapter.

**ABOUT SPRITE BUTTONS**

**231**

Chapter 10

# About Scripting Sprites

At some point, buttons and behaviors alone will just not be enough to provide the interactivity that you need. When that day comes, you will have to turn to the Sprite sample's script editor and begin creating QScripts of your very own.

## Scripting sprites

*QScripts* are a set of instructions that tell sprites what to do. Scripts can animate sprites over time or cause them to react to the pointer. Scripted sprites can play sounds when clicked, launch Web pages, shake, spin, or rock. In fact, sprites can do whatever you can dream up.

Although sprites are very talented, they are not good at thinking on their own. Just like actors on a stage, they need a script to dictate their actions. To write that script, open the sprite's script editor, select an event, and write your QScripts. To learn more about writing QScript, see Chapter 4, "The Script Editor," or Chapter 13, "Advanced QScript."

### To script a sprite:

1. In the Timeline, double-click a sprite sample to open it.

2. In the Sprites tab, select the Scripts subtab (**Figure 10.40**).

    The Scripts subtab opens, revealing the script editor and the Event Handler list.

3. In the Sprite list on the left side of the Sprites tab, select a sprite.

    This sprite is the one to which your QScripts will be attached.

4. Select an event handler in the Event Handler list.

5. Write a QScript in the script edit field (**Figure 10.41**).

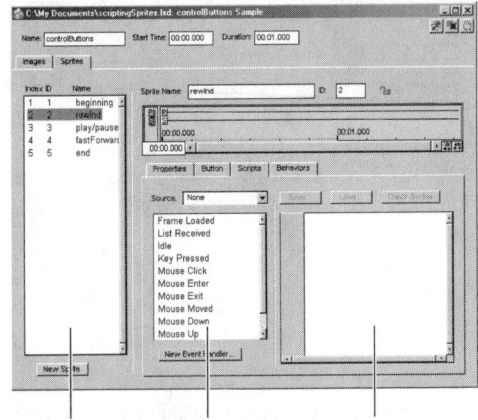

**Figure 10.40** The Scripts subtab holds the script editor.

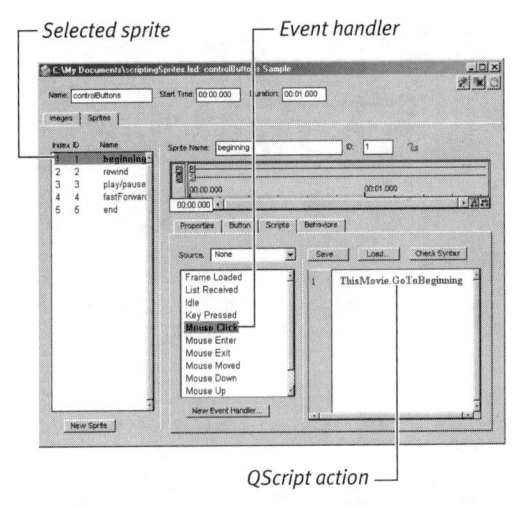

**Figure 10.41** The script that you write in the script edit field is attached to whichever sprite is selected in the Sprite list. The script in this figure sends the movie back to its beginning each time the sprite named beginning is clicked.

232

# Sprite Tracks

In either the preview movie or the final compiled movie, the action that you've wired executes each time the appropriate event is triggered, and your sprite behaves accordingly.

## Using the Idle event

The `Idle` event has a special relationship with a very important sprite-track property called the idle frequency. The *idle frequency* is like a localized clock that ticks away inside the sprite track whether or not the movie is playing. For each idle frequency tick, one `Idle` event is triggered. Because the idle frequency continues to tick even when your movie is stopped, the `Idle` event executes continuously for as long as your movie is open.

The idle clock ticks 60 times per second. By default, idle frequency is set to 1, which means that the `Idle` event executes 60 times per second. That setting fires a lot of events, and each one consumes a bit of processor power. If too many events are firing, the processor becomes overtaxed, and your movie starts to drag and stutter. You can prevent this problem by setting the idle frequency so that it executes `Idle` events only as often as they are needed. To learn more about idle frequency, see Chapter 4, "The Script Editor."

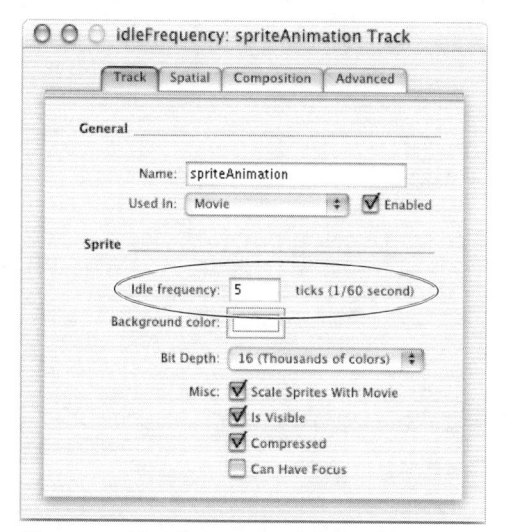

**Figure 10.42** The Idle Frequency text box defines how often the `Idle` event executes. An idle frequency of 5 (12 times/second) generally is fast enough to ensure that sprite animations play smoothly.

### To change the idle frequency:

1. In the Tracks tab, double-click the sprite track's header in the Track list.

   The Track Properties window opens, displaying the Track tab.

2. In the Sprite section, enter a new value in the Idle Frequency text box (**Figure 10.42**).

   The `Idle` event now executes at the rate you've specified.

*continues on next page*

## Chapter 10

### ✔ Tips

- The `Idle` event does not execute like a quartz clock. If the movie becomes bogged down with other events, the `Idle` event will execute slower than its idle frequency demands.

- You'll find that `Idle` events are ideal for animating sprites. By placing the `ToggleVisible` QScript in a sprite's `Idle` event handler, for example, you can make the sprite blink. As the idle frequency ticks along, it executes the `Idle` event over and over and over. Each time the event executes, the sprite's visibility switches to the opposite of its current state, causing the sprite to flash on or off.

- As you become more comfortable with QScript, you'll find it a good idea to use the `SetIdleFrequency(Frequency)` QScript action to control the `Idle` event. When the `Idle` event is not needed, turn it off by setting the idle frequency to −1. This setting frees the computer's processor, which can improve your movie's overall performance.

# Sprite Tracks

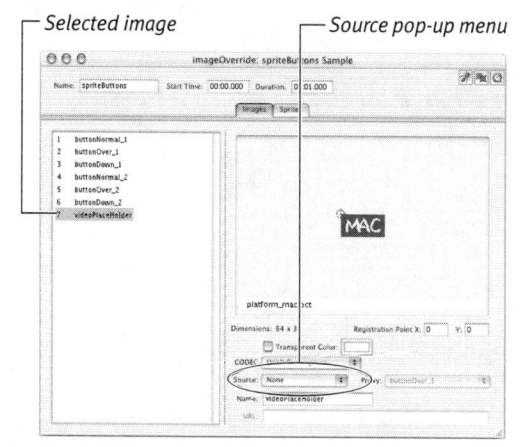

**Figure 10.43** To override a sprite image with the content from another track, select the image in the Image list and then choose a source track from the Source pop-up menu.

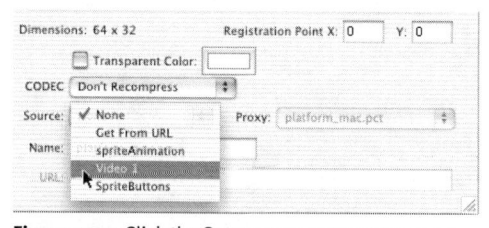

**Figure 10.44** Click the Source pop-up menu to see a list of all the tracks that you can use to override the sprite image.

## About Image Override

Normally, sprites display images. Although sprites can move around freely inside the sprite track, the images that they wear as faces are static. Images are still pictures; they do not move.

But what if you want to make an animated button or a video clip that the viewer can interact with? In these cases, you will need to use one of LiveStage's coolest sprite features: image override. With image override, you can replace a sprite's image with content from another track, called a *source track*. The source track could be a picture, movie, video, text, or even another sprite track. In the final compiled movie, the source track becomes a sprite, which you manipulate, animate, and otherwise wire as though it were a normal sprite.

### To override a sprite image source:

1. In the Timeline, double-click a sprite sample to open it.

2. Select the Images tab to open it.

3. In the Image list, select the sprite's image. The image is displayed in the image preview area (**Figure 10.43**).

4. From the Source pop-up menu, choose a source track for this image (**Figure 10.44**). The Source pop-up menu lists all project tracks that you can use as image-override source tracks.

5. In the sprite sample's top-right corner, click the Run Wired Movie button.
   LiveStage compiles your project into a preview movie, which displays the source track instead of the original sprite image.

### ✔ Tip

- If you've used image override, and you can't see all of the source track, try making the sprite track bigger.

235

# Animations and Manipulations

# 11

LiveStage contains a special track, called a *tween track*, that makes creating animations child's play. Tween tracks can spin VR objects or fly a plane across your project's sky. If set up correctly, a tween track can even fade in a visual track.

But this chapter doesn't stop at showing you how to add eye-catching animations. Because LiveStage is so well suited for wiring interactivity into your movies, it's easy to forget that LiveStage is also a full-featured video editor. In fact, through effect tracks, LiveStage mimics many features used in high-end video editing programs, such as Apple's Final Cut Pro and Adobe's Premiere. With effect tracks, you can create a plethora of cross-fades, transitions, and filter effects to blur, sharpen, color-correct, and otherwise manipulate the appearance of your visual media.

This chapter does not show you how to use every aspect of tween or effect tracks. It does, however, introduce their main features through step-by-step explanations and examples.

# About Source Pop-Up Menus

You've probably noticed the Source pop-up menus (**Figure 11.1**) spread throughout LiveStage and wondered, "What do those do?" Source pop-up menus are used to specify *data* tracks that animate or automate certain object properties, such as a track's position, a sprite image's index number, or a graphics mode's color values. In fact, wherever you see a Source menu, you'll also find a property you can animate.

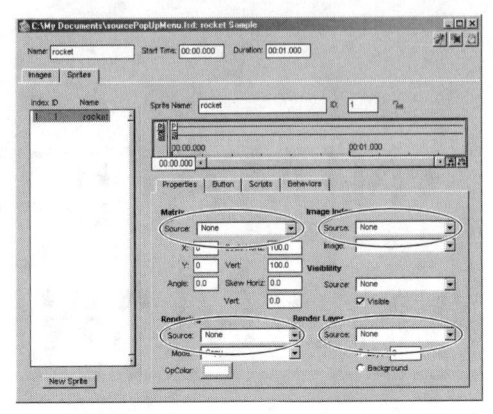

**Figure 11.1** Source pop-up menus allow you to select a data track to animate certain object properties, such as a sprite's position, a sprite image's index number, or a sprite's layer number.

---

### What Are Data Tracks?

Data tracks have no visual or audio content. A data track does nothing more than generate a series of numbers used by other project tracks.

There are two types of data tracks: tween and modifier tracks. Tween tracks are purposely built to animate movie object properties. Modifier tracks can also be used for animations, but they excel at defining a repetitive string of numbers that execute QScript custom events (To learn about custom events, see Chapter 13, "Advanced QScript."). Modifier tracks are a fairly advanced topic and are not covered in this book. The LiveStage manual, however, does outline their use.

# Animations and Manipulations

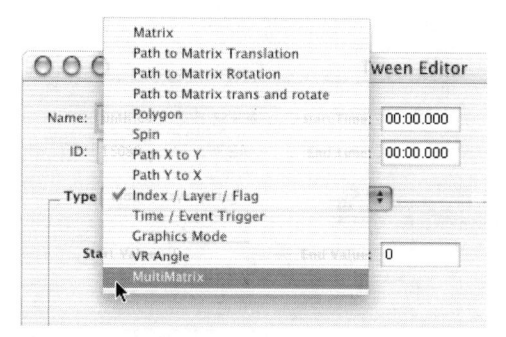

**Figure 11.2** LiveStage's tween editors.

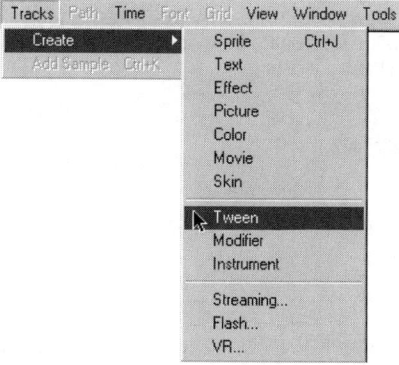

**Figure 11.3** To create a tween track, choose Tracks > Create > Tween.

## About Tween Tracks

Tween tracks simplify animations by taking a start and an end value and then mathematically calculating (interpolating) a series of numbers that join those two values over time. Take an animation of a sprite plane flying across your movie. Without a tween track, you would need to define the plane's position manually at each step of its flight. This procedure would take a lot of QScript and also a lot of time. But with a tween track, you need specify only the start and end position of the plane's flight path. The tween track takes care of the rest—no QScript needed!

Tween tracks create animations through special user interfaces (UIs) called *tween editors*. There are many of these tween editors available, each designed to serve a unique purpose (**Figure 11.2**). A path tween editor, for example, lets you draw a path for an object to follow as it travels across the movie, whereas a VR tween editor automates a VR track's pan angle, making the track spin all by itself. The graphics mode tween editor fades in visual objects, and the polygon tween editor stretches out an object's corners, making it warp and skew.

This chapter covers several, but not all, of LiveStage's tween editors. Most tween editors work similarly to the ones discussed in this chapter, so when you're comfortable using these tween editors, you can transfer your knowledge to the others easily.

### To create a tween track:

1. In the Project window, select the Tracks tab. The Tracks menu becomes active.

2. Choose Tracks > Create > Tween (**Figure 11.3**).

   A new tween track is created, and a default tween sample is placed in the Timeline.

239

Chapter 11

## Using path tweens

A *path* is a trail that leads from one point to another. In a similar fashion, a *path tween* specifies a trail for a sprite (or even an entire track) to follow as it travels across your movie.

For the remainder of this example, you will explore the Path to Matrix Translation tween editor. If you open the Path to Matrix Translation tween editor, you'll notice that it contains an exact representation of the stage (**Figure 11.4**), including all of your project's visual tracks and sprites. To animate an object without this editor, you would need to write a very complex QScript. With the Path to Matrix Translation tween editor, you simply draw a path for the object to follow, saving the hard scripting for other parts of your project.

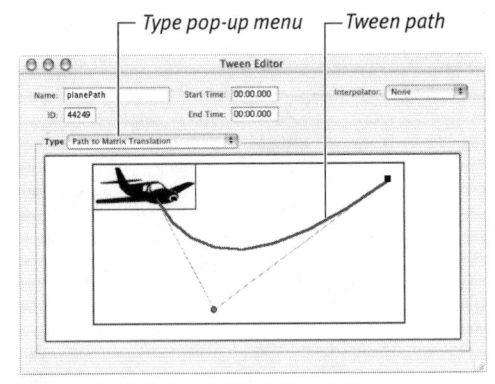

**Figure 11.4** The Path to Matrix Translation tween editor lets you chart a course for an object to follow. You can draw smooth, arced lines by pressing Option (Mac) or Ctrl+Alt (Windows) as you click to create points in the tween's path.

### To use a Path to Matrix Translation tween:

1. Create a sprite track and a sprite.

    For information on creating sprites, see Chapter 10, "Sprite Tracks."

2. Choose Tracks > Create > Tween.

3. In the Tracks tab, double-click the tween track sample to open it (**Figure 11.5**).

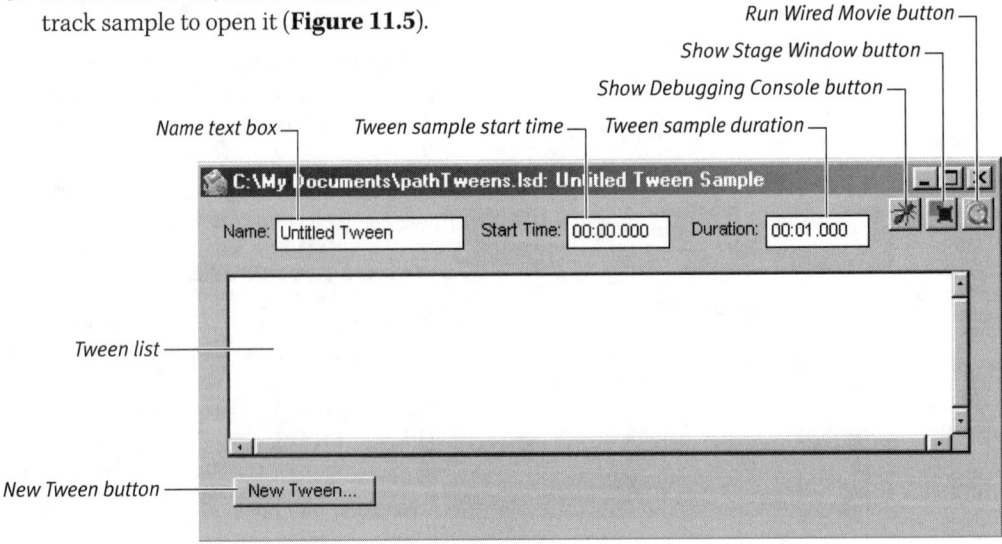

**Figure 11.5** An open tween sample.

240

**ABOUT TWEEN TRACKS**

# Animations and Manipulations

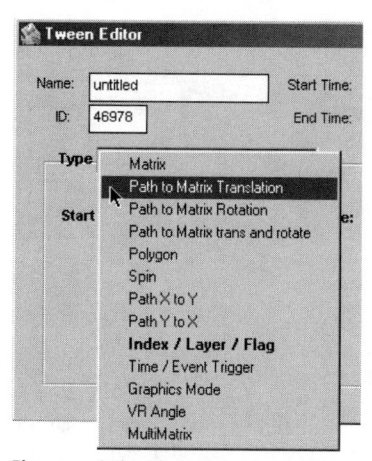

**Figure 11.6** The Type pop-up menu lists all the tweens available in LiveStage. The three path tweens let you draw a trail for an object to follow across the stage.

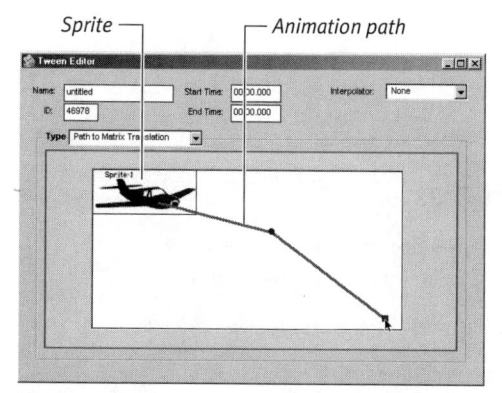

**Figure 11.7** The Path to Matrix Translation tween reveals its own representation of the stage, which makes it easy to click and create a path for the sprite to follow.

4. Click the New Tween button.

   The tween editor opens.

5. From the Type pop-up menu, choose Path to Matrix Translation (**Figure 11.6**).

   A representation of the stage appears in the tween editor.

6. On the tween editor's stage, click to create points that define a path for the sprite to follow (**Figure 11.7**).

7. In the Name text box, enter a name for the tween.

   The name that you enter will identify the tween in any of LiveStage's compatible Source pop-up menus.

8. In the Tracks tab, double-click the sprite sample to open it.

9. In the Sprite list, select the sprite that you want to animate.

*continues on next page*

10. Select the Properties subtab.

11. In the subtab's Matrix section, click the Source pop-up menu and choose the Path to Matrix Translation tween by name, using the name you specified in step 7 (**Figure 11.8**).

12. In the top-right corner of the sprite sample, click the Run Wired Movie button.

    LiveStage compiles a preview of your movie. When played, the preview movie shows the sprite moving across the stage.

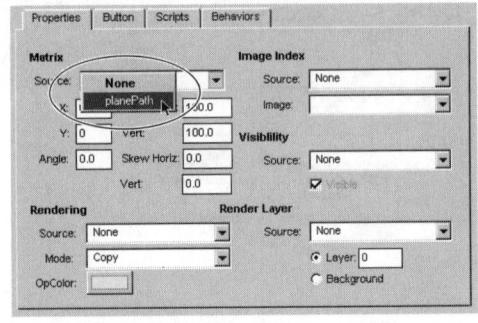

**Figure 11.8** After you've set the tween path by using the Path to Matrix Translation tween editor, you must choose the Path to Matrix Translation tween from the Source pop-up menu of the sprite's Properties subtab. In this example, the Path to Matrix Translation tween is named planePath.

### Path Tween Tips

Although each path tween is designed to serve a particular purpose, all these tweens draw paths exactly the same way. Keep these tips in mind as you use path tween editors:

- To delete a point in the path tween editor, select it and then press the Delete key.

- To change the position of a point in a path, drag it to a new position.

- When you click the stage to create a path for the tween, you create points that LiveStage joins with straight lines. This process creates a jagged tween, and your objects will lurch noticeably as they hit each point. To smooth out the tween (creating arcs for your object to follow), hold down Option (Mac) or Ctrl+Alt (Windows) as you click the points for your tween (refer to Figure 11.4).

- To alter the duration of the Path to Matrix Translation tween, change the length of the tween sample. You can also adjust the duration of the tween directly in the Path to Matrix Translation tween editor by entering values in the Start Time and End Time text boxes.

- The stage inside the path tween editor responds to all the normal stage draw settings (which you access from the View menu). Additionally, the Don't Draw stage draw setting works only with path tween editors. If you don't see a representation of the stage inside a path tween editor, open the View menu and make sure that Don't Draw is not checked.

# Animations and Manipulations

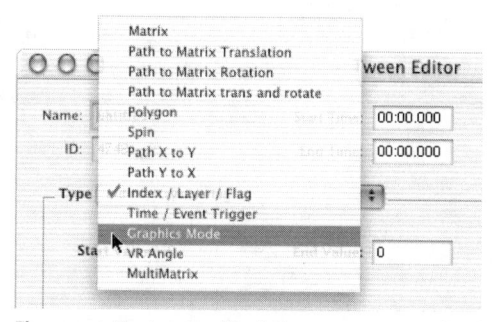

**Figure 11.9** The tween editor's Type pop-up menu lists the types of tweens you can create.

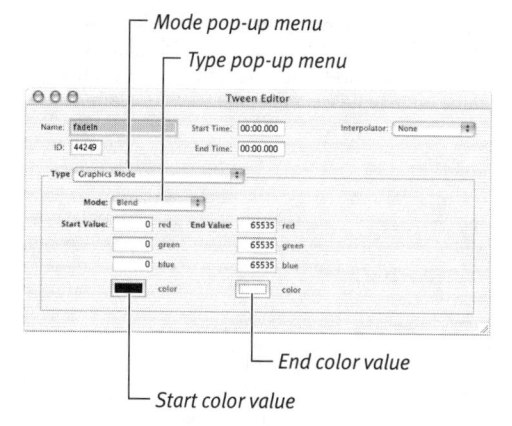

**Figure 11.10** The Graphics Mode tween editor blends a track from the start color to the end color over time.

## Tweening a visual fade-in

Fade-ins gradually introduce new visual content and are common at the beginning of video clips. Under normal circumstances, a fade-in blends a track from black to full visibility over a period of about 1 second. Although a fade-in takes time to create, it is a professional touch that adds that little bit of extra gloss to your movie.

You create a LiveStage fade by animating the grayscale value of the Blend graphics mode. If you're not familiar with this graphics mode, see Chapter 3, "Setting Track Properties."

### To tween a fade-in:

1. Drag an image or video into the Tracks tab of the Project window.

   A new picture or video track is created, and a media sample is placed in the Timeline. For simplicity, this example uses a picture or video track, though fade-ins work with any visual track, including VR and Flash tracks.

2. Choose Tracks > Create > Tween.

   A tween track is created, and a default sample is placed in the Timeline.

3. In the Tracks tab, double-click the tween sample to open it.

4. Click the New Tween button.

   The tween editor opens.

5. From the Type pop-up menu, choose Graphics Mode (**Figure 11.9**).

   The Graphics Mode tween editor opens (**Figure 11.10**).

   *continues on next page*

**ABOUT TWEEN TRACKS**

243

Chapter 11

6. From the tween editor's Mode pop-up menu, choose Blend (**Figure 11.11**).

7. In the Name text box, enter a name.
   Naming tweens makes it easy for you to choose the correct one from the Source pop-up menu later.

8. In the Tracks tab, double-click the track header of the visual track that you want to fade in.
   The Track Properties window opens.

9. Select the Composition tab.

10. From the Mode pop-up menu, choose Blend (**Figure 11.12**).

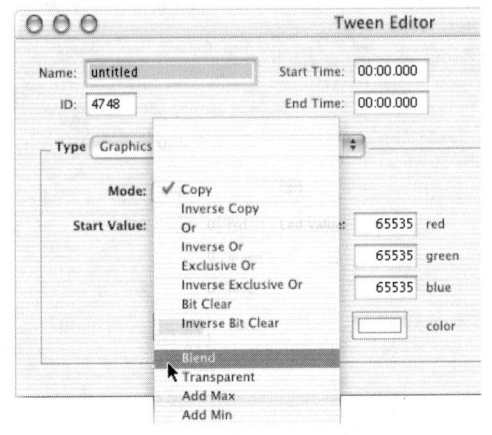

**Figure 11.11** The Blend graphics mode adjusts the translucency of an entire track or sprite globally. If you automate this blend to turn the track from fully transparent to fully opaque, the result is a fade-in.

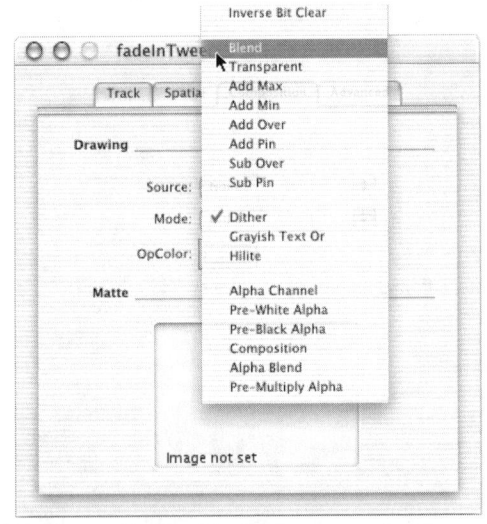

**Figure 11.12** The Graphics Mode tween works in conjunction with the Blend graphics mode. To select the Blend graphics mode, choose it from the Mode pop-up menu located in the Composition tab of the Track Properties window.

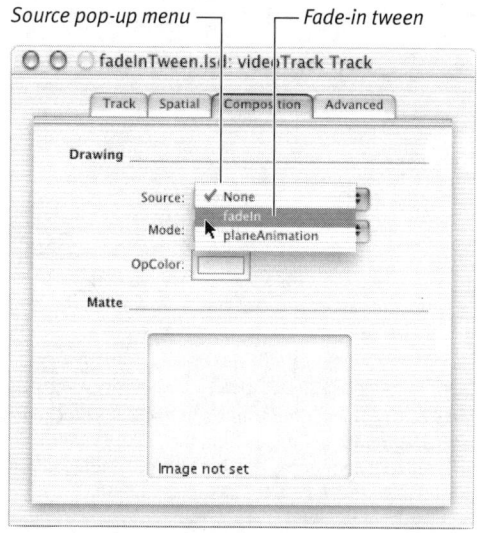

**Figure 11.13** Use the Source pop-up menu to specify the Graphics Mode tween that will automate the track's fade-in.

*Source pop-up menu* — *Fade-in tween*

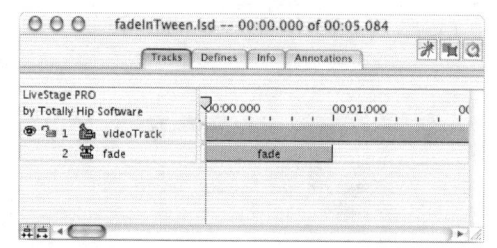

**Figure 11.14** In this figure, the fade tween track exactly covers the first second of the video track. As the movie plays back, the video track will fade in over a 1-second period.

11. From the Source pop-up menu, choose the Graphics Mode tween by name, using the name you specified in step 7 (**Figure 11.13**).

12. In the Tracks tab's Timeline, position the tween track so that it lines up exactly with the portion of the visual track that you want to fade in (**Figure 11.14**).

    The fade-in will occur over the duration of the tween track, so the tween track must be only as long as you want the fade to last. If the fade should take 1 second, the tween track should cover the first second of the visual track in the Timeline.

13. In the top-right corner of the Project window, click the Run Wired Movie button.

    LiveStage compiles a preview of your movie. As the movie plays, your visual track fades in.

### ✔ Tips

- If you notice that your track fades in from whiteness, not blackness, try putting a black color track on the bottom of your project. To change the color of the fade-in, change the color of the color track.

- Using a Graphics Mode tween, you can also fade tracks out. In the Graphics Mode tween editor, switch the start color to white and the end color to black. Back in the Timeline, move the tween track so that it covers the end of the visual track instead of the beginning. When the movie plays, the visual track fades out.

- You can use the Graphics Mode tween to tweak other graphics modes and create wild effects for your movies. With a little experimentation, you can create some interesting and complex blend effects.

245

# About Cel-Based Animations

When animators first began making cartoons, they used a technique called cel-based animation. In *cel-based animation*, animators actually painted their graphics on celluloid film one frame, or *cel*, at a time. As they moved along the strip of film, they painted slight variations into each picture. When played back at speed, the pictures looked like they were moving. A strip of film is a perfect example of a cel-based animation. As the film rolls, each frame changes slightly, and the result is a moving picture.

Using a sprite track, you can create cel-based animations in LiveStage out of a series of sprite images. When played in sequence, these images flip through a sprite like film frames, creating the illusion of motion.

This section explores two ways to create cel-based animations. The first method uses a tween track to generate a series of numbers that switch a sprite's image according to its image index number. The alternative relies on QScript to do the same thing.

## Setting up the animation

Before you create a cel-based animation, you must assemble a series of images. Any series of images will work, from a sequential collection of photos to a set of images generated in a 3D program such as Discreet 3D Studio Max. If you don't have a series of images handy, the LiveStage library comes stocked with a selection.

After you've settled on your images, collect them in the Images tab of one sprite sample (**Figure 11.15**). (To learn more about sprite tracks, see Chapter 10, "Sprite Tracks.") The Images tab's Image list must display your images in the correct order. In each of the cel-based animation techniques this section

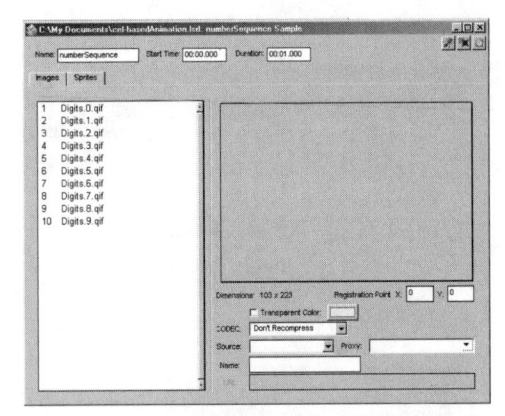

**Figure 11.15** The sprite sample's Image list is stocked with a sequence of images from the Library window. This number sequence, starting at 0 and ending at 9, will be used to create a cel-based animation.

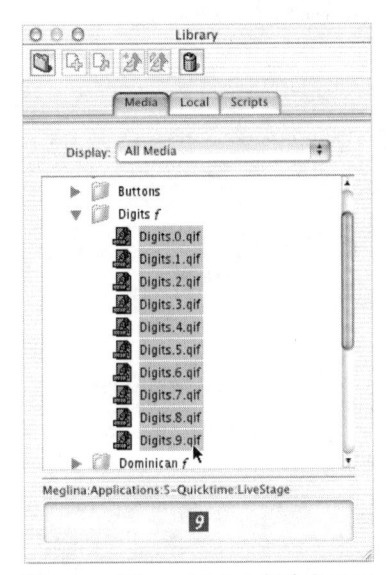

**Figure 11.16** If you select multiple images in the library, you can drag all of them into a sprite sample's Image list at the same time.

## Animations and Manipulations

*New sprite created in the Sprite list*

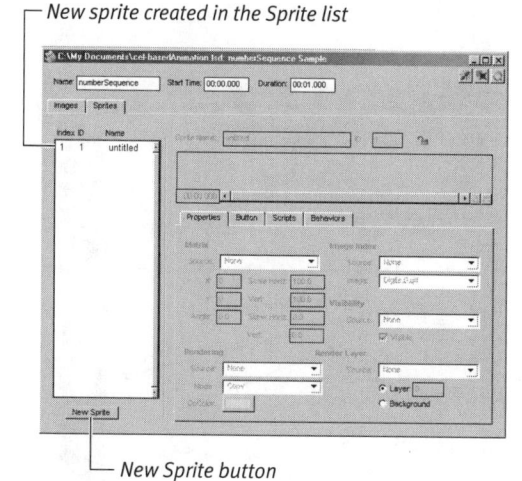

**Figure 11.17** Because you can switch a sprite's image easily with image index numbers, sprites are perfectly suited for cel-based animations.

*New Sprite button*

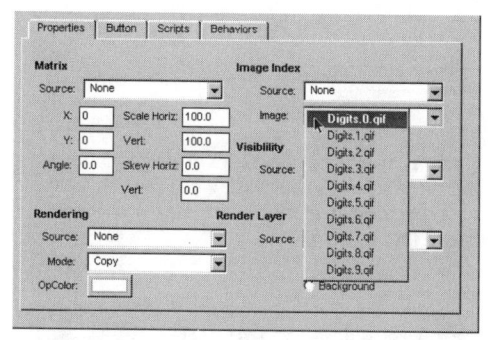

**Figure 11.18** Use the Image pop-up menu to choose the first image for your cel-based sprite animation.

covers, LiveStage cycles through the images from the top of the Image list to the bottom. If any of your images are out of order, you'll see a noticeable bump or lurch in your animation.

### To add a series of images to the Image list:

1. In the Project window, select the Tracks tab.

2. Choose Tracks > Create > Sprite.

   A sprite track is created, and a default sprite sample is placed in the Timeline.

3. Double-click the sprite sample.

   The sprite sample opens with the Images tab expanded.

4. Holding down the Shift key, choose all the images for your animation from the library, Finder (Mac), or desktop (Windows) (**Figure 11.16**).

5. Drag the images into the Images tab's Image list (refer to Figure 11.15).

6. Select the Sprites tab.

7. At the bottom of the Sprite list, click the New Sprite button.

   A new sprite is created in the Sprite list (**Figure 11.17**).

8. In the Image Index section of the Properties subtab, click the Image pop-up menu and choose the first image in your cel-based animation, which will be the image at the top of the Images tab's Image list (**Figure 11.18**).

   This image becomes the default image for the sprite and the one that appears first in the animation.

**ABOUT CEL-BASED ANIMATIONS**

247

## Tweening cel-based animations

Tween samples contain a tween editor that's perfectly suited for creating cel-based animations: the Index/Layer/Flag tween editor.

The Index/Layer/Flag tween editor causes a sprite's image to flip over time. This tween basically turns a sprite into a sequential series of frames, similar to the pages of a child's flip book. As the movie plays, the Index/Layer/Flag tween continuously switches the current sprite image with the next image down in the sprite sample's Image list, creating an animation (**Figure 11.19**).

### To tween a cel-based animation:

1. Set up a sprite track for cel-based animation, as described in "Setting up the animation" earlier in this chapter.

2. Choose Tracks > Create > Tween.

   A tween track is created, and a default tween sample is placed in the Timeline.

3. Double-click the tween sample to open it (**Figure 11.20**).

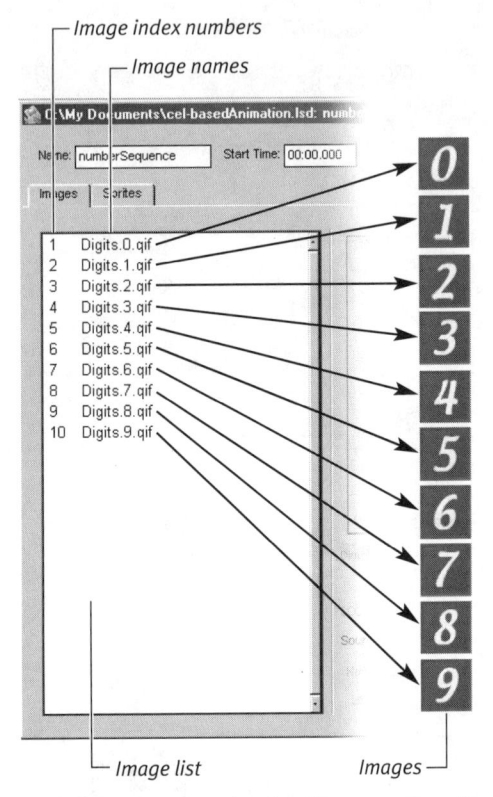

**Figure 11.19** A sequential series of images collected in the sprite sample's Image list. When used as the basis for a cel-based animation, these images will cycle from 0 through to 9.

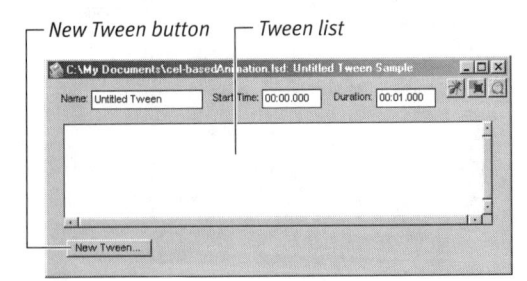

**Figure 11.20** A new tween sample does not have any tweens in the Tween list. To create a tween, click the New Tween button.

## Animations and Manipulations

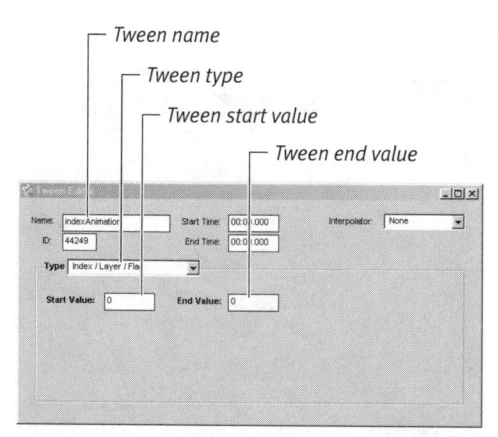

- Tween name
- Tween type
- Tween start value
- Tween end value

**Figure 11.21** The Index/Layer/Flag tween takes a start and end value and then interpolates a series of sequential whole numbers linking the two values. The start and end values must also be whole numbers; LiveStage does not let you enter decimals or fractions.

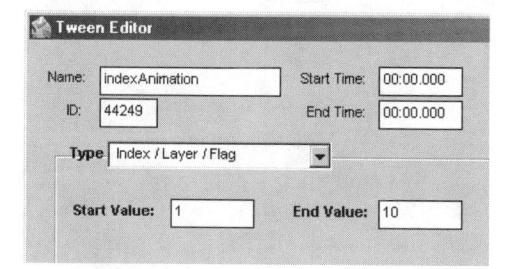

**Figure 11.22** The tween's start and end values must equal the start and end index numbers of the images (from the sprite sample's Image list) that make up your cel-based animation.

4. Click the New Tween button.

   The tween editor opens, displaying the Index/Layer/Flag tween, which is the correct one (**Figure 11.21**).

5. In the Name text box, enter a name for this tween.

   The name you enter will show up in any Source pop-up menu that works with this tween.

6. In the Start Value text box, enter the index number of the first image from the sprite sample's Image list (**Figure 11.22**).

   This image is the first one used in the cel-based sprite animation. The index numbers in the Image list start at 1, so the number in the Start Value text box should be equal to or greater than 1.

7. In the End Value text box, enter the index number of the last image in the sprite sample's Image list.

   This image is the last one used in the cel-based sprite animation.

8. In the Tracks tab, double-click the sprite sample to open it.

9. Select the Sprites tab.

   *continues on next page*

**ABOUT CEL-BASED ANIMATIONS**

249

# Chapter 11

10. In the Sprite list, select the sprite that you want to animate.

11. From the Source pop-up menu in the Image Index section, choose the Index/Layer/Flag tween by name, using the name you specified in step 5 (**Figure 11.23**).

12. In the Project window, select the Info tab.

13. In the Play section, check the Auto Start checkbox (**Figure 11.24**).

    If your movie does not play, the tween does not function. When you choose Auto Start, your movie begins playing as soon as it is opened or compiled into a preview movie.

14. In the top-right corner of the Project window, click the Run Wired Movie button.

    LiveStage compiles a preview movie, which begins playing automatically. As it plays, LiveStage cycles through the images in the sprite sample's Image list.

### ✔ Tip

- Make sure that the tween sample's duration and position in the project Timeline equal the duration and position of the Sprite sample; otherwise, the tween will not play back correctly.

*Selected sprite*   *Source pop-up menu*

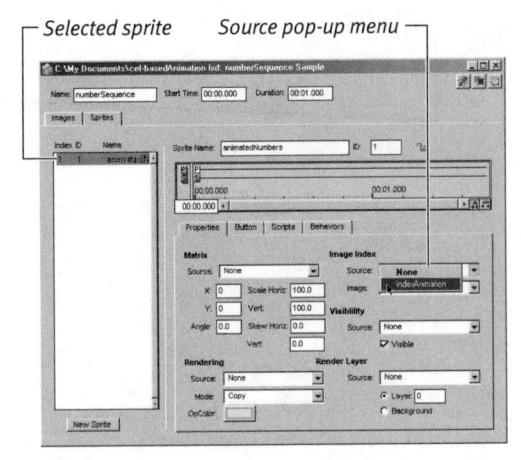

**Figure 11.23** The sprite sample's Image Index Source pop-up menu specifies the tween track that will switch the sprite images selected in the Sprite list.

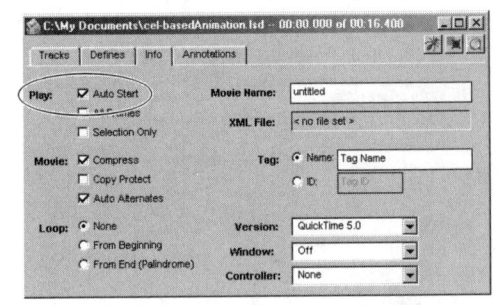

**Figure 11.24** Choosing Auto Start causes your preview movie to start playing as soon as it compiles. As you test your tweens, this option can be a handy time-saving feature, as you don't have to click Play each time you run a preview movie.

# Animations and Manipulations

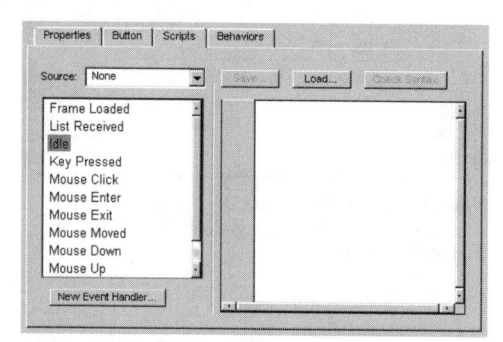

**Figure 11.25** The `Idle` event is a perfect event for animating sprites, as it executes regularly as time passes in your movie.

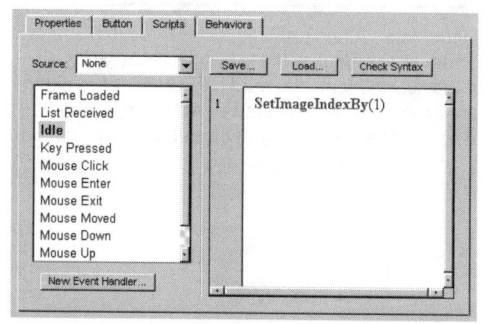

**Figure 11.26** The `SetImageIndexBy(1)` QScript action causes the index number of the sprite image to increase by 1 every time the action executes.

## QScripting cel-based animations

Cel-based animations cycle as time passes. If you've read Chapter 10, "Sprite Tracks," you might be reminded of a certain event handler that executes as time passes: the `Idle` event handler. Indeed, by using a combination of the `Idle` event handler and a single QScript action statement, you can create a cel-based animation that cycles for as long as your movie is open.

The secret of QScript cel animations is the `SetImageIndexBy(index_change)` QScript sprite action. Notice that this action contains the word `By`. When placed in an `Idle` event handler, this QScript causes a sprite's image index number to change *by* a set amount every time the `Idle` event executes. Like a film projector, the sprite skips through a series of images sequentially. If you also attach the `MIN`, `MAX`, and `WRAPAROUND` QScript action options, you can make the QScript animation loop forever (or as long as your movie is open).

### To QScript a cel animation:

1. Set up a sprite track for cel-based animation, as described in "Setting up the animation" earlier in this chapter.

2. With the sprite sample still open, click the Scripts tab.

   The Scripts tab displays the sample's script editor.

3. In the Event Handler list, select the `Idle` event (**Figure 11.25**).

4. In the script edit field, type the following QScript (**Figure 11.26**):

   `SetImageIndexBy(1)`

   Each time the `Idle` event executes, this QScript takes the index number of the current sprite image and increases it by 1. Because the `Idle` event executes as time passes, the sprite's image changes constantly, creating an animation.

   *continues on next page*

**ABOUT CEL-BASED ANIMATIONS**

251

But there's one problem: If you test your animation at this point (by clicking the Run Wired Movie button to create a preview movie), your animation would cycle from the first image to the last and then stop. To make your animation cycle for as long as the movie is open, you need to supply a MIN and a MAX value and also use the WRAPAROUND QScript action. The MIN and MAX values specify a range of index numbers. When the QScript reaches the MAX number, it jumps back to the MIN number and begins the animation all over again.

5. On the same line, directly after the SetImageIndexBy(1) QScript, enter the following text (**Figure 11.27**):

   MIN(1) MAX(maxIndexNumber)

   Change maxIndexNumber to the index number of the last image in the Images tab's Image list. The MIN and MAX values set the range of images for LiveStage to cycle through.

6. Finish the line by entering this keyword (**Figure 11.28**): WRAPAROUND

   The WRAPAROUND keyword tells LiveStage to cycle through to the last image, and then wrap around and begin the cycle all over again at the first image.

7. Click the Run Wired Movie button.

   LiveStage compiles your project into a preview movie. Check to see that your animation plays smoothly and at the right speed.

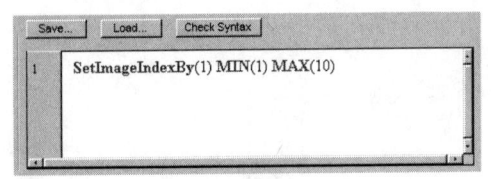

**Figure 11.27** The MIN and MAX QScript keywords set a range of values for LiveStage to cycle through as it executes a QScript.

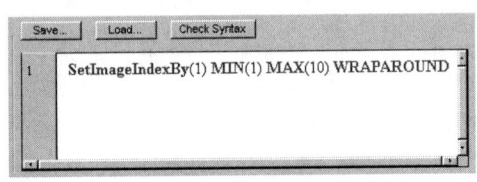

**Figure 11.28** After LiveStage cycles through the range of values specified by the MIN and MAX keywords, the WRAPAROUND QScript keyword tells LiveStage to begin the cycle all over again, starting at the beginning. When you use WRAPAROUND, your cel-based animation plays for as long as the movie is open.

✔ **Tip**

- Chances are that the preview movie will blaze through your animation at a breakneck pace. To slow the animation, you must increase the sprite track's idle frequency, which decreases the number of Idle events that are triggered per second. (To learn more about idle frequency, see Chapter 10, "Sprite Tracks.")

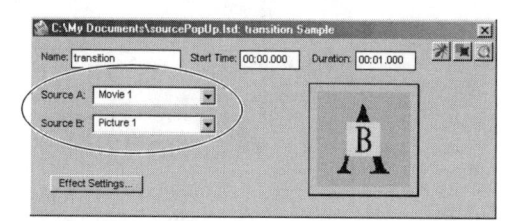

**Figure 11.29** The Source A and Source B pop-up menus.

## About Effect Tracks

LiveStage effect tracks provide access to all the filters, transitions, and special effects that come bundled with QuickTime. Effect tracks are one of QuickTime's best kept secrets—and for a reason. In QuickTime Pro, creating a filter or transition is difficult and time-consuming. But with LiveStage, complex visual effects are only a few clicks away.

An effect track itself contains no visual content. Instead, you feed a separate picture, video, or movie track into one or both of the effect sample's Source A and Source B pop-up menus (**Figure 11.29**). The effect track takes the source tracks and works its magic upon them.

Effect tracks can take one, two, or (under special circumstances) even no source tracks. If only one track is in the effect sample's Source A pop-up menu, the effect track turns into a filter—such as the Sharpen filter, which makes blurry graphics crystal-clear, or the Blur filter, which does the opposite.

### Why Real Time?

QuickTime renders all effects in real time, which can reduce your movie's bandwidth requirements significantly. To understand why, think about how transitions are created in a typical video editing program, such as Final Cut Pro.

To make a transition in Final Cut Pro, you blend the end of one track with the beginning of another. When you render your final strip of video, Final Cut goes through the transition frame by frame, progressively mixing the second track into the first until the first fades from view. All of this color-blending means that each pixel of each frame of the transition may be different.

When you compress your video, you discover that squeezing the video down to an acceptable file size causes the transition to become blocky and to stutter. Why? The simple answer is that most video compression codecs compress video over time. Think of compression on a pixel-by-pixel basis. If a pixel is red and doesn't change color for the next 300 frames, the codec can define its color one time and then tell it to stay the same for its next 300 instances. If the pixel changes color for each frame, the codec has to record each of these changes, which devours file size.

Think about the Final Cut fade, in which each pixel changes color constantly. When combined, these ever-changing pixels present a compression nightmare. QuickTime solves this problem by applying its effects in real time as the movie plays. Your source file contains no color blends, making compression easier and resulting in smaller files.

## Chapter 11

When tracks are set in both the Source A and Source B pop-up menus, the effect track lets you create transitions. Transitions smoothly cross-fade between two visual tracks, creating a blend that subtly introduces new video segments or images.

When no tracks are specified in the Source A or Source B pop-up menu, the effect track defaults to one of three special effects: Fire, Cloud, or Ripple. These effects definitely demonstrate QuickTime's quirky side, but with some imagination, you can make them do very interesting things.

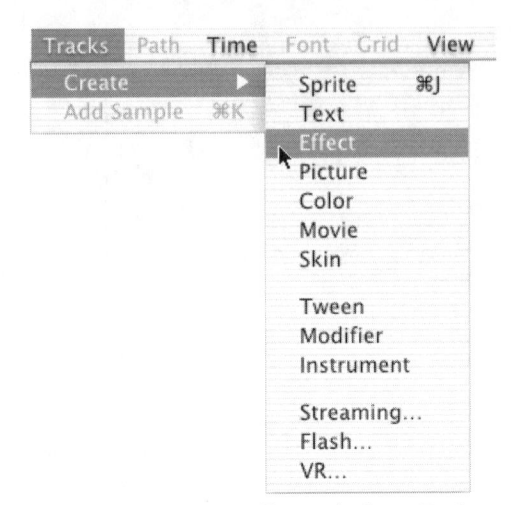

**Figure 11.30** To create an effect track, choose Tracks > Create > Effect.

### To create an effect track:

1. In the Project window, select the Tracks tab. The Tracks menu becomes active.

2. Choose Tracks > Create > Effect (**Figure 11.30**).
   A new effect track is created, and a default effect sample is placed in the Timeline.

### ✔ Tips

- Effect tracks do not scale to meet the dimensions of their source tracks. In fact, the opposite happens, as source tracks are expanded or crunched into the effect track's dimensions. As a result, you must ensure that the effect track's dimensions match those of the source track(s); otherwise, unexpected results will occur. To learn more about changing track dimensions, see Chapter 3, "Setting Track Properties."

- Effect tracks render in real time. This arrangement keeps files small but also consumes processor power. If you're going to use an effect track, do so prudently, and test your movie on a wide range of computers to ensure that it plays smoothly. As a rule, the larger an effect track, the more processor power you'll need.

- Effect tracks must be placed on top of the tracks that they affect. If an effect track is below its source tracks, it will be hidden.

*Effect preview area*  *Effect properties area*

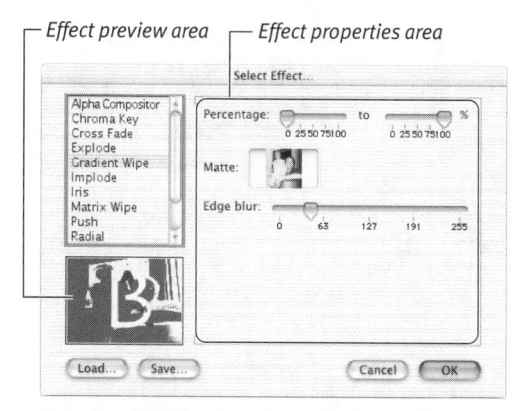

**Figure 11.31** On the right side of the Select Effect dialog, the effect properties area lets you control how the transition looks and animates. In this example, I've used a Gradient Wipe transition with a black-and-white matte image of two boys. In the effect preview area, you can see the transition morphing around the shapes in the picture.

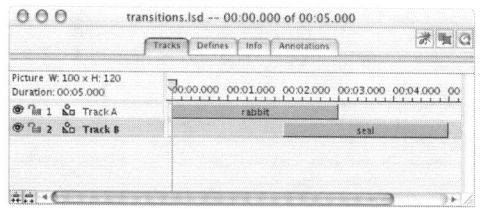

**Figure 11.32** Transitions blend the end of one visual track smoothly with the beginning of a second one. To set up a transition, drag the second visual track in the Timeline so that it overlaps a small portion of the first visual track. The length of the overlap determines the length of the transition.

# About Transitions

A *transition* takes the end of one visual track and blends it smoothly with the beginning of a second. When created correctly, transitions can "explode" one track into another or have the second track push the first from view.

Transitions are highly customizable and can add motion and elegance to still-image slide shows. They are also great for use in video projects, such as an instructional movie that cross-fades between a close-up of an instructor speaking and a visual demonstration of the topic that she's explaining.

LiveStage contains myriad popular transition effects that are common to all video-editing programs, including cross-fades, wipes, slides, and push transitions. With 13 different transitions to choose among, you're bound to find one that you like. But LiveStage doesn't stop there. After you choose a transition, try changing some of its properties (**Figure 11.31**).

## To create a transition:

1. In the Project window, select the Tracks tab.

2. From the library, Finder (Mac), or desktop (Windows), drag two visual tracks into the Tracks tab.

   For ease of explanation, the first visual track will be called Track A, and the second will be called Track B.

3. In the Timeline, move Track B so that it overlaps the end of Track A (**Figure 11.32**).

   The length of the overlap determines how long your transition lasts. If you want the transition to be 1 second long, Track B must overlap the last second of Track A.

*continues on next page*

# Chapter 11

4. Choose Tracks > Create > Effect.

   A new effect track is created, and a default sample is placed in the Timeline.

5. Drag the effect track sample to the area where Track B overlaps Track A in the Timeline.

6. Adjust the duration of the effect track sample so that it matches the duration of the overlap between Track A and B (**Figure 11.33**).

   The fastest way to adjust the effect track's duration is to grab its left or right edge and drag it along the Timeline. For more detailed information on changing sample duration, see Chapter 1, "The Tracks Tab."

7. Double-click the effect sample to open it.

8. From the Source A pop-up menu, choose Track A (**Figure 11.34**).

9. From the Source B pop-up menu, choose Track B.

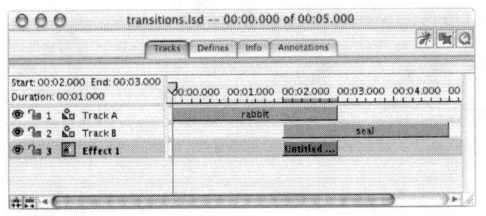

**Figure 11.33** For a transition to work properly, the effect track must cover the same duration in the Timeline as the overlap between Track A and Track B.

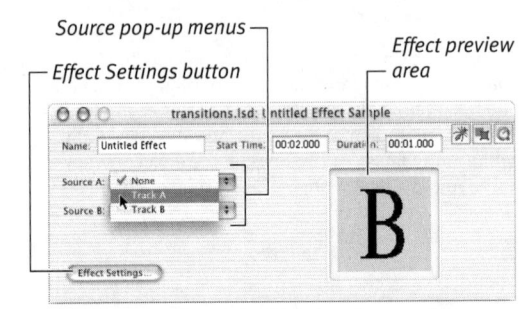

**Figure 11.34** In the open effect sample, use the Source A pop-up menu to specify the first track for your transition and the Source B pop-up menu to specify the second.

# Animations and Manipulations

*Effect preview area*
*Effect list*
*Effect properties area*

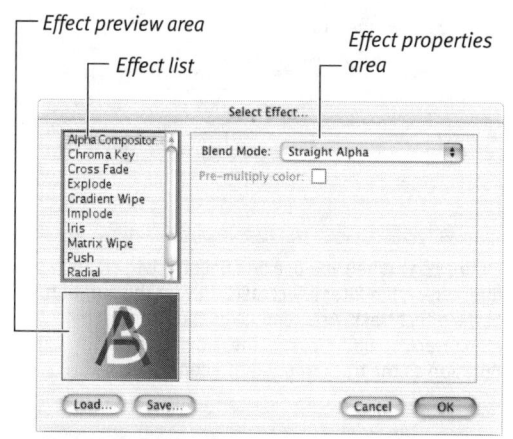

**Figure 11.35** The Select Effect dialog. If tracks are assigned to both the Source A and Source B pop-up menus in the main effect sample, the Select Effect dialog lists only transitions.

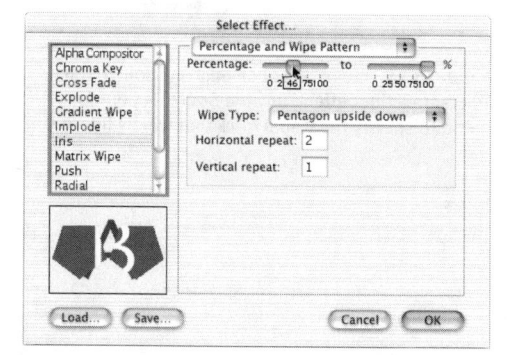

**Figure 11.36** The effect properties area contains property editors that you can use to tailor any transition to your needs.

10. Click the Effect Settings button.

    The Select Effect dialog opens (**Figure 11.35**). The left side of the Select Effect dialog holds an Effect list, and the right side (the effect properties area) displays properties for whichever effect is selected in the Effect list.

11. Select a transition in the Effect list.

    A preview of the transition appears in the effect preview area below the Effect list.

12. In the effect properties area, adjust the properties of the selected transition (**Figure 11.36**).

    The properties that appear in the effect properties area depend on which transition is selected in the Effect list.

13. Click OK.

    The Select Effect dialog closes.

14. In the top-right corner of the effect sample, click the Run Wired Movie button.

    When the preview movie plays, a transition occurs where Track B overlaps Track A.

## ✔ Tips

- Make sure that your transitions are long enough that viewers can see them. In general, transitions should be no shorter than 1/2 second; 1-second transitions are fairly standard.

- Don't forget that transitions also work on picture tracks. To add interest to any still-image slide show, make one picture blend smoothly into the next, or use some of LiveStage's less-subtle transitions to catch your viewer's eye and hold it.

**ABOUT TRANSITIONS**

257

# Chapter 11

## About Filter Effects

A filter takes a picture, video, or movie track and alters it, often in drastic ways. A brightness and contrast filter, for example, can make an overexposed video look darker. Lens flares animate points of light, adding ambiance. Another animated filter effect, Film Noise, introduces a grainy, worn-film look reminiscent of a 1920s black-and-white movie.

Filter effects operate on only one track. To create a filter effect, choose a picture, video, or movie track from the effect sample's Source A pop-up menu, but leave the Source B pop-up set to None. This technique puts the effect sample into filter mode, and when you open the Select Effect dialog, only filter effects will be available.

### To create a filter effect:

1. In the Project window, select the Tracks tab.

2. From the library, Finder (Mac), or desktop (Windows), drag a visual track into the Tracks tab.

   For ease of explanation, this track will be called Track A.

3. Choose Tracks > Create > Effect.

   A new effect track is created, and a default sample is placed in the Timeline.

4. In the Timeline, drag the effect track sample so that it starts at exactly the same point as Track A.

5. Adjust the duration of the effect track sample so that it matches the duration of Track A (**Figure 11.37**).

6. Double-click the effect sample to open it.

7. From the Source A pop-up menu, choose Track A (**Figure 11.38**).

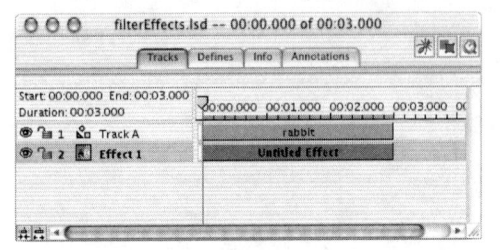

**Figure 11.37** When you use an effect track to create a filter effect, the filter effect lasts only for the duration of the effect track. As a result, you must stretch the effect track so that it covers the same Timeline duration as the track that it is affecting.

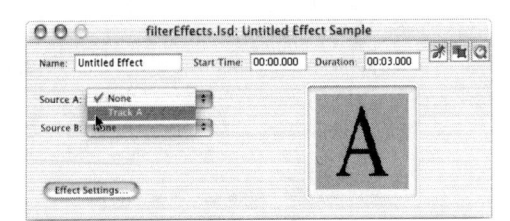

**Figure 11.38** Filter effects use only one source track. To create a filter effect, use the Source A pop-up menu to specify the visual track that will be filtered.

# Animations and Manipulations

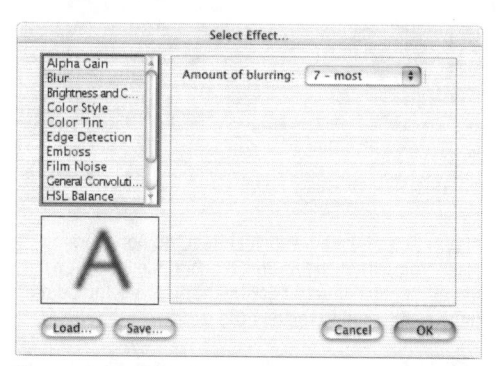

**Figure 11.39** With only one visual track selected in the Source A pop-up menu of the main effect sample, the Select Effect dialog displays only filter effects in the Effect list.

**Figure 11.40** The result of the Blur filter effect on a picture track.

Filter effects work on only one track at a time, so you don't need to choose a second track from the Source B pop-up menu; in fact, you must leave that menu at its default setting of None. Also, be sure that you assign Track A to the Source A pop-up menu. If you assign it to the Source B pop-up menu (leaving the Source A pop-up menu set to None), the effect will not work.

8. Click the Effect Settings button.

   The Select Effect dialog opens (**Figure 11.39**). The left side of the Select Effect dialog holds the Effect list, while the right side displays properties for whichever effect is selected in the Effect list.

9. Select a filter in the Effect list.

   A preview of the filter appears below the Effect list.

10. In the effect properties area, adjust the selected filter's properties.

11. Click OK.

    The Select Effect dialog closes.

12. In the top-right corner of the effect sample, click the Run Wired Movie button.

    LiveStage compiles a preview of your movie, which displays your filter effect when played (**Figure 11.40**).

**ABOUT FILTER EFFECTS**

259

Chapter 11

## About Special Effects

With a LiveStage effect track, you can access three QuickTime special effects: Fire, Cloud, and Ripple. These effects are somewhat esoteric, but they can provide interesting results if you set the effect track's graphics mode to Add Min or Add Max. (To learn more about graphics modes, see Chapter 3, "Setting Track Properties.") The Add Min and Add Max graphics modes are well suited to maintaining the visual integrity and color of the tracks below the effect track, but you can use any graphics mode that fits the effect you are trying to create.

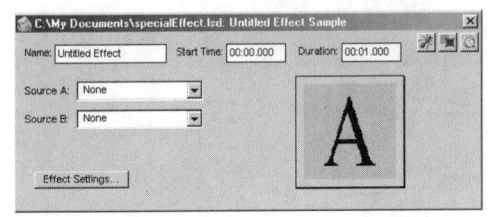

**Figure 11.41** To use a special effect, do not choose a track from either the Source A or Source B pop-up menu. Special effects work by themselves and do not need to be applied to any other track.

### To use a special effect:

1. In the Project window, select the Tracks tab.

2. Choose Tracks > Create > Effect.

   A new effect track is created, and a default effect sample is placed in the Timeline.

3. Double-click the effect sample to open it (**Figure 11.41**).

   Do not choose a track from either the Source A or Source B pop-up menu. Special effects do not need an assigned track to work.

4. Click the Effect Settings button.

   The Select Effect dialog opens (**Figure 11.42**). The left side of the Select Effect dialog holds the Effect list, and the right side displays properties for whichever effect is selected in the Effect list.

5. Select a special effect in the Effect list.

   A preview appears below the Effect list.

6. In the effect properties area, adjust the special effect's properties.

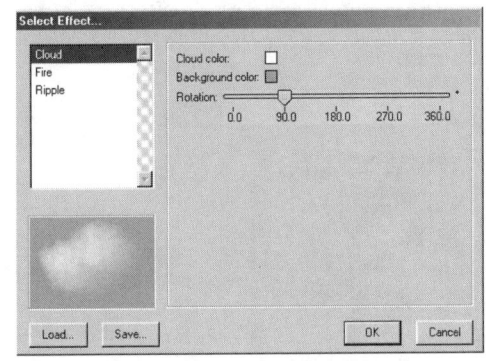

**Figure 11.42** With no source tracks selected in the effects sample, the Select Effect dialog opens to display three special effects. These special effects are particularly useful when used with a graphics mode (set in the Composition tab of the effect track's Track Properties window).

# Animations and Manipulations

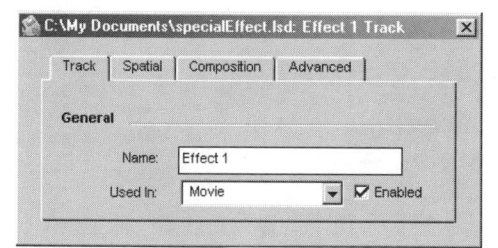

**Figure 11.43** The effect track's Track Properties window.

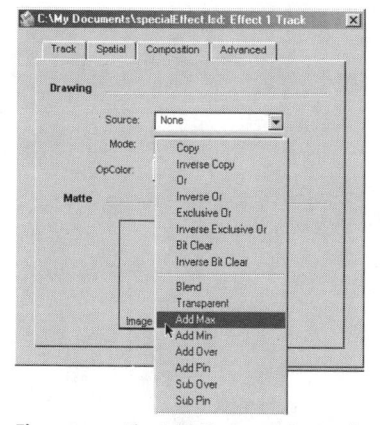

**Figure 11.44** The Add Max graphics mode is particularly effective when used with a special effect, as it lets tracks below the effect track shine through without changing their colors drastically.

**Figure 11.45** This preview movie shows the Cloud special effect positioned above the stem of a teapot.

7. Click OK.

   The Select Effect dialog closes.

8. In the Tracks tab, double-click the effect track's header in the Track list.

   The Track Properties window opens (**Figure 11.43**).

9. Select the Composition tab.

10. From the Mode pop-up menu, choose Add Max (**Figure 11.44**).

11. In the top-right corner of the Project window, click the Run Wired Movie button.

    When the preview movie plays, the special effect is displayed (**Figure 11.45**).

## ✔ Tips

- Special effects are very processor-intensive; the larger the effect track, the more the CPU has to work. Use special effects wisely, and keep the effect track's dimensions to the exact size of the area that it's intended to affect.

- If you need to confine the special effect to a non-rectangular shape, use a track matte. For more information on track mattes, see Chapter 3, "Setting Track Properties."

ABOUT SPECIAL EFFECTS

261

# WORKING WITH AUDIO

## 12

A movie without audio is like a cake without icing—tasty, but just not as sweet as it could be. This chapter demonstrates how to give your projects flavor by using recorded digital audio (AIFFs, WAVs, and MP3s) and/or QuickTime MIDI instruments.

Digital audio files sound great but can weigh movies down with their huge file sizes. You can combat this problem by compressing the files into tiny MP3s with an application such as Digidesign Pro Tools or Apple's iTunes. In some cases, however, no amount of compression can make the file small enough. QuickTime comes to the rescue with *MIDI* (Musical Instrument Digital Interface) instruments, which you can use to create low-bandwidth, high-fidelity audio that won't slow your downloads.

QuickTime hosts more than 200 MIDI instruments (sound samples representing everything from drums and basses to ringing telephones and gunshots). The instruments not only sound great, but also, because they're part of QuickTime, you don't have to include them in your movie file. Instead, you can use a MIDI or instrument track to access the MIDI instruments that you want played. When your compiled movie hits one of these tracks, it looks inside QuickTime, finds the MIDI instruments, and plays them on the fly.

# About Sound Tracks

A sound track houses digital audio, which comes in many forms. The songs on an audio CD are digital audio, as are the MP3 files that you download from the Internet. If you work on a Mac, you've very likely seen AIFF files; if you use a Windows system, you're probably familiar with WAVs. LiveStage understands them all and many, many more.

When you add a digital audio file to your project, LiveStage creates a sound track, places a sample in the Tracks tab's Timeline, and fills that sample with the audio file. LiveStage automatically sets the duration of the sound track to match that of the added digital audio file. If the audio file is 16 seconds long, for example, the sound track's sample will occupy 16 seconds of the Timeline.

**Figure 12.1** To create a sound track, drag a digital audio file into LiveStage.

### To add a sound track:

◆ Drag an AIFF, WAV, MP3, or any other QuickTime-compatible digital audio file into the Tracks tab of the Project window (**Figure 12.1**).

A new sound track is added to the Tracks tab, and a sound track sample is placed in the Timeline (**Figure 12.2**).

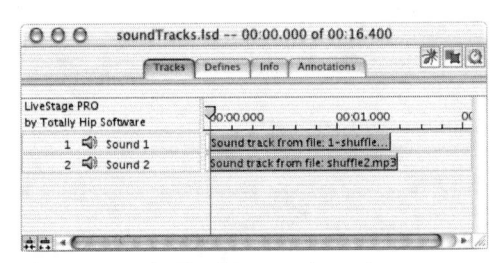

**Figure 12.2** In the Timeline, sound samples are green.

Working with Audio

**Figure 12.3** To make sure you've added the correct digital audio file to your project, in the Timeline, double-click the sound track sample to open a preview window. Because sound tracks have no visual content, the preview window consists of nothing more than a controller you can use to play, pause, forward or rewind the digital audio file.

### Making Sound Tracks

To make a sound track, you need to use a third-party program such as Digidesign Pro Tools or Propellerhead's Reason. Pro Tools stands out because it allows you to record and create both audio and MIDI files. Also, its MP3, AIFF, and WAV compression algorithms are second to none, and perfectly suited for compressing your sound files for Web delivery. Best of all, you can download a free, full-featured, eight-track version of Pro Tools from the Digidesign Web site. The free version comes stocked with a full range of Pro Tools' Digital Signal Processing (DSP) plug-ins, such as compressors, noise gates, and reverbs—and the demo's not time-limited! Go to http://www.digidesign.com and follow the links to Get Pro Tools Free.

### ✔ Tips

- To change the duration of a sound-track sample, grab its right edge and drag it along the Timeline. You should know, however, that when you change the duration of a sound track sample, you're also reducing or expanding its audio, which will change the way it sounds. Shortening a sound-track sample makes the audio play back faster, whereas lengthening it has the opposite effect, causing the audio to sound slow and labored.

- If you intend to use a small audio loop to provide background music, avoid MP3 compression. MP3 compression often tacks a tiny bit of silence onto the end of the audio file, which causes a noticeable stutter as the audio loops. Instead, use QuickTime Pro to compress your audio with the IMA 4:1 codec. The IMA 4:1 codec makes your new audio file four times smaller than the original. IMA 4:1 compression sounds great and loops perfectly.

- Double-click a sound-track sample to open a preview window you can use to listen to (audition) the sample's audio file (**Figure 12.3**).

**ABOUT SOUND TRACKS**

265

# About Track Volume

Sound, instrument, Macromedia Flash, MIDI, and movie tracks all have a volume setting that you can adjust in the Track Properties window (**Figure 12.4**). Track volume ranges from 0 (silent) to 256 (full volume). By default, any track that can make noise is set at a volume of 256—as loud as the track can get. If your movie has several audio tracks, such as a background loop and a vocal narration, you'll need to adjust their volumes so that one track doesn't overpower the others. Help your viewers hear, and understand, the movie's message by always setting background audio tracks to a lower volume than the narration.

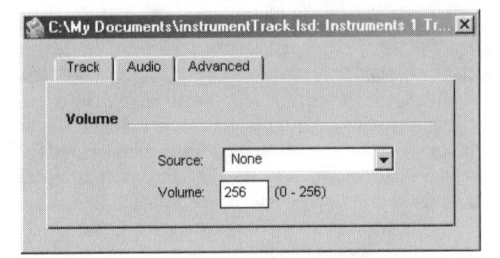

**Figure 12.4** The Volume option sets the relative loudness of any track containing audio.

## To set track volume:

1. In the Tracks tab of the Project window, double-click the track header of the track whose volume you want to change (**Figure 12.5**).

   The Track Properties window opens, with the Track tab showing. If your track is a movie, Flash, or sound track, a Volume text box appears in the Track tab (**Figure 12.6**).

2. If your track is a movie, Flash, or sound track, enter a new value in the Volume text box.

   *or*

   If your track is an instrument, MIDI, or streaming track, select the Audio tab of the Track Properties window (refer to Figure 12.4).

   The Audio tab opens to reveal a Volume text box.

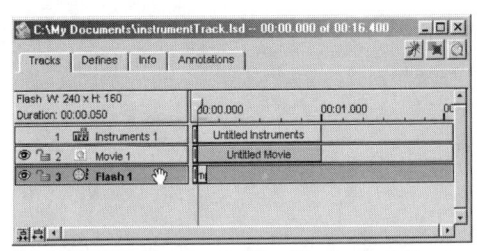

**Figure 12.5** Track volume is a track property that you can set in the Track Properties window. To open the Track Properties window, double-click the track's header in the Track list.

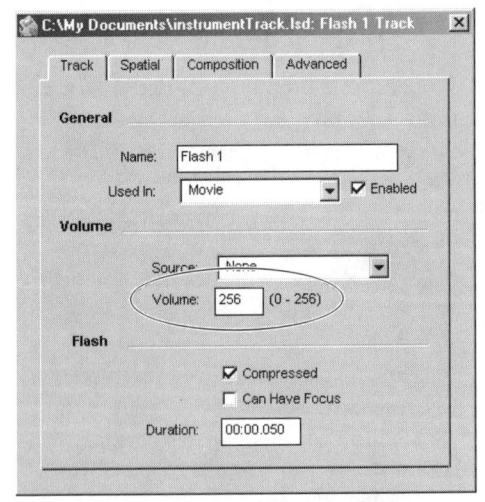

**Figure 12.6** The Volume text box accepts values between 0 (silent) and 256 (full volume).

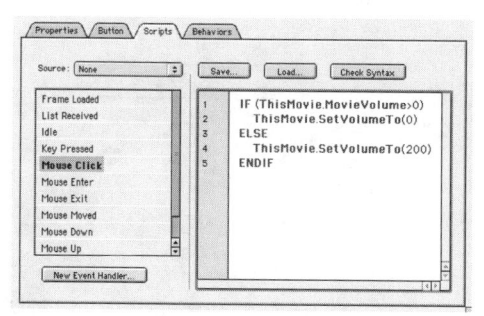

**Figure 12.7** When placed in the Mouse Click event handler of a sprite button, this QScript toggles a movie's volume on and off. First, it checks to see if the movie's volume is greater than 0 (playing). If so, the volume is set to 0 (off). If the volume is already at 0 (or less), this QScript sets the volume to 200.

3. Enter a new value in the Volume text box.

   By default, the Volume option is set to 256. If you lower the value in the Volume text box, the track seems quieter than normal in your compiled movie.

### ✔ Tips

- You can enter values higher than 256 in any Volume text box, but they won't make the track's audio any louder.

- MIDI tracks sound louder than recorded audio tracks, even if they're set to the same volume. If you're using a combination of MIDI and recorded audio, make sure that the MIDI instruments do not drown out any AIFFs, WAVs, or MP3s that you might also be using.

- Viewers don't always want loud, blaring audio, so give them a way to turn it off. Make a sprite Volume Off button, and place the following QScript in the button's `Mouse Click` event handler: `ThisMovie.SetVolumeTo(0)` (**Figure 12.7**).

---

### Clipping Sound Cards

If track volume, movie volume, and the output on the viewer's computer are all set to full, there's a chance that the viewer's sound card will overload, resulting in *clipping* (crackling and popping). Although clipping does no damage to the sound card, it torments the eardrum and, in rare circumstances, blows up speakers. To prevent your movie from clipping sound cards, never use a volume setting higher than 200. By lowering your tracks' volume slightly, you make it virtually impossible for your audio to cause a screeching overload.

# About MIDI

MIDI is an electronic system of communication that allows computers to talk to synthesizers, samplers, and other electronic instruments. A MIDI file itself contains no sounds; it is simply a string of numbers representing musical notes. To play a MIDI file, you need a MIDI-equipped synthesizer, such as QuickTime, to turn the numbers into sounds.

MIDI takes its inspiration from early player pianos, which played songs by reading tiny holes punched in a roll of paper. MIDI represents the modern, electronic version of that roll of paper, and QuickTime takes the role of the player piano.

When you install QuickTime, more than 200 MIDI instruments are placed on your hard disk, and all are available for use in your LiveStage projects. All you need to trigger them is a MIDI track.

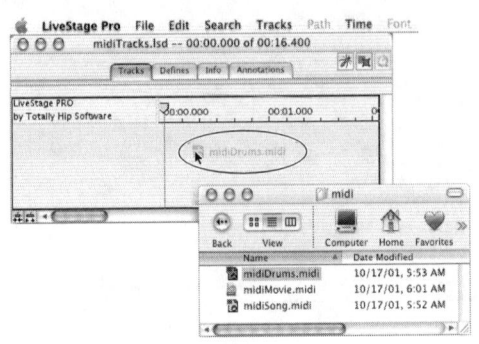

**Figure 12.8** To add audio to your project instantly, drag a MIDI file into the Tracks tab.

## Using MIDI tracks

LiveStage is not a MIDI sequencer, and you cannot use it to create MIDI files. To make a MIDI file, you need a third-party sequencing application, such as Steinberg Cubase or Digidesign Pro Tools. If you're on a budget, you can download several free shareware sequencers at: http://www.hitsquad.com/.

After you've created a MIDI file, drag it into your project to add a rolling dance beat, a smooth R&B groove, or whatever electronic soundscape your MIDI file contains.

### To add a MIDI track:

◆ From the library, Finder (Mac), or desktop (Windows), drag a MIDI file into the Tracks tab of the Project window (**Figure 12.8**).
A new MIDI track (external music track) is created, and a sound track sample is placed in the Timeline.

### ✔ Tip

- For some real fun, try adding two or more MIDI tracks of the same tempo and duration. If you align them exactly in the Timeline, you can enable and disable different MIDI tracks, making variations on your song. To learn more about enabling and disabling tracks, see Chapter 4, "The Script Editor."

## Changing MIDI instruments

If you go scouting on the Internet, you will find a wealth of MIDI files just waiting to be downloaded and added to your project. These files can be lifesavers when you need copyright-free background music, for example, but don't have the time to make it yourself. Just fire up your favorite search engine, type MIDI, and see what pops up.

After downloading a MIDI file, you might need to change some of its default MIDI instruments so that the music better suits your movie's atmosphere. Perhaps the lead synthesizer is too shrill, or the piano doesn't sound quite real. With QuickTime Pro, you can change these instruments without altering the structure of the song file. (You cannot change MIDI instruments inside LiveStage.) The lead synthesizer could be switched to an organ, the piano to a cello or any other QuickTime MIDI instrument. If you don't have QuickTime Pro, all MIDI sequencing applications let you change instrument sounds (try Pro Tools Free).

**Figure 12.9** To change the instrument used in a MIDI file, you need to open the file in QuickTime Pro. In QuickTime Pro, choose Movie > Get Movie Properties to open the Movie Properties window.

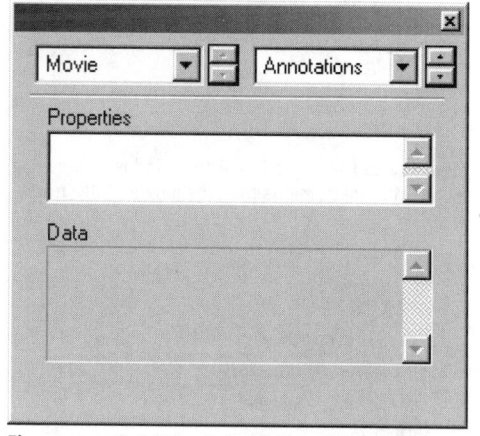

**Figure 12.10** QuickTime's Movie Properties window.

### To change a MIDI instrument:

1. Open the MIDI file in QuickTime Pro.

2. Choose Movie > Get Movie Properties (**Figure 12.9**).

   The Movie Properties window opens (**Figure 12.10**).

   *continues on next page*

Chapter 12

3. Choose Music Track from the left pop-up menu; and from the right pop-up menu, choose Instruments (**Figure 12.11**).

   A list of the music track's instruments appears in the Movie Properties window (**Figure 12.12**).

4. Double-click an instrument in the list.

   The New Instrument For Part (Mac)/ Instrument Picker (Windows) dialog opens (**Figure 12.13**). This dialog is widely referred to as the Instrument Picker and is labeled as such in the Windows version of QuickTime Pro. I will refer to this dialog as the Instrument Picker throughout the rest of this chapter.

5. Leave Default Synthesizer selected in the top pop-up menu.

6. Choose a group of instruments from the Category pop-up menu.

7. From the Instrument pop-up menu, choose an instrument.

8. Do not change the MIDI channel in the MIDI Channel pop-up menu at the bottom of the Instrument Picker.

   MIDI channels ensure the correct note information is provided to the correct MIDI instrument. These channels are set when the MIDI file is created and you don't need to specify a new channel if you're simply changing the MIDI instrument.

9. Click the OK button to close the Instrument Picker.

10. Choose File > Save to save the altered MIDI file to your hard disk.

    The new MIDI file is ready for use in any LiveStage project.

✔ **Tip**

- To audition an instrument, click or drag the pointer across the keyboard in QuickTime's Instrument Picker dialog.

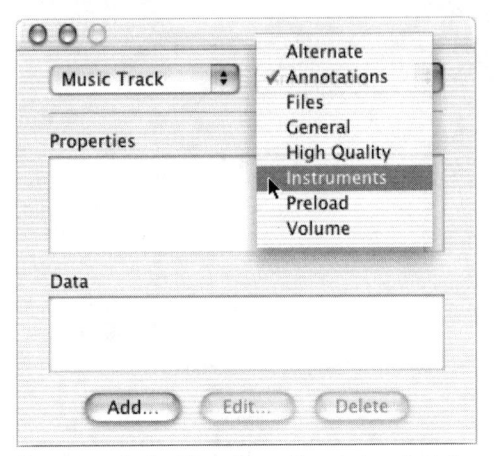

**Figure 12.11** In the Movie Properties window, the left pop-up menu lists all the tracks contained in the movie, and the right pop-up menu lets you adjust the properties of the track selected in the left menu.

**Figure 12.12** The Movie Properties window, displaying all the MIDI instruments from the movie's MIDI track.

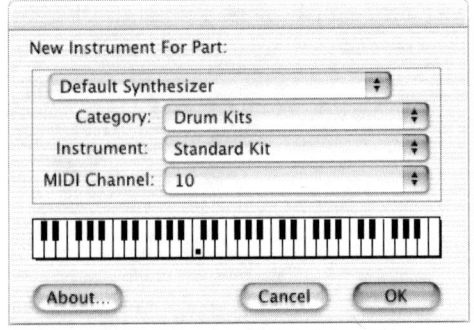

**Figure 12.13** The Instrument Picker dialog. The Category and Instrument pop-up menus work in tandem to let you select an individual instrument from a list of more than 200 MIDI instruments installed with QuickTime.

## About Instrument Tracks

Instrument tracks give your LiveStage projects access to QuickTime's MIDI instruments—no MIDI file needed. They are great for creating button rollover sounds, game noises, interactive pianos, alerts, and other audio special effects.

But there is one catch: Instrument tracks only define MIDI instruments, they don't actually contain instruments in the track itself. To play the MIDI instruments, you must write a QScript action statement. At the end of this chapter, you'll learn more about writing scripts that play instruments. First, take a moment to explore instrument tracks and create a few instruments of your own. After all, you must have an instrument before you can play it.

## Using instrument tracks

Instrument tracks are pointers that tell your movie how to locate the proper MIDI instruments inside QuickTime (sort of like MIDI tracks without the note information). The MIDI instruments themselves (the sounds) are not part of the instrument track or even your movie.

MIDI instruments work similarly to text fonts in QuickTime. If you've read Chapter 8, "Text Tracks," you know that QuickTime does not use embedded text fonts; instead, it supplies your movie with a reference to the correct font. When the movie is opened, it looks for the font on the viewer's computer, and if the font is present, it displays the text correctly.

In the same fashion, when LiveStage compiles your final movie, it leaves out all the MIDI instruments, safe in the knowledge that these MIDI instruments will be waiting and ready whenever the movie is opened in QuickTime. As a result, instrument tracks add very little to your movie's overall file size.

# Chapter 12

## To add an instrument track:

1. In the Project window, select the Tracks tab.

2. Choose Tracks > Create > Instrument (**Figure 12.14**).

   A new instrument track is created, and an instrument sample is placed in the Timeline.

## Creating instruments

Instrument tracks hold references to QuickTime MIDI instruments. If you open an instrument sample, you'll see a window displaying the Instrument list (**Figure 12.15**). You can add as many instruments as you like to the list, thereby making each one available to your project.

Using an instrument track is like assembling your own little band. You start by visualizing what type of music your band will play. After you've got an idea of the sound you're after, you build the band by adding instruments to the Instrument list. Need a bass? Add one. What about a guitar, a violin, or even a special effect, such as a helicopter? Add, add, add, and keep adding MIDI instruments until all the members of your band are assembled.

## To add an instrument:

1. In the Tracks tab of the Project window, double-click an instrument sample.

   The sample opens (**Figure 12.16**). By default, the instrument sample contains no instruments, and the Instrument list is empty.

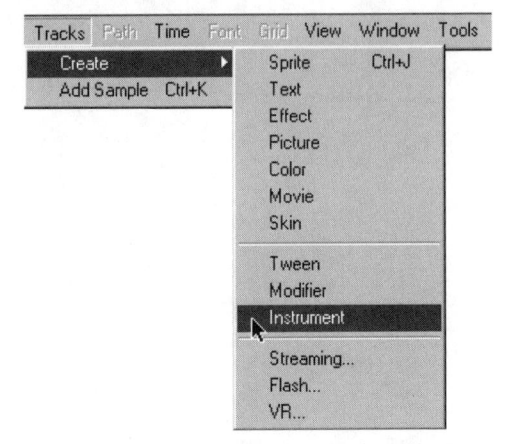

**Figure 12.14** You create instrument tracks in LiveStage by choosing Tracks > Create > Instrument.

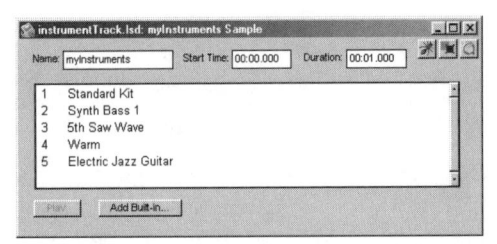

**Figure 12.15** An open instrument sample with five MIDI instruments added to it.

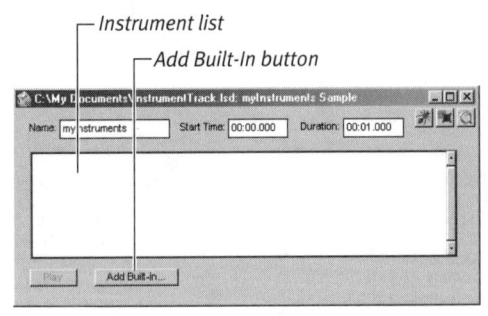

**Figure 12.16** By default, an instrument sample holds no MIDI instruments, and the Instrument list is empty. To create a MIDI instrument, click the Add Built-In button.

Working with Audio

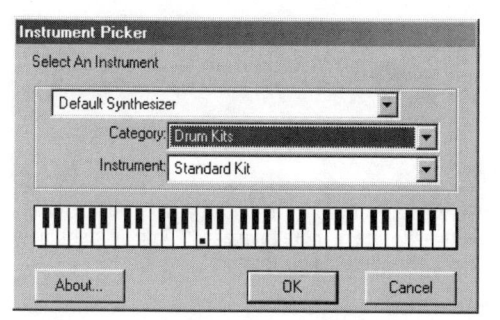

**Figure 12.17** Use the Instrument Picker to choose a MIDI instrument from QuickTime's default synthesizer.

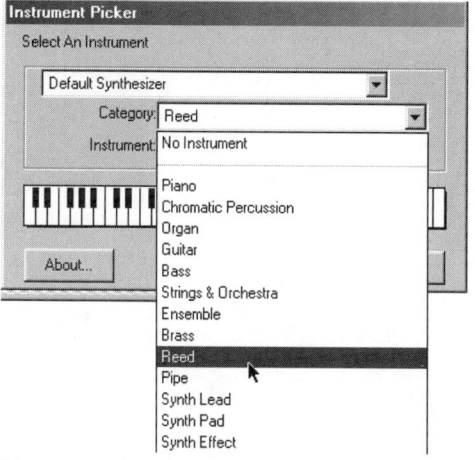

**Figure 12.18** The Instrument Picker's Category pop-up menu lists the QuickTime MIDI instruments by group.

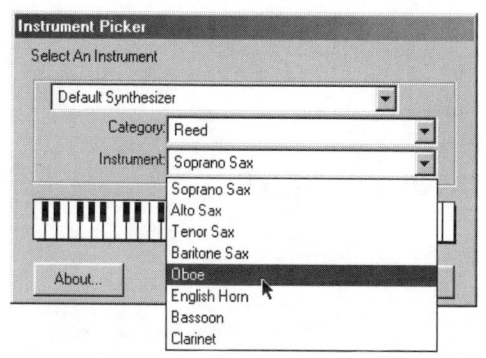

**Figure 12.19** After choosing a group of MIDI instruments from the Instrument Picker's Category pop-up menu, use the Instrument pop-up menu to choose an individual MIDI instrument.

2. Click the Add Built-In button.

 The New Instrument For Part (Mac)/Instrument Picker (Windows) dialog opens (**Figure 12.17**).

3. Leave Default Synthesizer selected in the top pop-up menu.

 If you have a synthesizer-equipped sound card or any other synthesizers installed and properly configured on your hard disk, these synthesizers will appear in this pop-up menu. Because most viewers will be using the Default Synthesizer inside QuickTime, you should, too. If you select a different synthesizer, the MIDI sounds you hear will be different from those the majority of your audience will hear.

4. Choose a group of instruments from the Category pop-up menu (**Figure 12.18**).

 QuickTime puts more than 200 instruments at your disposal. The Category pop-up menu gathers MIDI instruments in groups (Pianos, Bass, Drum Kits, etc.) letting you focus on a specific instrument type.

 After you choose an instrument category, the Instrument pop-up menu is activated.

5. From the Instrument pop-up menu, choose an instrument (**Figure 12.19**).

6. Click OK.

 The Instrument Picker closes, and the MIDI instrument is added to the instrument sample's Instrument list.

ABOUT INSTRUMENT TRACKS

273

## Using sampled sounds

If none of QuickTime's MIDI instruments plays the sound that you need, you can record your own digital audio file and add it to an instrument sample. This procedure creates a *sampled instrument*. LiveStage treats sampled instruments and normal QuickTime MIDI instruments the same way, with one difference: When you compile your project, LiveStage embeds all sampled instruments in the final QuickTime movie. No matter how you distribute that movie, the sampled instruments go with it, ready for action whenever the movie is opened.

Use sampled instruments when you need to create a unique sound. If your movie has an Enter button, for example, you can record your neighbor saying "Enter," load the recording into an instrument track, and trigger it whenever the pointer moves over the Enter button.

Sampled instruments are a bit of a Faustian bargain; your movie sounds great, but its file enlarges with each sampled instrument you add. You also face a couple of restrictions:

- You can't add any sampled instrument with a file size greater than 250 KB. You can try, but LiveStage quickly reprimands you with the alert dialog shown in **Figure 12.20**.

- Sampled instruments *must not be compressed*. Use AIFFs and WAVs, not MP3s. If you compress the audio used for a sampled instrument, it will not compile into your final movie and will not be available when the movie is played.

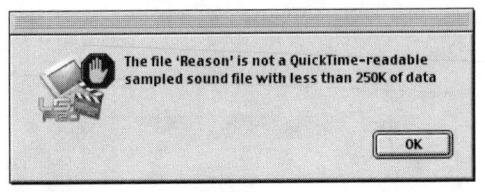

**Figure 12.20** If you try to embed a sampled instrument with a file size of more than 250 KB into an instrument track, this alert dialog appears.

# Working with Audio

Uncompressed, 250 KB is less than 2 seconds of stereo digital audio. Keep this in mind when you add sampled instruments to your movie.

## To add a sampled instrument:

1. In the Tracks tab of the Project window, double-click an instrument sample to open it.

2. From the library, Finder (Mac), or desktop (Windows), drag a digital audio file into the instrument sample's Instrument list (**Figure 12.21**).

   The digital audio file becomes a sampled instrument, and its name appears in the instrument sample's Instrument list.

## ✔ Tip

- To audition your sampled sound after you've added it to an instrument track, select it in the Instrument list and click the Play button, located in the bottom-left corner of the open instrument sample.

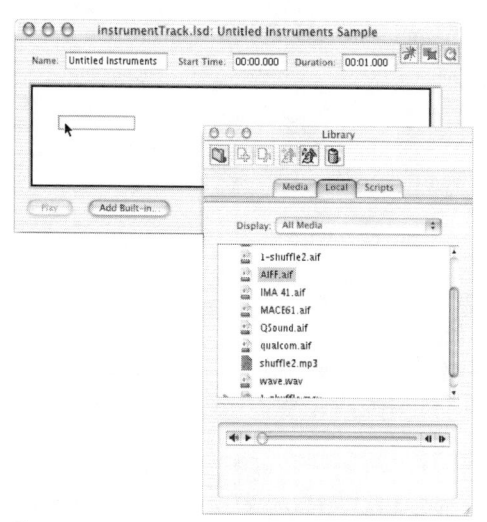

**Figure 12.21** To embed a sampled instrument in an instrument sample, drag it into the Instrument list from the library, Finder (Mac), or desktop (Windows).

ABOUT INSTRUMENT TRACKS

275

# About Playing Instruments

After you've created some instruments, use the PlayNote QScript action to play them (**Figure 12.22**). This action takes five parameters, all of which must be set for your MIDI instrument to play:

**Instrument ID.** As you add MIDI instruments to an instrument sample, each new instrument is given a distinct ID number, starting at 1 for the first instrument, 2 for the second, and so on.

**Delay.** The delay parameter is specified in a time scale of 600 ticks per second. Normally, when the PlayNote QScript is executed, you want the MIDI instrument to play immediately, which requires you to set delay to 0. If you want to delay the sound by 1 second, set delay to 600. The instrument now plays 1 second after the PlayNote QScript is triggered.

**Pitch.** *Pitch* refers to the frequency of a note. In the PlayNote QScript, pitch is defined as a number. A pitch value of 60 is the instrument's normal pitch and is equal to C3 on the MIDI keyboard. If you're playing a sampled instrument, a pitch value greater than 60 will increase its frequency (turning a tenor into a chipmunk soprano), whereas a lower value decreases its frequency and slows it (turning a tenor into a deeper, richer baritone).

**Volume.** When the note is played, its loudness is determined by the volume value. The number 0 represents silence, and 127 is as loud as the instrument gets.

**Duration.** Duration, like delay, is measured in a time scale of 600 ticks per second. To make a note play for 2.5 seconds, enter a duration of 1500 (2.5 X 600). For 1/4 second, enter 150 (0.25 X 600).

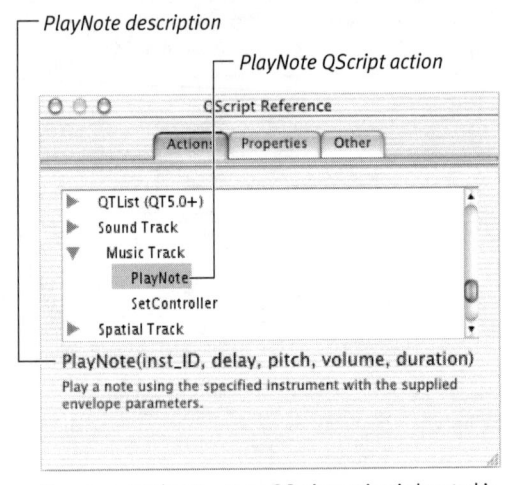

**Figure 12.22** The PlayNote QScript action is located in the Music Track folder of the QScript Reference window's Actions tab.

Working with Audio

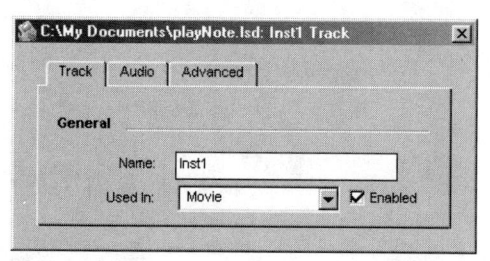

**Figure 12.23** The name you give the instrument track will later be used to target it so that the PlayNote QScript action finds and plays the correct MIDI instrument.

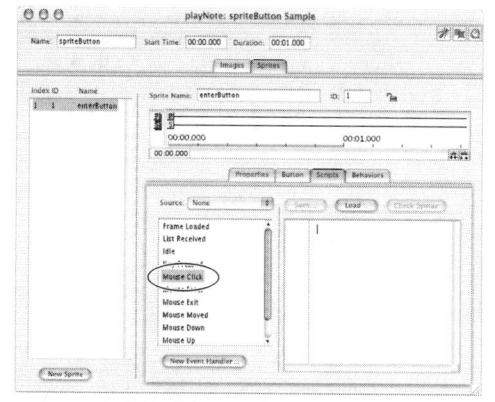

**Figure 12.24** Sprite buttons can be clicked to create an object event that plays a MIDI instrument. In this example, the Mouse Click event handler has been selected as the event that will trigger the note.

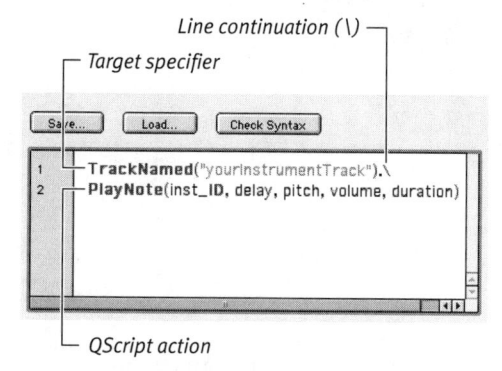

*Line continuation (\)*
*Target specifier*
*QScript action*

**Figure 12.25** The PlayNote QScript action takes many parameters.

The following example shows you how to create a button sound (a sound that plays when the viewer interacts with a button). This is only one use of the PlayNote QScript, with a little experimenting you are sure to find many more.

### To play a note:

1. Create an instrument track and define an instrument, as described in "About Instrument Tracks" earlier in this chapter.

2. In the Tracks tab, double-click the instrument track's track header.
   
   The Track Properties window opens, displaying the Track tab.

3. In the Name text box, enter a name for the instrument track (**Figure 12.23**).
   
   Later, a QScript will use this name to target the instrument track.

4. Create a sprite button.
   
   This sprite button will be the movie object that triggers your sound. To learn how to create a sprite button, see Chapter 10, "Sprite Tracks."

5. In the Event Handler list of the sprite button's script editor, select an event, such as Mouse Click (**Figure 12.24**).

6. In the sprite button's script edit field, type the following QScript statement (**Figure 12.25**):
   
   TrackNamed("yourInstrumentTrack"). PlayNote(inst_ID, delay, pitch, volume, duration).
   
   The PlayNote QScript action takes several parameters. The following steps address these parameters in succession.

*continues on next page*

ABOUT PLAYING INSTRUMENTS

277

Chapter 12

7. Replace "yourInstrumentTrack" with the name of your instrument track, which you set in step 3.

8. Replace inst_ID with your instrument's ID number, as reflected by its position in the instrument sample's Instrument list (**Figure 12.26**).

9. Replace delay with a time delay for your instrument.

10. Replace pitch with a note value, as defined by the keyboard in **Figure 12.27**

11. Replace volume with a number between 0 and 127.

12. Replace duration with a value indicating the duration of the note (**Figure 12.28**).

13. In the top-right corner of the sprite sample, click the Run Wired Movie button.

    LiveStage compiles a preview of your movie. When you click the sprite button, the sound plays.

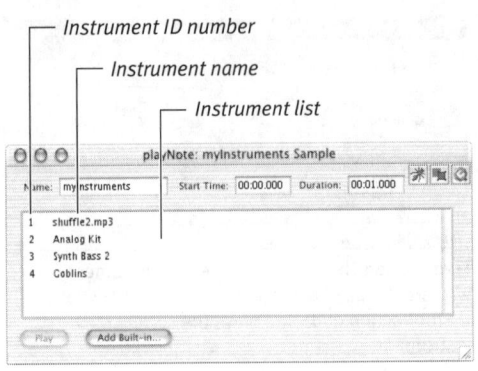

**Figure 12.26** As you add instruments to the Instrument list, each new instrument is given an ID number, starting at 1 for the first instrument in the list and increasing by 1 for every instrument added thereafter. This ID number is used to target the correct instrument via QScript.

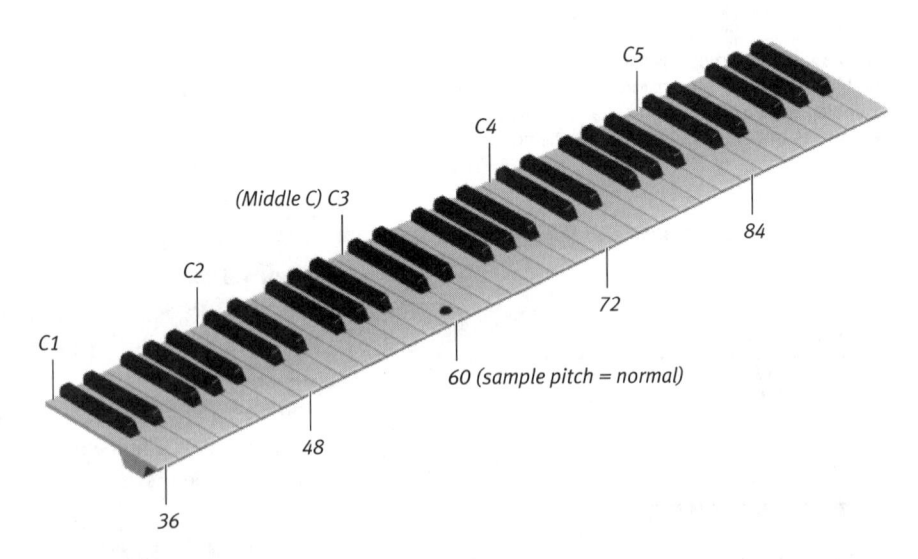

**Figure 12.27** This figure shows the relationship between octave ranges and pitch numbers. The numbers along the bottom of the keyboard represent the pitch of each C note, as understood by LiveStage. Pitch is a parameter that must be set when using the PlayNote QScript.

# Working with Audio

*Delay before note starts*
*Instrument ID number*
*Instrument track name*

`TrackNamed("inst1").PlayNote(3, 0, 60, 100, 150)`

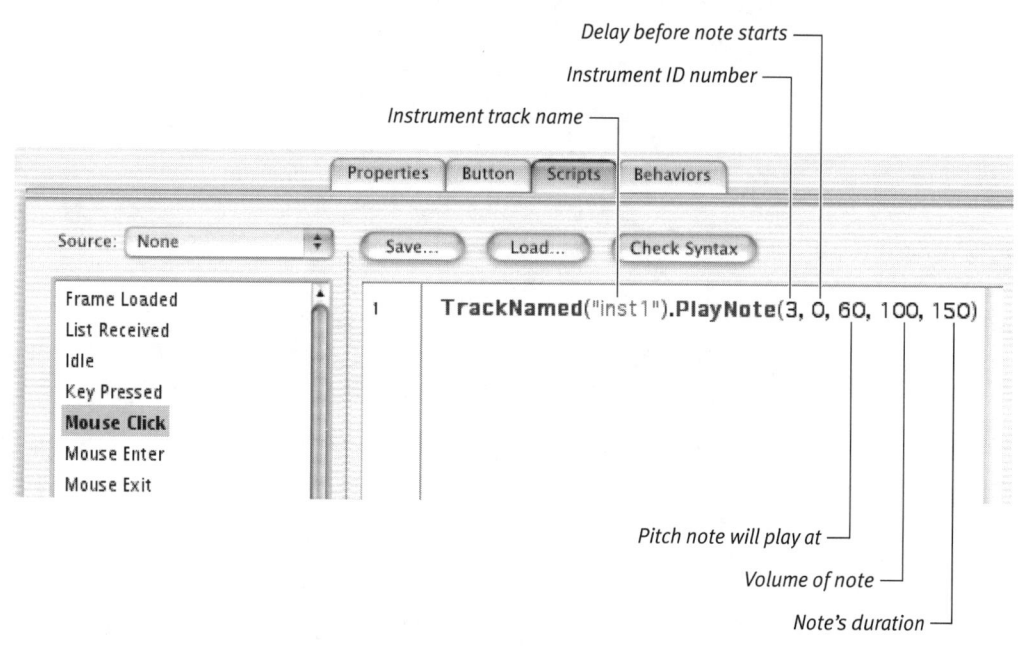

*Pitch note will play at*
*Volume of note*
*Note's duration*

**Figure 12.28** The finished `PlayNote` QScript action. This example will play the third instrument in the Instrument list with no delay, at a pitch of 60 (default pitch for sampled instruments), at a volume of 100, for 1/4 second.

## Thickening MIDI Sounds

One general complaint about MIDI sounds is that they are *thin* (lacking texture). To make your MIDI effects thicker, try layering different instruments to make new sounds. You might layer a Synth Pad, for example, with a violin sound to make an angelic "ahhhhhhhh."

Another way to add texture to your MIDI instruments is to use chords. A *chord* is two or more notes of a different pitch played at the same time. Picture pressing down three keys on a keyboard or strumming the strings of a guitar. To program a chord, write a `PlayNote` QScript action; then copy and paste that action into the script editor several times. Change the pitch value of each note, and test your chord by running a preview movie.

A third way to add complexity to your audio involves creating arpeggios. An *arpeggio* occurs when the notes of a chord are played in rapid succession, rather than simultaneously. An example of an arpeggio is a "ding-dong" sound, in which a high note is followed quickly by a lower one. To make an arpeggio, follow the instructions for making a chord, but slightly alter the delay value of each `PlayNote` action statement. Now you can really make those angels sing.

**ABOUT PLAYING INSTRUMENTS**

# Advanced QScript

QScript is a very colloquial scripting language. In fact, it's practically written in plain English, and one glance at any keyword tells you exactly what the script does. Although several intimidating scripting languages are out there, QScript is not one of them. Syntactical issues aside, the biggest challenge in learning QScript is building your vocabulary and coming to terms with the phenomenal wealth of keywords and language elements available to you. After that, writing QScripts is as simple as snapping keywords together.

Chapter 4, "The Script Editor," introduced you to many QScript concepts, providing a strong foundation for the advanced concepts discussed in this chapter. If you haven't yet read Chapter 4, do so now. If you have read Chapter 4, your QScript horizons are about to broaden.

This chapter delves deeper into QScript syntax and language elements that let you program complex interactivity into your projects. The chapter starts with a discussion of LiveStage's two main forms of data: constants and variables. Then you'll learn how to debug your QScripts before moving on to conditional statements that give decision-making intelligence to your movies. So, without further ado, plug the kettle in, put the dog out, and get ready to supercharge your QScript.

# Chapter 13

## About Constants

*Constants* are data that never changes over the course of your movie. The value of a constant is simply the constant itself. Following are a few examples:

- 12321. A numeric constant.
- "Hello world." A string constant.
- TRUE. A Boolean constant.

You use constants wherever you need to set a value or text string explicitly. An example of a constant is the URL that you enter in the GotoURL("URL") action statement (**Figure 13.1**), or the true/false value you assign to a SetEnabled(True/False) action statement (**Figure 13.2**).

## Understanding the Defines tab

As you write your QScripts, you will often use the same constants over and over again. You may have several sprite buttons, for example, that link to the same URL, which is a constant. Instead of writing out the URL in each QScript statement, you can use the Defines tab to attach a simple name to the URL (**Figure 13.3**), and then use the newly defined name in place of the constant in your QScripts. This special constant name is called a *define*.

Defines can save you time writing as well as editing scripts. If you reference the same URL in several of your project's QScripts, but later find that the URL is incorrect, you must hunt down each script that uses the URL and change the script manually. Furthermore, updating the URL by hand is dangerous. What if you accidentally misspell one URL? By using a define, you only need to change the URL once, in the Defines tab. LiveStage automatically changes the URL in each QScript that it's used, decreasing the chances of making a project-crashing mistake.

**Figure 13.1** This QScript statement links to a URL. Because the constant (the URL) is a string, it must be enclosed in quotation marks.

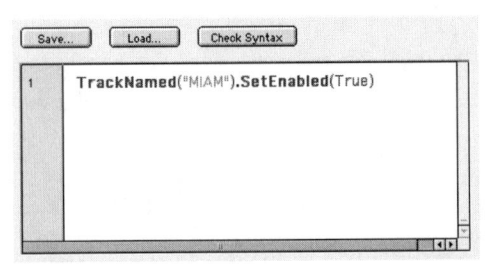

**Figure 13.2** To turn the track named MIAM off (disable it), use this statement. TRUE is a Boolean constant and does not need to be enclosed in quotation marks.

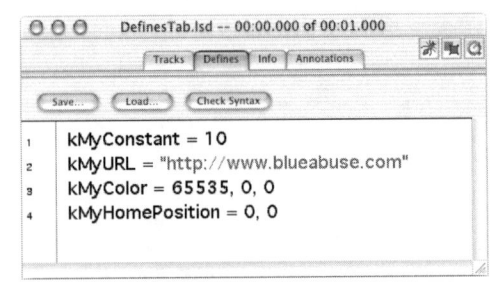

**Figure 13.3** The Defines tab collects your project's constants in one easy-to-find place.

# Advanced QScript

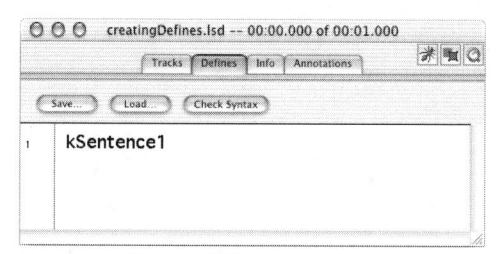

**Figure 13.4** Give each define a name that is easy to remember. If you place a *k* in front of the name, the define becomes easier to spot in your QScripts.

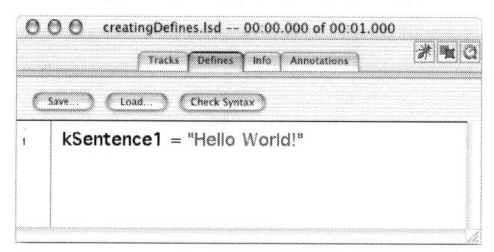

**Figure 13.5** A completed define.

Using defines takes forethought and planning, but the time you'll save is worth the effort. If you know that you'll use the same constant repeatedly in your project, make it easy on yourself; turn the constant into a define.

## To create a define:

1. In the Project window, select the Defines tab.

2. Enter a name in the script edit field (**Figure 13.4**).

    Remember to always follow the LiveStage convention of placing a "k" at the beginning of the define name.

3. After the define name, type an equal sign (=).

    You don't have to leave a space between the define and the equal sign, but doing so makes your scripts easier to read.

4. After the equal sign, enter your constant (**Figure 13.5**).

    From now on, you can refer to the constant in your QScripts by its define name.

## ✔ Tip

- The Defines tab's script edit field holds only defines. If you enter any other QScript in the Defines tab, your movie will not compile.

## Why the *k*?

In LiveStage, the convention is to place a *k* in front of any define that you create: kMyDefine.

You should follow this convention for three reasons:

- The *k* makes scripts easier to spot. As you search through your vast collection of QScripts, you can find your defines in a glance.

- The *k* distinguishes defines from variables, preventing confusion.

- The *k* is a convention that programmers always use (if you're reading this sidebar, you are now officially a programmer).

ABOUT CONSTANTS

## Using defines

After you've created a define, you can use it in any of your QScripts (bearing in mind, of course, that the constant the define represents must also make sense within the context of the QScript). To use the define, place a dollar sign ($) in front of it:

$kMyDefine.

When LiveStage compiles your movie, the dollar sign lets it know that what follows is a reference to a constant in the Defines tab. LiveStage then jumps to the Defines tab and grabs the constant. In other words, when LiveStage compiles your movie, it replaces each define with the constant that it represents.

### To use a define:

1. Create a define (refer to Figure 13.5).
   For more information on creating defines, see "To create a define" earlier in this chapter.

2. Write a QScript that uses the define's constant (**Figure 13.6**).

3. Replace the constant with a dollar sign ($), followed by the define (**Figure 13.7**).
   When LiveStage compiles your project into a finished movie, it goes through all your scripts, finds all the defines, and replaces them with their corresponding constant values.

### ✔ Tip

- To prevent confusion, don't leave any spaces between the words of your define names. If you do leave spaces, you must encase the define in quotation marks, both in the Defines tab and in your QScripts:

    "My Deep Blue" = 0, 0, 65535
    SetTextColor($"My Deep Blue").

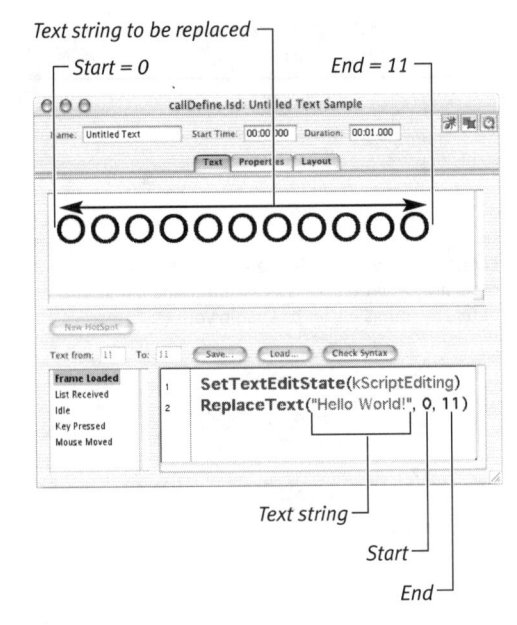

**Figure 13.6** The ReplaceText(string, start, end) QScript in this example takes several parameters (string, start, end). All these parameters are constants, and each can be replaced with a define.

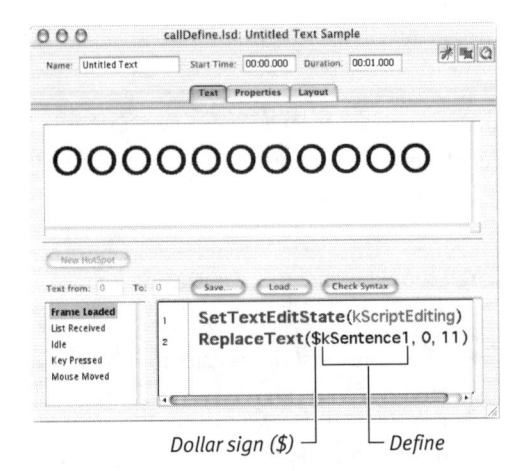

**Figure 13.7** The "Hello World!" text string has been replaced by a define. The dollar sign ($) lets LiveStage know that a define follows.

284

# Advanced QScript

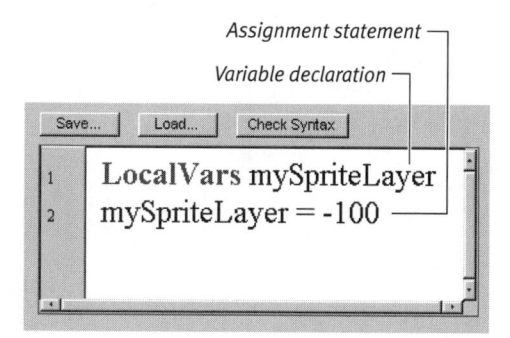

**Figure 13.8** Assignment statements attach a value to a variable. In this example, the variable `mySpriteLayer` has been declared and assigned the value of –100.

## About Variables

In general, a *variable* is something that is subject to change. In LiveStage, a variable is a name associated with a data value.

To use a variable, you must do three things:

◆ Determine the variable's scope

◆ Declare the variable with a variable declaration statement

◆ Assign the variable a value using an assignment statement (**Figure 13.8**)

This section goes through each step in detail, beginning with variable scope.

### ✔ Tip

■ You are free to name your variables anything you like, with one restriction: You must not use any LiveStage QScript keywords as variable names.

## Understanding variable scope

*Scope* refers to a variable's sphere of influence, or *persistence*, in your QScripts. You can restrict a variable's scope so that the variable affects only scripts inside its event handler, or you can expand the variable's scope so that it is available to an individual sprite, sprite track, or even the whole movie.

Setting variable scope helps prevent the introduction of errors into your QScripts. Your project, for example, may need to use a variable named Y in two sprites. If you restrict the scope of each variable to the sprite that contains it (sprite scope), when the Y value of one sprite changes, the Y value of the other remains unaffected. If the variables are assigned a larger scope (global or movie scope), when the Y value of one sprite changes, the Y value of the second also changes.

*continues on next page*

The following list outlines the four different levels of variable scope:

- **Local scope.** A variable with local scope is only available to QScripts inside the current sprite event handler. Local scope is available only to sprites.

- **Sprite scope.** If a variable has sprite scope, any QScript in the same sprite may access its value. Sprite scope is available only to sprites.

- **Global scope.** If a variable has global scope, all QScripts in the same sprite track have access to its value. Global scope is available only to sprites.

- **Movie scope.** If a variable has movie scope, any QScript in the movie can access its value. Variables in Flash, text, and VR tracks must be assigned movie scope; otherwise, your project will not compile.

## Declaring a variable

Before you can use a variable in LiveStage, you must declare it. A variable declaration looks like this:

`LocalVars myVariable.`

This declaration does two things: it sets the variable's scope (`Local`) and defines its name (`myVariable`).

As you saw in "Understanding Variable Scope" earlier in this chapter, a variable can have local, sprite, global, or movie scope. Four variable declaration keywords represent each type of scope:

- `LocalVars`. Represents local scope.
- `SpriteVars`. Represents sprite scope.
- `GlobalVars`. Represents global scope.
- `MovieVars`. Represents movie scope.

# Advanced QScript

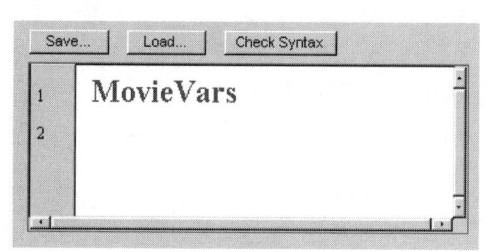

**Figure 13.9** The `MovieVars` keyword allows a variable to be used by any script in the movie.

**Figure 13.10** To make it easy to tell what a variable does, give it a name that reflects its purpose.

## To declare a variable:

1. At the top of the script edit field that will contain the variable, enter the QScript keyword representing the variable's scope (**Figure 13.9**).

2. Press the spacebar.

   The variable's name must be separated from the variable-scope keyword by a space. Otherwise, LiveStage does not understand that the variable-scope keyword and the variable itself are both separate QScript language elements.

3. Enter the variable's name (**Figure 13.10**).

   The variable is declared and can be used in any event handler that falls within its scope.

## ✔ Tips

- Always use a variable scope that encompasses only the sphere of influence you want your variable to have. If the variable in a sprite does not need to be available to scripts outside that sprite, make sure that you assign it sprite scope only.

- If several variables inside the same event handler have the same scope, you can declare all of them at the same time by separating names with a comma (,):
  `GlobalVars i,j,SpriteYPosition`.

- In a sprite, text, or VR track, if you need to set a variable to a certain value as soon as the track loads, restrict the variable to sprite scope and declare it in the `Frame Loaded` event handler. When the track loads, the variable is set to this initial value and can be called from any QScript event handler in the same sprite.

## Using assignment statements

After you've declared a variable, you must assign it a value; if you don't assign it a value, your QScripts will not know what to do with it. To assign a value to a variable, use an assignment statement (**Figure 13.11**):

Variable = Expression.

An assignment statement is made up of a declared variable, an equal sign (=), and an expression. The expression can be a constant:

X = -1

an object property:

X = ThisMovie.MovieVolume

or a combination of the two, joined by operators:

X = (ThisMovie.MovieVolume)*(-1).

After you've assigned a value to a variable, you can use the variable in any of your QScript statements.

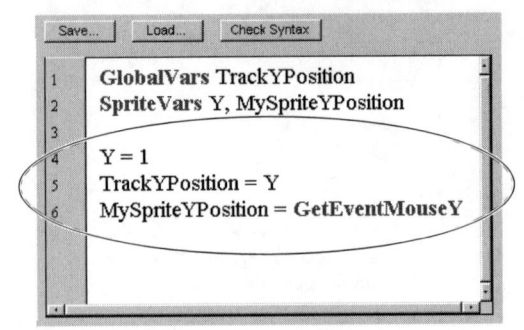

**Figure 13.11** An example of assignment statements.

Advanced QScript

# About Debugging Projects

Sometimes, your QScripts just don't behave the way you want them to. In those situations, wouldn't it be great if you could get under the hood and see what's going on? With the LiveStage Debugging Console, you can (**Figure 13.12**).

The Debugging Console can be open while you run your preview movies. As the preview movie's event handlers execute, the Debugging Console shows each action that occurs and keeps a list of all QScripts that are executed.

The Debugging Console itself won't explicitly tell you what's wrong with your QScript. No lights flash, and no alarms go off. The console simply keeps track of what's going on in the movie's scripts. To uncover the root of the suspicious events, you may have to do some detective work.

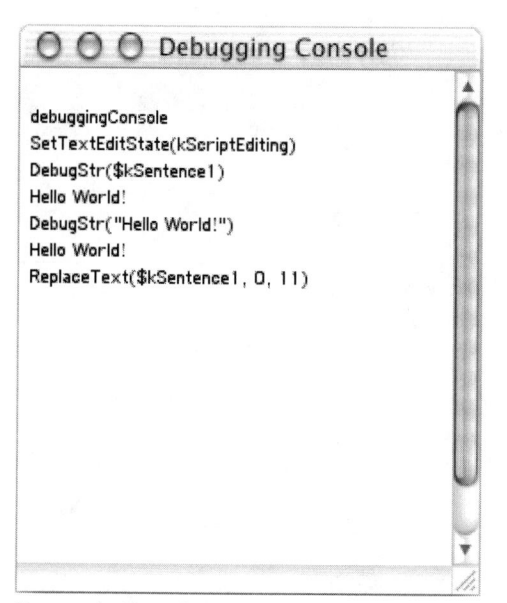

**Figure 13.12** The Debugging Console lets you watch your QScripts as they execute, making it easier to spot errors in your scripts.

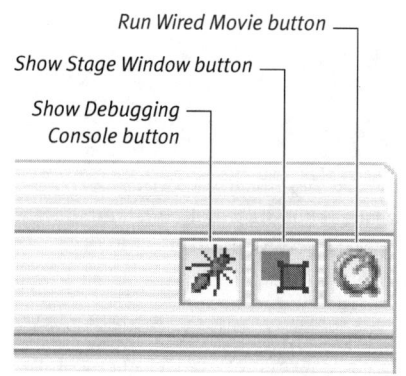

**Figure 13.13** To open the Debugging Console, click the Show Debugging Console button.

### To open the Debugging Console:

1. In the top-right corner of the Project window, click the Show Debugging Console button (**Figure 13.13**).

    The Debugging Console opens (refer to Figure 13.12).

2. In the top-right corner of the Project window, click the Run Wired Movie button.

    LiveStage compiles a preview of your project. If you look at the Debugging Console, you see a list of all the event handlers that execute as the movie plays.

    *continues on next page*

289

## ✓ Tip

- If you can't see the preview movie's event handlers in the Debugging Console, choose Edit > Preferences > Compiler, and check the Default to Show Source in Debugger checkbox. While you're in the Compiler section of the Preferences window, check the Clear Console Before Running checkbox (**Figure 13.14**). This option causes the Debugging Console to start fresh every time you run a preview movie, making it easy to scroll back to the top and examine scripts from when you first launched the preview.

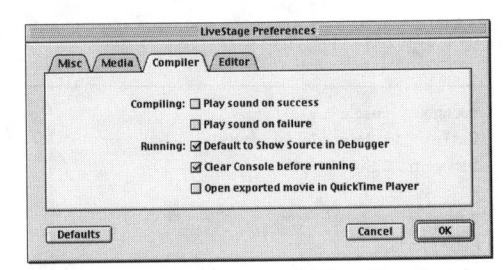

**Figure 13.14** The Preferences window's Compiler tab.

---

### About DebugStr(string)

The `DebugStr(string)` QScript action displays the value of object properties and variables. Knowing these values can help you zero in on problem QScripts. If you have a sound track named Sound that you cannot hear, for example, check its volume by placing the following QScript in an event handler:

`DebugStr(TrackNamed("Sound").TrackVolume).`

In the Debugging Console, when the event executes, the `DebugStr` QScript action lists the volume of the track named Sound. If the `DebugStr` QScript action returns a value of 0, you know that the sound track is not making any noise and can take the appropriate actions to fix it. If the `DebugStr` QScript action returns a value greater than 0, but you still cannot hear the sound track, you know that your problem lies elsewhere.

You can also enter a text string in the `DebugStr` QScript action, but you must encase it in quotation marks:

`DebugStr("Button Clicked").`

This example lets you make sure that a button is interacting properly with the pointer. If the button is clicked, `Button Clicked` is listed in the Debugging Console.

# About Conditional Statements

A *conditional statement* lets your movie make decisions. Conditional statements use an if/then statement to check for a condition. If the condition is true, the conditional statement executes a QScript action statement. A sprite's `Idle` event handler, for example, might use a conditional statement to see whether a movie has played past a certain point in the Timeline. If the movie has passed that point, the conditional statement could stop it from playing (**Figure 13.15**).

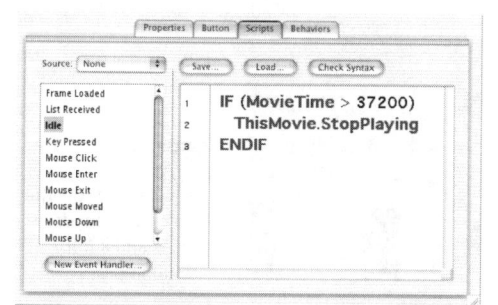

**Figure 13.15** This conditional statement checks to see whether the current time in the movie is greater than 1 minute and 2 seconds (62 seconds X 600 ticks per second = 37200). If so, the movie stops playing.

In its most basic form, a conditional statement looks like this:

```
IF (expression)
    Statement
ENDIF.
```

When your movie encounters a conditional statement, it evaluates the expression. If the expression is false, nothing happens. If the expression is true, the statement executes.

Conditional statements can make more complex decisions if you add an `else` clause (**Figure 13.16**):

```
IF (expression)
    Statement 1
ELSE
    Statement 2
ENDIF.
```

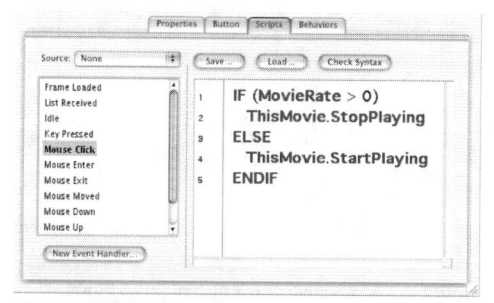

**Figure 13.16** The `else` clause allows your movie to choose one action from two possible choices. This conditional statement checks to see whether a movie is playing (`MovieRate > 0`). If the movie is playing, the statement stops the movie. If the movie is not playing, the statement starts it (perfect for a Play/Pause button).

This conditional statement evaluates the expression and checks to see whether it's true. If the expression is true, `Statement 1` executes. If it isn't true, `Statement 2` executes.

## ✔ Tip

- Don't forget to include parentheses around the conditional statement's expression. Parentheses are a necessary part of the statement's syntax, and your project will not compile without them.

## About Custom Events

*Custom events* are like complex defines. (To learn more about working with defines, see "Using defines" earlier in this chapter.) A define lets you assign a name to a constant. Similarly, a custom event lets you assign a name to an entire block of QScript.

Use a custom event whenever you need to trigger the same QScript in more than one event handler. In the QuickTime tile game in **Figure 13.17**, the viewer reorganizes sprite tiles to make a picture. When the viewer clicks any of the sprite tiles, a MIDI instrument plays a hit sound, and the sprite tile's graphics mode changes (altering the color of the sprite). You could program these QScript actions into each sprite tile, but if you want to alter the instrument or graphics mode, you would have to hunt down each QScript and make the change manually.

When you use a custom event, you create one event handler to trigger the instrument *and* change the sprite's graphics mode (**Figure 13.18**). You can then execute that event from any of the sprite tiles (**Figure 13.19**). If you decide to change the MIDI instrument or the graphics mode, you need only alter the custom event to make the change globally.

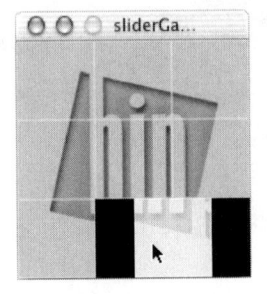

**Figure 13.17** In this tile game, when the viewer selects a sprite tile, the tile's graphics mode changes and a MIDI instrument plays.

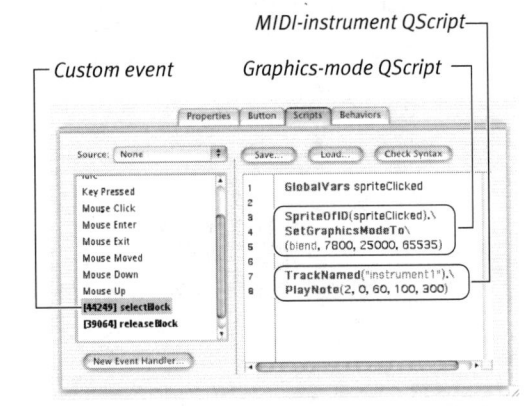

**Figure 13.18** This custom event contains a block of QScript that plays a MIDI instrument and changes a sprite's graphics mode.

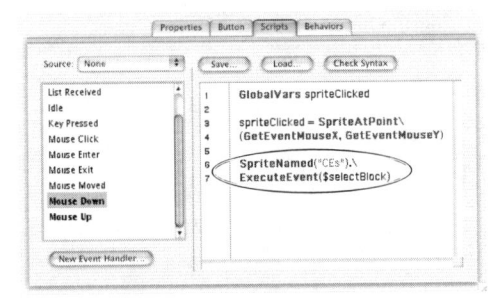

**Figure 13.19** The Mouse Down event handler of each sprite tile contains this block of QScript. When the viewer selects any sprite tile in the puzzle, the custom event is executed, and the sprite tile enters its hit state.

## Creating a custom event

Custom events live in sprites, so to create a custom event, you need to have at least one sprite in your project.

### To create a custom event:

1. Create a sprite.

   To learn more about creating sprites, see Chapter 10, "Sprite Tracks."

2. From inside your newly created sprite, select the Scripts tab (**Figure 13.20**).

3. Below the Event Handler list, click the New Event Handler button.

   The Edit Event Handler dialog opens (**Figure 13.21**).

4. In the Name text box, enter a name for your custom event.

5. Click the OK button.

   The Edit Event Handler dialog closes, and a new event handler is created at the bottom of the Event Handler list (**Figure 13.22**). This custom event handler can be scripted just like any other event handler.

6. Type a QScript statement in the script edit field.

   Your custom event is ready to be triggered. To learn more about triggering a custom event, see "Executing a Custom Event" later in this chapter.

### ✔ Tip

- If you have one or more custom events that several sprites use, create a special sprite and use it as a custom event holder. If you place all your custom events in one sprite, you know exactly where to go when you need to change them.

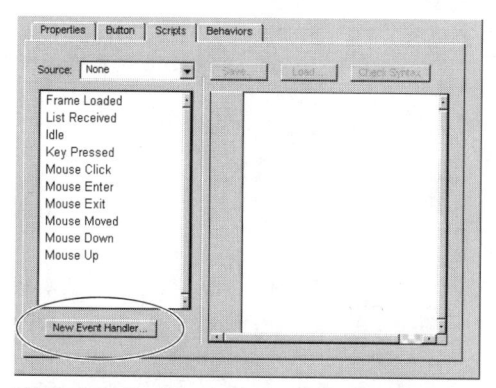

**Figure 13.20** The New Event Handler button at the bottom of the Scripts tab (below the Event Handler list) allows you to create custom events.

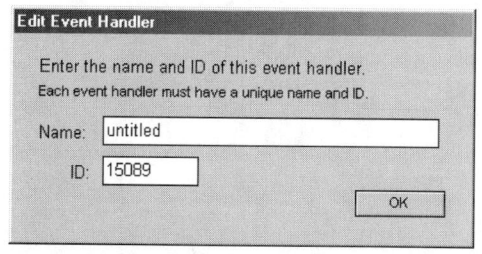

**Figure 13.21** The Edit Event Handler dialog lets you name your custom events. If you want to switch the custom event's ID number, enter a new value in the ID text box.

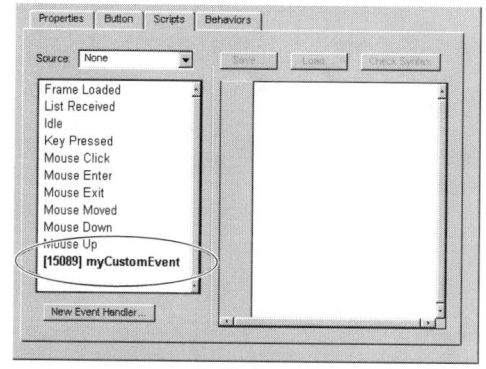

**Figure 13.22** New custom events are placed at the bottom of the Event Handler list.

## Chapter 13

### Executing a custom event

After you've created a custom event, you can trigger it from any event handler in your project (including Flash buttons, text hotspots, and VR hotspots) by typing the following QScript in the script edit field (**Figure 13.23**):

ExecuteEvent(event_ID).

LiveStage assigns each custom event a unique event ID, located in brackets to the left of the custom event's name in the Event Handler list. The ExecuteEvent(event_ID) QScript action uses this ID number to trigger the correct custom event.

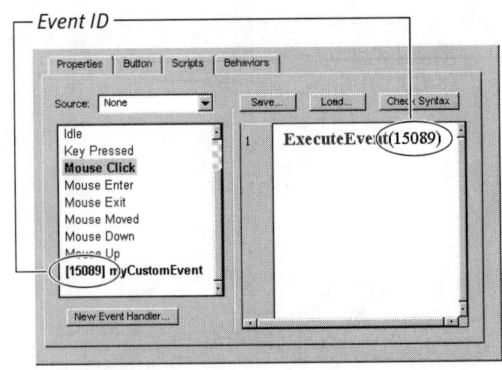

**Figure 13.23** This QScript action executes the custom event of ID 15089.

### ✔ Tips

- If you're triggering the custom event from a sprite other than the one it lives in, you must target the sprite first as in the following example:

    SpriteNamed("mySprite").\
    ExecuteEvent(event_ID).

- LiveStage automatically creates a define from a custom event's name. Instead of referring to the custom event by its ID number, you can enter a dollar sign ($) and then type the custom event's name, just as you would do with any other define.

# Keyboard Shortcuts

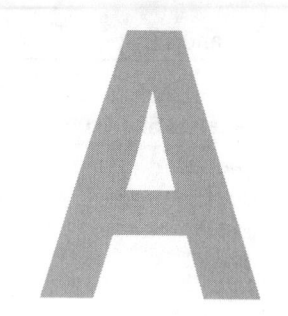

## Menu Shortcuts

| Command | Macintosh | Windows | Menu |
|---|---|---|---|
| New Project window | ⌘N | Ctrl N | File > New Project |
| Open LiveStage project | ⌘O | Ctrl O | File > Open |
| Close window | ⌘W | Ctrl W | File > Close |
| Save LiveStage project | ⌘S | Ctrl S | File > Save |
| Compile preview movie | ⌘R | Ctrl R | File > Run Wired Movie |
| Compile QuickTime movie | ⌘M | Ctrl M | File > Export Wired Movie |
| Quit LiveStage | ⌘Q | Ctrl Q | File > Quit |
| Undo previous action | ⌘Z | Ctrl Z | Edit > Undo |
| Redo undone action | Shift ⌘ Z | Shift Ctrl Z | Edit > Redo |
| Cut selection to Clipboard | ⌘X | Ctrl X | Edit > Cut |
| Copy selection to Clipboard | ⌘C | Ctrl C | Edit > Copy |
| Paste Clipboard selection | ⌘V | Ctrl V | Edit > Paste |
| Duplicate selection | ⌘D | Ctrl D | Edit > Duplicate |
| Select all text | ⌘A | Ctrl A | Edit > Select All |
| Create new sprite track | ⌘J | Ctrl J | Tracks > Create > Sprite |
| Create new sample | ⌘K | Ctrl K | Tracks > Add Sample |
| Open Library window | ⌘Y | Ctrl Y | Window > Show Library Window |
| Open QScript Reference window | ⌘T | Ctrl T | Window > Show QScript Reference |

295

Appendix A

## Timeline Shortcuts

| Command | Macintosh | Windows |
|---|---|---|
| Jump to last sample | ← | ← |
| Jump to next sample | → | → |
| Zoom in | ⌘ ] | ⌘ ] |
| Zoom out | ⌘ [ | ⌘ [ |
| Snap playhead or sample to edge of other samples | Option-drag | Ctrl Alt-drag |

## Stage Shortcuts

| Command | Macintosh | Windows |
|---|---|---|
| Select sprite track | ⌘ Option-click | Ctrl Shift-click |
| Remove selected object | Delete | Delete |
| Zoom in | ⌘ ] | ⌘ ] |
| Zoom out | ⌘ [ | ⌘ [ |
| Open sample or sprite editor | Double-click track or sprite | Double-click track or sprite |
| Open Flash button from stage | Double-click Flash button | Double-click Flash button |

# ONLINE RESOURCES

## LiveStage

### Blue Abuse
www.blueabuse.com

The official LiveStage home page. Find tips and tutorials, or ask questions in the forum. If you have questions, you'll find the answers here.

### The LiveStage Developer Network
www.totallyhip.com/lsdn

If you're having serious technical problems, look to the developers for sure solutions.

### LiveStage Talk discussion list
www.totallyhip.com/lsdn/community/join_mail.html

Join the LiveStage Talk discussion list. Ask questions and see what other LiveStage users have to say about the product.

### Totally Hip Software
www.totallyhip.com

Totally Hip Software's corporate site. Find out about the company and learn about its suite of QuickTime-enabled applications.

## QuickTime

### Embedding QuickTime for Web Delivery
http://developer.apple.com/quicktime/quicktimeintro/tools/embed2.html

A list of <embed> tag parameters used by the QuickTime plug-in.

### Internet Explorer and QuickTime
http://developer.apple.com/quicktime/compatibility.html

You'll find important information about embedding QuickTime movies in Microsoft Internet Explorer.

### QuickTime
www.apple.com/quicktime

Apple Computer's official QuickTime Web page.

### QuickTime Development Resources
http://developer.apple.com/quicktime/quicktimeintro

Find sample code, QuickTime tools, and other resources.

## Audio

### The Beta Lounge
www.betalounge.com

Something to listen to during those long, long midnight hours.

### Digidesign
www.digidesign.com

Download Digidesign Pro Tools free.

### Hit Squad
www.hitsquad.com

Download more than 3,800 free audio programs from the Shareware Music Machine.

### Propellerheads Software
www.propellerheads.se

Propellerheads Reason and other audio tools; demo versions are available.

### Steinberg
www.steinberg.net

Steinberg is the maker of Cubase.

# C

# USEFUL QSCRIPTS

This appendix details four handy QScripts that many LiveStage authors find useful. While every project is different, these scripts cover common queries that you're likely to face as your scripting skills mature and your projects become increasingly complex.

# Switching Fonts Based on Platform

In Chapter 8, "Text Tracks," you learned that Windows fonts can display up to 33 percent larger (96 dots per inch) than Macintosh fonts (72 dots per inch). To give your text a uniform size across all platforms, create two text tracks: one for Macintosh and one for Windows. Disable them both, and use the `Platform` QScript property and a conditional statement to check what platform the viewer is using. Use this information to enable the correct text track dynamically (**Figure C.1**).

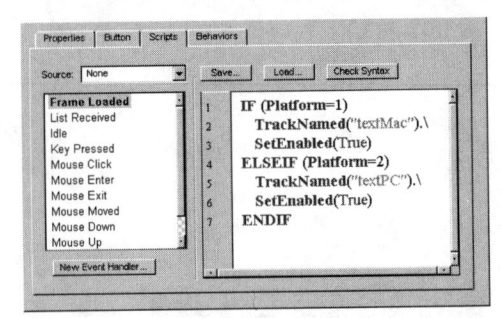

**Figure C.1** This conditional statement checks whether the viewer is using a Macintosh or a PC and enables a text track specifically formatted for that platform.

### ✔ Tip

- The `Platform` QScript property returns a value of 1 on the Macintosh and a value of 2 in Windows.

# Checking Connection Speed

When you set up QuickTime, you must specify your Internet connection speed. This connection speed is stored as a QuickTime preference. What's more, your movies can read it by using the following QScript property:

ConnectionSpeed

Movies can use this property to select content dynamically based on the viewer's connection speed. A movie could have several movie tracks, for example, each containing child movies optimized for a particular bandwidth (referenced by URL). Disable all the movie tracks (movie tracks don't load if they're not enabled). After you've performed this step, create a conditional statement that determines the viewer's connection speed and enables the correct movie track dynamically (**Figure C.2**).

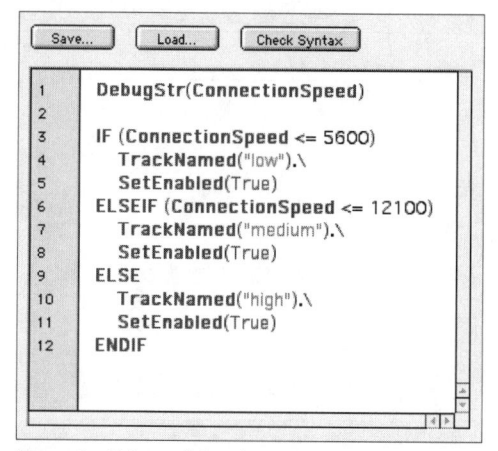

**Figure C.2** This conditional statement determines the viewer's connection speed before enabling the appropriate movie track.

LiveStage reads connection speed in bits per second, whereas QuickTime specifies it in kilobits per second. **Table C.1** lists the values of several common QuickTime connection speeds, along with the corresponding bits-per-second conversions used by LiveStage.

## ✔ Tip

- The ConnectionSpeed QScript property does not return the actual Internet connection speed of the computer displaying your movie. Instead, it returns the connection speed as specified by the QuickTime connection-speed preference. If viewers set their connection speed incorrectly, they will not see your movie as you intend them to.

**Table C.1**

| QuickTime Connection-Speed Conversions ||
|---|---|
| QUICKTIME CONNECTION SPEED | LIVESTAGE BITS PER SECOND |
| 28.8/33.6Kbps modem | 2800 |
| 56Kbps modem/ISDN | 5600 |
| 112Kbps Duyal ISDN/DSL | 11200 |
| 512Kbps DSL/cable | 51200 |
| 1Mbps cable | 100000 |

```
1   DebugStr(ConnectionSpeed)
2
3   IF (ConnectionSpeed <= 5600)
4     TrackNamed("low").\
5     SetEnabled(True)
6   ELSEIF (ConnectionSpeed <= 12100)
7     TrackNamed("medium").\
8     SetEnabled(True)
9   ELSE
10    TrackNamed("high").\
11    SetEnabled(True)
12  ENDIF
```

# Making a JavaScript Pop-Up Window

If your movie is playing in a Web browser, you can add buttons that open JavaScript pop-up windows. The JavaScript function that opens the window sits at the head of the HTML file (**Figure C.3**). To tell QuickTime to trigger that function, use the GotoURL(URL) QScript, but instead of linking to another Web page or movie, replace URL with the following text string (**Figure C.4**):

JavaScript: openWindow()

### ✔ Tips

- This technique is not limited to opening pop-up windows; you can use it to trigger any JavaScript function in your HTML document.

- JavaScript syntax is very finicky. If your JavaScript function doesn't work, make sure that all your capitals and semicolons (;) are where they should be. Netscape users can also type javascript: in the location bar to see a list of JavaScript errors.

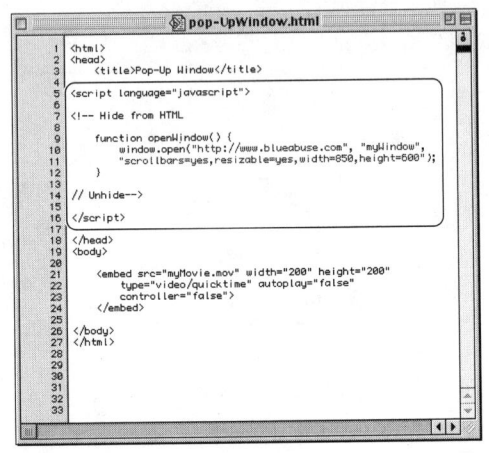

**Figure C.3** To open a JavaScript pop-up window, you must write this JavaScript function in the head section of your HTML file. The QuickTime movie embedded in this HTML file contains a button that triggers the JavaScript function, opening a new browser window.

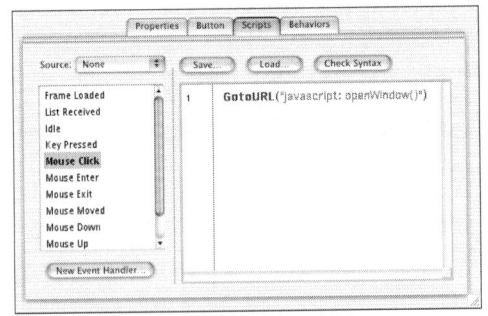

**Figure C.4** To trigger a JavaScript function from the HTML page of an embedded QuickTime movie, use this QScript.

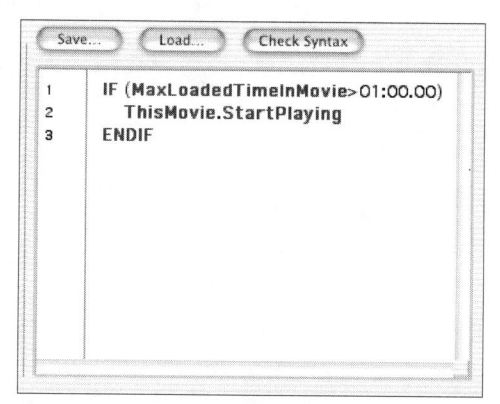

```
Save...    Load...    Check Syntax
1    IF (MaxLoadedTimeInMovie>01:00.00)
2        ThisMovie.StartPlaying
3    ENDIF
```

**Figure C.5** This QScript starts playing the movie automatically after one minute of it has downloaded.

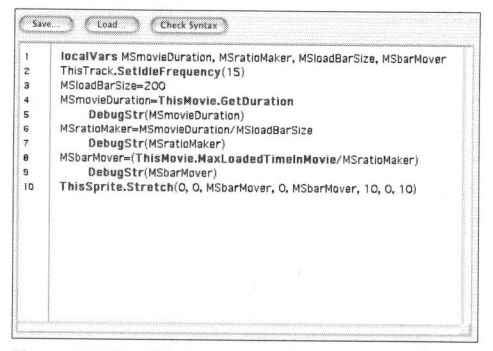

```
Save...    Load...    Check Syntax
1     localVars MSmovieDuration, MSratioMaker, MSloadBarSize, MSbarMover
2     ThisTrack.SetIdleFrequency(15)
3     MSloadBarSize=200
4     MSmovieDuration=ThisMovie.GetDuration
5         DebugStr(MSmovieDuration)
6     MSratioMaker=MSmovieDuration/MSloadBarSize
7         DebugStr(MSratioMaker)
8     MSbarMover=(ThisMovie.MaxLoadedTimeInMovie/MSratioMaker)
9         DebugStr(MSbarMover)
10    ThisSprite.Stretch(0, 0, MSbarMover, 0, MSbarMover, 10, 0, 10)
```

**Figure C.6** This QScript stretches a progress-bar sprite as the movie downloads. When the movie has fully downloaded, the progress bar is 200 pixels wide by 10 pixels high.

# Monitoring a Movie's Download Progress

The MaxLoadedTimeInMovie QScript tells you how much of your movie has downloaded. But this QScript is useful only if you're delivering your movies over the Internet, as movies running off a hard disk or CD-ROM don't need to be downloaded. If you are distributing your movie over the Web, this QScript property lets you do really cool things. You can set a movie to start playing after a set amount of it has downloaded (**Figure C.5**), for example, or create a progress bar to track the movie's download status (**Figure C.6**).

## ✔ Tip

- A *load sequence* is a still image or short animation that plays while your movie downloads in the background. To create a simple load sequence, open Macromedia Flash and make a one-frame animation. Add this animation to LiveStage, placing it on top of all the other tracks in your movie. By monitoring your movie's download progress, you can disable the Flash track after a certain amount of your movie has downloaded, revealing the tracks below.

# INDEX

## A

Action statements. *See also* Actions
    data, 74
    defined, 71
    properties, 75–77
    targets and commands, 72–73
Actions, QScript, 68, 70. *See also* Action statements
Adobe's Premiere, 237
Advanced tab, Track Properties window
    Alternates settings, 51
    offsetting tracks, 9
    Playback settings, 51–52
Aliases for files/folders, Library window, 33
Alignment toolbar, Stage window, 26–27
Alpha channels, graphics modes, 44–45
Alternates settings, tracks, 51
Animation
    cel-based, 246–247
        QScripts, 251–252
        tweening, 248–250
    data tracks
        basics, 238
        Source pop-up menus, 238
    tween editors, 239
    tween tracks
        basics, 239
        fade-ins, 243–245
        path tweens, 240–242
Antialiased text, 155

Apple
    AppleScripts, 30
    Final Cut Pro, 237
        real time rendering, 253
    iTunes, 263
    QuickTime Player Pro, 177
    QuickTime VR Authoring Studio, 177
Arpeggios, MIDI sounds, 279
Assignment statements, QScript, 71, 288
Audio online resources, 298
Auto Scaled text, 154

## B

Backdrops, 104
Backgrounds
    boxes for text, 153
    sprite tracks
        color, 223
        transparent, 224–225
Behaviors
    assigning, 227–228
    creating new, 228
    installing, 229
    library, 30
    opening Behaviors folders, 226
Blending tracks, graphics modes
    alpha channels, 44–45
    basics, 42–43
    Blend mode, 47, 243–245
    Dither mode, 48–49
    Transparent mode, 45–46

305

# Index

Boolean constants, QScript, 69, 74
Buttons
    Flash
        FSCommand action, 195–198
        opening from stage, 194
        scripting, 192–193
    sprites
        basics, 230
        changing idle frequency, 233–234
        creating, 231
        loading child movies, 138
        scripting, 232–233

## C

Caching tracks, 51
CD-ROM movie updates, 125
Cel-based animation, 246–247
    tweening, 248–250
Chapter tracks
    basics, 173
    creating, 174–175
Child movies
    defined, 119
    embedding directly, 122–123
    layout settings, 135–136
    loading
        from relative paths, 126–127
        from URLs, 124–125
        multiple, 137–138
    previewing, 128–129
    slaving
        audio settings, 131
        duration, 132
        graphics mode, 132
        time settings, 130
Chords, MIDI sounds, 279
Color
    grid settings for stage, 25
    text, 148
        background boxes, 153
        color values, 167
        highlights, 157–158
    text hotspots
        changing color, 165–167

        changing rollover color, 170–171
    Tracks Properties settings
        Blend mode, 47
        Dither mode, 48–49
        OpColor, 43
        track mattes, 49–50
        Transparent mode, 45–46
Color (visual) tracks
    creating, 104
    defining, 105–106
    gradients
        altering alignment, 108
        multiband, 106–107
    properties, 111
Commands, QScript, 70, 72
Comments, QScript, 71
Compiling QScript, disabling compile
    sounds, 67
Compositing. *See* Blending
Composition tab, Track Properties window
    graphics modes
        alpha channels, 44–45
        basics, 42–43
        Blend, 47
        Dither, 48–49
        Transparent, 45–46
    OpColor settings, 43
    track mattes, 49–50
Compressing
    movie resources, 87
    picture samples, 111–112
    sprite images, 213
Conditional statements, QScript, 291
Constants, QScript, 69, 74
    defines, 282–283
        k convention, 283
        using, 284
    types, 282
Containers. *See* parent movies
Continuous scrolling text, 161
Control statements, QScript, 71
Controllers, QuickTime, 94
Coordinates, tracks
    repositioning in Stage window, 20
    setting in Matrix editor, 40

# Index

Copy-protecting movies, 88
Copying
   QScripts, 63
   tracks, 8
Cross-fade transitions, 255
Custom events, QScript
   basics, 292
   creating, 293
   executing, 293

## D

Data tracks. *See also* Modifier tracks;
    Tween tracks
   basics, 238
   Source pop-up menus, 238
Data, QScript, 69
   action statements, 74, 75
Debugging Console, QScript, 289–290
`DebugStr(string)` QScript action, 290
Deleting
   files/folders in Library window, 34
   gradient colors, 107
   QScripts, 63
   samples, 12
   text hotspots, 164
   tracks, 8
Digidesign Pro Tools, 263
   creating sound tracks, 265
Dimensions, tracks
   repositioning in Stage window, 20
   setting in Matrix editor, 39
Dither graphics mode, 48–49
Dot syntax, QScript, 72, 74
Drag masks, 113, 116
Draw settings for tracks, Stage window,
    28–29
Drop shadows, text, 156
Duration changes
   Flash tracks, 186
   samples, 11
   slaving child movies, 132
   streaming tracks, infinite duration,
    182–183
   Timeline external, 118

## E

Effect tracks
   basics, 253–254
   creating, 254
   filter effects, 258–259
   special effects, 260–261
   transitions, 255–257
Electricrain's Swift 3D, 177
Event handler
   custom events, 292–294
   defined, 57
   object events, 57–58
   script editor section, 54
   track events, 57, 59
     `Idle`, 60–61
Exporting QuickTime movies, 97–98
Expressions, QScript, 70
External (visual) tracks, 117–118
   properties, 111

## F

Fade-ins, 243–245
Files/folders in Library window
   adding alias files to folders, 33
   adding files to folders, 32
   creating, 31
   deleting, 34
   filtering, 34
   moving files between folders, 34
Filter effects, 258–259
Filtering files/folders in Library window, 34
Final Cut Pro (Apple), 237
   real time rendering, 253
Flash (Macromedia), 177
Flash tracks, 177–178
   basics, 184
   buttons
     `FSCommand` action, 195–198
     opening from stage, 194
   changing duration, 186
   changing volume, 187
   importing files, 184–185

# Index

Flash tracks *(continued)*
  scripting
    frame events, 190–191
    object events, 192–193
  stretching files, 187
  text, 187
Folders/files in Library window
  adding alias files to folders, 33
  adding files to folders, 32
  creating, 31
  deleting, 34
  filtering, 34
  moving files between folders, 34
Fonts (text)
  Macintosh and Windows display problems, 145
    QScript to switch fonts, 300
  sizes, 144–145
  type, 146
`Frame Loaded` events, 59
Frequency of idles, 60

## G

GIF file compression, picture samples, 112
Global scope, 285–286
Gradient Editor, color
  defining, 105–106
  gradients
    alignment, 108
    multiband, 106–107
Graphics modes
  alpha channels, 44–45
  basics, 42–43
  Blend, 47, 243–245
  Dither, 48–49
  slaving for child movies, 132
  Transparent, 45–46
Grids on stage
  enabling/disabling
    display, 23–24
    snap to grid function, 24
  settings
    new color, 25
    new size, 24

## H

Hiding Stage window tracks, 22
Highlights for text, 157–158
Horizontal scrolling text, 161
Hotspots
  text
    changing color, 165–167
    changing length, 163
    changing pointers, 171–172
    deleting underling, 165
    scripting, 163
    simulating rollover color, 170–171
    style, 168–169
  VR
    changing pointers, 204–205
    naming, 205

## I

`Idle` events, 59, 60–61, 202
  time scale, 61
Images. *See* Sprite tracks, images
Importing Flash files, 184–185
Instrument tracks
  basics, 271–272
  instruments
    creating, 272–274
    sampled, 274–275
  play parameters, 276–277
  playing notes, 277–279
Invisible/visible text, 154
ITunes (Apple), 263

## J

JPEG file compression
  picture samples, 111–112
  sprite images, 213
Justifying text, 149

# Index

## K

K convention, defining QScript constants, 283
Key Pressed events, 59
Keyboard shortcuts
  menus, 295
  stage, 296
  Timeline, 296
Keyed text, 155
Keywords, QScript target specifiers, 68, 69, 72
Keywords, QScript, Reference window, 78–80

## L

Language tracks, movies, alternate tracks, 88–90
Library window
  folders/files
    adding alias files to folders, 33
    adding files to folders, 32
    behaviors, 226–229
    collecting movie projects, 99
    creating, 31
    deleting, 34
    filtering, 34
    moving files between folders, 34
  tabs, 30
Linear controllers, QuickTime, 94
Linear progression, movies, Timeline, 13–15
LiveStage
  online resources, 297
  *versus* other video-editing programs
    stage properties, 19
    time scales, 14
Local scope, 286
Local tab, library, 30
  populating local folder, 33
Locking tracks in Stage window, 21–22
Looping movies, 91
  child movies, 134

## M

Macintosh and Windows font display differences, 145
  QScript to switch fonts, 300
Macromedia Flash, 177
Margins, text, 150–152
Matrix editor, track settings
  coordinates, 40
  dimensions, 39
Media samples. *See* Samples
Media skins. *See* Skin tracks
Media tab, library, 30
Menu keyboard shortcuts, 295
MIAM projects. *See also* Movie tracks; Movies
  child movies
    embedding directly, 122–123
    loading from relative paths, 126–127
    loading from URLs, 124–125
    previewing, 128–129
    slaving audio settings, 131
    slaving graphics mode, 132
    slaving time settings, 130
  defined, 119
  playback parameters, 133–134
  testing, 129
MIDI tracks
  adding, 268
  basics, 268
  instruments
    basics, 263
    changing, 269–270
  thickening sounds, 279
Modes
  graphics
    alpha channels, 44–45
    basics, 42–43
    Blend, 47, 243–245
    Dither, 48–49
    slaving for child movies, 132
    Transparent, 45–46
  movies, 93
Modifier tracks. *See also* Data tracks; Tween tracks

**309**

# Index

Movie in a Movie projects. *See* MIAM projects
Movie tracks. *See also* MIAM projects; Movies
  basics, 119–120
  child movies
    embedding directly, 122–123
    layout settings, 135–136
    loading from relative paths, 126–127
    loading from URLs, 124–125
    loading multiple, 137–138
    previewing, 128–129
    slaving audio settings, 131
    slaving duration, 132
    slaving graphics mode, 132
    slaving time settings, 130
  creating, 121
  filter effects, 258–259
Movies. *See also* MIAM projects; Movie tracks
  collecting project files, 99
  download monitoring with QScript, 303
  exporting to QuickTime files, 97–98
  Info tab, Loop section, 91
  Info tab, Movie section
    Auto Alternate (tracks), 88–90
    Compress, 87
    Copy Protect, 88
  Info tab, Play section
    All Frames playback, 82–84
    Auto Start, 82–83
    Sections Only playback, 82, 84–86
  intermovie communication, 95–96
  modes, 93
  pointers to streaming tracks, 179–180
  QuickTime properties
    controllers, 94
    present movie mode, 93
    version compatibility, 92
  scope, 285–286
  tag names and ID numbers, 95–96
  Timeline's playhead, 13–15
  updating CD-ROM, 125

Multi-node VRs
  basics, 206
  deleting hotspot behaviors, 206–207
  linking, 207–208
Musical Instrument Digital Interface. *See* MIDI

# N

Naming
  movies, 98
  sprites, 216
    images, 212
  tracks, 36–37
  VR hotspots, 205
Node IDs, VR tracks, 206–208

# O

Object VR tracks, 199
  multi-node VRs
    deleting hotspot behaviors, 206–207
    linking, 207–208
  scripting, 203
Object-oriented scripting languages
  basics, 70
  QScript, 68
Object/Event Handler list, Flash tracks, 188–189
Online resources
  audio, 298
  LiveStage, 297
  QuickTime, 298
OpColor settings, tracks, 43
Opening
  Library window, 31
  QScript Reference window, 78
  script editor, 55–56
  Stage window, 18–19
    sample editors, 22
  Track Properties window, 35
Operators, QScript, 70
Owner tracks, 173

# Index

## P

Palindrome looping, 91
   child movies, 134
Panoramic VR tracks, 199–200
   multi-node VRs
      deleting hotspot behaviors, 206–207
      linking, 207–208
Parent movies
   defined, 119
   loading child movies with relative paths, 126–127
Pasting
   QScripts, 63
   tracks, 8
Path tweens, 240–242
Paths (relative), loading child movies, 126–127
Picture (visual) tracks
   creating, 109
   filter effects, 258–259
   properties, 111
   setting/switching picture samples, 110–111
Ping-pong looping, 91
Playback settings
   tracks, 51–52
Playback settings
   MIAM projects, 133–134
Playhead, movies, Timeline
   current time, 13
   jumping to specific point, 14
   moving along Timeline, 15
PNG file compression
   picture samples, 111–112
   sprite images, 213
Posters (tracks), 37–38
Premiere (Adobe), 237
Previews
   child movies, 128–129
   tracks, 37–38
Propellerhead's Pro Tools, 265
Properties
   action statements, 68, 70, 75–77

QuickTime movies
   controllers, 94
   present movie mode, 93
   version compatibility, 92
   stages, *versus* other video-editing programs, 19
   Track Properties window
      Advanced tab, 9, 51–52
      basics, 35
      color settings, 43, 45–50
      Composition tab, 42–50
      opening, 35
      Spatial tab, 39–41
      Track tab, 36–38, 61
   visual tracks, 111
Push transitions, 255

## Q

QScripts. *See also* Script editor
   actions, 68, 70
   basics, 53–54
   cel-based animation, 251–252
   constants
      defines, 282–284
      types, 282
   custom events
      basics, 292
      creating, 293
      executing, 293
   Debugging Console, 289–290
   disabling compile sounds, 67
   Flash tracks
      buttons, 194
      frame events, 190–191
      FSCommand action, 195–198
      object events, 192–193
      Object/Event Handler list, 188–189
   Internet connection speed, 301
   JavaScript pop-up windows, 302
   language elements, 69–70
   library, 30
   Macintosh/Windows font switching, 300

311

# Index

QScripts *(continued)*
    managing, 64–65
    manipulating, 62–63
    movie download monitoring, 303
    sprites
        behaviors, 226–229
        idle frequency, 233
        registration points, 218–219, 218–2197
        scripting, 232–233
    statements
        assignment, 288
        conditional, 291
    syntax
        action statements, 71, 72–74
        action statements, properties, 75–77
        basics, 68
        checking, 66
        statements, types, 71
    target specifiers, 68, 69
        action statements, 75–77
        child movies, 139
        none specified, 169
        Reference window, 78–80
    text hotspots, 163
        changing hotspot color, 165–167
        changing pointers, 171–172
        changing rollover color, 170–171
        changing style, 168–169
        deleting underlining, 165
    text, color values, 167
    variables
        basics, 285
        declaring, 286–287
        scope, 285–286
    VR tracks
        object events, 203
        track events, 201–202
QuickTime (Apple), online resources, 298
QuickTime Player Pro (Apple), 177
QuickTime VR Authoring Studio (Apple), 177

## R

Real time rendering, 253
Reference window, QScript, 78–80
Registration points, sprites, 218–219
Relative paths, loading child movies, 126–127
Removing. *See* Deleting
Resizing. *See* Sizing
Reverse scrolling text, 161

## S

Sample editors, opening in Stage window, 22
Sampled instruments, 274–275
Samples
    defined, 5
    Flash, 188–189
    manipulating, 10–12
Scope of variables, 285–286
Script editor. *See also* QScripts
    event handler, 54
        defined, 57
        object events, 57–58
        track events, 57, 59
    opening, 55–56
    script edit field, 54
Scripts tab, library, script types, 30
Scrolling text, 159–161
Sizing
    text field, 142–143
    Track list, 8
    tracks in Stage window, 21
Skin (visual) tracks
    basics, 113–114
    creating, 114
    masks
        drag, 113, 116
        window, 113, 115
Skinned movies, 113
Slaving child movies
    audio settings, 131
    graphics mode, 132
    times, 130

# Index

Slide transitions, 255
Sound online resources, 298
Sound tracks
   basics, 264–265
   clipping sound cards, 267
   instrument tracks
      basics, 271–272
      creating instruments, 272–274
      play parameters, 276–277
      playing notes, 277–279
      sampled instruments, 274–275
   MIDI tracks
      adding, 268
      basics, 268
      changing instruments, 269–270
      thickening sounds, 279
   volume settings, 266–267
Source pop-up menus, data tracks, 238
Source tracks, sprites, 235
Spatial tab, Track Properties window
   drawing layers values, 41
   Matrix editor
      coordinates, 40
      dimensions, 39
Special effects, 260–261
Sprite tracks. *See also* Sprites
   backgrounds
      color, 223
      transparent, 224–225
   defined, 55
   idle frequency, time scale, 61
   images
      adding, 211–212
      cel-based animation, 246–250
      changing, 216
      compressing, 213
      naming, 212
      overriding image sources, 235
      registration points, 218–219
   opening script editor, 56
Sprites. *See also* Sprite tracks
   behaviors
      assigning, 227–228
      creating new, 228
      installing, 229

      opening Behaviors folders, 226
   buttons
      basics, 230
      changing idle frequency, 233–234
      creating, 231
      loading child movies, 138
      scripting, 232–233
   creating, 215
   multiple, 214
   naming, 216
   positioning, 220–221
   properties, 222
   scope, 285–286
   stacking order, 217
      changing layers, 221–222
Stage
   keyboard shortcuts, 296
Stage window
   basics, 17–19
   opening sample editors, 22
   Timeline's playhead, 13
   tracks
      alignment toolbar, 26–27
      draw settings, 28–29
      hiding, 22
      locking, 21–22
      repositioning, 20
      resizing, 21
Stages
   grids
      enabling/disabling display, 23–24
      enabling/disabling snap to grid function, 24
      setting new color, 25
      setting new size, 24
   properties, *versus* other video-editing programs, 19
Start times, samples, 10
Statements, QScript
   action statements, 71, 72–73
   data, 74
   assignment, 288
   conditional, 291
   dot syntax, 72, 74
   types, 71

# Index

Streaming tracks, 177–178
   adding files, 181
   basics, 179
   pointer movies, 179–180
   setting infinite duration, 182–183
   using, 182
Swift 3D (Electricrain), 177
Syntax, QScript
   basics, 68
   checking, 66
   statements
      action statements, 71, 72–74
      types, 71

## T

Tag names and ID numbers, movies, 95–96
Target objects, QScript, 75
Target specifiers, QScript, 68, 69
   action statements, 75–77
   child movies, 139
   none specified, 169
   Reference window, 78–80
Testing movie language tracks, 90
Text. *See also* Text tracks
   appearance, 154–155
   background boxes and box color, 153
   color, 148
      color values, 167
   effects
      drop shadows, 156
      highlights, 157–158
   entering, 142
   Flash tracks, 187
   fonts
      Macintosh and Windows display problems, 145, 300
      sizes, 144–145
      type, 146
   hotspots
      changing color, 165–167
      changing length, 163
      changing pointers, 171–172
      deleting underling, 165
      scripting, 163

      simulating rollover color, 170–171
      style, 168–169
   justification, 149
   margins, 150–152
   scrolling, 159–161
   sizing text field, 142–143
   style, 147
Text tracks. *See also* Text
   basics, 141–143
   chapter tracks
      basics, 173
      creating, 174–175
   idle frequency, time scale, 61
Thin/thick MIDI sounds, 279
Time scale
   idle frequency, 61
   LiveStage's scale *versus* other video-editing program's scales, 14
Timeline
   external track duration, 118
   keyboard shortcuts, 296
   playhead, movie's current time, 13
   samples
      defined, 5
      manipulating, 12
Track Properties window
   Advanced tab
      Alternates settings, 51
      offsetting tracks, 9
      Playback settings, 51–52
   basics, 35
   color
      Dither mode, 48–49
      OpColor, 43
      track mattes, 49–50
      Transparent mode, 45–46
   Composition tab
      Blend graphics mode, 47
      Dither graphics mode, 48–49
      graphics modes and alpha channels, 44–45
      graphics modes, basics, 42–43
      OpColor settings, 43
      track mattes, 49–50
      Transparent graphics mode, 45–46

# Index

opening, 35
Spatial tab, 39–41
Track tab, 36–38
  basics, 3–5
  Idle Frequency setting, 61
  poster and previews, 37–38
  Timeline, media samples, 5
  tracks, 36–37
tracks
  caching, 51
  creating, 6
  display quality, 52
  idle frequency, time scale, 61
  manipulating, 7–8
  mattes, 49–50
  movies, alternate tracks, 88–90
  offsetting, 9
  preloading, 52
  samples
    adding, 10
    altering duration, 11
    altering start times, 10
    defined, 5
    deleting, 12
    duplicating, 12
    repositioning, 12
  Stage window
    alignment toolbar, 26–27
    draw settings, 28–29
    hiding tracks, 22
    locking tracks, 21–22
    repositioning tracks, 20
    resizing tracks, 21
Transitions, 255–257
Transparent graphics mode, 45–46
Tween tracks. *See also* Data tracks;
  Modifier tracks
basics, 239
cel-based animation, 248–250
fade-ins, 243–245
path tweens, 240–242
tween editors, 239

## V

Variables, QScript, 69, 74
  basics, 285
  declaring, 286–287
  scope, 285–286
Version compatibility, QuickTime
  movies, 92
video-editing programs, *versus* LiveStage.
  *See also* Effect tracks
  stage properties, 19
  time scale, 14
Visible/invisible text, 154
visual tracks
  color tracks
    creating, 104
    defining, 105–106
    gradients, alignment, 108
    gradients, multiband, 106–107
  external tracks
    basics, 117–118
  filter effects, 258–259
  picture tracks
    creating, 109
    properties, 111
    setting/switching picture samples,
      110–111
  skin tracks
    basics, 113–114
    creating, 114
    drag masks, 113, 116
    window masks, 113, 115
Volume settings, sound tracks, 266–267
VR controller, QuickTime, 94, 205
VR tracks, 177–178
  basics, 199–200
  changing idle frequency, 202
  hotspots
    changing pointers, 204–205
    naming, 205
  multi-node VRs
    basics, 206
    deleting hotspot behaviors, 206–207
    linking, 207–208

VR tracks *(continued)*
   scripting
      object events, 203
      track events, 201–202

# W
Window masks, 113, 115
Windows and Macintosh font display
    differences, 145
   QScript to switch fonts, 300
Wipe transitions, 255

X and Y coordinates, sprites, 220–221
X-, Y-, and Z-axis track settings, 39–40

# Z
Zooming in/out, Stage window, 19

# WHEN YOU ARE READY TO TAKE YOUR VIDEO TO THE NEXT STAGE...LOOK TO PEACHPIT PRESS FOR YOUR DIGITAL VIDEO NEEDS!

**Adobe After Effects 5.0 Classroom in a Book**
Adobe Creative Team
ISBN: 0-201-74131-8 • 384 pages • $45.00

**After Effects 5 for Macintosh and Windows: Visual QuickPro Guide**
Antony Bolante
ISBN: 0-201-75043-0 • 608 pages • $34.99

**Adobe Premiere 6.0 Classroom in a Book**
Adobe Creative Team
ISBN: 0-201-71018-8 • 480 pages • $45.00

**Editing Techniques with Final Cut Pro**
Michael Wohl
ISBN: 0-201-73483-4 • 400 pages • $44.99

**Final Cut Pro 2 for Macintosh: Visual QuickPro Guide**
Lisa Brenneis
ISBN: 0-201-71979-7 • 624 pages • $24.99

**FireWire Filmmaking**
Scott Smith
ISBN: 0-201-74163-6 • 176 pages • $39.99

**iMovie 2 for Macintosh: Visual QuickStart Guide**
Jeff Carlson
ISBN: 0-201-78788-1 • 216 pages • $19.99

**The Little Digital Video Book**
Michael Rubin
ISBN: 0-201-75848-2 • 192 pages • $19.99

**LiveStage Professional 3 for Macintosh and Windows: Visual QuickStart Guide**
Martin Sitter
ISBN: 0-201-77142-X • 416 pages • $21.99

**Making iMovies**
Scott Smith
ISBN: 0-201-70489-7 • 156 pages • $39.99

**QuickTime 5 for Macintosh and Windows: Visual QuickStart Guide**
Judith Stern and Robert Lettieri
ISBN: 0-201-74145-8 • 440 pages • $19.99

**Premiere 6 for Macintosh and Windows: Visual QuickStart Guide**
Antony Bolante
ISBN: 0-201-72207-0 • 592 pages • $19.99

**Video on the Web with Adobe Premiere**
Thomas Luehrsen
ISBN: 0-201-77184-5 • 352 pages • $39.99

**WWW.PEACHPIT.COM**

# PEACHPIT PRESS

Quality How-to Computer Books

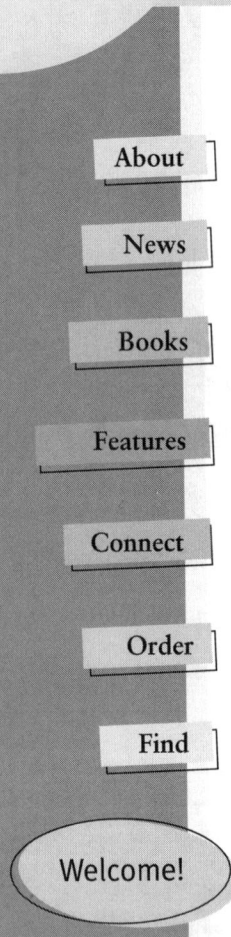

- About
- News
- Books
- Features
- Connect
- Order
- Find
- Welcome!

## Visit Peachpit Press on the Web at www.peachpit.com

- Check out new feature articles each Monday: excerpts, interviews, tips, and plenty of how-tos

- Find any Peachpit book by title, series, author, or topic on the Books page

- See what our authors are up to on the News page: signings, chats, appearances, and more

- Meet the Peachpit staff and authors in the About section: bios, profiles, and candid shots

- Use Connect to reach our academic, sales, customer service, and tech support areas and find out how to become a Peachpit author or join the staff

- Click Order to enter the online store; order books or find out how to find Peachpit books anywhere in the world

## Peachpit.com is also the place to:

- Chat with our authors online
- Take advantage of special Web-only offers
- Get the latest info on new books